New Issues in Islamic Finance and Economics: Progress and Challenges

New Issues in Islamic Finance and Economics: Progress and Challenges

Hossein Askari, Zamir Iqbal,
and Abbas Mirakhor

John Wiley & Sons (Asia) Pte. Ltd.

Published in 2009 by John Wiley & Sons (Asia) Pte. Ltd.
2 Clementi Loop, #02-01, Singapore 129809

Other Wiley Editorial Offices

John Wiley & Sons, 111 River Street, Hoboken, NJ 07030, USA
John Wiley & Sons, The Atrium, Southern Gate, Chichester, West Sussex, P019 8SQ, United Kingdom
John Wiley & Sons (Canada) Ltd, 5353 Dundas Street West, Suite 400, Toronto, Ontario, M9B 6HB, Canada
John Wiley & Sons Australia Ltd, 42 McDougall Street, Milton, Queensland 4064, Australia
Wiley-VCH, Boschstrasse 12, D-69469 Weinheim, Germany

Library of Congress Cataloging-in-Publication Data

ISBN 978-0-470-82293-7

Typeset in 10.5/13pt Palatino by Laserwords Private Limited, Chennai, India.
Printed in Singapore by Markono Print Media Pte. Ltd.

10 9 8 7 6 5 4 3 2 1

In the Name of Allah, the All Merciful, the All Beneficent

Contents

Acknowledgment

We acknowledge the contributions of Dr. Nadeem ul Haque and Dr. Kazem Sadr in Chapters 7 and 8 respectively. We are also grateful to our research assistant, Shahrzad Daneshvar, for her excellent work.

Glossary of Arabic Terms

ahadith — Plural of *hadith* (for meaning, see *hadith*).

ahkam — Plural of *hukm* (for meaning, see *hukm*).

ajr-un-kareem — A generous reward.

al-adl — Justice.

al-ghurm bil ghunm — The principle that one is entitled to a gain only if one agrees to bear the responsibility for the loss. For example, if someone gives finance to someone else, he is only entitled to a share in the profit resulting from the use of that finance if he is also prepared to bear any resultant loss.

al-kharaj bil daman — The principle in Islamic jurisprudence that entitlement to return or yield (*al-kharaj*) is for the one who bears the liability (*daman*) for something, say an asset, and one who does not bear the liability has no claim to the yield.

al mal — Wealth, property.

al-mu'minun — Those who believe through the heart.

amanah — Trust.

awqaf — Plural of *waqf* (for meaning, see *waqf*).

ayah — A verse of the *Qur'an*.

bay' — Stands for "sale." It is often used as a prefix in referring to different sales-based modes of Islamic finance, such as *murabahah, istisna'*, and *salam*.

bay' al-'ayan — Sale of tangible objects such as goods (as opposed to sale of services or rights).

bay' al-dayn — Sale of debt. According to a large majority of *fuqaha'*, debt cannot be sold for money, except at its face value, but can be sold for goods and services.

bay' al-kali bil kali — A sale in which both the delivery of the object of sale and the payment of its price are delayed. It is similar to a modern forward sale contract.

bay' al-'inah The sale of something to someone at a given price (usually on credit) and then the purchase back from the buyer, at the same time, at a different price (usually lower but cash). This kind of sale and buyback is prohibited because it effectively means exchanging a given amount of money with a different amount of money, which amounts to *riba*. It can be used as a subterfuge for *riba* dealings.

bay' bithaman ajil A sales contract where payment is made in instalments after delivery of goods. Sale could be for long-term and there is no obligation to disclose profit margins.

bay' al-mudaf A sales contract in which delivery of both the commodity and the payment is deferred—for example forward sales in modern times. Such contracts are not permitted by the *Shari'ah*.

bay' al-mulamasah A form of sale prevalent in the days of the Prophet (peace be upon him) in which the sales contract was finalized by the simple act of touching the object of sale. The prophet (peace be upon him) prohibited this kind of sale since the buying party did not have a fair chance of inspection and hence the practice involved *gharar*.

bay' al-munabazah A form of sale prevalent in the days of the Prophet (peace be upon him) in which the sales contract was finalized by the simple act of throwing the object of sale towards the buying party. The prophet (peace be upon him) prohibited this kind of sale since the buying party did not have a fair chance of inspection and hence the practice involved *gharar*.

bay' al-salaf An alternative term for *bay' al-salam*.

bay' al-salam A sale in which payment is made in advance by the buyer and the delivery of the goods is deferred by the seller.

bay' al-sifah A sale based on a detailed description of the object of sale.

bay' bi thaman al-'ajil	Another term used for *bay' mu'ajjal.*
bay' mu'ajjal	Sale on credit, that is, a sale in which goods are delivered immediately but payment is deferred.
bay' muzayadah	Sale by auction.
buyu'	Plural of *bay'* (for meaning, see *bay'*).
daman	Guarantee, security.
Dar al-Islam	The world (or the abode) of Islam.
darar	Damage, harm, injury.
darurah	Necessity. (Usually used for the "Doctrine of Necessity," whereby something otherwise prohibited becomes temporarily permissible).
dhimmah	Liability, responsibility.
faqih	Jurist who gives rulings on various juristic issues in the light of the *Qur'an* and the *sunnah.*
fasad	Mischief, troublemaking, corruption.
fatwa	Religious verdict by *fuqaha'.*
fatawi	Plural of *fatwa* (for meaning see *fatwa*).
fiqh	Refers to the whole corpus of Islamic jurisprudence. In contrast to conventional law, *fiqh* covers all aspects of life—religious, political, social, commercial, and economic. *Fiqh* is based primarily on interpretations of the *Qur'an* and the *sunnah* and secondarily on *ijma'* (consensus) and *ijtihad* (individual judgement) by the *fuqaha'.* While the *Qur'an* and the *sunnah* are immutable, *fiqhi* verdicts may change due to changing circumstances.
fiqhi	Relating to *fiqh.*
fuqaha'	Plural of *faqih* (for meaning, see *faqih*).
gharar	Literally, it means deception, danger, risk, and uncertainty. Technically, it means exposing oneself to excessive risk and danger in a business transaction as a result of uncertainty about the price, the quality and the quantity of the countervalue, the date of delivery, the ability of either the buyer or the seller to fulfil their commitment, or ambiguity in the terms of the deal—thereby, exposing either of the two parties to unnecessary risks.

gharar yasir	A little bit of *gharar*. This is tolerable because it may be unavoidable.
hadanah	The right of custody of a child after the divorce.
hadith	Saying, deed, or endorsement of the Prophet Muhammad (peace be upon him) narrated by his Companions.
Hajj	The pilgrimage to Mecca.
halal	Things or activities permitted by the *Shari'ah*.
Hanafi	A school of Islamic jurisprudence named after Imam Abu Hanifa.
Hanbali	A school of Islamic jurisprudence named after Imam Ahmed bin Hanbal.
haq	A right.
haq al-irtifaq	Literally, the right of utilization or easement. Technically, the right to derive free benefit from the immovable property of someone else. The right has been recognized by the *Shari'ah* in the spirit of generosity that members of a community should display toward each other.
haram	Things or activities prohibited by the *Shari'ah*.
hawalah	Literally, it means transfer. Technically, it refers to an arrangement whereby a debtor transfers the responsibility for payment of a debt to a third party who owes that debtor a debt. It is also used for a cheque or draft.
hazar	Danger, caution.
hibah	Gift.
hikmah	Wisdom.
hilah	Legal trick or device to avoid the imposition of a law in a particular case.
Hisbah	Literally, it means reward or calculation. Technically, it refers to an institution that existed through most of Islamic history for implementing what is proper and preventing what is improper. The main role of *al-hisbah* was the regulation and supervision of markets to ensure proper market conduct by all concerned.
hiyal	Plural of *hilah* (for meaning, see *hilah*).
hukm	*Shari'ah* ruling having general applicability.
'ibadat	Duties of man due to God.

'ibadah	Worship.
ibahah	Permissibility from a *Shari'ah* point of view.
ihsan	Beneficence, kindness, virtue.
ijarah	Leasing. The sale of usufruct of an asset. The lessor retains the ownership of the asset with all the rights and the responsibilities that go with ownership.
ijarah muntahiyyah bil-tamlik	Lease ending in ownership.
ijma'	A consensus (of *fuqaha'*). *Ijma'* is one of the sources of Islamic Law.
ijma' al-nas	General consensus of "*ulama.*"
ijma' sukuti	Tacit consensus (of *fuqaha'*), that is, an opinion carried without any contest from any known scholar.
ijma' qawli	Consensus expressed verbally.
ijtihad	In technical terms, it refers to the endeavor of a jurist to derive a rule or reach a judgement based on evidence found in the Islamic sources of law, predominantly, the *Qur'an* and the *sunnah*.
ikrah hukmi	An "unpleasant ruling."
'illah	Reason or characteristic behind a *Shari'ah* ruling such that if a particular reason or characteristic is found in other instances, the same ruling will apply.
ilm	Knowledge.
imama	Spiritual and temporal leadership.
iman	Belief through the heart in addition to oral profession of faith.
infaq	Spending. In the literature of Islamic economics, it usually refers to spending in the way of Allah (*swt*).
iqtisad	It refers to Islamic approach to economic problems.
irfaq	An act of benevolence or charity for seeking the pleasure of Allah (*swt*).
irshad	Providing moral guidance.
israf	Extravagance or excessiveness (especially in expenditure).

istihsan It refers to the departure from a ruling in a particular situation in favor of another ruling, which brings about ease. This is done by taking a lenient view of an act which would be considered a "violation" on a stricter interpretation of the action based on earlier *qiyas*.

istislah An unprecedented judgement within the overall *Shari'ah* framework though not having explicit support from the *Qur'an* or *sunnah*. Motivated by broader public interest, *istislah* is accepted as a source of Islamic Law.

istisna' (short form for *bay' al-istisna'*) Refers to a contract whereby a manufacturer (contractor) agrees to produce (build) and deliver a well-described product (or premise) at a given price on a given date in the future. In *istisna'* as opposed to *salam*, the price need not be paid in advance. It may be paid in instalments in step with the preferences of the parties or partly at the front end and the balance later on as agreed.

ithm A sinful act.

jahl Ignorance, lack of knowledge. In contracts, it refers to lack of information on the subject, or the terms and conditions, of the contract.

jihad Striving to better oneself spiritually. One specific application is participation in defense of one's faith against aggression.

jizyah A levy on those who prefer to keep their own faith in lieu of zakat which all Muslims are required to pay.

ju'alah Performing a given task for a prescribed fee in a given period.

kafalah A contract whereby a person guarantees, or takes responsibility for, a liability or duty of another person.

kafil Guarantor.

karahiyyah Dislike, aversion. In *Shari'ah* terms, something that is not completely prohibited but is abhorred.

kharaj A levy on land use.

khilafa	Vice-regency.
khiyanah	Breach of faith, cheating, deception.
khiyar	Option.
khiyar al-'ayb	Option to rescind a sales contract if a defect is discovered in the object of sale.
khiyar al-ru'yah	Option to rescind a sales contract after physical inspection of the object of sale.
khiyar al-shart	The option to rescind a sales contract based on certain conditions. One of the parties to a sales contract may stipulate specific conditions, which, if not met, would grant the stipulating party the option to rescind the contract.
khula'	A divorce in return for either the husband foregoing the dower of the wife or a monetary compensation by the wife to the husband.
khums	A 20 percent levy on net annual income.
maad	The event of "end-of-time return," indicating the "day of reckoning," the time when all stand before their Creator to be judged.
mafasid	Plural for *mafsadah* (for meaning, see *mafsadah*).
mafsadah	Anything declared harmful by the *Shari'ah* or anything hampering the achievement of the *maqasid al-Shari'ah*.
makrooh	Abominable. In *Shari'ah* terms, something that is not completely prohibited but is abhorred.
mal	Asset, property.
Maliki	A school of Islamic jurisprudence named after Imam Malik.
manfa' ah	Usufruct. Benefit flowing from a durable commodity or asset.
maqasid al-Shari'ah	The basic objectives of the *Shari'ah*. These are protection of faith, life, progeny, property, and reason.
masalih	Plural of *maslahah* (for meaning, see *maslahah*).
masalih mursalah	Public interest as determined in the light of the rules of the *Shari'ah*.
maslahah	Literally, it means benefit. Technically, it refers to any action taken to protect any one of the five basic objectives of the *Shari'ah*, that is, protection of faith, life, progeny, property, and reason.

maysir	Literally, it refers to an ancient Arabian game of chance with arrows used for stakes of slaughtered animals. Technically, gambling or any game of chance.
milkiyyah	Ownership.
mu' amalat	Relationships or contracts among human beings as against *'ibadat* which define the relationship between God and His creatures.
mudarabah	A contract between two parties—a capital owner or financier (*rabb al-mal*) and an investment manager (*mudarib*). Profit is distributed between the two parties in accordance with the ratio upon which they agree at the time of the contract. Financial loss is borne only by the financier. The investment manager's loss lies in not getting any reward for his services.
mudarib	An investment manager in a *mudarabah* contract.
muhtasib	Ombudsperson.
mujtahid	A religious scholar qualified to give *Shari'ah* rulings.
mukhatarah	Risk.
muqaradah	Carries the same meaning as *mudarabah.*
murabahah	Sale at a specified profit margin. This term, however, is now used to refer to a sale agreement whereby the seller purchases the goods desired by the buyer and sells them at an agreed marked-up price, the payment being settled within an agreed time frame, either in instalments or as a lump sum. The seller bears the risk for the goods until they have been delivered to the buyer. *Murabahah* is also referred to as *bay' mu'ajjal.*
musharakah	Partnership. A *musharakah* contract is similar to a *mudarabah* contract, the difference being that in the former both the partners participate in the management and the provision of capital and share in the profit and loss. Profits are distributed between the partners in accordance with the ratios initially set, whereas loss is distributed in proportion to each one's share in the capital.

muzara'ah	A contract whereby one party agrees to till the land owned by the other party for an agreed share in the produce of the land.
nafaqah	Allowance.
nafaqat	Plural of *nafaqah*, (for meaning, see *nafaqah*).
nafs	The inner, primordial self.
Najash	In reference to a sales contract, it means contriving with the seller and bidding a higher price, not with an intention to buy but simply to fetch a higher price from other potential buyers.
nas	Text from the *Qur'an* or *sunnah*.
nisab	With reference to *Zakah*, the limit of wealth that marks the beginning of the imposition of *Zakah* liability. Wealth below this limit is exempt.
niyyah	Intention.
nubuwwah	Prophethood.
qabd	Possession.
qadar	Provision of exact measure by the Creator of what His creation needs, individually and collectively, for the life on this plane of existence.
qadi	Judge.
qard-ul-hassan (short form qard)	A loan extended without interest or any other compensation from the borrower. The lender expects a reward only from God.
qasada	The term refers to the concept of "the golden mean."
qimar	Gambling.
qirad	See *mudarabah*.
qiyas	Derivation and application of a rule or law on the analogy of another rule or law if the basis (*'illah*) of the two is the same. It is one of the secondary sources of Islamic Law.
qur'an (also written as *al-qur'an*)	The Holy Book of Muslims, consisting of the revelations made by God to the Prophet Muhammad (peace be upon him). The *Qur'an* lays down the fundamentals of the Islamic faith, including beliefs and all aspects of the Islamic way of life.

qurud hasanah	Plural of *qard ul-hassan (for meaning, see qard ul-hassan).*
rabb al-mal	Capital owner (financier) in a *mudarabah* contract.
riba	Literally, it means increase, addition or growth. Technically, it refers to the "premium" that must be paid by the borrower to the lender along with the principal amount as a condition for the loan or an extension in its maturity. Interest, as commonly understood today, is regarded by a predominant majority of *fuqaha'* to be equivalent to *riba.*
riba al-fadl	*Riba* pertaining to trade contracts. It refers to the exchange of different quantities or qualities of the same commodity. As defined by the *Shari'ah*, there are particular commodities for which such exchanges are not allowed. Different schools of *fiqh* apply this prohibition to different commodities.
riba al-nasa'	*Riba* pertaining to loan contracts.
sadaqah	An act of charity.
sadaqat	Plural of *sadaqah* (for meaning, see *sadaqah*).
sadaqah jariyah	An act of charity with perennial benefits.
sadd al-zara'i	Prohibition of a deed which, if permitted, may lead to another prohibited deed.
salaf	The short form of *bay' al-salaf.*
salah	A verbal noun referring to the best course of action in accordance with the behavioral rules of Islam.
salam	The short form of *bay' al-salam.*
sarf	Currency exchange.
Shaf'i	A school of Islamic jurisprudence named after Imam Shaf'i.
Shari'ah	Refers to the corpus of Islamic law based on Divine guidance, as given by the *Qur'an* and the *sunnah*, and embodies all aspects of the Islamic faith, including beliefs and practices.
sharikat tawzif al-amwal	A partnership with assigned property delegation.
shirakah	Partnership. Technically, it is equivalent to *musharakah.*

shuf'ah	Right of preemption.
shura	Islamic institution of consultation in the process of decision-making.
subhanahu wa-ta'ala	Deviotional phrase appearing after the mention of *Allah*' meaning "glorious and exatted is He." Often abbreviated to *swt*.
sukuk al-ijarah (short form sukuk)	A negotiable financial instrument issued on the basis of an asset to be leased. The investors provide funds to a lessor (say an Islamic bank). The lessor acquires an asset (either existing or to be created in future) and leases it out if it is not already leased out. *Sukuk al-ijarah* are issued by the lessor in favour of the investors, who become owners of the leased asset in proportion to their investment. These *sukuk* entitle the holders to collect rental payments from the lessee directly. *Sukuk* can also be made tradable in the stock exchange.
sukuk al-salam	A negotiable instrument issued on the basis of a *salam* contract. A *salam* sale creates an in-kind debt payable on a future date. *Sukuk al-salam* represent common shares in that debt. Trading *salam* debt for money is controversial among Islamic scholars.
sunnah	The *sunnah* is the second most important source of the Islamic faith after the *Qur'an* and refers to the Prophet's (peace be upon him) example as indicated by his practice of the faith. The only way to know the *sunnah* is through the collection of *ahadith*, which consist of reports about the sayings, deeds, and endorsements of the Prophet (peace be upon him).
surah	A chapter of *Qur'an*.
swt	Abbreviation of *subhanahu wa-tasla*.
ta'am	Eatables.
ta'awun	Cooperation (for good).
tabarru'at	Actions or contracts, the purpose of which is not commercial but is seeking the pleasure of *Allah* (*swt*).
tabdhir	Unreasonable (impermissible) and wasteful expenditure.

tafseer	Interpretation of the *Qur'an*.
takaful	An alternative to the contemporary insurance contract. A group of persons agree to share a certain risk (for example, damage by fire) by collecting a specified sum from each. In the case of loss to any of the group, the loss is met from the collected funds.
takhrij	Deducing rules of *fiqh* from existing and varied sources, that is, from various schools of thought.
tamwil	Financing.
tandid	Liquidation.
taqwa	Ever-present consciousness of the presence of *Allah (swt)*.
tawakkul	Trust in God for results after one has undertaken all necessary effort. It is one of the important values for Muslims. After making all necessary efforts, a Muslim believes that the results are in the hand of God.
tawarruq	Reverse Murabaha. Buying an item on credit on a deferred payment basis and then immediately reselling it for cash at discounted price to a third party.
tawhid	Belief in the unity of God, both in terms of the person as well as in His attributes.
'ulama'	Scholars.
Ummah	The nation of Muslims.
'urf	Established usage, custom. *'Urf* is one of the sources of Islamic law as long as it does not contradict the basic sources, the *Qur'an* and *sunnah*.
ushr	Referring to the law of *Zakah*, it means a rate of 10 percent leviable on certain types of wealth, output, or income.
usul	Principles, basics.
wa'd	A time-bound promise to deliver on terms contracted.

wadi' ah	A contract whereby a person leaves valuables with someone for safekeeping. The keeper can charge a fee, even though Islamic culture encourages this service to be provided for nothing, or to recover only the costs of safekeeping without any profit.
wa'id	Warning.
wakalah	Contract of agency. In this contract, one person appoints someone else to perform a certain task on his behalf, usually for a fixed fee.
waqf	Appropriation or tying up a property in perpetuity for specific purposes. No property rights can be exercised over the corpus. Only the usufruct is applied towards the objectives (usually charitable) of the *waqf*.
Zahiri	A school of Islamic jurisprudence.
Zakah	The amount payable by a Muslim, on his net worth, as a part of his religious obligations, mainly for the benefit of the poor and the needy. It is an obligatory duty on every adult Muslim who owns more than a threshold wealth.
zanni	Based on conjecture.
zulm	Injustice, encroaching upon the rights of anyone else.

Source: Islamic Research and Training Institute (IRTI), Jeddah, Saudi Arabia.

CHAPTER 1

The Development and Progress of Islamic Finance

Islamic finance has emerged on the international financial landscape in a relatively short time. From a humble beginning in the 1960s, the concept was put into practice in the 1970s when the first commercial Islamic bank, Dubai Islamic Bank, was launched, followed by the establishment of the Jeddah-based multilateral development institution, the Islamic Development Bank, in 1975. Since then, the Islamic financial industry has enjoyed consistently high growth (10–15 percent annually) and continues to grow rapidly. There are now more than 300 institutions in more than 65 countries engaged in some form of Islamic finance, and, according to some conservative estimates, total assets classified as Islamic exceed US$600 billion.

Islamic finance is a relatively new term which denotes engaging in financial and business transactions according to the principles of Islamic Law—*Shari'ah*.[1] The most critical and distinguishing feature of such a system is the prohibition of *riba*, which includes the payment and receipt of interest as understood in today's financial markets. The most significant implication of this prohibition is the removal of pure "debt-based" contracts from the financial transactions. In modern history, interest in conducting *Shari'ah*-compliant business rose with the first sign of expansion of conventional "interest-based" commercial banking into the Arab and Muslim world. As early as the late nineteenth century, a formal critique and opposition to the element of "interest" started in Egypt when Barclays Bank was established in Cairo to raise funds for the construction of the Suez Canal. Further, a formal opposition to the institution of "interest" can be found as early as 1903 when the payment of interest on post office saving funds was declared contrary to Islamic values and, therefore, illegal by *Shari'ah* scholars in Egypt.

During the first half of the twentieth century, there were several attempts to highlight the differences between the emerging conventional financial system and the areas where it conflicted with Islamic values. By the 1950s and 1960s, several Muslim countries began to gain freedom from years of colonialism, and with this newly found freedom there were attempts to rediscover Islamic values and heritage. By 1953, Islamic economists had offered the first description of an interest-free bank. By the start of the 1960s, there was substantial demand for *Shari'ah*-compliant banking, resulting in the establishment of the Mit Ghamr Local Savings Bank in Egypt in 1963 by the noted social activist Ahmad-al-Najjar. It is worth noting that Dr. Najjar chose not to label this institution as an "Islamic bank" but promoted it as a social welfare institution.[2] Unfortunately, this experiment lasted for only four years. In the same year, there were parallel efforts in Malaysia to develop a saving scheme for Muslims to perform Pilgrimage.

The establishment of the Dubai Islamic Bank by some traders in 1974 is considered to be one of the earliest private initiatives in the United Arab Emirates. The 1970s witnessed a rise in the price of oil, leading to rising oil revenues and financial assets in several oil-rich Muslim countries, especially in the Middle East. The oil revenues of the 1970s, sometimes referred to as "petrodollars," offered strong incentives for creating suitable investment outlets for Muslims wanting to comply with the *Shari'ah*. Interest-free or Islamic banking, which was only a conceptual idea by the early 1970s, was given a strong business foundation. Both domestic and international bankers, including some of the leading conventional banks in the world, exploited this business opportunity.

In 1975, the Islamic Development Bank (IDB) was established, along the lines of other regional development institutions, with the objective of promoting economic development in Muslim countries as well as offering development finance according to the rules of the *Shari'ah*. Since its inception, the IDB has played a key role in expanding Islamic modes of financing and in undertaking valuable research in the area of Islamic economics, finance, and banking. The 1980s proved to be the beginning of a trend of rapid growth and expansion for the emerging Islamic financial services industry. The major developments of the 1980s included the continuation of serious research on the conceptual and theoretical level, constitutional protection in three Muslim countries, and the involvement of conventional bankers in offering *Shari'ah*-compliant services. The Islamic Republics of Iran, Pakistan, and Sudan announced that they would transform their overall financial systems to make them compliant with the *Shari'ah*. Other countries, such as Malaysia and Bahrain, started Islamic banking within the framework of their existing systems. The International Monetary Fund (IMF) initiated research into understanding the macroeconomic implications of an economic system operating without the basis of interest. Similar research was conducted to understand the issues of profit–loss sharing contracts and the financial stability of a system based on the sharing of profit and loss.

During the early stages of Islamic financial market growth in the 1980s, Islamic banks faced a dearth of quality investment opportunities. This created business opportunities for conventional Western banks to act as intermediaries to deploy Islamic banks' funds according to the guidelines given by the Islamic banks. Western banks realized the importance of the emerging Islamic financial markets and started to offer Islamic products through "Islamic windows" in an attempt to attract clients directly, without having an Islamic bank as intermediary. The number of conventional banks offering Islamic windows grew, and several leading conventional banks, such as the Hong Kong and Shanghai Banking Corporation (HSBC) and Citibank, began to pursue this market aggressively.

By the early 1990s, the market had gained enough momentum to attract the attention of public policymakers and of institutions interested in introducing innovative products. Citibank is one of the first Western banks to have established a separate Islamic bank—Citi Islamic Investment Bank (Bahrain) in 1996. HSBC has a well-established network of banks in the Muslim world. With the objective of promoting Islamic asset securitization and private equity and banking in OECD countries, HSBC Global Islamic Finance (GIF) was launched in 1998. With the growth of Islamic products and services, the need for regulation and standards increased, resulting in the establishment of a self-regulatory agency—the Accounting and Auditing Organization for Islamic Financial Institutions (AAOIFI)—in Bahrain which has played an important role in promoting growth.

1.1 RECENT DEVELOPMENTS

By the late 1990s and early 2000s, Islamic finance began to catch attention at international level and more and more countries began to embrace the concept that a system without interest (debt) is workable. This recognition can be attributed to two major factors. First, during its history of more than 30 years, no major Islamic bank failed; on the contrary, these banks proved to be as efficient and profitable as their conventional counterparts. There were cases of bank failures but those failures were caused by, and attributed to, bad governance and lack of risk management. In none of the failed banks was the issue of Islamic financial products or the design of financial intermediation questioned. This success of 30 years gave confidence and trust to customers and removed the doubts of skeptics. Second, the advancement of financial theory, in both conventional and Islamic literature, in the area of portfolio theory and the understanding of financial intermediation has been supportive. Such advancement in theory showed that a system without interest can be designed, and, under certain conditions, such systems may prove to exhibit more stability than the conventional system.[3]

As the science of financial engineering developed, its application in Islamic finance also led to innovation. The first wave of innovation came in the form of Islamic funds where portfolios of commodities, equities, Islamic leases, and other Islamic products were established. In the case of equities, special screening and filters were developed to comply with *Shari'ah*, and research showed that application of such screens or filters does not impact on the benefit of diversification. The other significant breakthrough came in the form of *sukuk* (Islamic bonds), where pools of *Shari'ah*-compliant financial instruments are securitized in the form of a fixed-income security. The issuers of *sukuk* include both sovereign and corporate entities, and the success of *sukuk* is evident by the high growth this market has enjoyed. *Sukuk* have also proved to be a bridge between Islamic and conventional markets and have led to the gradual development of capital markets, as discussed in the following section. As demand for infrastructure increased in the region, innovative structures to finance infrastructure projects were introduced. The years 2006 and 2007 proved to be the most active for the project finance market in the Middle East, attracting Western banks and law firms to structure Islamic tranches for major energy, infrastructure, and real estate projects.

Another noticeable development is the awareness of Islamic finance in non-Muslim countries and acceptance of Islamic products at major financial centers in the West. Leading Western financial intermediaries were engaged in Islamic transactions from the early stages, and the majority of the deals were done discretely; but by the mid-2000s, competition increased and both Islamic and conventional financial institutions began to position themselves aggressively to capture market share. Islamic finance gained attention in academic circles as well. Many well-regarded academic institutions—including

Harvard University (United States), Durham University (United Kingdom), and Loughborough University (United Kingdom)—organized seminars and conferences, and offered degree programs and certifications. During this decade, major publishing houses, such as Euromoney, John Wiley, and Edward Elgar, began to commission commercial and academic books on the subject.

More recently, there has been another wave of interest in Islamic finance. Similar to the surge of 1970s, the recent surge has been stimulated by increased oil revenues in the Middle East. Whereas during the 1970s interest in Islamic finance was limited to the high-net-worth class, current growth is the result of demand by much wider groups, including small investors and retail consumers. Several countries where Islamic finance was dormant are experiencing a sudden surge in demand for *Shari'ah*-compliant products. One example is Saudi Arabia, where, for a long time, there was skepticism of Islamic finance and no encouragement for its growth, but it has suddenly seen increasing public pressure to embrace Islamic finance. For example, Saudi Arabia's largest bank, National Commercial Bank, has converted its entire branch network to *Shari'ah* principles. Saudi Arabia has also issued three new licenses for *takaful* (Islamic insurance) companies.[4]

Both Bahrain and Malaysia have taken an active role in the development of Islamic finance and made serious efforts to establish world class financial centers to promote Islamic finance. The government of Malaysia has developed this industry, using a phased approach and this can be used as a roadmap for others who are interested in developing this sector.[5] The Islamic Banking Act was enacted in 1983, which led to the establishment of the first Islamic Bank—Bank Islam Malaysia Berhard—in the same year *Shari'ah*-compatible investment certificates were introduced to supplement the liquidity needs of the Islamic banking sector. In the second phase, three conventional banks were allowed to open Islamic windows. In January 1994, Bank Negara Malaysia established the Islamic Interbank Money Market to allow Islamic institutions to adjust their portfolios according to their short-term financing needs. In the third phase, some conventional banks, with a sufficient critical mass of Islamic customers, transitioned to full-fledged Islamic banks in the late 1990s. Finally, the government began to promote development of Islamic capital markets, Islamic insurance businesses, and other supporting institutions.

There is no formal or systematic source of statistics on Islamic finance but several estimates are often quoted by different commercial and noncommercial sources.[6] According to the 10 Year Master Plan for Islamic Financial Industry prepared by the IDB and the Islamic Financial Services Board (IFSB), by the end of 2005 more than 300 institutions in over 65 jurisdictions were engaged in Islamic finance. In a broad sense, the Islamic financial industry consists of different sectors such as Islamic banks, Islamic windows, capital markets, Islamic insurance (*takaful*), and other non-bank financial institutions. Islamic banking usually refers to offshore and onshore deposit-taking commercial and investment banking, and is the most dominant sector of the market. Islamic windows are specialized windows available through conventional banks catering to the demand for Islamic products. Historically, Islamic banking and windows have been the most active sector, but in the last decade other forms of financial products and services are gaining momentum. Activities in the capital markets in the form of Islamic funds or Islamic bonds (*sukuk*) are increasing, and there are institutions specializing in asset management, mutual funds, and brokerage houses. Islamic non-bank financial institutions include specialized institutions offering financial services through leasing (*ijarah*) or partnership (*mudarabah*), similar to conventional fund management companies. There are limited but growing numbers of institutions engaged in microfinance, venture capital, and private-equity financing.

Table 1.1 shows the total size of different segments of the market, compiled from different sources. Due to a lack of transparency of financial disclosure by financial institutions in developing countries these estimates are on the conservative side, and the actual size of assets under management is considered to be significantly larger.

Earlier this year, *The Banker* (2008) compiled a comprehensive listing of financial institutions engaged in Islamic finance and

Table 1.1 Total assets under management (as of 2007)

Sector	Amount (US$ billion)
Islamic banks	300
Islamic windows	200
Sukuk	70
Islamic funds	20
Takaful	4
Total	594

published a list of 500 top Islamic institutions, including Islamic banks, Islamic windows, Islamic investment banks, and insurance companies.[7] According to this report, the global total of *Shari'ah*-compliant assets grew at an impressive rate of 29.7 percent in 2007, compared to the previous year, to reach US$500.4 billion. Although this size is relatively small compared to the US$74,232.2 billion in total assets managed by the top 1,000 conventional banks worldwide, the massive growth taking place in Islamic institutions is almost double the growth rate of 16.3 percent for conventional banks.

Globally, the MENA (Middle East and North Africa) region accounts for the largest share of total *Shari'ah*-compliant assets at 70.9 percent, followed by Asia with market share of 22.7 percent. Within MENA, market share is split almost evenly between the GCC (Gulf Cooperation Council, consisting of Bahrain, Kuwait, Oman, Qatar, Saudi Arabia, and the United Arab Emirates) states with 35.6 percent and the non-GCC MENA states with 35.3 percent. Table 1.2 shows the size and growth rate of assets under management by the top 500 Islamic financial institutions as compiled by *The Banker* (2008). An interesting observation is that the top 15 countries by size of Islamic assets includes a non-Muslim country—the United Kingdom—at tenth place, with *Shari'ah*-compliant assets of US$10.4 billion, mainly due to successful operations by HSBC Amanah with total assets of US$9.7 billion.

Table 1.2 Islamic finance assets (US$m)

Region	2007	2006	% Change
GCC	178,129.55	127,826.55	39.4%
Non–GCC MENA	176,822.17	136,157.64	29.9%
MENA Total	354,951.72	263,984.19	34.5%
Sub-Saharan	4,707.98	3,039.32	54.9%
Asia	119,346.46	98,709.56	20.9%
Australia/Europe/America	21,475.72	20,300.24	5.8%
Global Total	500,481.88	386,033.33	29.6%

Source: The Banker (2008).

1.2 THEORETICAL DEVELOPMENT[8]

Siddiqi (2006) recalls conducting a survey of writings on Islamic economics and banking in English, Arabic, and Urdu languages in the early 1970s, and makes the following observations:

> Out of the items included in the bibliography only 8 date before 1920. Out of these, only 2 deal with the subject of interest, the remaining dealing with distribution of wealth (2) history (2) trade (1) and *waqf* (1). Of the 14 entries in the following decade only one deals with interest, the remaining are spread over other subjects. The first writings on interest-free banking appear in the nineteen-forties. Out of a total of 28 writings on Islamic economics during this period, three are on interest-free banking. Among the remaining, *zakat* and the Islamic economic system in general has the largest number of writings. Though the writers in this period include *Ulema* [scholars] trained in traditional schools, the writings on interest-free institutions are not by them. We have 156 entries for the nineteen-fifties which include several writings on interest and interest-free institutions but the writings on socialism, capitalism and on some other aspects of Islamic economy far outnumber these.

Modern scholars began thinking about Islamic finance in the second half of the last century, and focused on explanations of the prohibition of *riba* (interest), and to a lesser extent *gharar* (information asymmetry), and on their economic and social impact.[9] The main question of whether the prevailing fixed, predetermined rate of interest on loans in conventional banking constituted *riba* was debated well into the 1980s, when a consensus was reached among scholars that indeed the prohibition did include such interest receipts or payments. In the 1970s research also began on how Islam proposes to organize an economy, with the now classic works of Baqir al-Sadr (1987) who provided groundbreaking ideas on the main features of an Islamic economy in comparison with those of socialism and capitalism. Al-Sadr also provided original ideas on how a modern Islamic bank can be organized and operated without resorting to an interest rate mechanism. His work on an Islamic economy was followed by that of, among others, Chapra (1975, 1979), Siddiqi (1981), Khan and Mirakhor (1985), and Mirakhor (1989), who provided further groundbreaking research on why there is a need for an alternative system, what are the essential features of an Islamic economic system, and how a system will function in the absence of interest. This research gradually moved to more formal discussions on designing an alternative economic system, which led to the laying out of alternatives to the conventional banking system by exploring *Shari'ah*-complaint contracts, especially equity partnerships. Finally, a model of a financial intermediary based on two-tier *mudarabah* emerged, where the financial intermediary, acting as a *mudarib* (agent), would accept deposits from investors (principals) on the basis of profit and loss-sharing agreements and will deploy funds in suitable investment vehicles. Using a principal-agent framework, Nadeem ul Haq and Mirakhor (1989), followed by Presley and Sessions (1994), showed that a *mudarabah* contract is an efficient form of financial intermediation.[10]

Increasing demand for Islamic financial products and services and the emergence of Islamic banks stimulated further research on intermediation and especially on banking. As a result, most of the limited research resources were consumed by the growing business of Islamic banking, and work on so-called Islamic economics took a back seat. As banking business expanded, the need for investigation into risk management, regulation, and corporate governance also increased. This led to the production of some high-quality research in these areas, and significant progress has been made by institutions such as the Islamic Research and Training Institute (IRTI), the IFSB, the AAOIFI, and the World Bank.[11] Archer and Karim (1997) convincingly argued for special regulations of Islamic banks and, therefore, for special capital adequacy requirements. Errico and Farahbakhs (1998), Sundararajan and Errico (2002), and Khan and Ahmed (2001) provided a regulatory and risk-management framework, which was developed further by others, laying the foundations for standards on risk management and capital adequacy by the IFSB. Chapra and Ahmed (2002) initiated discussion on the corporate governance of Islamic financial institutions. Iqbal and Mirakhor (2004) developed a stakeholder-based model of corporate governance, arguing that any corporate governance structure in Islam will be stakeholder-centered, ensuring each stakeholder's property rights are protected and that they are held accountable for any explicit, as well as implicit, contract.

By the late 1990s and early 2000s, there began discussion on the scope of financial engineering and derivatives. Financial engineering did not receive much attention in the literature, primarily because most of the deals and transactions were designed by lawyers and *Shari'ah* experts and were executed in private by financial institutions who did not discuss the structure in a transparent manner. Iqbal (1999) argued that with the availability of basic building blocks in Islam and with the freedom to contract within the perimeters of *Shari'ah*, financial engineering should be encouraged. As an example, he discussed the scope and benefits of securitization of assets in Islamic finance. Successful securitization was introduced in the form of *sukuk* (Islamic bonds), and became an instant success.

Discussion on Islamic derivative products is rare, and even what is available in the literature is not very favorable. One difficulty is that derivatives are a new phenomenon for which one does not find any precedent in the classical authority of *fiqh*. Kamali (1999) attempts to make a case for commodity derivatives on the grounds that derivatives are clear of the wrongful devouring of the properties of others and such contracts are concluded through the mutual consent of the trading parties.[12] He also argues that commodity derivatives should be viewed under the broad scope of public interest or *maslahah*, which is a recognized proof and basis of judgment in *Shari'ah*. Al-Suwailem (2006) discusses hedging and the scope of derivatives and financial engineering in Islam. He does not seem to be convinced that derivatives satisfy the aspect of "tolerable risk" in Islam and, therefore, concludes that these may not add much value to the financial system.

With increasing globalization, Muslim scholars began to understand the impact of globalization on Islamic finance. Mirakhor (2005b) presented the thesis of a convergence of Islamic finance and globalization based on the risk-sharing feature of Islamic finance. He argues that whereas the central proposition of Islamic finance is the prohibition of debt-based contracts, it offers an alternative by encouraging exchange—*al-bay'* (البيع)—which ultimately leads to sharing of risks. He concludes that whereas positive features of globalization, such as risk sharing, are compatible with Islam, negative impacts of globalization, such as inequality, can be overcome by following Islam's tenets of justice—thus leading to a convergence.

Progress in Islamic finance and economics has not been without criticism; for example, Kuran (1995, 1996) has questioned the very nature of Islamic finance and economics, as well as the motivation of scholars working in this area (see also Mirakhor 2005a, who responds to his criticism). Others have questioned the role of *Shari'ah* scholars and the transparency of their relations with the financial institutions they advise (Siddiqi 2006, El-Gamal 2006). El-Gamal (2006) has questioned the legitimacy and validity of certain rulings and practices by some of these scholars. While there has yet to appear objective, informed, and intellectually worthwhile criticism to the theoretical foundation of Islamic finance, given the comparatively short history of Islamic finance and economics, even those that have been offered thus far are important to their theoretical and empirical evolution.

1.3 INSTITUTIONAL DEVELOPMENT

The private sector has been much more active than the public sector in the growth of this market. Governments, such as those in Bahrain and Malaysia, have made serious efforts to establish financial centers for Islamic financial institutions. An institutional infrastructure to support the development of the financial sector is slowly emerging. This includes institutions to deal with accounting and regulatory standards, corporate governance, credit ratings, and capital markets. These efforts to develop institutions are also supported by several stakeholders such as the IMF, central banks of leading Muslim countries, international standard setting bodies, and financial centers.

The IDB was established in 1975 as a regional development institution to promote economic development in Muslim countries through Islamic finance. It has also been active in providing financial and infrastructure support to promote Islamic finance. Since its creation, the IDB has established several sister institutions to develop private sector insurance facilities and trade and export financing.[13] Additionally, the IDB has played a very important role in developing institutional infrastructure to promote Islamic financial systems. Some notable contributions are institutions to enhance the regulatory framework and standardization of the Islamic banking industry, such as: the AAOIFI; the IFSB; the General Council of Islamic Banks and Financial Institutions (GCIBFI); the International Islamic Financial Market (IIFM); the Islamic International Rating Agency (IIRA); the Liquidity Management Center (LMC); and the International Islamic Center for Reconciliation and Commercial Arbitration (IICRCA).

The IRTI—the research arm of IDB—was established in 1981 to undertake research, training, and knowledge generation activities on economic, financial, and banking issues according to Islam. The main activities of the IRTI include organizing seminars and conferences on these subjects in collaboration with national, regional, and international institutions, undertaking theoretical and empirical research for the application of *Shari'ah* in the fields of economics, banking, and finance, and developing human capital capacities in Islamic economics and finance through training. The IRTI has become a center of knowledge dissemination by developing a rich resource center for research through collection of in-house research papers, background and discussion papers, seminar proceedings, lectures, translations, journals, and articles, which are available through its Web site. The role the IRTI has played, despite limited resources, is commendable, and the fruits of its efforts are beginning to show as research in the areas of banking, risk management, regulation, and corporate governance has helped the growth of industry in new territories. The IRTI played a critical role in developing the 10 Year Master Plan for Islamic Financial Industry by collaborating with the leading stakeholders in the industry.

Another sister organization of the IDB is the Islamic Corporation for the Insurance of Investment and Export Credit (ICIEC), which was established in 1994 with the objective of enlarging the scope of trade transactions and the flow of investments among member countries. The ICIEC's main objectives are to provide *Shari'ah*-compliant export credit insurance and reinsurance to cover the nonpayment of export receivables resulting from commercial (buyer) and noncommercial (country) risks, and to provide investment insurance and reinsurance against country risk, emanating mainly from foreign exchange transfer restrictions, expropriation, war and civil disturbance, and breach of contract by the host government.

The Islamic Corporation for the Development of the Private Sector (ICD) was established in 1999 to promote the development of the private sector in member countries. Its objectives are to: identify opportunities in the private sector that could function as engines of growth; provide a wide range of productive financial products and services; mobilize additional resources for the private sector in member countries; and encourage the development of Islamic financial and capital markets.

One of the latest institutions established by the IDB is the International Islamic Trade Finance Corporation (ITFC) in 2006, to promote trade among OIC (Organization of Islamic Countries) countries through the Islamic mode of financing. The principal objective of the ITFC is to supplement the activities of the IDB by providing *Shari'ah*-compliant trade finance, promoting trade in member countries through increased intra-trade among member countries, enhancing the export capabilities of member countries, and increasing the developmental impact of trade financing on member countries. In 2006, IDB member countries also decided to establish a special "solidarity" fund for reducing poverty within their territories. The objectives of this fund are to reduce poverty, eliminate illiteracy, eradicate major communicable diseases such as malaria, tuberculosis, and

AIDS, and to build the human and productive capacities, particularly in the least developed OIC countries. This fund is expected to have capital of US$10 billion and is organized as an endowment (*waqf*) fund.

In 1991 the AAOIFI was established as a self-regulation agency for the industry to tackle the problem of *Shari'ah* compliance and gaps in applying conventional financial reporting standards to Islamic banks. The AAOIFI's membership consists of about 97 institutions spanning over 24 countries, and it has issued 50 standards on accounting, auditing, governance, ethical, and *Shari'ah* standards. The AAOIFI's *Shari'ah* board is paving the way towards *Shari'ah* harmonization of banking practices throughout the world.[14] The banking supervisors in a number of countries, such as Bahrain and Sudan, require Islamic banks to comply with the AAOIFI's standards or, as in the case of Qatar and Saudi Arabia, are specifying the AAOIFI's standards as guidelines.

The AAOIFI was successful in defining the accounting and *Shari'ah* standards which were adopted or recognized by several countries. However, with the growth of the market, the regulatory and supervisory authorities—with the help of the IMF—established a dedicated regulatory agency, the IFSB in 2000, to address systemic stability and various governance and regulatory issues relating to the Islamic financial services industry. The IFSB took on the challenge and started working in the area of regulation, risk management, and corporate governance, which are discussed further in the section on regulations.

The GCIBFI focuses on media and awareness, information and research, policies and strategic planning, and Islamic financial products. The Arbitration and Reconciliation Centre for Islamic Financial Institutions (ARCIFI) aims to settle financial and commercial disputes between financial or commercial institutions that have chosen to comply with the *Shari'ah* to settle disputes. It also settles disputes between these institutions and third parties through reconciliation and arbitration.

The major objectives of the Bahrain-based IIFM are: to enhance cooperation among the regulatory authorities of Islamic banks; to address the liquidity problem by expanding the maturity structure of instruments; and to explore the possibility of sovereign, asset-backed securities. Recently, the IIFM has signed a Memorandum of Understanding (MoU) with the International Capital Markets Association (ICMA) to work together for further development of primary and secondary markets for Islamic bonds (*sukuk*). Both associations have established working groups to coordinate efforts to facilitate standardized documentation and industry practices for floating and trading *sukuk*. The IIFM is also working with the ICMA to develop a master repurchase (repo) agreement to help central banks manage liquidity in the *sukuk* market, as well as a master agreement for commodities *murabahah* contracts, which are used in interbank transactions between Islamic banks and between Islamic and conventional banks.[15]

The IIRA aims to assist in the development of regional financial markets by providing an assessment of the risk profiles of entities and instruments that can be used for investment decisions. The IIRA is sponsored by multilateral finance institutions, several leading banks and other financial institutions, and rating agencies from different countries. The organization has a board of directors and an independent rating committee as well as a *Shari'ah* board. The IIRA also provides a unique service for rating the quality of the *Shari'ah* committee of a financial institution. The *Shari'ah* quality rating provided does not aim to give a *Shari'ah* opinion on Islamic financial products or to comment on the decisions of the *Shari'ah* committees of banks and financial institutions, or to correct their *fatawi* (proclamations). The IIRA's role is to assess the level of compliance by the institutions with the stipulations adopted by their *Shari'ah* committee in good faith, both in letter and in spirit. They also examine whether there is a mechanism within the institution to evaluate its compliance with the *Shari'ah* and whether the *Shari'ah* committee has enough authority, information, and resources to perform the examination and evaluation.

The LMC was established to facilitate investment of the surplus funds of Islamic banks and financial institutions into quality short- and medium-term financial instruments structured in accordance with *Shari'ah* principles. The shareholders include Bahrain Islamic Bank, Dubai Islamic Bank, Islamic Development Bank, and Kuwait Finance House. The LMC assists Islamic financial institutions in managing their short-term liquidity and supports the interbank market. In addition, the center attracts assets from governments, financial institutions, and corporations in both the private and public sectors in many countries. The assets are securitized into readily transferable securities or structured into other innovative investment instruments. The LMC also provides short-term liquid, tradable, asset-backed treasury instruments (*sukuk*) in which Islamic financial institutions can invest their surplus liquidity. The center also offers Islamic advisory services dealing with structured, project, and corporate finance as well as equity flotation.

Table 1.3 lists the key stakeholder institutions in the Islamic financial sector.

Table 1.3 Key institutions in the Islamic financial industry

Acronym	Organization	Function
IDB	Islamic Development Bank	Development institution formed in 1975 to promote Islamic finance and economic development **Member/sister organizations** **ICD**—Islamic Corporation for the Development of the Private Sector **ICIEC**—Islamic Corporation for the Insurance of Investment and Export Credit; Islamic insurance company, providing insurance products for investments and export credits **IRTI**—Islamic Research and Training Institute; Research and training arm **ITFC**—International Islamic Trade Finance Corporation **Solidarity Fund**—To reduce poverty in OIC countries **ARCIFI**—Arbitration and Reconciliation Centre for Islamic Financial Institutions
AAOIFI	Accounting and Auditing Organization for Islamic Financial Institutions	Accounting and *Shari'ah* standard setting body
IFSB	Islamic Financial Services Board	Standard-setting institution to ensure best practices and help member countries with regulating Islamic financial institutions
IIFM	International Islamic Financial Markets	Trade association to promote capital markets
IIRA	Islamic International Rating Agency	Rating agency
LMC	Liquidity Management Center	Institution to provide liquidity enhancement to the financial system
CIBAFI	General Council of Islamic Banks and Financial Institutions	Trade association of Islamic banks to enhance member institutions' ability to better serve customers around the world through transparent banking practices

1.4 ISLAMIC BANKING

Islamic banking—consisting of commercial and investment banking—is one of the oldest sectors of Islamic finance. Although Islamic banking has firm roots in the Middle East, it also has a presence in South and East Asia. Bahrain in the Middle East and Malaysia in Southeast Asia are trying to establish themselves as centers for Islamic finance and thus offer special incentives for Islamic banks. Islamic banking assets in Bahrain grew from US$1.3 billion to US$8.0 billion at the compounded annual growth rate (CAGR) of 28.99 percent from 1998 to 2005. Similarly, Islamic banking assets in Malaysia grew from US$19.4 billion to US$31.5 billion at a CAGR of 17.48 percent from 2002 to 2005.[16]

Table 1.4 shows the percentage market share of total Islamic banking assets of different countries as of 2006.

Financial intermediation performed by Islamic banks is based on the principle of profit and loss sharing. The depositors agree to share profits and losses with a bank that uses its skills and market knowledge to invest depositors' funds in *Shari'ah*-compliant assets. Figure 1.1 shows a stylized balance sheet of a typical Islamic bank. Depositors'

Table 1.4 Islamic banking market share by country

Saudi Arabia	19.54%
Bahrain	18.97%
Malaysia	16.30%
Kuwait	14.64%
UAE	14.39%
Qatar	3.79%
Egypt	2.83%
Iran	2.82%
Switzerland	1.86%
Jordan	1.73%
Bangladesh	1.24%
Indonesia	1.11%
Pakistan	0.35%
United Kingdom	0.25%
Palestine	0.09%
Yemen	0.06%
Rest of the world	0.03%

Source: ISI (2006). This list excludes Sudan where the total banking system is conforming to *Shari'ah*.

Figure 1.1 Theoretical balance sheet of Islamic bank

Assets	*Liabilities*
Cash balances	Demand deposits (*amanah*)
Financing assets (*murabahah, salam, ijarah, istisna'*)	Investment accounts (*mudarabah*)
Investment assets (*mudarabah, musharakah*)	Special investment accounts (*mudarabah, musharakah*)
Fee-based services (*ju'alah, kafalah,* and so forth)	Reserves
Non-banking assets (property)	Equity capital

Source: van Greuning and Iqbal (2007).

funds are invested in either financing instruments used to finance trade activities, leasing or manufacturing/construction activities, or in investment instruments through partnership and equity-partnership arrangements.

Distinct intermediation raises two concerns. First, Islamic banks' assets are dominated by short-term, trade- and leasing-based, financial instruments. These instruments tend to be of short-term maturity and are not very liquid assets. This poses a serious problem to Islamic banks that are unable to transfer illiquid assets in the secondary markets, and due to this illiquidity Islamic banks tend to shy away from medium- to long-term financial instruments. Second, Islamic banks are often characterized by being small in terms of asset size and capitalization. Several studies have suggested that the industry should seriously consider consolidating smaller banks to reap the benefits from the economics of scale and scope. Table 1.5 provides the key performance indicators of the top ten Islamic banks. Significant differences in capitalization are visible as one goes down the list.

Over the last decade, all leading rating agencies have come to understand the distinct features of Islamic banks. Agencies have developed special rating models to incorporate the distinct financial instruments and the nature of "pass-through" of profits and losses by Islamic banks. For example, realizing that the depositors of Islamic banks are loss absorbing, Standard & Poor's Ratings Services cannot use their classic credit ratings. Therefore, they have developed stability ratings to provide the depositors with a useful opinion about these instruments. These stability ratings represent Standard & Poor's opinion about the expected stability of cash flow distributable to the profit-and-loss-sharing account holders of an Islamic financial institution. A stability rating offers a current opinion about the prospective relative stability of cash flow distributable to profit-sharing depositors based on sustainability and variability, and an outlook, which expresses their opinion about the trend for the stability

Table 1.5 Top ten Islamic banks – capitalization and key indicators

Rank	Commercial Islamic bank	Country	Acct. period	Total assets (US$'000)	Market capitalization (US$'000)	Share capital (US$'000)	Reserves (US$'000)	Net profit (US$'000)	Non-performing loans (US$'000)	Capital adequacy ratio (%)	EPS (US$)	ROE (%)
1	Al Rajhi Bank	Saudi Arabia	2005	24,344,543	65,031,329	1,200,051	1,348,946	1,502,285	441,358	18.2	16.0	47
2	ABC Islamic Bank	Bahrain	2005	17,588,000	115,000,000	1,000,000	430,000	129,000	262,000	17.6	1.3	18
3	Kuwait Finance House	Kuwait	2005	16,112,894	9,006,048	376,556	788,421	444,300	342,186	n/a	12.2	21
4	Dubai Islamic Bank	UAE	2005	11,709,612	11,904,438	408,491	441,707	289,586	n/a	n/a	19.1	34
5	Malayan Banking Berhad	Malaysia	2006	6,650,135	n/a	168,956	99,361	93,816	274,047	9.2	n/a	1
6	Al Baraka Banking Group	Bahrain	2005	6,276,343	1,845,900	387,998	34,262	−133,651	n/a	n/a	0.2	20
7	Abu Dhabi Islamic Bank	UAE	2005	6,042,784	3,866,050	272,327	320,125	233,181	14,097	14.1	0.9	17
8	Bank Islam Malaysia	Malaysia	2005	4,171,314	199,409	157,916	255,316	140,710	627,886	10.9	−5.1	−6
9	Bank Al Jazir	Saudi Arabia	2005	3,778,503	6,347,154	200,009	110,596	39,120	53,348	25.4	15.5	32
10	Faisal Islamic Bank of Egypt	Egypt	2005	2,862,895	902,180	102,226	2,466	10,858	n/a	n/a	n/a	21

Source: ISI Analytics (2007).

rating over a one- to three-year horizon: stable, negative, positive, or developing.[17]

Several studies have been undertaken to evaluate the cost and production efficiency of Islamic financial institutions (IFIs) in different countries where Islamic finance is practiced. The majority of such studies have measured efficiency by using accounting ratios and comparing the same with the ratios of conventional banks of similar size and location. The results of the studies are mixed. Although Islamic banks are found to be performing efficiently when compared to similar conventional financial institutions in similar market conditions, some degree of inefficiency has also been observed. Metwally (1997) compared the performance of 15 interest-free banks with 15 conventional banks for structural difference between the two groups of banks in terms of liquidity, leverage, credit risk, profit, and efficiency. The study found that although profitability and efficiency differences are not statistically significant between the two types of banks, Islamic banks tend to be more conservative in utilizing funds for lending and were disadvantaged in terms of investment opportunities. Similar findings of constraining investment opportunities were observed by Samad and Hassan (1999), who looked at the interbank performance of Bank Islam Malaysia Berhad in terms of profitability, liquidity, risk, and solvency, as well as community involvement, for the period 1984 to 1997, and concluded that the average profit of the Islamic bank was significantly lower than that of conventional banks mainly due to the limited investment opportunity set for the Islamic bank.

Based on data from 1993 to 2000, Majid, Nor, and Said (2003) concluded that there was no statistically significant difference in the level of efficiency between Islamic and conventional banks operating in Malaysia. In a comparative study of conventional and Islamic banking, Iqbal (2000) measured the efficiency of 12 IFIs by comparing their trends and profitability ratios with a "control group" of 12 conventional banks of similar size from the same countries. Islamic banks included in the sample accounted for more than 75 percent of the total assets as well as the total capital of the whole Islamic banking industry, and were accordingly a reasonable proxy and representative of the entire sector. The study found that from 1990 to 1997, IFIs turned out to be more cost effective and made better use of their resources than the banks in the control group, as indicated by significantly higher deployment ratios.

Hussein (2003) estimated the operational efficiency of 17 Sudanese Islamic banks from 1990 to 2000, and found that Islamic banks did not create inefficiency *per se* but there were wide efficiency differences across domestic Islamic banks. Yudistira (2004) analyzed the efficiency of 18 Islamic banks for the period 1997 to 2000, and concluded that the overall efficiency results showed low levels of inefficiency (around 10 percent) across the banks, which is considerable comparable to many conventional counterparts. The study also found that Islamic banks in the sample suffered from the global crisis in 1998–99 but performed very well after the difficult periods. Hassan (2006) looked at the relative efficiency of the Islamic banking industry in Pakistan, Iran, and Sudan by employing a panel of banks during 1994 to 2001, and found that, on average, the Islamic banking industry was relatively less efficient compared to their conventional counterparts in other parts of the world. Although Islamic banks were relatively more efficient in containing cost, they are relatively inefficient in generating profit.

Recently, IMF staff conducted a first-of-its-kind study on empirical analysis of Islamic banks' impact on financial stability.[18] Using z-scores as a measure of stability, Eihák and Hesse (2008) found that: small Islamic banks tend to be financially stronger than small conventional commercial banks; large conventional commercial banks tend to be financially stronger than large Islamic banks; and small Islamic banks tend to be financially stronger than large Islamic banks. The study speculates that the reason why Islamic banks, while relatively more stable when operating on a small scale, are less stable when operating on a large scale could be because it is significantly more complex for Islamic banks to adjust their credit risk monitoring system as they become bigger. The study suggests that monitoring the various profit–loss arrangements becomes rapidly much more complex as the scale of the banking operation grows, resulting in problems relating to adverse selection and moral hazard becoming more prominent.

1.5 CAPITAL MARKETS

Compared to Islamic banking, *Shari'ah*-compliant capital markets are relatively new. During the early stages of development, the capital market activities were limited to syndicated financing and Islamic funds. One main reason was the absence of a *Shari'ah*-approved structure which was tradable in the market. Therefore, the initial focus of capital market activities was on fund management, especially during the boom in the world equities markets. Islamic funds were introduced in the late 1980s and early 1990s. These funds were a portfolio of different asset classes such as funds specializing in commodities, equities, and Islamic instruments such as leases (*ijarah*). For equities, special screening filters were defined to satisfy requirements of *Shari'ah*. For example, shares of those companies that dealt with interest-based income, carried extensive debt in their capital structure, or engaged in not "socially responsible" activities—such as alcohol production or gambling—were excluded from the fund.

Islamic funds have enjoyed considerable success, but not all investors were willing to invest in the risky equities asset class. Typical investors in Islamic banks were looking for less-risky security where the principal is protected and the security offered some steady stream of cash flows. In short, the investors were looking for a security that is *Shari'ah*-compliant but had the risk/return characteristics of a conventional fixed-income security; that is, a bond. Meanwhile, conventional finance witnessed an explosion of securitization of assets, ranging from accounts receivables to mortgages. Considering that Islamic finance promotes security linked to an asset and the success with securitization in conventional finance, finally a security in the form of an Islamic bond called *sukuk* was designed, and it immediately became a success. Within a short period of time, several different structures of *sukuk* had been introduced into the market.

Figure 1.2 shows rapid growth of the market from approximately US$1 billion in 2002 to US$47 billion in 2007. The volume of new issuance almost doubled in size from 2006 to 2007. The number

Figure 1.2 Global *sukuk* issuance (US$ million)

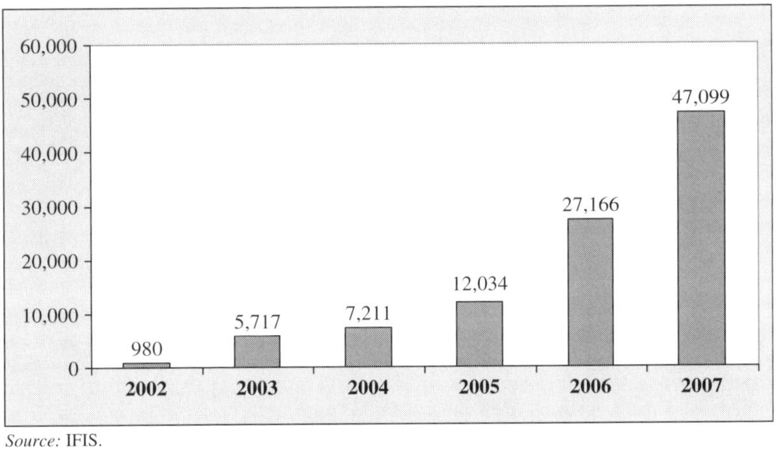

Source: IFIS.

of *sukuk* issued did not grow significantly in 2007 as compared to the previous year. Only 207 *sukuk* were issued globally in 2007, compared to 199 in 2006 and 89 in 2005.[19] Some observers attribute this slow growth in issuance to turmoil in the financial markets due to the subprime crisis. It should, however, be pointed out that although the number of issues did not increase significantly, the average issuance size of a *sukuk* did increase.

There was diversity of structures issued during 2007, and this included structures based on *bay' bithaman ajil*, *istisna'*, *mudarabah*, *ijarah*, *musharakah*, and *wakalah* contracts. Table 1.6 lists *sukuk* issuance by different countries and sectors. It is interesting to note that whereas in conventional markets sovereign bond issuance dominates the market, in case of the *sukuk* market, 79.2 percent of issuance was by the corporate sector with Malaysian corporations being the most active. This shows that sovereign entities have yet to exploit this market but is also indicative of the fact that when it comes to structuring a *sukuk*, sovereign entities have fewer options as compared to corporations who have more tangible assets to securitize.

Table 1.7 lists the top ten investment banks that acted as lead managers for the issuance of *sukuks* in 2007. It is clear that the list is dominated by leading conventional investment banks. Of the top ten,

Table 1.6 *Sukuk* issuance by country and sector for year 2007

Country	Sovereign	Corporate	Quasi-sovereign	Grand total
Bahrain	617	400	...	1,017
Brunei Darussalam	222	...	...	222
Cayman Islands	...	100	...	100
Indonesia	81	113	...	193
Kuwait	...	993	...	993
Malaysia	3,777	22,752	...	26,529
Pakistan	339	725	...	1,065
Qatar	...	450	...	450
Saudi Arabia	...	4,350	1,333	5,683
Sudan	...	130	...	130
United Arab Emirates	3,425	7,292	...	10,717
Total	**8,461**	**37,306**	**1,333**	**47,100**
Percentage	**18.0%**	**79.2%**	**2.8%**	

Source: IFIS.

Table 1.7 2007 Islamic bonds bookrunners/lead managers league table — issued

Ranking	Bookrunner/Lead manager	Amount—US$m	Issues
1	CIMB Islamic	7,490	33
2	HSBC Amanah	3,583	15
3	Barclays Capital	2,479	6
4	ABN-Amro Bank Bhd	2,292	3
5	Deutsche Bank	1,980	6
6	Citigroup	1,762	5
7	JP Morgan	1,283	2
8	Dubai Islamic Bank	1,097	6
9	Standard Chartered Bank	1,083	17
10	Riyadh Bank	1,050	1

Source: IFIS.

only three banks—Malaysian-based CIMB Islamic, Dubai Islamic Bank, and Riyadh Bank—are local as well as Islamic, while the rest are Western banks. There are several reasons for conventional banks to play this leading role. First, conventional banks are more experienced and knowledgeable about financial engineering and structuring transactions. Second, conventional banks have more sophisticated sales channels to market the issues. There is a growing trend of conventional investors investing in *sukuks* as they see better value. Third, conventional banks are working more aggressively to capture this growing field, especially in GCC countries.

Growth in the *sukuk* market led to the development of the *sukuk* Index by Dow Jones Indexes and Citigroup Corporation in 2006. An index plays a critical role in portfolio management as it serves as a proxy for the market and is used as a benchmark by portfolio managers to measure their performance. The Dow Jones Citigroup *Sukuk* Index includes *sukuk* with a minimum issue size of US$250 million, minimum maturity of one year, and a minimum rating of BBB–/Baa3 by leading rating agencies. Furthermore, *sukuk* must comply with the Bahrain-based AAOIFI standards for a tradable *sukuk*. This constraint excludes most of the Malaysian corporate issuances, which are primarily Islamic private debt securities (IPDS), which are based on the sale of receivables—a structure yet to be approved by *Shari'ah* scholars in the Middle East. At the time of inception, the index was tracking seven *sukuk* issuances, including the US$400 million AAA-rated IDB Solidarity Trust Services issue, the US$250 million A-rated BMA International *Sukuk*, and the US$700 million A+ rated Qatar Global *Sukuk*.[20] It is expected that with increasing *sukuk* issuance, fund managers and wealth managers will be able to use such an index as a benchmark and will be able to offer investment opportunities measured against this index.

In the Islamic funds domain, property funds have recently gained popularity and interest among investors in the Middle East and Europe. In addition, there are also Islamic real estate investment trusts (REITs) which invest their portfolios in listed real estate securities—subject to *Shari'ah* compliance—that own and operate real estate such as residential, commercial, and retail properties, storage facilities, warehouses, and car parks.[21] Although the number of Islamic funds available on the market has expanded in recent years (see Figure 1.3), most are relatively small in terms of size. For example, approximately 50 percent of the funds have less than US$50 million of assets under management. A significant segment of Islamic funds is concentrated in equity investments (see Figure 1.4), mainly because this is relatively easy to set up and a conventional equity mutual fund manages can apply the filter and construct such funds. However, there are gaps across other asset classes, including sector-specific funds and fixed-income funds.[22]

In 1998, the FTSE Group launched the first series of Islamic equity indices, the FTSE Global Islamic Index Series (GIIS). The GIIS are a subset of the FTSE All-World index group, which includes stocks from 29 countries. The FTSE has 15 Islamic indices; classification is based

Figure 1.3 Growth of Islamic equity funds (1996–2007)

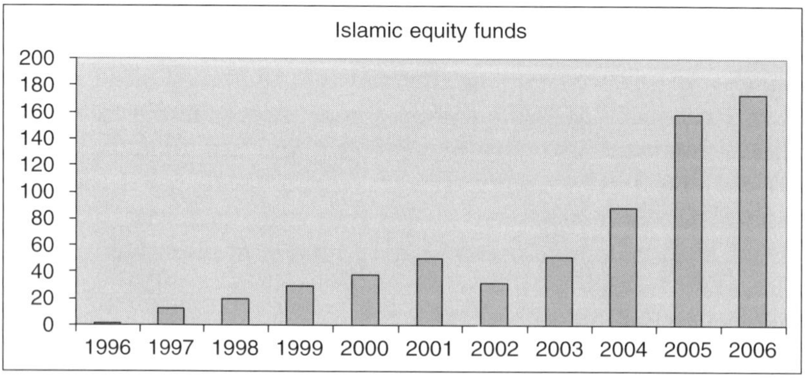

Source: ISI, Falaika.

Figure 1.4 Types of Islamic equity funds (2006)

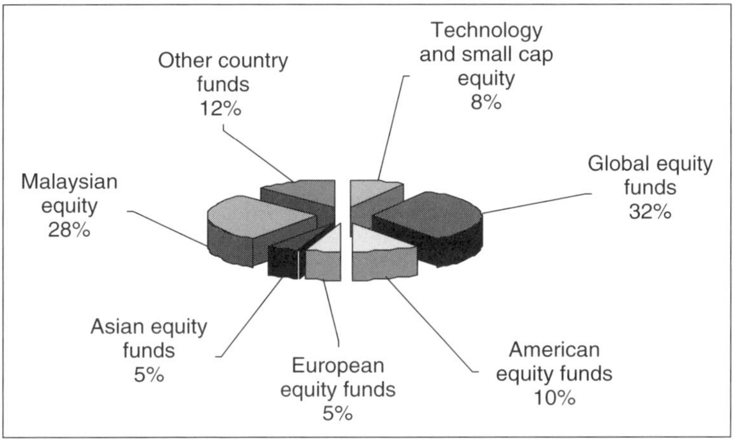

Source: ISI.

on industry (ten indices) and region (Global, the Americas, Europe, Pacific Basin, South Africa). This was followed by the first Dow Jones Islamic Market Index (DJIMI) in 1999, created to track the performance of companies whose activities are consistent with *Shari'ah* principles. More recently, Standard & Poor's has also introduced similar indices. The performance of all these indices is regularly monitored and reported.

When the idea of Islamic equity portfolios with special screens was developed, critics objected that by imposing such screens the investors will be constrained, with limited diversification benefits. However, this has been proven wrong both theoretically and empirically. Lightstone (2002) argues that quantitative methods of stock selection are well suited to the selection of active Islamic strategies that track established equity styles and which can be evaluated against their benchmarks. The paper claims that by using quantitative analysis of estimate revisions to develop Islamic strategies they can strongly outperform conventional benchmarks in 20 years of backtesting in up and down markets. The paper shows that given the availability of these strategies, there are now opportunities for asset allocation and style rotation.

Since the introduction of Islamic indices, several empirical studies have looked at the efficiency and performance of these indices. Hussein (2005) undertook a comparison of the relative performance of the Dow Jones Islamic Index and FTSE Global Islamic Index with the Dow Jones World Index and FTSE All-World Index respectively to investigate if they are significantly different. The study reviews the returns over different periods to control for behavior in different market conditions. The period from December 1993 to December 2004 is further divided into bull period I (December 1993 to December 2000), bear period (December 2000 to September 2002), and bull period II (September 2002 to December 2004). The study finds that the application of *Shari'ah* screens does not have an adverse impact on the Islamic indices' performance. In the short run, a comparison of raw and risk-adjusted performances show that the Islamic indices perform as well as their counterparts over the entire period and in the second bull market period. In the long run, there is clear evidence that the Islamic indices have a superior performance compared with their counterparts in the entire and first bull market periods. On the other hand, the Islamic indices fail to sustain their better performance over the bear and second bull market periods since the counterpart indices achieve higher returns.

Hassan and Girard (2005) looked at Dow Islamic indices for the period of 1992 to 2005 and did not find any noticeable performance differences between Islamic and non-Islamic indices from January 1996 to December 2005. The Dow Islamic indices outperformed their conventional counterparts from 1996 to 2000 and underperformed them from 2001 to 2005. They suggest that the period-specific performance of Islamic indices could be attributed to style differences between the two types of series because they observed that Islamic indices are growth and small-cap oriented and conventional indices are relatively more value and mid-cap focused. They also conclude that, overall, similar reward to risk and diversification benefits exist for both types of index.

Elfakhani, Hassan, and Sidani (2007) perform an empirical study of a sample of 46 Islamic mutual funds to investigate the difference in behavior of Islamic and conventional mutual funds. The study concludes that the behavior of Islamic mutual funds does not differ from that of other conventional funds, with some *Shari'ah*-compliant mutual funds overperforming their benchmarks and others underperforming them. The total number of overperforming funds ranges between 29 funds (63 percent of the sample) and 11 funds (24 percent), depending on the performance measure used and the market benchmark. This study makes two interesting observations: there is not any statistically significant risk-adjusted abnormal reward or penalty associated with investing in *Shari'ah*-compliant mutual funds, and thus with following one's belief in financial investment; and

Islamic funds can be considered by conventional fund managers since investing in *Shari'ah*-compliant funds offers some form of diversification and hedging benefits, especially during downturn times for the economy.

Hassan and Antonios (2006) examine the relative performance of the Dow Jones Islamic Index and the Data Stream Global Index and confirm earlier findings that in no way are Islamic equity investments less profitable than conventional types of investments given relatively major differences between Sharpe and Treynor measures and significant positive Alpha over the positive returns period. The study also observes a bias of Islamic indices towards technology stocks which proved beneficial during bull markets but adversely affected the performance during the bear period.

1.6 FINANCIAL ENGINEERING

Whereas financial engineering in conventional finance was driven by breakthroughs in financial theory, financial engineering in Islamic finance is driven by innovative application of *Shari'ah* rules. *Shari'ah* scholars have worked closely with the practitioners to develop products demanded by the market. In its early days, financial engineering was limited to the development of a product for a financial intermediary such as an Islamic bank, but with the development of capital markets the focus of product development has shifted more towards marketable securities. A relevant example is the introduction of *sukuk* (Islamic bonds), which have become an overnight success. There are more than ten different structures of *sukuk*, and the instrument has been welcomed by both Islamic and conventional market players. Following the success of *sukuk*, there is more financial engineering activity in customized and structured products.

As compared to conventional finance, the pace of innovation and application of financial engineering in Islamic finance is slow and limited. The main reason for the slow pace is that a conventional financial engineer has access to highly liquid debt and derivatives markets, which offer sufficient borrowing, investing, and hedging opportunities at relatively low transaction costs. However, a financial engineer in Islamic finance does not have access to debt or interest-based securities or to basic hedging instruments. Developing new products with profit–loss- and risk-sharing characteristics, as advocated by Islamic finance, requires extensive resources and efforts. The result is limited innovation, most of which is in the form of reverse engineering where the objective is to replicate the behavior and risk/return profile of a conventional security.

Despite the abovementioned obstacles, Islamic financial engineering is taking place in several Western institutions that have extensive market and financial engineering knowledge and experience and are trying to capture market share. Most of such activities are taking place through "wrapping" in the form of structured deposits, funds, or bilateral contracts. While these products are labeled as *Shari'ah*-compliant, details of the structures are often not available publicly. Below are some examples of recent applications of financial engineering:

- Deutsche Bank (DB) is offering a structure that enables DB to issue *Shari'ah*-compliant securities linked to a wide range of asset classes, such as commodities, fixed-income, and money market funds with a range of different payoffs, such as capped and leveraged returns. These securities are also transferable at market value which enhances market liquidity. Through this instrument, investors deposit funds with DB which are invested in *Shari'ah*-compliant securities such as shares selected from a Dow Jones Islamic benchmark, and both investors and DB exchange promises (*wa'd*) to sell securities at predetermined levels. The net effect is that from an economic or derivatives aspect, the *wa'd* arrangement amounts to an outperformance put or call option, even though such options are not normally considered to be *Shari'ah*-compliant.[23]
- BNP Paribas is offering an Islamic version of Constant Proportion Portfolio Insurance (CPPI), which is a well-known strategy in conventional finance. Whereas in the conventional version of CPPI a portion of funds is placed in zero-coupon bonds and a marketable, risky security with complex rebalancing rules to ensure protection of the principal amount, in the Islamic version the zero-coupon asset is replaced by investment in a *murabahah* and the assets offering the "risky" return are Islamic equities or funds. The allocation mechanism is driven by predefined trigger rules (to switch between risky and non-risky assets) based on the difference between the value of the basket of Islamic underlyings and the value of the cash assets. Several variations of *Shari'ah*-compliant CPPI exist, such as income-paying, look back, profit lock-ins, and open-ended structures.[24]

- Standard Chartered Bank, Malaysia has introduced several hedging instruments that are *Shari'ah*-compliant. For example, the Islamic Profit Rate Swap (IPRS) was introduced to assist in the management of profit rate risks. A profit rate swap is a mechanism structured to allow bilateral exchange of profit streams using two parallel and back-to-back Islamic marked-up sale (*murabahah*) transactions. In simple IPRS, a series of *murabahah* sale and purchases are conducted, allowing parties to swap or exchange profit rates from fixed to floating rates or vice versa. In another version, called Islamic Cross-Currency Swap (ICCS), the same mechanism is applied for the purpose of cross-currency swaps. The pricing of all these Islamic hedging solutions depends on the expected rate of profit, which is agreed upon by the bank and the client. The period of the swap ranges from one to five years.[25]
- Deutsche Bank executed the first Islamic Collar Profit Rate Swap with Dubai Islamic Bank (DIB) in October 2007. The transaction was over US$500 million in notional, and is the largest such structure done in the Islamic markets. The transaction was customized to the needs of DIB, which had specific hedging requirements which could not be done through plain-vanilla Islamic profit rate swaps. DB worked with DIB and their *Shari'ah* teams to design an off-balance-sheet profit-rate swap with caps and floors to provide desirable protection for DIB.[26]

Although there are several other applications of financial engineering in the market, there is a sense of a lack of transparency in constructing some of these deals. Internal details of most of the deals are a highly guarded secret, and although a respectable *Shari'ah* committee has blessed the transaction, there is still some confusion about the applicability of certain *Shari'ah* principles in some cases.[27]

1.7 ISLAMIC INSURANCE *(TAKAFUL)*

An insurance conforming to *Shari'ah* is known as *takaful*, literally meaning "mutual guarantee," and its design is based on the solidarity and cooperation among its members. Whereas Islamic finance grew rapidly, *takaful* business did not spread as swiftly. The primary reason was a division of opinion among *Shari'ah* scholars with respect to the legitimacy of underwriting an event in the future, which was considered similar to speculation and thus gambling. Such objection was particularly applicable to underwriting life insurance, which was considered totally unacceptable as it involves gambling and uncertainty, and goes against the Islamic concept of predestination (*qadar*).[28] Due to this internal debate, the *takaful* industry did not take off smoothly, but over time some of the internal *Shari'ah* issues have been resolved and a consensus has emerged on the permissibility of insuring business losses and—to a lesser extent—loss of life.

Even after one convincingly argues that insurance does not amount to gambling, the issue is raised of how to invest premium funds in a manner which is compliant with *Shari'ah*; that is, investments without involving *riba*. Unlike conventional insurance underwriters that had access to liquid money and capital markets to construct efficient portfolios of fixed-income securities with desirable risk and return profiles, *takaful* companies did not have access to similar markets. Therefore, during the early stages of development of Islamic finance, *takaful* companies had difficulties in placing funds in liquid securities. As the market for *Shari'ah*-compliant products is expanding, this constraint has become a lesser issue.

The first *takaful* company was established in 1979—the Islamic Insurance Company of Sudan—followed by Malaysia in 1984, before spreading to Saudi Arabia and other Middle East countries. The *takaful* industry has been growing at a rate of 10–20 percent per annum, compared to the global average growth of the conventional insurance industry of 5 percent per annum. A large number of *takaful* companies exist in the Middle East, Far East, and even in some non-Islamic countries. Re-*takaful* business has also been developed in Malaysia, Bahrain, Saudi Arabia, and United Arab Emirates.[29]

The *takaful* industry has witnessed high growth in recent years (see Table 1.8). The total gross premiums underwritten by *takaful* companies were worth US$530 million in 2000; this rose close to US$3 billion by the end of 2006.[30] As of 2005, there were 82 companies engaged in *takaful* business. Of these 82 companies, 77 were dedicated *takaful* companies and 5 were offering *takaful* products through Islamic windows. At the same time, there were 8 companies engaged in re-*takaful* business.[31] In terms of market share, as of 2005, South and East Asia held 56 percent of the market, followed by the Middle East with 36 percent, Africa with 7 percent, and Europe, America and others with 1 percent share.

Table 1.8 Islamic insurance (*takaful*) market

Year	Size (US$m)	General *takaful*	Family *takaful*
2002	1,396	98%	2%
2003	1,648	98%	2%
2004	1,749	98%	2%
2005	1,980	98%	2%
2006	3,000	98%	2%

Source: ISI (2007).

Industry growth is forecast to maintain at approximately 15 percent to until 2015.[32]

There are two main lines of *takaful*—General (non-life) and Family (life). General *takaful* businesses offer protection for losses due to accidents, fire, and other incidents, and compensate the participants for any material loss, damage, or destruction of properties or belongings. Family *takaful* businesses (Islamic "life" insurance) are a combination of long-term investment and mutual financial assistance schemes. These are designed to attract investments by participants over a fixed period of time and are invested in *Shari'ah*-compliant investment vehicles. The objective is to save up to a target amount, and if a mishap occurs before that the remainder is covered by other participants on a mutual cooperation basis. Some *takaful* schemes include family, health, education, and mortgage insurances.[33]

There are three models of Islamic insurance, based on *mudarabah*, *tabarru*, and *waqf*. The *mudarabah* model is based on the concept of a solidarity fund where participants mutually share losses. An annual premium is paid into a fund which is invested in *Shari'ah*-compliant assets. The losses are covered through the profits generated by the assets. The members are allowed to withdraw accumulated investments but also agree to share losses of other members if there are not sufficient funds to cover the losses. The reason it is called "solidarity *mudarabah*" is that the participants have the right to share surplus profits (after paying for collective losses), but at the same time they are jointly liable for any shortfall in liabilities due to excessive losses not covered by original premiums.

In the *tabarru*-based model the contributions or premiums of the participants into the general *takaful* fund are wholly on the basis of donations. *Tabarru* is the agreement by a participant to relinquish as a donation a certain proportion of the *takaful* contribution that he or she agrees or undertakes to pay, thus creating a joint guarantee should any of the fellow participants suffer a defined loss. Funds from the donations are invested, and at the end of the period an assessment is made of profits, if any, after discharging any obligation of assisting the fellow participants has been fulfilled.[34] The third model is based on *waqf*, which operates as a public foundation or as an endowment fund for the mutual benefit of all members.

Going forward, *takaful* has promising prospects in the future. With the development of Islamic finance, there has been a significant increase in the lease or *ijarah*-based financing of physical assets and mortgages which necessitates demand for *Shari'ah*-compliant insurance protection. At the same time, there is growing demand for products to cover personal assets, healthcare expenses, and family finances. Therefore, *takaful* has become an integral part of the financial system conforming to *Shari'ah*. However, before its full potential is realized, several obstacles need to be overcome: the development of liquid money and capital markets; the existence of a proper regulatory framework to give *takaful* companies a level playing field; and the existence of re-insurance or re-*takaful* companies to mitigate and diversify aggregate risks over different geographical regions.[35]

1.8 REGULATIONS, SUPERVISION, RISK MANAGEMENT, GOVERNANCE

With the growth of institutions providing Islamic financial services, considerable research and practical advancement has taken place in the area of regulatory framework, supervision, risk management, and corporate governance issues of such institutions. In this arena, close collaboration between the industry, public sector, multilaterals, and other stakeholders is evident. The results of these efforts are beginning to show as many countries that were averse to the idea of nonconventional financial institutions are now more open to it, and the fear of the unknown is less due to dissemination of practical experience and knowledge. This area has attracted more research and valuable contributions have been made.

Establishing standards in this respect was the first priority, and this started with the establishment of the self-regulation agency, the AAOIFI, which undertook the task of defining accounting, regulatory capital, and *Shari'ah* standards. The AAOIFI's main contribution is to increase the awareness of the need for special standards and treatments for Islamic financial instruments. Realizing the benefits of harmonization of accounting standards—such as cost savings, enhanced comprehensiveness, the ability to make informed comparisons of alternative investment opportunities, and to promote best practices—AAOIFI has now issued 50 standards on accounting, auditing, governance, ethical, and *Shari'ah* standards.[36] Today AAOIFI's membership spans over 24 countries and its standards are implemented in the Islamic banking and finance centers globally, such as Bahrain, Sudan, Jordan, Malaysia, Qatar, and Saudi Arabia, where they are either mandatory or used as a guideline by the regulators.[37]

As the number of financial institutions and their geographical reach spread and expanded, there was a need to formalize the self-regulatory aspect of AAOIFI and to establish the IFSB with a wider scope. The IFSB was established in 2000 with the efforts of the IMF and more than ten central banks of Muslim countries that showed strong commitment to this industry. Since its inception, the AAOIFI has made significant contributions by issuing standards on capital adequacy, risk management, and corporate governance.[38] These standards are issued after consultations of all stakeholders and follow a thorough process of peer review. A working group of technical experts in the relevant area is formed, which reviews and drafts a document before it is approved. The IFSB's standard on capital adequacy was issued in December 2005, which offered a comprehensive framework for the identification of risk weights for *Shari'ah*-compliant products and the methodology for computation and determination of capital requirements for Islamic financial institutions.

The IFSB issued guiding principles of risk management for institutions offering Islamic financial services in December 2005. These guiding principles deal with risk profiles of different products and make suggestions on how to deal with credit, market, and operational risk of Islamic products. The guiding principles also identify risks specific to Islamic instruments and the ways to control such risks. The IFSB strongly urges Islamic financial institutions to have in place a comprehensive risk-management and reporting process, including appropriate board and senior management oversight, to identify, measure, monitor, report, and control relevant categories of risks and, where appropriate, to hold adequate capital against these risks. In December 2006, the IFSB issued guiding principles on corporate governance for institutions offering Islamic financial services. The IFSB defines seven guiding principles classified into four broad categories: general governance approach; rights of investment account holders (IAH); compliance with Islamic *Shari'ah* rules and principles; and transparency of financial reporting in respect of investment accounts. These principles—which exclude Islamic insurance (*takaful*) institutions and Islamic mutual funds—are considered merely for the purpose of guidance as the IFSB recognizes that there is no "single model" of corporate governance that can work well in every country or every organization.

In December 2007, the IFSB issued guidance on key elements in the supervisory review process of institutions offering Islamic financial services. The objective is to offer guidance on the practices that supervisory authorities are expected to apply concerning capital adequacy, risk management, internal controls, and corporate governance. The guidelines take a risk-based approach to the process of supervisory review. The IFSB recommends that the supervisory authority shall satisfy itself as to the adequacy of various compliance aspects, including the *Shari'ah* rules and principles, with reference to the IFSB's standards, including those on capital requirements, risk management, governance structure and processes, transparency, and market discipline. The latest achievement of the IFSB is the establishment of the Prudential Islamic Finance Database (PIFD), with the purposes of facilitating macroprudential analysis and to help assess the structure and state of development of the Islamic financial services industry. Some key standards and drafts are shown in Table 1.9.

Shari'ah scholars play an important role in the governance of Islamic financial institutions. *Shari'ah* scholars provide guidance to the institution on product development and work closely with the management to ensure that the institution is conforming to the principles of *Shari'ah*. Once a product or financial instrument is cleared or certified by the *Shari'ah* scholars, it gives comfort to other stakeholders that the financial institution is not engaged in any activity that is against the essence of their beliefs. During the early stages of Islamic finance, there were limited numbers of *Shari'ah* experts and most of them were not very well versed in the English language and/or the rules of economics, finance, or banking. Each institution formed its own *Shari'ah* board and made every effort to attract prominent names to establish credibility for the institution. With the entry of Western institutions, demand for *Shari'ah* scholars who were reasonably conversant in the English language also increased, and with the increased demand payoffs also increased.

With the continuing growth of Islamic finance and the scarcity of properly trained *Shari'ah* scholars, competition among *Shari'ah* scholars increased and many started to represent multiple *Shari'ah*

Table 1.9 Key Islamic Financial Services Board (IFSB) standards and drafts

	IFSB issued standards
2007	Guidance on Key Elements in the Supervisory Review Process of Institutions offering Islamic Financial Services (excluding Islamic Insurance (*takaful*) Institutions and Islamic Mutual Funds)
2006	Guiding Principles on Corporate Governance for Institutions Offering Only Islamic Financial Services (Excluding Islamic Insurance (*takaful*) Institutions and Islamic Mutual Funds)
2005	Capital Adequacy Standard for Institutions (other than Insurance Institutions) offering only Islamic Financial Services (IIFS)
2005	Guiding Principles of Risk Management for Institutions (other than Insurance Institutions) offering only Islamic Financial Services (IIFS)
	Exposure drafts (work-in-progress)
	Guiding Principles on Governance for Islamic Collective Investment Schemes
	Capital Adequacy Requirements for *Sukuk* Securitisations and Real Estate Investment
	Guidance Note in Connection with the Capital Adequacy Standard: Recognition of Ratings by External Credit Assessment Institutions (ECAI) on *Shari'ah*-compliant Financial Instruments

boards. This sharing of resources raised concerns about the transparency and confidentiality of decision-making by scholars representing multiple institutions. Siddiqi (2006) makes very pertinent observations that in the beginning, during the 1970s, issuing a *fatwa* (religious proclamation) was considered a sacred duty and an action of public good, as compared to legal experts in conventional banking charging significant fees. However, this changed over time when competition and compensation created a lucrative market for experts who could bless a transaction and make it *Shari'ah*-compliant. With this commercialization, innovation went from the public domain to behind the closed doors of financial institutions that guarded their deals to maintain their competitive advantage.

Today, it is standard practice for financial institutions to maintain a *Shari'ah* Supervisory Board (SSB) that provides an oversight of the institution's dealing in *Shari'ah* matters. Each SSB is subject to an institution's internal procedures and processes to ensure compliance. From the governance point of view, the functioning of SSBs raises five main issues of corporate governance: independence in decision-making; confidentiality of decision-making; competence of members; consistency of decision-making; and disclosure requirements.[39] In addition to internal corporate governance arrangements, national regulators and international standard setters in several countries have implemented guidelines for SSBs. These often refer to SSBs' general duty to ensure *Shari'ah* compliance of transactions and, less frequently, indicate areas of competence, composition, and decision-making. For example, regulators in Bahrain, Malaysia, Pakistan, Kuwait, Jordan, Lebanon, and Indonesia have defined terms of reference for SSBs, and Bahrain, Pakistan, Jordan, Lebanon, and Indonesia have guidelines for the appointment and dismissal of members of SSBs.[40] There is more awareness of the importance and the role of *Shari'ah* boards, and there is realization that the industry should move towards defining *Shari'ah* standards. The need for standards stems from the existence of different schools of Islamic jurisprudence and different practices in different jurisdictions. The AAOIFI took early initiatives in defining *Shari'ah* standards, and as of 2007 it has drafted around 30 standards. Similarly, the idea of a centralized *Shari'ah* Supervisory Board (also referred to as a High *Shari'ah* Authority or *Fatwa* Board) has been implemented in some countries. For example, Malaysia, Sudan, Kuwait, Pakistan, United Arab Emirates, and Indonesia have established centralized boards to provide guidelines and to perform an oversight function over individual *Shari'ah* boards.[41]

Two ideas have been floated with respect to the practices of *Shari'ah* boards. The first is similar to the practice of credit rating by independent sources and, therefore, calls for the development of independent institutions to rate the performance of *Shari'ah* boards. The critical criteria for a good rating would be consistency and transparency in decision-making and a review of procedures to ensure proper compliance. Malaysia has established a rating agency on similar lines. The other idea is to conduct independent audits of practices and decisions of *Shari'ah* boards. This independent source is expected to conduct a thorough audit of the processes and procedures followed by the board and to give independent reports on the degree of transparency and a comparison with industry's best practices. The topic of governance frameworks for *Shari'ah* boards and standardization of contracts and practices is expected to attract the attention of researchers, regulators, and policymakers in the coming years.

1.9 THE GLOBALIZATION OF ISLAMIC FINANCE

Islamic finance is gradually being introduced in countries that are not Muslim. Although Western financial centers and financial intermediaries have always played an important part in executing and innovating Islamic transactions, such activities have been mostly carried out in the private sector and in a discrete fashion. By early 2000, this trend began to change, and several non-Muslim countries began to take interest in the emerging market. This can be attributed to several factors, such as booming oil revenues leading to accumulation of investible funds looking for attractive investment opportunities, increased awareness of regulatory issues relating to Islamic financial intermediaries, and the desire to tap into alternative funding resources by sovereign and corporate entities. Islamic finance going global is evidenced by the wide distribution of subscribers investing in *sukuk*, as shown in Table 1.10. *sukuk* issued by institutions based in Malaysia, Saudi Arabia, and United Arab Emirates are held in significant portions by investors in Asia, Europe, and the United States.

Given the historical significance of London as a financial center, its reputation, sound regulatory framework, well-reputed financial houses, financial depth, and attractive time zone with respect to the Middle East it has become a popular choice for Islamic financial transactions. It is claimed that more money flows through the London financial center in terms of most-widely used Islamic financial instruments and commodity *murabahah* than any other center.[42] With a Muslim population of almost two million in the United Kingdom,

Table 1.10 Global investor base for *sukuk*

	Middle East	Asia	Europe	US
Malaysia *sukuk* – 2002	51.0%	30.0%	15.0%	4.0%
IDB *sukuk* – 2004	32.0%	35.0%	26.0%	7.0%
Emirate Airline *sukuk* 2005 – I	59.6%	8.4%	32.0%	
Emirate Airline *sukuk* 2005 – II	72.0%	11.0%	14.0%	3.0%

Source: Ismael (2007).

there was enough demand to establish the Islamic Bank of Britain in September 2004; by the end of 2006 the bank had attracted deposits of £83 million from 30,000 customers and its assets stood at £120 million.[43] Similarly, the European Islamic Investment Bank began its operations in April 2006 with the objective of promoting *Shari'ah*-compliant investment banking. In 2008, European Finance House, a unit of Qatar Islamic Bank, was awarded a banking license in the United Kingdom to provide *Shari'ah*-compliant banking. European Finance House plans to target the European Union's 14 million Muslims who will have access to Islamic financial products.[44]

Realizing the significance and potential for Islamic finance domestically and internationally, the UK government has taken steps to make its markets "Islamic finance friendly." To facilitate Islamic finance for the residents, the government has lifted double stamp duty on Islamic residential mortgages and commercial property loans. Previously, if a financial institution offered Islamic mortgages by first buying the property with the purpose of selling to the client, it was subject to stamp duty at each buy and sell transaction, which raised the cost of the transaction. Similarly, the tax regime has also been restructured to remove the negative treatment of non-interest-based products.

In 2007, the UK government, to tap into increased liquidity and the search for *Shari'ah*-compliant venues for investments, started evaluating the possibility of launching a sovereign *sukuk* with the objective of encouraging the domestic Islamic finance market and to develop a global benchmark. It was also declared in the 2007 Budget that *sukuk* are to be accorded the same tax status as conventional debt instruments and the income to *sukuk* investors is to be treated as interest income. These measures were introduced to send positive signals to potential *sukuk* issuers and to ensure a level playing field with conventional securities. As more steps are taken to develop London as a hub for Islamic finance, it poses serious threats for regional financial centers such as Bahrain and Malaysia that are working hard to develop dedicated Islamic financial centers. Some argue that this may lead to capital flight, which can hamper the development of regional financial centers. However, others argue that London can play a complementary and enhancing role through financial innovations, cost-effective execution, and access to other markets.

Islamic finance has a long history of silent presence in Europe. The major early development was the establishment in 1981 of the Dar al Maal al Islami Trust in Geneva, an investment company that holds stakes in several Islamic banks.[45] Many high-net-worth clients demanding *Shari'ah*-compliant investments deal directly with European banks, notably with UBS of Switzerland, the leading provider of *Shari'ah*-compliant, wealth-management services. The pioneering *sukuk* in Europe was by the German Federal State of Saxony-Anhalt, which raised €100 million through an issuance of five-year *sukuk* in July 2004.[46] Although London has been active in the market, in the rest of Europe the idea of Islamic finance has yet to attract attention on a large scale. For example, in France where the Muslim population of six million is three times the size of the United Kingdom's, the authorities and regulators have been slow to realize the potential of this market.[47]

In the rest of the world, Japan and Hong Kong are also considering engaging in Islamic finance. Tokyo has taken concrete steps to capture a slice of the Islamic finance market. For example, Japan's trade promotion body, The Japan Bank for International Cooperation (JBIC), has announced plans to issue a *sukuk* to attract Middle East petrodollars.[48] Several Japanese banks and their securities divisions are keen to establish themselves as a gateway to Malaysia for Japanese investors to tap into this market. More recently, Japan announced that it will issue its first sovereign *sukuk* of between US$300 million and US$500 million in Malaysia in 2008.[49]

The presence of Islamic finance is felt all over the globe, and multilateral institutions are also engaging with the market. Although the World Bank and the IMF have made contributions to this field through research, other institutions are getting involved also. The International Finance Corporation (IFC)—the private sector arm of the World Bank—has executed several *Shari'ah*-compliant transactions. In a notable transaction, in 2006 the IFC worked as a structuring investor to enable its client Kingdom Installment Company (KIC) in Saudi Arabia to issue the first true-sale securitization from a GCC member country.[50] The *sukuk*, backed by *ijarah* contracts, provided an important alternative source of funding for KIC as well as a *Shari'ah*-compliant, fixed-income investment product similar to a mortgage-backed security to GCC-based and other international investors. KIC issued US$18.3 million *sukuk* backed by a US$23.5 million pool of mortgage receivables. The IFC provided a *Shari'ah*-compliant guarantee of 10 percent of the outstanding principal balance of *sukuk*, which led to a rating of A– from Capital Intelligence, an international credit rating agency.

In 2007, the Multilateral Investment Guarantee Agency (MIGA)—one of the agencies of the World Bank Group—provided its first-ever guarantee for *Shari'ah*-compliant project financing.[51] The US$427 million guarantee is to support investments in construction of a new container terminal in Djibouti, which is expected to significantly improve port facilities and help the country become a major business hub in East Africa. MIGA's participation facilitated the syndication of a significant amount of financing provided by several banks on favorable terms and conditions under an Islamic financing structure. MIGA's guarantees are protecting the investments of Dubai Port World as well as those of the financing banks—Dubai Islamic Bank, Standard Chartered Bank, and West LB—against the risks of transfer restriction, war and civil disturbance, expropriation, and breach of contract. MIGA plans to reinsure US$50 million with the ICIEC—an arm of the IDB.

1.10 THE FUTURE

The future of Islamic finance will depend in large part on the success of privatization programs, on the extent and quality of economic and financial reform and liberalization, on institutional reform (especially in the judiciary and establishing the rule of law), on the quality of governance and supervision, on the pace of sustained economic growth in OIC countries, and on oil price developments and the size of available investment funds in oil-exporting countries.

There is a well-recognized synergy between the real and financial sectors in an economy. Rapid economic growth stimulates financial development and growth, and rapid financial development and growth fuels economic growth. The OIC embraces some of the poorer countries in the world, such as Bangladesh, Gambia, and Guinea-Bissau, and some of the richest, such as Qatar, Kuwait, and the United Arab Emirates. Focusing on the oil-rich Persian Gulf countries, economic growth, GDP, and GDP per capita were not impressive in comparison to other country groups over the last 30 or so years. Real GDP growth (in average percent per year) over the period 1975–2002 was Iran 2.2, Kuwait 1.0, Saudi Arabia 2.1, United Arab Emirates 4.4, and 2.3 for all the countries in the region, in comparison to the world average of 2.9. In per capita terms, because of rapid population growth their performance was even less impressive: Iran 0.4, Kuwait 1.2, Saudi Arabia 2.5, United Arab Emirates 2.8, and 4.0 for all countries in the region, in comparison to the world average of 1.3. The subpar economic performance is particularly disturbing for the oil-exporting countries, which have, and could generate, sizeable investment funds.

Their economies have suffered under the weight of large government sectors and excessive regulation. However, in the period since 2003 their performance has been much better, in large part due to spiraling oil prices, as indicated in economic growth indicators: for the GCC countries as a group, the average annual GDP growth rate for 2003–2007 is estimated at a rapid 9.5 percent, and Iran's is estimated at 6.2 percent.

Because of higher oil prices and enhanced economic performance, the oil-rich countries of the Persian Gulf have also accumulated surplus funds available for foreign investment at a higher rate than before (see Table 1.11). Our own estimates of the largest sovereign wealth funds (SWF) are somewhat different to those in the table. These

Table 1.11 Sovereign wealth funds (SWF)*

Country	Fund	Assets (US$bn)	Inception Year	Type of SWF
United Arab Emirates	Abu Dhabi Investment Authority (ADIA)	875	1976	Government holding management companies
Saudi Arabia	Various funds	300	N/A	Various
Kuwait	Kuwait Investment Authority	250	1953	Government holding management companies
Qatar	Qatar Investment Authority	50	2000	Government holding management companies
Libya	Libyan Investment Authority	40	2007	Government holding management companies
Brunei	Brunei Investment Agency	30	1983	Government holding management companies
Malaysia	Khazanah	18.3	1993	
Kazakhstan	National Fund	23	2000	
Iran	Oil Stabilization Fund	12.9	1999	Stabilization fund
Nigeria	Excess Crude Account	11	2004	
Oman	State General Reserve Fund	8.2	1980	Stabilization fund

Source: Wikipedia (http://en.wikipedia.org/wiki/Sovereign_wealth_funds) and others.

*Some sources also suggest that Qatar Investment Authority's holdings are rapidly approaching US$100 billion, and Saudi Arabia is planning to establish a sovereign fund with holdings of US$900 billion.

funds represent only the state holdings of these countries; the private sector's external assets are huge, and may exceed government holdings in Kuwait, and especially in Saudi Arabia where private holdings could exceed US$500 billion. The large public and private holdings of these countries will afford Muslims a much larger influence and presence in global finance. This may in turn motivate greater supply of *Shari'ah*-compliant investment instruments and generate even more interest in the development of Islamic finance.

The higher oil prices have helped, but there are also indications that the OIC countries, especially the major oil exporters, have realized their economic shortcomings. They have embarked on economic reforms. They have embraced deregulation and privatization. They have recognized the importance of institutions, especially the rule of law, regulatory frameworks, and supervision in promoting sustained economic growth. They have appreciated the important role of finance in the growth of the real sector. They are trying to stick to consistent macroeconomic policies. They realized that success will require a long-term commitment to these policies. If these policies bear fruit, as they have started to in recent years (as partially confirmed by recent growth figures), and if the regulatory and supervisory administration of Islamic finance is enhanced, then the future of Islamic finance is much brighter than anything we have seen in the past 30 or so years. Moreover, as the richer Muslim countries succeed in their economic development and accumulate vast external assets, the less fortunate Muslim countries may provide a safe (from expropriation) and profitable investment outlet for *Shari'ah*-compliant investments. This prediction is further reinforced by the fact that Muslims the world over are seeing the diverse possibilities open to them to practice their faith by increasing their savings, investing in *Shari'ah*-compliant assets, promoting economic growth in Muslim countries, and ultimately improving the lives of the disadvantaged members of their community. Non-Muslim countries can be expected to join the recent efforts of the United Kingdom in providing services to this rapidly growing financial market.

As economic performance improves in OIC countries, as financial liberalization and growth continues, as financial regulatory and supervisory administration of Islamic financial practices matures, and as Muslims are afforded diverse and better opportunities to save and invest in accordance with their religion (both in Muslim and non-Muslim countries), the growth of Islamic finance should be more rapid than anything we have seen in the past.

ENDNOTES

1 For an introductory text on Islamic economics and finance, please consult Iqbal and Mirakhor (2007).

2 Martin, Matthew, "The Globalisation of Islamic Banking," *Middle East Economic Digest*, (September 7, 2007), 51, no.36: 33–36.

3 Khan, Mohsin, "Islamic Interest-Free Banking: A Theoretical Analysis," in Khan and Mirakhor (eds.), *Theoretical Studies in Islamic Banking and Finance*, (Houston: IRIS Books, 1987).

4 "The 2007 guide to Opportunities and Trends in Islamic Finance," *Euromoney* (London: Euromoney Institutional Investor PLC, 2007).

5 Sole, Juan, "Introducing Islamic Banks into Conventional Banking Systems" *IMF Working Paper* no. 07/175, (Washington, DC: International Monetary Fund, 2007).

6 The General Council of Islamic Banks and Financial Institutions is making efforts to maintain statistics on Islamic financial institutions.

7 The list of 500 Islamic institutions includes 292 commercial banks (both fully Islamic and those offering Islamic windows or selling Islamic products), 115 Islamic investment banks and finance companies, and 118 insurance companies, adding up to a total of 525 institutions from which the Top 500 were drawn.

8 For a summary of the history of economic thought in Islam, see: Siddiqi, *Recent Works on History of Economic Thought in Islam: A Survey* (Jeddah: International Center for Research in Islamic Economics, King Abdul Azziz University, 1982).

9 Some of the early Muslim scholars who made significant contributions in highlighting and realizing the need for an economic and banking system are Maulana Syed Abul Ala Maudoodi (Pakistan), Imam Muhammad Baqir al-Sadr (Iraq), Anwar Iqbal Qureshi (Pakitan), Mohammad Nejatullah Siddiqi (India), Muhammad Uzair (Saudi Arabia), Umer Chapra (Saudi Arabia), and Ahmad al-Najjar (Egypt). See Ahmad Khurshid, "Islamic Finance and Banking: The Challenges and Prospects," *Review of Islamic Economics*, no. 9 (Leicester: The Islamic Foundation, July 2000): 59.

10 Presley, J. R. and J. G. Sessions, "Islamic Economics: The Emergence of a New Paradigm," *The Economic Journal: The Quarterly Journal of the Royal Economic Society*. 104, no. 424 (May 1994): 584–596.

11 For example, see World Bank publication, El-Hawary, Grais, and Iqbal (2005).

12 Kamali gives reference to verse 4:29 of the *Qur'an ("devour not each other's properties wrongfully unless it be by means of trading through your mutual consent")* to develop his argument. Mohammad Hashim Kamali, "Prospects for an Islamic Derivatives Market in Malaysia," *Thunderbird International Business Review*, 41 (July–October 1999): 523–540.

13 For further details on the role of the Islamic Development Bank, see IDB (2005).

14 Alchaar, Mohamad N., "Developments in International Financial Reporting: Implications for Islamic Banks," in ed. Tariqullah Khan and Dadan Muljawan, *Islamic Financial Architecture: Risk Management and Financial Stability* (Jeddah: IRTI, 2006).

15 Kerr, Simeon, "New battleground to reassert credentials," FT Report—Islamic Finance, May 23, (2007), *Financial Times*, (London, UK).

16 ISI Analytics, Islamic Financial Services Industry, (London: ISI Emerging Markets, 2007).

17 Standard & Poor's, "Standard & Poor's Islamic Finance Outlook 2008," (New York: Standard & Poor's, 2008).

18 Martin Eihák and Heiko Hesse, "Islamic Banks and Financial Stability: An Empirical Analysis," *IMF Working Paper* WP/08/16 (Washington, DC: International Monetary Fund, 2008).

19 Islamic Financial Information Services (ISI Emerging Markets, 2007).

20 Parker, Mushtak, "Dow Jones Citigroup sukuk Index Launched," *Arab News* (2006).

21 ISI Analytics (2007).

22 Ernst & Young, "Ernst & Young Islamic Funds and Investment Report," The World Islamic Funds and Capital Markets Conference, Dubai, UAE (2007).

23 Deutsche Bank, "Pioneering Innovative Shari'a Compliant Solution," Deutsche Bank Academic Paper, Deutsche Bank.

24 Euromoney, "The 2007 guide to Opportunities and Trends in Islamic Finance" (*Euromoney*, London, Euromoney Institutional Investor PLC, 2007).

25 Aziz, Azrulnizam Abdul, "The Evolution of Islamic Hedging Solutions," *Islamic Finance News*, (Kuala Lumpur, Singapore: RedMoney, 2007). Please note that many structures which are acceptable in the Malaysian market may not be acceptable in the Middle Eastern market.

26 http://www.db.com/presse/en/content/press_releases_2007_3654.htm?month=3

27 Siddiqi, Mohammad Nejatullah, "*Shari'ah*, Economics and the Progress of Islamic Finance: The Role of Shari'ah Experts," Seventh Harvard Forum On Islamic Finance, Cambridge, Massachusetts, USA, April 21, 2006.

28 Saleh (1992). According to him, the proponents of the contract of insurance argue that gambling and insurance have distinct features. In the case of the former, a gambler pursues, through unlawful means such as betting and wagering, risks which could be easily avoided if he so wanted. As for insurance, the insured person seeks protection from danger over which he has no control. Moreover, gambling has very detrimental social effects whereas insurance is very desirable and sometimes vital for trade and commerce.

29 Ayub, Muhammad, *Understanding Islamic Finance*, (Singapore: John Wiley & Sons (Asia), 2007).

30 Ernst & Young, *The Islamic Funds and Investments Report 2007* (IFIR), The World Islamic Funds and Capital Markets Conference (Dubai, 2007). IRTI and IFSB, *Islamic Financial Services Industry Development: Ten-Year Framework and Strategies*, (Jeddah: 2006). ISI Analytics, Islamic Financial Services Industry, ISI Emerging Markets (London).

31 ISI Analytics, Islamic Financial Services Industry, ISI Emerging Markets (London).

32 Ibid.

33 Ibid.

34 Ibid.

35 Ayub (2007).

36 Alchaar, Mohamad N., "Developments in International Financial Reporting: Implications for Islamic Banks," in ed. Tariqullah Khan and Dadang Muljawan, *Islamic Financial Architecture: Risk Management and Financial Stability*, (Jeddah: IRTI, 2006).
37 Ibid.
38 For further details, see http://www.ifsb.org.
39 Grais, Wafik L. and M. Pellegrini, "Corporate Governance and Shari'ah Compliance in Institutions Offering Islamic Financial Services," World Bank Policy Research Working Paper 4054, (November 2006).
40 Ibid.
41 Ibid.
42 Oakley, David, "Capital Takes a Leading Role," FT Report—Islamic Finance, *Financial Times*, (London: May 23, 2007).
43 Martin, Mathew, "The Globalization of Islamic Banking," *Middle East Economic Digest*; (September 7, 2007) 51, no.36: 33–36.
44 Spikes, Sarah, "Qatar Islamic Unit Wins UK banking license," *Financial Times*, February 3, 2008.
45 Wilson, Rodney, "Islamic Finance in Europe," *RSCAS Policy Papers* no. 2007/02, (Florence: Robert Schijman Centre for Advanced Studies, European University Institute, 2007).
46 Ibid.
47 Oakley (2007).
48 Martin (2007).
49 *Euromoney Magazine* (Islamic Finance), (January 1, 2008).
50 http://www.ifc.org/ifcext/treasury.nsf/AttachmentsByTitle/SF_Kingdom+Installment+Company+(KIC)/$FILE/KIC.pdf.
51 http://www.miga.org/news/index_sv.cfm?aid=1696.

CHAPTER 2

Issues and Challenges

As is invariably the case in any emerging market, the emerging Islamic financial industry faces several challenges. The nature of these challenges is diverse, as there are numerous issues concerning theoretical foundation, infrastructure development, systemic implementation, integration with external systems, and enhancing the efficiency of operations. To foster the growth and stability of Islamic finance and financial markets, additional challenges are to achieve sustained economic development and growth of the real sector while maintaining sound public finances. There are challenges at both macro and at micro levels that require a careful analysis before a solution can be suggested. The approach to overcome some of these challenges will determine the future success or failure of the industry. Although the Islamic financial industry has enjoyed handsome growth, the sustainability of this success and the future growth of the industry will largely depend on which challenges are addressed and the degree of success that is achieved. If due attention is not paid to addressing these issues, Islamic finance will fail to achieve its full potential and will also fail to deliver its promise. Therefore, the stakes are very high and demand serious discussion of the issues.

A complete coverage of all the issues and challenges would be a lengthy and voluminous academic exercise. However, in this chapter we attempt to provide a short overview of some of the major challenges, and selected topics are discussed in some detail in the subsequent chapters of this volume.

2.1 THE DEVELOPMENT OF THEORETICAL FOUNDATION

Conventional economics is the result of decades of rigorous theoretical and empirical research and has gone through many iterations of debates and analytical arguments. This has led to solid and time-tested development of models that provide a foundation for further analytical work. This is evident in all aspects of economics, whether micro or macro issues or in fields such as economic development or international trade and finance. This collective understanding is evolving every day, and has become a valuable asset in understanding the economic behavior of individuals as well as of societies. Similar rigorous analytical work, especially in areas of core economics, is seriously lacking in the case of Islamic economics. The research in Islamic finance has primarily been driven by business needs to establish an Islamic banking and financial system, and less attention has been paid to developing a comprehensive analytical framework based on the economic principles of Islam. The progress in understanding and describing economic behavior, as envisioned by Islam, is slow and needs more attention. Without a solid foundation and rigorous analytical work, it would be difficult to present viable solutions to economic and social problems. In Chapter 9 we discuss this challenge in further detail.

The development of a theoretical foundation of finance in Islam also needs attention. Several areas—such as asset pricing, corporate finance, derivatives, and hedging—require further research. For example, in the absence of a risk-free asset, how will the Capital Asset Pricing Model (CAPM) behave, or using Black's zero-beta model, how will the model behave with restrictions on short selling?[1] Several such issues have not been researched. In the development of conventional economics, finance was not seen as a separate field until relatively recently. In conventional economics the importance of investment has been long recognized. Financial markets were seen as important in attracting savings, and as a channel to allocate savings to investors and to do this in the most efficient way. The health of financial markets was appreciated largely in accommodating the financing of the real economy. The importance of finance was perceived from this very narrow perspective. Thus earlier finance was not treated as an important and separate field of endeavor.

The appreciation of risk was the important building block in the development of modern conventional finance. Early in the twentieth century, Irving Fisher, one of the giants of economics, was the first to appreciate the importance of risk in the functioning of financial markets. In the 1930s a number of renowned economists, most notably John Maynard Keynes, saw the importance of risk in the selection of a portfolio. But in their analysis and discussion the role of risk was largely limited to affecting expected capital gains and speculative and hedging activities. This strain of analysis led to results covering the relationship of futures prices and expected spot prices (normal backwardation), the price stabilizing effect of speculation, the impact of risk on assessing the value of future streams of income, and eventually leading to the development of portfolio theory.

These developments in turn led to the realization that arbitrage was one of the two fundamental features of conventional finance; this is supported by the Black-Scholes-Merton option pricing model and by the Modigliani-Miller Theorem. In the case of option pricing, if a portfolio of other assets can reproduce the return from an option, then the price of the option must be equal to the value of the portfolio; if not there will be arbitrage opportunities. The Modigliani-Miller Theorem also uses arbitrage reasoning to examine the impact of corporate financial structures for arriving at a market value for a firm. If the production outlook of two firms (with differing financial structures) is the same, then the market value of the firms must be the same; if not, there is opportunity for arbitrage.

The second important development in the modern theory of finance was initiated by the empirical finding that commodities and asset prices behaved randomly. Paul Samuelson came up with an ingenious explanation for this observation that asset prices had to behave randomly; if this was not the case then arbitrageurs could exploit the opportunity to make a profit. For asset prices to behave randomly, all available and relevant information would have to be immediately translated into asset price changes in markets that behaved "efficiently." Thus the Efficient Market Hypothesis was born. In sum, appreciation of the importance of risk, arbitrage pricing, and efficient markets are the relatively recent foundations of conventional finance. At its core, conventional finance is seen today as the management of risks.

In Islam, the importance of risk is clearly acknowledged. While conventional finance, with its roots in economic theory, has developed instruments to identify risk and trade risk to those willing to assume it, in Islam risk cannot be sold in any manner. The study of finance in Islam is built on the foundation that risk must be *shared* between parties in any endeavor (as opposed to being all assumed by one party or the other). Finance in Islam can benefit from the same theoretical developments in conventional economics and finance but with two important differences. First, Islam prohibits the notion of a "risk-free, interest-bearing debt." Thus conventional finance and its instruments can be applied in Islam if they are developed without reliance on risk-free, interest-bearing debt. Second, instruments that partition risk contrary to Islamic teachings cannot be allowed. Finance can be developed in Islam along conventional lines but with these two important constraints. On the face of it, modern finance should provide practitioners of Islamic finance added tools to achieve their central goal of better risk sharing. Moreover, as Islam prohibits financial gain without the assumption of some measure of risk it would appear that efficient markets and the random walk behavior of financial assets and commodities are implicitly, if not explicitly, subsumed in Islamic teachings.

In short, for Islamic finance to make further progress it needs to devote resources and efforts to develop analytical models and a theoretical foundation in economics and finance which distinguishes it from conventional economics and finance. Without it, there is danger of it being marginalized as a small subset of the conventional system.

2.2 GLOBALIZATION AND ISLAMIC FINANCE: A CONVERGENCE?

Globalization is a multifaceted process that is connecting the nations and peoples of the world. Its main dimensions are cultural, sociopolitical, and economic. Its economic dimensions include growing trade flows, unhindered movements of finance, investment and production, and standardization of processes, regulations, and institutions—all facilitated by the free flow of information and ideas. Globalization is the result of lower costs of information and transportation, and liberalization of trade, finance, investment, capital flows, and factor movements.

As globalization gathers momentum and as more economies liberalize and integrate into the global economy, the new finance will grow and so will risk-sharing and asset-based securitization, both of which are at the core of Islamic finance. So far, globalization is considered unfair because the risks and rewards of the process are not shared equitably. But as equity-based and asset-backed financing grows, the fruits of globalization could be distributed more widely and more equitably among participants, at least in terms of the financial linkages. Issues such as protectionism in industrial countries, segmented labor markets, impediments to the transfer of technology, and the like remain, and will require full international cooperation if they are to be addressed and mitigated.

As globalization proceeds, its main engines—the new finance and advances in information technology—will shift the methods and instruments of financing trade, investment, and production in favor of spreading and sharing risk rather than shifting risk via fixed-price debt contracts. This will be the result of financial innovations that are dissecting, analyzing, and pricing risk better, so that—combined with efficient availability of information and the adoption of best international standards of transparency, accountability, and good governance in public and private sectors—the raison d'être of fixed-price debt contracts will erode. This will pave the way for risk-sharing financial contracts, such as those promoted by Islamic finance. As risk-sharing financial instruments gain wider acceptance and earn the confidence of investors, a financial system founded on the risk-sharing principles promoted by Islamic finance will become more and more feasible. In Chapter 3 we address the possibility of convergence between Islamic and conventional finance.

2.3 FINANCIAL SYSTEM ARCHITECTURE AND INFRASTRUCTURE

There is well-documented research suggesting strong positive linkages between financial development and the economic development of the real sector of a country. In addition, the existence of a robust financial system infrastructure leads to financial market development and financial system stability. Whereas development of a robust financial sector is essential for any country, the rapid growth of institutions offering *Shari'ah*-compliant financial products and services is posing challenges to the policymakers who are considering the bigger picture of developing a financial system supportive of such institutions. In addition, continuing globalization, emphasis on market discipline based on a regulatory environment, a shift towards a risk-focused supervisory approach, and increased competition by conventional financial institutions are the factors influencing the design of financial architecture conducive to Islamic finance. Finally, unique risk/reward characteristics of financial intermediation of Islamic financial institutions must be incorporated in the design of financial architecture to promote a sound regulatory environment and to develop seamless integrations with the broader financial landscape.

Financial system infrastructure can be classified into three categories:

- *Systemic liquidity infrastructure*, which covers institutional arrangements for money and government securities markets, payment settlement systems, monetary and foreign exchange operations, and liquidity risk management.

- *Information and governance infrastructure*, which includes accounting and disclosure standards and corporate governance arrangements for financial institutions.
- *Insolvency regime and safety net infrastructure*, which includes lender of last resort arrangements, deposit insurance, and the legal framework governing bank insolvency, loan recovery, and creditors' rights.[2]

Whereas financial architecture refers to the legal and institutional arrangements for a sound and well-functioning financial services industry, financial infrastructure is a subset of the architecture and is often referred to as the underlying foundation to facilitate the preconditions for the functioning of the industry and the effectiveness of supervision and regulation of different segments.

At the national level, financial architecture includes legal and institutional arrangements for regulation and supervision of the Islamic financial services industry. A robust legal infrastructure to define and enforce contracts, insolvency, and financial safety nets is essential. It should also include a framework for macro prudential surveillance, arrangements for efficient systemic liquidity, and a transparent and information-rich governance infrastructure.[3] At the international level, financial architecture improves coordination among various national policies and promotes financial and technical cooperation. This includes institutions such as the International Monetary Fund, World Bank, Bank for International Settlements, regional development banks such as the Asian Development Bank and the Islamic Development Bank (IDB), international standard setting institutions such as International Accounting Standards, and international associations of market players for self-regulation and industry promotion such as International Capital Markets Association.

Sundararajan (2006), Marston and Sundararajan (2006), and IDB/IFSB (2006) provide a detailed discussion on the issues and the missing elements in developing architecture and infrastructure for the Islamic financial industry, which we summarize below:

- Whereas there are distinct differences in conventional and Islamic financial systems, significant parts of conventional infrastructure elements are equally applicable and accessible to Islamic finance. Therefore, there is no need to duplicate components of infrastructure which can be shared with some adjustments to accommodate the specific operational requirements of Islamic finance.

- Financial architecture should be aligned with a vision for the industry, and it should start with a detailed policy designed to address issues of conforming financial sector laws—such as insolvency laws—with Islamic Law (*Shari'ah*), strengthening the environment for risk sharing—that is, equity-based financial instruments and intermediation—and enhancing corporate governance of institutions offering Islamic products and services.
- At the national level, financial architecture for Islamic finance is exposed to the same weaknesses as the conventional financial sector in many developing countries. Inadequate or nonexistent legal frameworks for regulation, weak observance of base core principles (such as a lack of independence, weak risk management, and weaknesses in disclosure), and ill-defined consolidated supervision affect both conventional and Islamic banks. In addition, there is a need for special treatment of the legal and institutional framework for the insolvency regime, investor rights, creditor rights, securitization, and judicial enforcement.
- As part of the systemic liquidity infrastructure, the microstructure of money and exchange and securities markets, payment settlement systems, and monetary and debt management operations are not yet well adapted to accommodate and integrate Islamic financial institutions into the broader financial system. These factors limit the development of securities markets, which is critical for promoting product innovations, risk management, and effective supervision of Islamic finance generally. *Shari'ah*-compatible money and capital markets are essential for the implementation of monetary and fiscal policies.
- There is a need for strengthening the international architecture of Islamic finance, as there are still gaps and overlaps in the support structure provided by international infrastructure institutions. International infrastructure institutions can and should, therefore, play a key catalytic role in promoting the industry at the national level. In this respect, the IFSB is expected to play the leading role in standard setting, and to coordinate with the Basel Committee on Banking Supervision (BCBS), International Organization of Securities Commissions (IOSCO), and International Accounting Standards Board (IASB). The AAOIFI

should continue to realign work programs and promote greater adoption of AAOIFI standards at the national level. The IIFM should focus on market practices and contract standards and strengthen its role as an association of market players. The LMC can play a role to promote national and regional strategy for money market development. The IIRA can play an important role in enhancing disclosure and transparency.

The design of financial infrastructure and architecture to promote Islamic finance is a challenge and demands serious commitment by the stakeholders. Some of these challenges are discussed below.

2.3.1 The Development of Economic Institutions

Optimal functioning of an Islamic financial system, or for that matter of any system, requires that underlying economic and legal institutions are in place. The Islamic economic system is a rule-based system which dictates rules concerning property rights, contracts, expected behavior of economic agents, and social capital according to the teaching of Islam. As a result of several years of inactivity in developing such economic institutions, any effort to build a financial system to comply with partial aspects of Islam is bound to face difficulties and result in suboptimal performance.

2.3.2 Promoting Risk-Sharing Instruments

In the long run, the design of an Islamic financial system requires that the necessary institutions, based on Islamic economic tenets, are developed to be a foundation for the system. Institutions to support risk-sharing, partnership-based, and equity-style financing and investment are the most critical. By design, such instruments require close monitoring by the financial intermediary, which also incurs additional costs. Therefore, there is a need to develop systemic-level mechanisms to perform collective monitoring of economic agents to reduce monitoring costs for the financial intermediary. Also, equity-based securities and their efficient trading should be encouraged; in this respect, a stock market operating according to *Shari'ah*, which prohibits the use of leverage (use of margin accounts) and excessive speculation (including short sales). Chapra (2006) suggests reforming the stock market in the light of Islamic teachings to ensure that share prices reflect underlying business conditions and do not fluctuate erratically as a result of speculative forces.

2.3.3 The Alignment of Financing and Trading Activities

Due to the nature of trade- and asset-based financing instruments, Islamic banks tend to act as more than mere financiers. Institutions are needed to facilitate the efficiency of these instruments and also to reduce extensive involvement of the financier so that the financier can focus on the financing function rather than being involved in the administration of the assets. For example, specialized institutions are needed to administer, maintain, and facilitate lease-related operations and to work closely with banks to provide the supply of funds. Standardizing the operations and instruments will pave the way for pooling heterogeneous assets for securitization purposes—a much-needed functionality for enhancing liquidity in the market.[4]

2.3.4 The Development of Supporting Infrastructure

Supporting institutions to facilitate financial contracting is a necessary ingredient of a robust financial system. Institutions such as rating agencies, audit agencies, trade associations, and dispute resolution organizations play a vital role. The function of rating agencies should not be limited to rating creditworthiness but should extend to evaluating and giving an opinion on the compliance and the quality of *Shari'ah* boards. Furthermore, although the IIRA is mandated to rate financial institutions, there is a need to rate large numbers of counterparties with whom a financial institution may engage in partnerships. Chapra (2006) proposes development of private, credit-rating agencies in all Muslim countries to facilitate the task of Islamic banks in choosing their counterparties. Similarly, the scope of an audit should include the effectiveness of controls on new product development to ensure *Shari'ah* compliance. Speedy and effective dispute resolution is a critical component of financial systems. Collectively, these institutions can provide the foundation required for a vibrant financial system.

2.3.5 Integration with the Global Financial Landscape

Increasing globalization has spread Islamic finance to many different geographical locations where the infrastructure does not support Islamic finance-friendly institutions. This poses a problem for policymakers and regulators and can create an obstacle for the growth of Islamic finance. For Islamic finance to integrate well with the conventional system there is a need to develop international institutions and standard-setting agencies that can provide the necessary support to local authorities and can also develop procedures and standards which can be adopted with ease.

2.3.6 Liquidity Risk and Lender of Last Resort

Several studies have highlighted the issue of liquidity risk associated with Islamic financial instruments and the resulting exposure to Islamic banks.[5] In addition, lack of a lender of last resort facility based on Islamic instruments further complicates the liquidity risk problem. Although, like conventional banks, a lender of last resort facility is usually available to Islamic banks, such arrangements are based on non-*Sharī'ah*-compliant financial instruments. For a fully functional financial system, a system of lender of last resort that complies with Islamic Law is another essential requirement. Very limited work has been done in this area and further research is required.[6]

2.3.7 The Payment System

The absence of risk-free or high-grade investment securities and the dominance of trade-financed, asset-backed securities are of concern to regulators, as they threaten the payment system and increase its vulnerability to risk and illiquidity. In this context, it has been suggested that the concept of narrow banking be applied to Islamic banks. Fisher originally presented the concept of narrow banking, which is banking that specializes in deposit-taking and payment activities but does not provide lending services. Stability and safety are achieved if deposits are invested only in short-term treasuries or their close equivalents. In the context of the Islamic financial system, Islamic banks do not have access to relatively risk-free securities such as treasuries. One alternative, suggested by El-Hawary, Grais, and Iqbal (2004), is to segment the balance sheet of Islamic banks so that demand and short-term deposits are invested only in high-grade, liquid asset-backed securities, reducing the risk to the payment system. This concept needs to be refined further by developing a secondary market to enhance the liquidity and standardizing contracts to reduce the riskiness of asset-backed securities.

2.3.8 The Development of Benchmarks

The practice of measuring the performance of an asset by comparing its return and risk to a well-defined benchmark is well established in a market-centered financial system. Markets are good at offering an efficient, measurable, and consistent benchmarks for different asset classes and securities. The dearth of transparent benchmarks that can be used to compare risk-adjusted returns complicates the task of evaluating the efficiency of financial institutions. Such benchmarks are valuable tools for measuring the relative performance of different asset classes and, ultimately, the performance of the financial intermediary. The economic system in Islam suggests the use of return in the real sector as a benchmark for the return on the financial sector. However, the current practice of using interest-based benchmarks such as the London Interbank Offer Rate (LIBOR) is certainly in direct conflict. Although this practice has been accepted on an ad hoc basis under the law of necessity and in the absence of better benchmarks, several researchers have correctly brought up the need to develop benchmarks based on the rate of return, reflecting Islamic modes of financing. An approach to developing such benchmarks is discussed in Chapter 7.

2.4 FINANCIAL INTERMEDIATION ISSUES

Islamic financial intermediation is dominated by deposit-accepting Islamic banks and windows, and as a result Islamic banking is the largest sector of the Islamic financial industry. Being the largest sector, it has received considerable attention by researchers who have identified various issues, as discussed below. Some of these issues are serious and pose a real threat to future growth.[7]

2.4.1 Reputational Risk

Islamic banks are exposed to reputational risk more than their counterparts in conventional banking. Depositors and other stakeholders of Islamic banks have placed a special "trust" in the management of these financial institutions, assuming that they are facilitating a *sacred obligation*, and any damage to this trust can lead to a breach of confidence. Furthermore, misconduct on the part of a single institution can bring the whole industry under the microscope and can result in irreversible damage to the industry's reputation. This risk is not afforded any attention in either academic or in practical circles, and therefore warrants a serious discussion, which is covered in detail in a subsequent chapter.

2.4.2 Illiquidity

Islamic banks are operating with a limited set of short-term traditional instruments, and there is a shortage of products for medium- to long-term maturities. One reason for these shortcomings is the lack of markets in which to sell, trade, and negotiate the financial assets of the bank. There are no venues for securitizing dormant assets and taking them off the balance sheet. In other words, the secondary markets lack depth and breadth. An effective portfolio management strategy cannot be implemented in the absence of liquid markets, as opportunities for diversification become limited. The most critical factor for the illiquidity is the composition of assets of Islamic banks which are dominated by trade-financing instruments. Such instruments are the result of a sale of commodities or goods and are, therefore, considered ineligible for sale in the secondary market due to the *Shari'ah* rule that a financing instrument cannot be treated as a negotiable financial claim.

Since the needs of the market regarding liquidity, risk, and portfolio management are not being met, the system is not functioning at its full potential. There is growing realization that the long-term, sustainable growth of Islamic financial markets will depend largely on the development of well-functioning secondary markets and the introduction of liquidity-enhancing and risk-sharing products. Alternatively, Islamic banks need to reduce the weight of such assets in their portfolios and switch to those products that are market tradable. In order to switch to market-tradable securities, the Islamic financial industry requires the development of efficient and transparent money and capital markets.

2.4.3 The Lack of Appetite for Risk-Sharing Assets

One of the major criticisms of Islamic banks is their reluctance to hold risk-sharing assets. By design, because of Islam's economic principles—prohibition of interest and pure debt, and sharing of risks—Islamic banks should engage in partnerships and equity-sharing financial assets, but in practice the portion of such assets on the balance sheets of Islamic banks is minimal. For example, Table 2.1 shows the asset composition of selected banks from 1999 to 2002; it is evident that Islamic banks' first preference is for financing instruments that are generated through sale contracts and leasing instruments. Informal observation of more recent balance sheets shows a similar picture. Islamic banks' heavy usage of the sale-based

Table 2.1 Asset composition of select Islamic banks

	1999	2000	2001	2002
Murabahah and deferred sales	80.1%	83.0%	86.7%	84.3%
Istisna	10.8%	8.7%	7.5%	7.0%
Ijarah (leasing and hire purchase)	2.5%	2.4%	1.9%	2.9%
Mudarabah (partnership)	1.6%	1.6%	1.2%	3.1%
Musharakah (equity participation)	0.9%	0.8%	1.3%	1.2%
Qard ul-hassan	0.2%	0.3%	0.4%	0.5%
Other	0.2%	0.2%	0.5%	3.0%

Source: Islamic Banks and Financial Institutions Information System (IBIS).

financing instrument, *murabahah*, has earned this practice the title of "*murabahah* syndrome."[8]

Islamic banks' reluctance in regards to risk-sharing instruments such as *musharakah* (equity partnership) and *mudarabah* (principal–agent partnership) is problematic for achieving the true potential and promise of the system. The reason for shying away from such instruments is a lack of appetite for risky assets, which in turn is due to Islamic banks trying to emulate conventional commercial banks where preservation of depositors' principal is their foremost objective. By investing in financing and trade-related instruments, Islamic banks are able to provide low-risk and safe investment opportunities. Islamic banks should change this business model and expand their portfolio to include risk-sharing instruments. Islamic banks often claim that their reluctance is a direct reflection of the reluctance of the depositors for risk-sharing instruments. However, it is possible that the depositors' low appetite for risk-sharing instruments is due to a lack of transparency and confidence in the ability of the financial intermediary. Therefore, Islamic banks should consider doing a better job of selecting and monitoring risk-sharing assets and enhance the transparency of the investment process by informing the depositors with good estimates of exposure to risks taken by the financial intermediary in investing in risk-sharing instruments.

2.4.4 Limited Scale and Scope

Although Islamic banks have grown in number, the average size of their assets is still small compared to that of conventional banks. The majority of Islamic banks are below the benchmark asset size of US$500 million considered to be the minimum for an efficient conventional bank. In Table 1.5 we listed the top ten Islamic banks;

there are only four banks with total assets in excess of US$10 billion, compared to the top six conventional banks, each of which has total assets in excess of US$1 trillion. Large institutions have significant potential for efficiency gains due to economies of scale and scope, organizational efficiency, and lower cost of funding. Due to their small size, Islamic banks are unable to reap these benefits.[9]

In the absence of debt markets, underdevelopment of equities markets, and lack of derivatives markets, financial intermediaries play a critical role in the provision of Islamic financial services. Financial intermediaries not only are the main source of capital and risk mitigation but also are expected to undertake activities with wider scope. The changing global financial landscape will require Islamic banks to go beyond their traditional role as commercial banks and develop areas such as securities, risk management, retail banking, assets management, and insurance that are either lacking or functioning on a limited scale.

The nature of financial intermediation and the style of financial products and services offered make Islamic banks a hybrid between commercial and investment banking, similar to a universal bank. Universal banking benefits from economies of scope due to its close relationship, established client base, and access to private information gained through the relationship. Combining different product lines (such as banking and insurance products) or commercial and investment banking lines may increase the relationship value of banking at a much lower average cost of marketing. Islamic financial institutions could realize the benefits of universal banking by strengthening this aspect of their business.

For example, by expanding the scope of services, Islamic banks could spread the fixed cost, in terms of both physical and human capital, of managing a client relationship over a wider set of products, leading to a more efficient use of resources. Through expansion, Islamic banks could use their branch networks and other channels to distribute additional products at low marginal costs. As universal banks, Islamic banks would be able to capitalize on their good reputation established in one product or service to market other products and services with relatively little effort. Finally, expanding the scope of Islamic banks would benefit consumers, who would save on searching and monitoring costs by purchasing a bundle of financial services from a single provider instead of acquiring them separately from different providers.

2.4.5 Concentrated Banking

Islamic banks tend to have a concentrated base of deposits or assets. They often concentrate on a few select sectors and avoid direct competition. For example, one Islamic bank may specialize in financing the agricultural sector, while another might do the same in the construction sector, and neither attempts to diversify into other sectors. This practice makes Islamic banks vulnerable to cyclical shocks in a particular sector. Dependence on a small number of sectors—lack of diversification—increases their exposure to new entrants, especially foreign conventional banks that are better equipped to meet these challenges.

This concentration in the base of deposits or assets reflects a lack of diversification, which increases exposure to risk. Islamic banks' assets are concentrated in a handful of products. Islamic banks are not fully exploiting the benefits that come from both geographic and product diversification. At present, they rely heavily on maintaining good relationships with depositors. However, these relationships can be tested during times of distress or changing market conditions, when depositors tend to change loyalties and shift to large financial institutions which they perceive to be safer. By diversifying their base of depositors, Islamic banks could reduce their exposure to displacement or withdrawal risks. With the changing face of banking and the introduction of Internet-based banking, achieving a high degree of geographic diversity on the liabilities side is conceivable and should be encouraged.

For Islamic financial institutions, geographic expansion of the depositor base could achieve diversification on the liabilities side. Diversification on the assets side could reduce the variance of the returns that accrue to claimholders of the financial intermediary. Also, geographic and sectoral diversification on the assets side could break up the financial institutions' concentration in a region or a sector and thus reduce its exposure by creating less perfectly correlated risks. Geographic spread of products can further help the financial intermediary to improve its credit risk by selecting borrowers with the best credit and avoiding those with the weakest. With diversification, Islamic banks would be able to extend the maturity frontier.

2.4.6 Risk Management Framework

Financial markets are becoming more integrated and interdependent, thus increasing the probability of expeditious contagion effects and leaving little room for swift measures against unexpected risk.

Insufficient understanding of the new environment can create a sense of greater risk even if the objective level of risk in the system remains unchanged or is even lower. The current wave of capital market liberalization and globalization is prompting the need for enhanced risk-management measures, especially for the developing economies and emerging markets. Whereas risk management is practiced widely in conventional financial markets, it is underdeveloped in Islamic financial markets.

Due to limited resources, Islamic banks are often unable to afford high-cost management information systems or the technology to assess and monitor risk in a timely fashion. With weak management and lack of proper risk-monitoring systems, the risk exposure of Islamic banks is high. Islamic financial intermediaries need to adopt appropriate risk management not only for their own portfolio but also for that of their clients. Diversification and risk management are closely associated with the degree of market incompleteness. In highly incomplete markets, financial intermediaries are in a better position to provide diversification and risk management for the client because the responsibility for risk diversification shifts from the investors to the financial intermediary, which is considered to be better at providing intertemporal risk management. Islamic financial institutions need to take immediate steps to devise an infrastructure for implementing proper measures, controls, and management of risk and to create innovative instruments to share, transfer, and mitigate financial risk so that entrepreneurs can concentrate on what they do best: managing exposure to business risk in which they have a comparative advantage.

Exposure can also be reduced by working closely with clients to reduce their exposure, which will ultimately reduce the intermediary's exposure. In other words, if the debtor of the bank has lower financial risk, this will result in better quality credit for the bank. Furthermore, monitoring becomes vital in cases where Islamic banks invest in equity-based instruments because an institution with limited resources may not be equipped to conduct thorough monitoring. An institution with adequate resources may develop processes, systems, and training to undertake effective monitoring. There is clearly a need for Islamic financial institutions that can offer guarantees, enhance liquidity, underwrite insurance against risks, and develop hedging tools for a fee.

Finally, Islamic financial institutions need to realize the importance not only of financial risk and its management but also of operational risk, which is risk due to the failure of controls and processes. Currently, there is a serious lack of a risk culture and of enterprise-level sponsorship of active risk management. Formulating a strategy for risk management in Islamic financial markets will require: holding comprehensive and detailed discussion of the scope and role of derivatives within the framework of the *Shari'ah*; expanding the role of financial intermediaries, with special emphasis on facilitating risk sharing; applying *takaful* (*Shari'ah*-compliant mutual insurance) to insure financial risk; and, finally, applying financial engineering to develop synthetic derivatives and off-balance-sheet instruments (van Greuning and Iqbal 2007).

2.5 REGULATORY AND GOVERNANCE ISSUES

Several studies have identified weaknesses and vulnerabilities among Islamic banks in the areas of risk management and governance.[10] Operational risk, which arises due to the failure of systems, processes, and procedures, is one area of concern. Weak internal control processes may present operational risks and expose an Islamic bank to potential losses. Governance issues are equally important for Islamic banks, investors, regulators, and other stakeholders. The role of *Shari'ah* boards brings unique challenges to the governance of Islamic financial institutions. Similarly, human resource issues, such as the quality of management, technical expertise, and professionalism, are also subject to debate.

Implementation of a risk-management framework requires close collaboration among the management of Islamic financial institutions, regulators, and supervisors. Implementation of risk management at the institutional level is the responsibility of management, which should identify clear objectives and strategies for the institution and establish internal systems for identifying, measuring, monitoring, and managing various risk exposures. Although the general principles of risk management are the same for conventional and Islamic financial institutions, there are specific challenges in the management of risk in Islamic financial institutions.

Corporate governance in Islamic finance entails implementation of a rule-based incentive system that preserves social justice and order among all members of society. Governance processes and structures inside and outside the firm are needed to protect the ethical and pecuniary interests of shareholders and stakeholders. Iqbal and Mirakhor (2002) present a stakeholder-centered model of corporate governance based on the principles of Islam and suggest that an institution operating within an Islamic system is expected to protect the rights of all stakeholders in the firm as well as in the society. At the operational level, there are serious issues relating to the rights of investment account holders (IAH)—that is, the depositors—as their participation in the governance structure is nonexistent. Similarly, Islamic banks maintain several reserves to smooth income and to compensate IAH in times when actual profits are below market expectations. However, there are no clear rules relating to the governance of such reserves.

Implementation of financial disclosure is another priority. Ideally, jurisdictions where Islamic banks are present should implement accounting and reporting practices in line with standards of the AAOIFI. This could be accomplished by adopting the official AAOIFI standards, creating AAOIFI-inspired national standards, or integrating select AAOIFI standards with existing accounting and auditing standards. AAOIFI standards present multiple advantages. First, the process of conducting periodic reviews ensures that only the best accounting and auditing practices are used. Second, they allow comparability across Islamic banks in different jurisdictions, although they may limit comparability between Islamic and conventional banks. Third, stakeholders involved in Islamic finance will find it easier to gain familiarity with a single accounting framework instead of multiple national ones. In spite of increased comparability across sectors, the simple extension of International Financial Reporting Standards (IFRS) or national conventional standards is not likely to bring the same clarity, because it may not allow the disclosure of relevant information.

Poor corporate governance imposes heavy costs, but the mere extension of international standards to Islamic banks may not be sufficient. The principles and practices of Islamic financial services require a thorough review from the corporate governance perspective. Sound corporate governance requires the formulation of principles and enforcement (for more, see van Greuning and Iqbal 2007). Many countries where Islamic finance is developing have weak contracting environments: regulators often lack the power to enforce rules, private actors are nonexistent, and courts are "underfinanced, unmotivated, unclear as to how the law applies, unfamiliar with economic issues, or even corrupt" (Fremond and Capaul 2002). Furthermore, a "law habit" culture—that is, a propensity to abide by the law—must be rooted in society. While the ability to enforce regulations is inextricably coupled with the overall process of development, legislation enabling transparency, private monitoring initiatives, and investments in the rule of law by willing authorities can pave the way to the emergence of regulatory frameworks.

2.6 *SHARI'AH* GOVERNANCE

The role of *Shari'ah* scholars is critical in Islamic finance, and to the growth of the industry; given that *Shari'ah* scholars are one of the most significant stakeholders, their code of conduct, mode of operation, and governance pose a serious challenge. During the last three decades, *Shari'ah* scholars have played a positive role in the growth and development of Islamic finance, but their role has also come under scrutiny and sometimes they have been unfairly attacked.[11] Respectable *Shari'ah* scholars such as Dr. Nejjatullah Siddiqi, Sheikh Yousaf DeLorenzo, and Mufti Taqi Usmani have often highlighted anomalies in the role and practices of *Shari'ah* scholars.

The first issue is how to ensure that the rulings by *Shari'ah* scholars do not inadvertently encourage a practice which is in conflict with the essence of Islam. As noted by Siddiqi (2006), the role played by *Shari'ah* experts has gone through a cycle. In the early stages of development of Islamic finance, issuing a *fatwa* (legal ruling) was considered a public good and no financial benefit was expected from the service. However, the expansion of business and the current wave of commercialization have created a competitive market for *Shari'ah* scholars at the expense of less transparency. Today's business world is changing rapidly and the circumstances and precedents familiar to *Shari'ah* scholars are very different. Siddiqi points out that there is no doubt that *Shari'ah* experts have been doing what their training equips them to do, and they have been doing it well, but unfortunately their training is no longer well designed to serve the *maqasid al-Shari'ah* (objectives of *Shari'ah*) in circumstances very different from the environment reflected in the books they study. Today's business environment calls for not only economic analysis but draws upon the latest developments in other social sciences such as sociology, psychology, political science, and management. Therefore, with a lack of proper institutional arrangements there is high probability of malfunction in *Shari'ah* advisement which can have dire consequences for this industry in its infancy.

For example, the practice of *tawarruq* (a controversial practice) is a glaring example of malfunction. Although it was necessary to evaluate the *masalih* (benefits) and *mafasid* (harms) associated with this practice on a large scale by financial institutions, the process that was followed was flawed. First, there were no precedents in the entire history of Islam for such application. Second, evaluating *masalih* and *mafasid* in case of widespread practice of *tawarruq* was beyond the capacity of *Shari'ah* experts, mainly because it required expertise across disciplines with the knowledge of the macroeconomic impact of decisions. According to Siddiqi (2006), the benefits cited by those approving the product mainly relate to the individuals, but its application at a grand scale without looking at the bigger picture was unjustified, resulting in approval of a practice that is in direct conflict with the spirit of Islam.

The second issue is how to avoid contamination in the application of *Shari'ah* principles. During the early stages of the development, *Shari'ah* scholars approved certain transactions by using the *Law of Necessity*, and treating certain aspects of the transactions as an exception provided they are convinced that these aspects are in the greater interests of the industry. However, the business community may have misused this permission and may have made exceptions the rule. For example, *Shari'ah* scholars allowed fund managers to invest in shares of companies where debt was less than one-third of the capital on the grounds that upon taking ownership the shareholders should exert their influence and pressure the management to reduce the debt to make it fully compatible with *Shari'ah*. The result is that the acceptability of one-third debt is becoming the rule with the fund managers and serves as another screening rule without any serious effort to reduce the debt from the capital structure. Similarly, approval by *Shari'ah* scholars to treat LIBOR as a benchmark rate of return has become a common practice among financial intermediaries. Whereas this practice is convenient for the financial houses, it creates a moral hazard in the long run as it is a disincentive to develop a benchmark that represents the rate of return in the real economy as opposed to opportunity cost in the debt markets.

DeLorenzo (2007) raises another very serious question: should a *Shari'ah* supervisory board approve any financial product that is "delivered" by *halal* means, even if what is being delivered by those means is derived from noncompliant investments? He questions the use of non-*Shari'ah*-compliant assets as a determinant for returns for a *Shari'ah*-compliant product. He reports that the term sheet for one such product states unequivocally that its purpose is to "wrap a non-*Shari'ah* compliant underlying (asset) into a *Shari'ah*-compliant structure." Such practices where the structure and the transactional basis are compliant with established *Shari'ah* rules but the end product is the result of prohibited investments are a serious concern and should be discouraged.

Usmani (2007) reviews the practice of structuring *sukuk* and raises certain concerns with some of the prevailing practices. As chairman of AAOIFI's *Shari'ah* Committee, he strictly takes notice that *sukuk* holders must have complete ownership in real assets as opposed to a simple ownership interest which occurs in the absence of a "true sale" of securitized assets. It was also observed that "actual" returns of underlying assets should be passed on to *sukuk* holders after necessary adjustments for manager fees and other expenses, instead of any predetermined or prepromised returns. Finally, the practice of lending money by the manager in case actual profits are less than the expected was declared unlawful.

The above examples remind us of the complexities involved with *Shari'ah* practices and why it is important to pay attention to these matters. This also highlights the severity of the challenge it poses for the future growth of the market. This brings us to the third issue of setting up a governance structure that is effective, efficient, consistent, and transparent. The functioning of internal *Shari'ah* boards raises five corporate governance issues: independence, confidentiality, competence, consistency, and disclosure. The first issue concerning the *independence* of the *Shari'ah* boards from management is critical. A competent and independent *Shari'ah* board, empowered to approve new instruments, would facilitate innovation within the firm. In issuing its *fatawi*, the board could be guided by standardized contracts and practices that could be harmonized by an international standard setting self-regulatory professionals' association. Such an approach would ensure consistency of interpretation and enhance the enforceability of contracts before civil courts. Review of transactions would mainly be entrusted to internal review units, which in collaboration with external auditors would be responsible for issuing an annual opinion on the *Shari'ah* compliance of the transactions. This process would be sustained by reputable agents—such as rating agencies, stock markets, financial media, and researchers—that would channel signals to market players. Such a framework would also enhance public understanding of the requirements of *Shari'ah*, and lead to a more effective participatory role by the stakeholders in the activities of the institution.[12]

Having an extensive structure of *Shari'ah* boards at individual financial institutions is inefficient because of a shortage of competent *Shari'ah* scholars, their inability to ensure transparency, and the resulting nonstandard practices and contracts.[13] Instead, a suggestion has been put forth to establish a system-wide *Shari'ah* board which can work closely with the regulators and supervisors to make sure that effective monitoring and supervisory controls are devised to protect the rights of all stakeholders. It will be the board's responsibility to ensure that compliance with the monitoring system will protect the rights of those stakeholders with whom the financial institution has "explicit" or "implicit" contracts. This structure of governance with a system-wide religious board will be more efficient and cost-effective because: each stakeholder will not be required to duplicate monitoring; each institution will not be required to maintain its own *fatwa*-issuing board; the *fatwa*-issuing board will consist of knowledgeable experts in *Shari'ah* as well as finance; and there will be uniformity of expected behavior which will set the standards to be followed by individual institutions.[14]

Furthermore, there is a need to have mechanisms in place for the external monitoring of *Shari'ah* compliance, either in the form of rating agencies or through external auditors. To enhance *Shari'ah* compliance further, relying on a body external to the institution is likely to improve the consistency of interpretation and application of *Shari'ah*. Chapra and Ahmed (2002) propose having chartered auditing firms acquire the necessary knowledge to undertake a *Shari'ah* audit. The idea of a market for *Shari'ah* audit firms presents some advantages if externalization is reconceptualized as a complement—rather than an alternative—to the internal *Shari'ah* audit. External *Shari'ah* companies would perform a role that reflects their chartered counterparts in conventional finance, thus introducing an additional layer in the *Shari'ah* verification process. This option would entail a clear separation of *ex ante* and *ex post* audits. However, it is unclear whether switching to a market for *Shari'ah* auditing firms would guarantee *Shari'ah* compliance.

The fourth issue is the outstanding resolutions on several critical *Shari'ah*-related issues that have serious impacts on the financial transactions. The foremost and critical one is to offer some guidance regarding the treatment of derivative contracts. There is need to have a healthy debate among *Shari'ah* scholars to offer solutions and alternatives to hedging to mitigate risks. Another issue is the treatment of receivables which constitute a large portion of Islamic banks' portfolios. Due to *Shari'ah*'s prohibition on sale of debt (other than its face value), the banks are unable to trade these assets in the secondary markets and, therefore, are unable to enhance their liquidity. This constraint is very costly for Islamic banks and there is need to think about viable solutions to this problem. Although *Shari'ah* scholars in Malaysia are less restrictive on the sale of debt, the same is not true elsewhere. There is need to develop a consensus on transferability and negotiability of a financial claim resulting from a sale contract (*murabahah*).

2.7 GOING BEYOND BANKING

The distinction between traditional commercial banking and investment banking is becoming blurred, and there is a global trend to mix financial services with non-banking services. Although this trend is prevalent in major industrial economies, it has not been embraced by many of the emerging markets where Islamic finance is practiced. For example, a recent study that ranks several countries in the Middle East according to their level of financial development finds that countries throughout the region have a weak institutional environment and a poorly developed non-bank financial sector.[15] Islamic finance has been dominated by commercial banking, and the relative size of investment banking, insurance, asset management, small and medium enterprise (SME) financing, and microfinance is very small.

Islamic finance that claims to promote social justice and advocates equal opportunity for less fortunate segments of society needs to develop the SME and microfinance industry. A well-developed microfinance industry will promote economic development in underdeveloped Islamic countries. As poor segments of society are economically empowered, they will move from being "non-bankable" to being "bankable," expanding the base of depositors and investors. Whereas microfinance institutions have been successful in conventional markets, there are only a few cases of such institutions operating on Islamic finance principles. This phenomenal success in conventional finance has forced even private investors to regard microfinance as a potential and viable asset class. In an Islamic system, instruments such as *qard-ul-hassan*, *sadaqah*, and *Zakah* can play a vital role in serving the poor, and the role each instrument can play needs to be reviewed.

2.8 ECONOMIC DEVELOPMENT

Besides the critical issues directly affecting the growth and development of Islamic finance outlined above, the growth of Islamic finance will be determined by the growth and development of the real sector of Muslim economies. By this we do not mean growth of gross domestic product (GDP) alone. Growth in GDP can be accompanied by little or no financial development, as for example would be the case if a country sells its oil abroad and imports all its needs. Broad-based economic development requires higher savings and investment, a more educated and better-trained labor force, adoption of modern technology and best practices, efficient institutions (especially the rule of law), consistent economic policies, and an environment where a vibrant private sector can grow and develop. The synergy between the real and financial sector has been readily acknowledged. Economic growth of the real sector in such a setting will stimulate the financial sector, and the financial sector will in turn provide financing for the growing real economy. The largest and most developed economies tend to have the largest and most efficient financial sectors.

Whereas Islamic finance has received considerable attention, no attempt has been made for system-wide implementation of economic tenets of Islam. The challenge for the Muslim countries wishing to embrace Islamic finance would be to understand the linkage between the economic tenets of Islam and economic growth. Islam's notions of justice in exchange and distribution, the role of the society and the state, instruments to promote social welfare, inclusiveness, and promotion of mutual and collective help can lead to an equitable and just economic system. Chapter 10 discusses some of the issues related to economic development in Islam.

2.9 PUBLIC FINANCE

One of the key elements for sustained growth and development of any modern economy is sound public finances; that is, adequate public revenues and prudent public expenditures that promote economic growth and social welfare. An overbearing government that runs large budgetary deficits and finances wasteful expenditures does significant harm to promoting economic growth and development, and social welfare. An overbearing public sector, relative to the private sector, crowds out private sector investment and growth. A government that runs large deficits reduces resources for the private sector, damages macroeconomic stability, and reduces available policy options. Wasteful government expenditures, such as harmful subsidies and excessive military expenditures, reduce economic growth and adversely affect social welfare.

On the revenue side, efforts aimed at improving the elasticity and efficiency of the tax system need to be supported by improvements in administrative efficiency and tax enforcement. On the expenditure side, an improvement in the quality of public expenditure programs, especially the elimination of indiscriminate subsidies and the adoption of a fair and just social safety net, would enhance their contribution to economic growth. However, while not all Muslim countries have warmed to the concept of the market economy and broad-based reforms, nearly all—to varying degrees—have taken timid steps to reduce fiscal costs and improve efficiency by tackling a variety of complex and politically sensitive issues, including the need: to broaden the tax base and to reduce budget deficits; to address spending on subsidies, public sector employment, pensions, and health; to use taxation and income transfers in order to achieve a fairer distribution of income and wealth; and to introduce greater transparency as part of governance reform. The attendant benefits of the improved fiscal conditions are also evident in lower inflation, smaller balance of payments deficits, more resources for private sector investment, and, quite recently, better growth rates. Chapter 11 touches upon the challenges of public finance in Islam.

2.10 SOCIAL SAFETY NET

While over the last few decades the international community has adopted the position that broad-based economic growth is necessary for stemming the effects of systemic poverty, a growing consensus has emerged that social safety nets and social protection are also essential elements of any comprehensive framework for poverty alleviation. Not only are resources that provide basic services, such as health and education, important in their own right, they are also critical drivers for economic growth and development and essential to achieving an equitable distribution of income and wealth. An adequate social safety net is a central feature of Islamic economic doctrines and it is acknowledged to have a positive impact on economic growth and development.

In the early 1980s, the general prescription for growth in developing countries was economic reform, focusing on developing a prudent combination of policies to enhance stabilization and adjustment, while little attention was placed on the potential social costs of such reforms; reforms were largely for reforms' sake and did not incorporate the particular conditions of individual countries. However, by the late 1990s the pendulum gradually shifted towards a model of economic growth that included more attention to relieving constraints that were binding to individual countries, including specific provisions for social welfare and protection. It has also been recognized that safety nets alone cannot serve effectively as an instrument for alleviating poverty without sound macroeconomic policies that enhance sustainable growth. While restructuring efforts may create economic efficiency gains over the long term, they oftentimes also lead to social dislocation, particularly over the short term. As Muslim countries adopt much needed economic reforms to promote fiscal discipline (eliminate government waste, reduce harmful subsidies), build effective institutions (enforce rule of law, reduce corruption), and promote economic justice in an effort to stimulate long-term growth, the development of a comprehensive structure to protect the vulnerable from declining deeper into poverty and improving the income distribution becomes even more pressing. Chapter 12 discusses this issue in detail and also presents a case study of the current state of the social safety net in selected Muslim countries.

2.11 HUMAN RESOURCES DEVELOPMENT

Education, or knowledge, is today seen as a major, if not the major, input for sustained economic growth and development. In the development of a modern financial sector there is a critical need for highly educated professionals in the fields of economics, finance, accounting, and IT. At the same time, effective and prudent supervision and regulation of the financial sector requires highly trained specialists. Unfortunately, all of these specialists are in high demand the world over and are highly mobile. High-quality university education, a good working environment, and appropriate remuneration are key factors. Efforts should also be made to develop a multitude of customized research and training programs with certification in areas such as financial engineering and risk management. One cannot emphasize enough developing cross-discipline activities to train *Shari'ah* scholars in economics and train the economists in the basics of *Shari'ah* principles.

ENDNOTES

1 Iqbal, Zamir, "Theoretical Foundations of Islamic Economics," in Habib Ahmed, ed., *Theoretical Foundations of Islamic Economics*, (Jeddah: IRTI, 2002).

2 Martson, David and V. Sundararajan, "Unique Risks of Islamic Banks: Implications for Systemic Stability," in ed. Tariqullah Khan and Dadan Muljawan, *Islamic Financial Architecture: Risk Management and Financial Stability*, (Jeddah: IRTI, 2006).

3 Macro prudential surveillance refers to monitoring the impact of plausible macroeconomic shocks on financial soundness and of the implications of financial soundness on the macroeconomy, and adjusting macro and financial policies, as needed.

4 Iqbal, Zamir and Abbas Mirakhor, *Introduction to Islamic Finance: Theory and Practice*, (Singapore: John Wiley & Sons (Asia), 2007).

5 See Salman S. Ali's, "Islamic Modes of Finance and Associated Liquidity Risks," paper presented at the Conference on Monetary Sector in Iran: Structure, Performance and Challenging Issues Tehran, February 2004. See also Umar M. Chapra, "Financial Stability: The Role of Paradigm and Support Institutions" in ed. Tariqullah Khan and Dadan Muljawan, *Islamic Financial Architecture: Risk Management and Financial Stability*, (Jeddah: IRTI, 2006).

6 Chapra (2006) puts forth the idea of creating a common pool at the central banks to provide mutual accommodation to banks in case of need. All banks may be required to contribute a certain mutually agreed percentage of their deposits to this common pool, just as they do in the case of statutory reserve requirements. They would then have the right to borrow interest-free from this pool with the condition that the net use of this facility is zero (that is, drawings do not exceed contributions) over a given period of time. In a crisis situation the central banks may allow a bank to exceed the limit, with appropriate penalties, a warning, and a suitable corrective program.

7 See Iqbal and Mirakhor (2002), Iqbal and Mirakhor (2007), and Hennie van Greuning and Zamir Iqbal (2007), *Risk Analysis for Islamic Banks*, (Washington, DC: World Bank).

8 Ali and Ahmed, "An Overview," in ed. Salman S. Ali and Ausaf Ahmad, *Islamic Banking and Finance: Fundamentals and Contemporary Issues*, (Jeddah: IRTI, 2006).

9 Iqbal, Zamir, "The Impact of Consolidation on Islamic Financial Services Industry," *Islamic Economics Studies*, 15, no.2 (January 2008).

10 See Chapra M. Umer and Tariqullah Khan. *Regulation and Supervision of Islamic Banks*, Occasional Paper no 3. (Jeddah: IRTI, 2000). Ed. Tariqullah Khan and Habib Ahmed, *Risk Management: An Analysis of Issues in Islamic Financial Industry*, Occasional Paper no. 9, (Jeddah: Islamic Development Bank, 2001). Dahlia El-Hawary, Wafik Grais and Zamir Iqbal, *Regulating Islamic Financial Institutions—The Nature of the Regulated*, Policy Research Working Paper No. 3227, (Washington, DC: World Bank, 2004). Wafik Grais and Zamir Iqbal, "Corporate Governance Challenges of Islamic Financial Institutions," 7th Harvard Forum on Islamic Finance, Boston, USA, April 22–23, 2006.

11 For example, El-Gamal labels some of their practices as "*Shari'ah*-Arbitrage." Mahmoud El Gamal, *Islamic Finance: Law, Economics and Practice* (New York: Cambridge University Press, 2006).

12 Grais, Wafik and M. Pellegrini, "Corporate Governance and Shari'ah Compliance in Institutions Offering Islamic Financial Services," World Bank Policy Research Working Paper 4054, (November 2006).

13 El-Hawary, Grais, and Iqbal (2004).

14 Grais and Pelligrini (2006) and van Greuning and Iqbal (2007).

15 Creane, S., Rishi Goyal, A. Mushfiq Mobarak, and Randa Sab (2003), Financial Development in the Middle East and North Africa, (Washington, DC: International Monetary Agency, 2003).

CHAPTER 3

Islamic Finance and Globalization: Convergence and a Boost for Rapid Growth?

"Neither your creation (was) nor your resurrection (will be) except as one united soul" The *Qur'an* (31:28)

Globalization has become an accepted fact of life. The forces of globalization have increasingly affected economic and financial developments in all countries: through trade in goods and services, financial flows, labor movements, distant policy decisions, and more. Given the rapid growth of both financial globalization and Islamic finance, in this chapter we look into whether it is possible that conventional and Islamic finance would converge, and thus reinforce the growth of Islamic finance. The underlying justification for this enquiry is that, from a theoretical point of view, an essential facet of globalization and Islamic finance is the enhancement of maximum risk sharing. The fundamental axiom of Islamic finance is the simultaneous prohibition of debt-based financing and promotion of equity financing: the first reduces risk sharing and the second increases it. Similarly, financial globalization aims at spreading the investor base, and diversifying and sharing risk globally. This could be done through reliance on the most effective vehicle: equity or equity-like finance. Therefore, at least from a theoretical standpoint, as conventional and Islamic finance progress through the development of sophisticated risk-sharing instruments (including in the field of risk insurance), it could be expected that they converge. From an empirical point of view, there is tantalizing evidence that, particularly in the last decade, the growth of financial globalization has been accompanied by increasing equity and equity-like cross-border flows. This growth has been faster than debt flows (bonds), especially to emerging markets (see Table 3.1 and Figures 3.1 to 3.4).

Table 3.1 Emerging markets and developing countries: Net capital flows[1]

(Billions of US dollars)

	1996–98	1999	2000	2001	2002	2003	2004	2005	2006
Total									
Private capital flows, net[2]	159.3	74.6	56.7	70.2	88.3	173.3	238.6	257.2	255.8
Private direct investment, net	142.3	177.4	168.6	182.8	152.2	165.3	190	266.3	266.9
Private portfolio flows, net	60	60.1	11.4	−80.5	−90.9	−12.1	25	29.4	−76.3
Other private capital flows, net	−43	−162.9	−123.4	−32.1	26.9	20.1	23.5	−38.5	65.2
Official flows, net[3]	20.2	22.4	−34.2	6.6	2.3	−44.5	−57.8	−122.6	−143.8
Change in reserves[4]	−72.6	−98.2	−131.2	−120.6	−198.9	−358.9	−508.2	−590.1	−738.4
Memorandum									
Current account[5]	−72.1	34.4	123.5	86.8	132.3	229.4	299.7	511.6	638.5
Africa									
Private capital flows, net[2]	6.5	9	−4.2	2.2	0.9	2.7	12.3	18.3	20.2
Private direct investment, net	5.8	8.6	7.6	23.1	13.5	15.4	16.8	27	19.1
Private portfolio flows, net	5	9.1	−1.8	−7.9	−1.6	−0.5	5.4	4.1	18.5
Other private capital flows, net	−4.3	−8.7	−10	−13	−11	−12.2	−9.8	−12.8	−17.4
Official flows, net[3]	5	4.1	7.7	6.5	8.6	6.4	4.3	−1.8	−3.8
Change in reserves[4]	−4.2	−0.4	−12.8	−9.7	−5.5	−11.4	−32.7	−42.3	−48.4
Central and Eastern Europe									
Private capital flows, net[2]	27.4	36.3	38.7	10.9	54	52.5	74.7	117.5	121.1
Private direct investment, net	14.9	22.7	24.1	24	24.1	16.2	34.5	50.1	65.8
Private portfolio flows, net	1.7	5.3	3.1	0.4	1.7	6.5	26.9	20.9	8.1

Table 3.1 *(continued)*

	1996–98	1999	2000	2001	2002	2003	2004	2005	2006
Other private capital flows, net	10.8	8.3	11.6	−13.4	28.3	29.9	13.3	46.4	47.1
Official flows, net[3]	−0.5	−2.4	1.6	6	−7.5	−5	−6.6	−8.3	−4.9
Change in reserves[4]	−8.8	−12.1	−6	−3	−18.5	−11.5	−13.6	−48.2	−21.2
Commonwealth of Independent States[6]									
Private capital flows, net[2]	−5.3	−13.5	−27.6	7.2	15.8	17.9	7.7	37.6	65.7
Private direct investment, net	5.5	4.7	2.3	4.9	5.2	5.4	12.9	14.4	33.1
Private portfolio flows, net	2.2	−0.9	−10	−1.2	0.4	−0.5	8.1	−3.1	13.9
Other private capital flows, net	−13	−17.3	−19.9	3.5	10.2	13	−13.4	26.3	18.8
Official flows, net[3]	−1	−1.8	−5.8	−4.9	−10.4	−8.9	−7.3	−22.1	−32.6
Change in reserves[4]	5.1	−6.4	−20.3	−14.5	−15.1	−31.8	−53.8	−75.6	−126.9
Emerging Asia[7]									
Private capital flows, net[2]	36.9	−1.9	4.5	23.5	25.4	69.2	142.5	69.7	53.9
Private direct investment, net	56	70.9	59.8	52	52.6	73.1	68	105.8	102.4
Private portfolio flows, net	16	54.1	19.6	−50.2	−60.1	7.8	11.2	−8.1	−99.4
Other private capital flows, net	−35.1	−127	−74.8	21.6	32.8	−11.6	63.4	−27.9	50.9
Official flows, net[3]	5.9	8.5	−10.9	−12	4.1	−16.6	−7	−2.8	−9.8
Change in reserves[4]	−45.1	−84.8	−59.1	−85.4	−154.3	−234.3	−339	−284.1	−365.6
Middle East[8]									
Private capital flows, net[2]	11.8	−3.8	−10	−5.5	−19.4	4.7	−12	−19.9	−15.5
Private direct investment, net	7	4.4	4.9	12.3	9.7	17.8	8.8	17.6	12

(continued overleaf)

Table 3.1 *(continued)*

	1996–98	1999	2000	2001	2002	2003	2004	2005	2006
Private portfolio flows, net	0.5	−8.6	−1.2	−13.5	−17.4	−14.9	−14	−14.9	−5
Other private capital flows, net	4.3	0.4	−13.7	−4.3	−11.6	1.8	−6.8	−22.5	−22.5
Official flows, net[3]	5.2	8	−20.5	−14.2	−9.8	−24.6	−32.5	−57.1	−75
Change in reserves[4]	−8.1	−2	−31.2	−11.6	−3.1	−33.7	−45.7	−106.6	−129.7
Western Hemisphere									
Private capital flows, net[2]	82	48.5	55.2	31.9	11.5	26.2	13.3	33.9	10.4
Private direct investment, net	53.1	66.1	70	66.5	47.2	37.5	49.1	51.4	34.5
Private portfolio flows, net	34.6	1	1.7	−8.1	−13.9	−10.5	−12.5	30.5	−12.4
Other private capital flows, net	−5.7	−18.6	−16.5	−26.5	−21.8	−0.9	−23.3	−48	−11.6
Official flows, net[3]	5.6	6.2	−6.4	25.2	17.4	4.3	−8.7	−30.4	−17.7
Change in reserves[4]	−11.4	7.4	−1.8	3.5	−2.4	−36.2	−23.4	−33.4	−46.5
Memorandum									
Fuel-exporting countries									
Private capital flows, net[2]	−5.4	−27.2	−57	−12.7	−11.2	12.7	−14.9	−6.8	−2.6
Other countries									
Private capital flows, net[2]	164.8	101.8	113.6	82.9	99.5	160.6	253.4	264	258.4

Source: IMF, World Economic Outlook, April 2007.

1 Net capital flows comprise net direct investment, net portfolio investment, and other long- and short-term net investment flows, including official and private borrowing. In this table, Hong Kong, Israel, South Korea, Singapore, and Taiwan are included.

2 Because of data limitations, flows listed under "private capital flows, net" may include some official flows.

3 Excludes grants and includes overseas investments of official investment agencies.

4 A minus sign indicates an increase.

5 The sum of the current account balance, net private capital flows, net official flows, and the change in reserves equals, with the opposite sign, the sum of the capital account and errors and omissions.

6 Historical data have been revised, reflecting cumulative data revisions for Russia and the resolution of a number of data interpretation issues.

7 Consists of developing Asia and the newly industrialized Asian economies.

8 Includes Israel.

Figure 3.1 Total global cross-border inflows

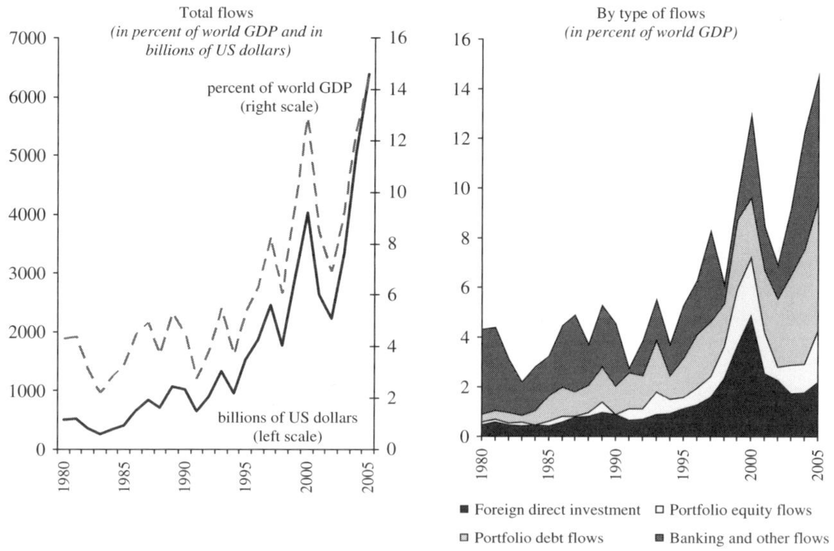

Source: IMF: Global Financial Stability Report, April 2007.
Other flows include derivative transactions.

Figure 3.2 Equity market capitalization (in percent of GDP)

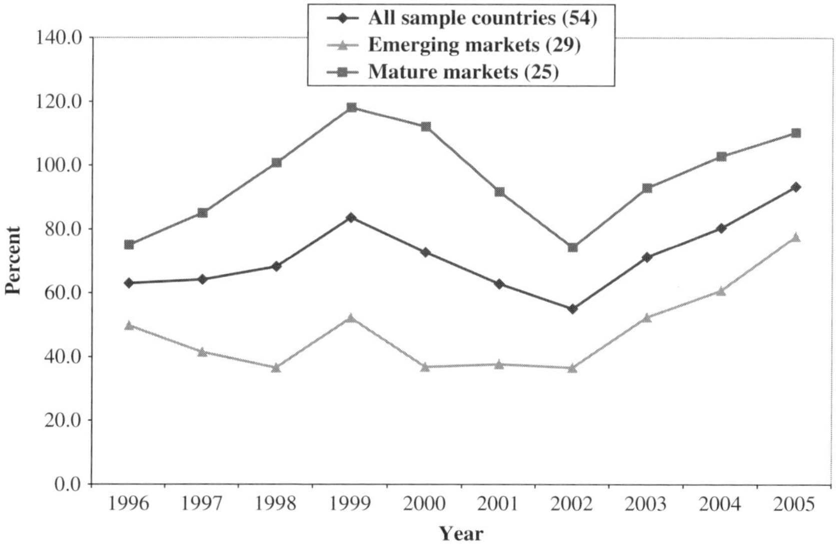

Figure 3.3 Bond market capitalization (in percent of GDP)

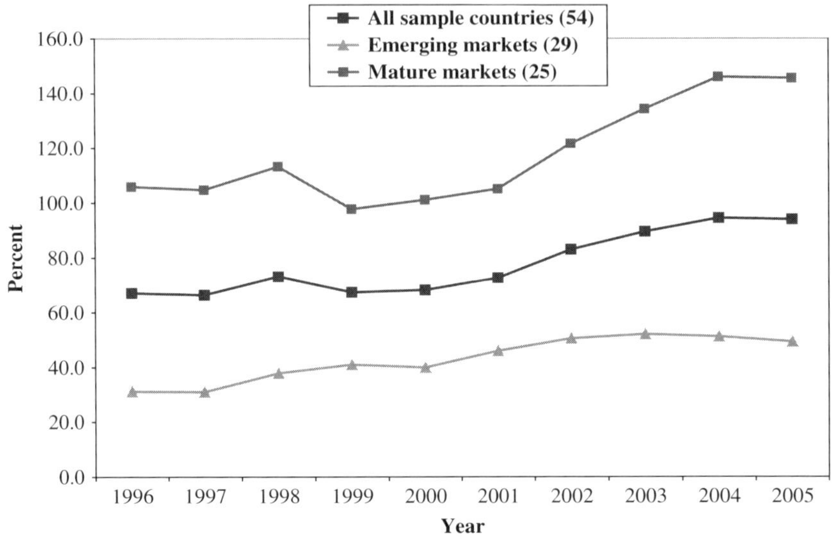

Figure 3.4 Equity markets: 2000–06

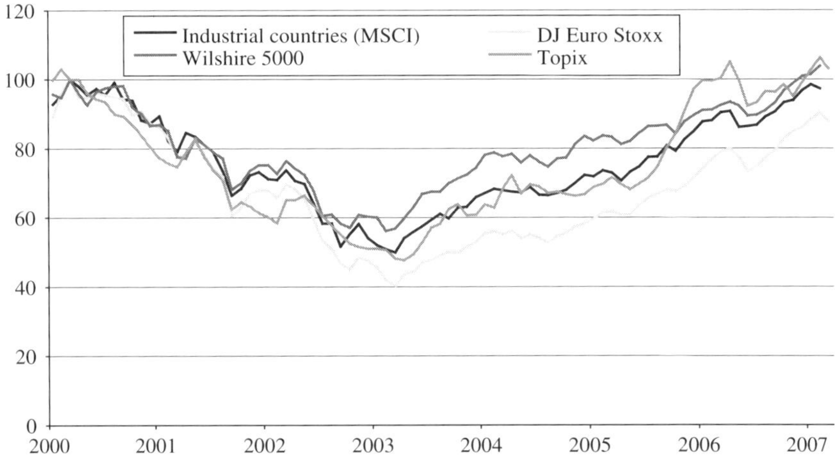

Source: IMF: World Economic Outlook, April 2007.

3.1 FINANCIAL GLOBALIZATION: BENEFITS, COSTS, AND RISK SHARING

Since 1990, the world has witnessed a dramatic and rapid change in the structure of financial markets and institutions. Advances in the theory of finance, rapid innovation in the practice of finance, revolution in information technology, deregulation and liberalization, and institutional reform have changed the nature of financial relations, leading to the emergence of the "new finance." As a result, investment in many instruments matching different risk/return profiles has been made possible, leading to better risk sharing among market participants across the world. Financial transactions have become more at arm's length, allowing broader participation in deeper and expanded markets.

Between 1991 and 2000, gross capital flows (the sum of the absolute value of capital inflows and outflows) expanded by 300 percent among industrialized countries alone, the bulk of which was due to the rise in foreign direct investment (FDI) and portfolio equity flows—both rising by 600 percent—while bond flows over the same period increased by only 130 percent.[1] Over the same period, both stocks and flows of capital movements have increased substantially, especially in relation to GDP and the size of financial markets.

More recent data (Table 3.1, and Figures 3.1, 3.5, and 3.6) show that, after the market turbulence of 2000–02, these trends have resumed, with FDI and portfolio equity flows assuming a larger share of the total flow. The largest increase in FDI in 2006 was in emerging Europe and the Middle East. Empirical evidence suggests that the composition of capital flows matters a great deal. Equity flows (portfolio equity flows + FDI + venture capital) promote better risk sharing, reduce volatility, and strengthen stability.[2] There is a

Figure 3.5 Portfolio equity and FDI flows (emerging markets: 2002–06)

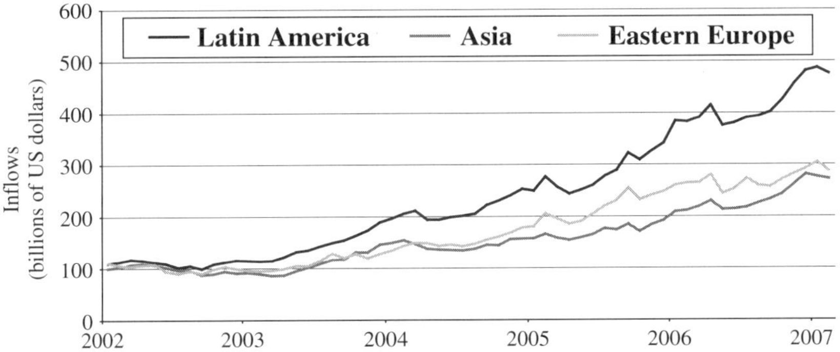

Source: IMF: World Economic Outlook, April 2007.

Figure 3.6 Global foreign direct investment inflows: 1996–2006

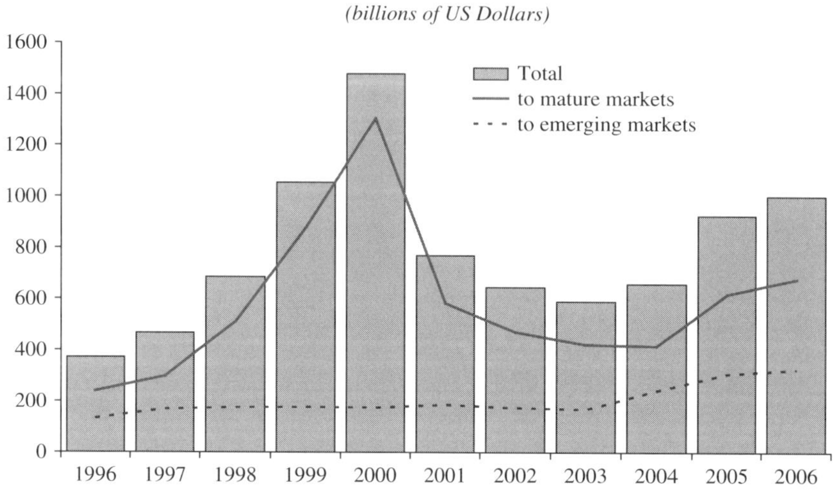

Source: IMF, World Economic Outlook, April 2007.

substantial body of evidence that these flows, especially FDI, are associated positively with economic growth.[3]

Over the past few decades, stock markets have also shown increasing vitality. Development of stock markets increases the rate of saving and leads to growth in investment, while enhancing its quality. Stock markets diversify the investor base while distributing risks across investors, which, in turn, increases the resilience of the economy to shocks (IMF, GFSR 2007). It has been demonstrated that greater reliance on debt flows exposes a country to a higher probability of sudden stops of international capital flows and to financial crises.[4]

3.1.1 Benefits

3.1.1.1 Financial globalization and financial integration have an interactive relationship

On the one hand, the degree of progress of financial integration depends on how well developed financial sectors are in countries. On the other hand, financial globalization plays an important catalytic role in the liberalization and development of the domestic financial markets.[5]

3.1.1.2 Credit and equity markets

An important dimension of the process of financial sector development is expansion and quality improvement in credit and equity markets.[6] The process of financial development deepens markets and services that channel savings to productive investment and strengthens risk sharing. Liberalization of the stock market reduces the cost of equity capital,[7] leading to a surge in the growth rate of investment and expansion of employment and output. The effect would be stronger when stock market development is accompanied by privatization as the latter would be a signal of the country's commitment to liberalization.[8]

3.1.1.3 Financial sector development results in economic growth

Financial sector development constitutes the most important channel of economic growth, particularly in countries that are finance-constrained.[9] Empirical research over the last two decades has established the strong link between financial development and economic growth: greater involvement of private sector and better risk sharing; reduced risks that lower expected returns, leading to lower cost of capital and resulting in investment in higher risk, higher return projects; enhancement of competition and innovation; improved productivity; lower output and income volatility; cost-efficiency gains in mobilizing resources for public investment; financial deepening as financial development leads to greater financial intermediation by banks, capital markets, and non-bank financial institutions; and reduced income inequality and poverty.[10]

3.1.1.4 Legal and institutional developments must accompany financial development

The benefits of economic growth will accrue if legal and institutional developments complement financial development. The most important dimensions of the former are legal protection of creditor, investor, and property rights, as well as contract enforcement.[11] Good governance, transparency, and accountability are the important institutional aspects that support financial development.[12] It is considered that, once a threshold level of availability of these legal and institutional developments is surpassed, the beneficial effects will accrue.[13] Empirical evidence suggests that countries with weak governance and low transparency receive less FDI and equity flows and have to resort to debt financing through bank loans that, as mentioned earlier, expose them to vulnerabilities and volatilities, leading to financial crises.[14]

3.1.1.5 Economic instability and macroeconomic policies (as an important determinant of the composition of capital flows) can exacerbate problems[15]

On the other hand, better legal institutions and improved governance and transparency reduce informational problems (adverse selection and moral hazard) and market frictions.[16] This, in turn, will assist in the process of integration and deepening in the financial sector, which, in their own turn, will allow the emergence of active and liquid equity markets, reduce the cost of capital, and improve credit rating.[17] As a result, more investment projects become viable, leading to greater risk sharing. More active equity markets are also associated with reduced volatility, again suggesting improved risk sharing. On the other hand, an equity market opening against a backdrop of a weak financial sector, inadequate institutional and legal development, and an unstable macroeconomy "may not reduce variability at all and may even increase it."[18] Research suggests that an interactive relationship exists between financial sector liberalization and the development of an active equity market when a country achieves a threshold level of higher bureaucratic quality, lower levels of corruption, and strengthened legal institutions.[19] Stulz (2006) states that "financial systems with a higher degree of legal and institutional development that support finance increase stock market trading volumes and enhance the effect of financial openness." In short, financial sector development—which is accompanied by legal and institutional developments that protect investor, creditor, property rights, enforce contracts, improve transparency, and lower corruption—promote equity markets that, in turn, increase risk sharing.[20]

* * * * *

Domestic financial sector development allows integration with the global market as it increases diversification opportunities and expands the set of financial instruments available for risk sharing. Economies that are open to two-way investments are said to be globally integrated, in turn facilitating global risk sharing. *There appears to be a symbiotic and interactive relationship between domestic financial development, financial integration, and financial globalization.*

Importantly, there is empirical evidence that financial development and integration reduce poverty through increased investment, employment, and income, and reduced income inequality. Recent research has found that: the impact of financial development on poverty exerts two independent influences, with half of the impact on economic growth and the other through reduction in income inequality; financial development leads to considerable deceleration in the rate of growth of income inequality; and as the process of financial development gathers momentum, the rate of reduction in the proportion of the population living in poverty accelerates.[21] In sum, there appears to be considerable benefit to financial sector development and financial integration. Muslim countries are in the early phase of such development and integration.

On the assumption that significant informational problems and transactions costs are absent, theory suggests that integration and globalization of finance allows better international diversification of portfolios, promoting capital flows into markets with the most favorable risk/return profiles. Thus, as risk sharing expands globally, capital is allocated more efficiently, enhancing global welfare. Empirical evidence, however, suggests that risk sharing within countries and across borders has a long way to go.[22] There are important paradoxes contradicting this theory: the Lucas paradox; the home equity bias puzzle; and the equity premium puzzle.

First, Lucas (1990) argued that theory would suggest capital-scarce countries should offer higher rates of return to capital and should be able to attract investment from rich countries. Data, however, showed that most international capital flows, especially FDI and portfolio equity flows, took place among rich countries.[23] Also equity flows were much more biased in favor of domestic (rather than international) markets than theory would suggest.[24] Research indicates that a very high percentage of aggregate stock market wealth is composed of domestic equity.[25] Furthermore, even in domestic markets of rich countries, investment in stock markets is a fraction of what theory suggests, given that the returns to equity are much larger than justified on the basis of aversion to risk.[26] Mehra and Prescott (1985) demonstrated that, over many decades, a large differential existed between the real rates of return to equity in comparison to safe assets; that is, U.S. Treasury bills. They also demonstrated that this differential was too large to be explained by existing theories of rational investor behavior. The implication presents a puzzle as to why rational investors, noting the differential, would not invest in equities up to the point where the remaining differential could be explained as the risk premium on equities. While Mehra and Prescott focused on the U.S. data in their 1985 paper, subsequent research emphasized that the same phenomenon existed in a number of other countries, including India.[27] Recent research has shown the global character of this puzzle and has attributed a significant part of it to institutional factors (Erbaş and Mirakhor 2007). Interestingly, in one of his recent papers Mehra (2003) reports that the real worth of one dollar invested in equity in 1802 would have been nearly US$560,000 in 1997, whereas the real worth of the same US$1 invested in Treasury bills in 1802 would have been only US$276 over the same period.

There is validity in the critics' arguments on globalization that—despite the fact that globalization was expected to help the poor—poverty has not been reduced and that measures of inequality reveal that it has not decreased.[28] Moreover, there is empirical evidence of increased risks of volatility and financial crises.[29] In answer, researchers argue that the process of globalization is far from complete and that, at present, global economy and finance are undergoing major structural changes that create a situation of "fluidity." These have changed the usual "determinants of market valuation, volatility, leverage, velocity, and liquidation." Each of these changes is significant on its own and in the way it interacts.[30] These structural changes are: positive productivity shocks associated with the growing integration of large segments of the labor force in developing economies, rendering them a significant portion of global expansion; significant increases in commodity prices, which has made their producers, as a whole, net global creditors; and considerable retrenchment in the barriers to entry.[31]

Even the rapid innovation in the design of instruments of risk sharing has focused on a fraction of possibilities, and significantly large potential markets that allow trade in broad claims on national income, called "macro markets," have yet to be developed and tapped. "Some of these markets could be far larger in terms of the value of the risks traded than anything the world has yet experienced, dwarfing today's stock markets."[32] Shiller (2003) notes, "stock markets are claims on corporate dividends which are only a few percent of national income." Researchers also suggest that, while the benefits of globalization have not been fully forthcoming with the scope and magnitude expected, the problem has not been the process of globalization, but rather the way in which it has proceeded, where the playing field has not been quite leveled and where many financial markets have a long way to develop to allow meaningful integration of wider and deeper risk sharing. Financial globalization does not automatically provide the benefits expected to many countries unless they have attained the threshold levels of legal and institutional development mentioned earlier.[33]

Evidence suggests that countries that attain the threshold levels of good legal and institutional development are likely to attract more FDI and portfolio equity flows. In one such study, Faria and Mauro (2004) measured institutional quality as the average of six indicators—voice and accountability; political stability and absence of violence; government effectiveness; regulatory quality; rule of law; and control of corruption—and found that countries that ranked higher on these indicators attracted more equity-like flows. Wei (2005) found evidence from a study on mutual funds that countries with a high degree of government and corporate transparency attract more equity investment because, as explained by Erbaş and Mirakhor (2007), transparency reduces adverse incentive and ambiguity effects. There is also empirical evidence that poor public institutions bias the composition of inflow of capital against equity-like flows and toward debt, exposing these countries to currency and financial crises and adversely affecting the country's ability to use a given amount of capital inflow to stimulate economic growth.

Stulz (2005) indicates that in many developing countries there is a "twin agency" problem stemming from poor corporate and state governance that feed on each other. In countries with a "twin agency" problem, the risk of expropriation by corporations and the state is high because "those who control a country's state can establish, enforce, and break rules that affect investors' payoffs within that country. When expropriation risks are significant, it is optimal for corporate ownership to be highly concentrated, which limits economic growth, risk sharing, financial development, and the impact of financial globalization."[34] One study found that one dollar of cash is, on average, worth US$0.91 in countries with low corruption and only US$0.33 in countries with high corruption.[35] Where the "twin agency" problem exists, diffusion of ownership is weak, the financial sector is poorly developed, and investment and economic growth are low.[36] Once a country begins to liberalize its financial market and improves legal institutions and governance, a virtuous circle becomes possible and globalization begins to play a positive role in encouraging further development of legal and institutional infrastructures that allows further development of the financial sector.[37] There is mounting evidence that in the last decade many developing countries have implemented reforms that promoted legal and institutional developments. They have improved governance, transparency, and accountability, and have adopted regulatory and supervisory standards of best international practice in accounting and data reporting. They have also stabilized their economy with sound macro policies and debt management. Some have even borrowed or rented additional credibility by cross-listing their domestic corporate shares in more advanced markets.[38] As a result, they have received increased capital inflows, with FDI and portfolio equity flows constituting a major portion of these flows.[39]

In addition to the evidence that many developing countries have improved their legal institutions and governance, there is some indication that the three paradoxes mentioned earlier—demonstrating the divergence between the theory and empirics of financial globalization—are beginning to lose strength. Lucas (2000) points out that the twenty-first century will witness a reversal of the widening inequality among nations. His assertion is based on an analysis of a Solow-type neoclassical model with global capital mobility, assuming that all countries have access to the same technology and institutions as well as to market-friendly economic policies. In this case, the "Lucas paradox"—that capital did not move from rich to poor countries—will no longer hold, and a "catch-up" process will rapidly narrow the income gap among countries. Despite critics of his model, Lucas contends that more capital will move to developing countries that adopt policy and institutional infrastructure to reduce the risk premium on investment.[40] Developing countries' adoption of sound macroeconomic policy, best-practice international standards of transparency, accountability, and good governance, as well as legal institutions that protect investor, creditor, property rights, and enforce contracts, will reduce risk premiums.[41] It is not unrealistic that, as their financial sectors develop and international financial integration proceeds, assets of identical risk will command the same expected return, irrespective of spatial or domicile differences. Moreover, data from 2000 show the increasing flow of capital to developing countries (see Table 3.1, and Figure 3.5). In recent years, equity flows to emerging markets have been much stronger than bond flows, and equity-market capitalization much stronger than bond-market capitalization (Figures 3.4, 3.5, and 3.6). Micro data are also beginning to reveal a perceptible shift of household assets portfolio allocation toward greater risk-sharing instruments. The data on the composition of households' financial assets in Europe, the United States, and Japan between 1995 and 2003 demonstrate that in the Euro area, the European Union, and the United States, households allocated a larger portion of their portfolio to risk-sharing instruments. While comparable figures are not available for other areas, similar behavior could be expected as policy, institutional, legal, and financial development progress in developing countries. Considering the Lucas paradox, Alfaro, et al. (2005) concluded that "institutional quality is the leading causal variable" in explaining the paradox based on their empirical study.

Recent empirical evidence also suggests that, since 2001, there has been a systematic decline in home bias, at least in U.S. equity investments.[42] There has also been some empirical evidence that social capital[43]—especially trust, institutional, and legal developments as well as greater transparency and availability of information—may, at least tentatively, explain the equity premium puzzle. In particular, the literature indicates that there is a high correlation between trust and development of the financial sector.[44] Importantly, if the level of trust is high, more reliance is placed on risky assets, such as equity. People invest a larger portion of their wealth in stocks, use more checks, and have access to a greater amount of credit than in low-trust societies. Over the last decade, a number of researchers have demonstrated the impact of trust on economic performance.[45] Arrow had suggested in

Figure 3.7 Emerging markets: FDI outflows by region: 1996–2006

(billions of US dollars)

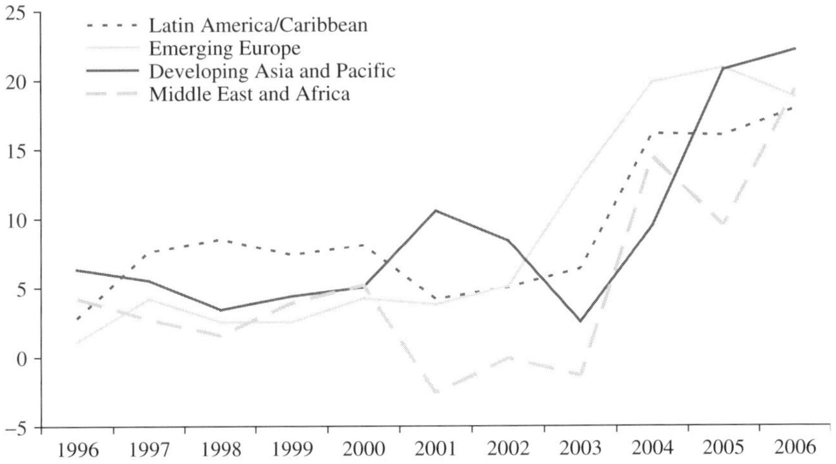

Source: IMF, World Economic Outlook, April 2007.

Figure 3.8 Cumulative net flows to emerging market funds: 2001–06

(billions of US dollars)

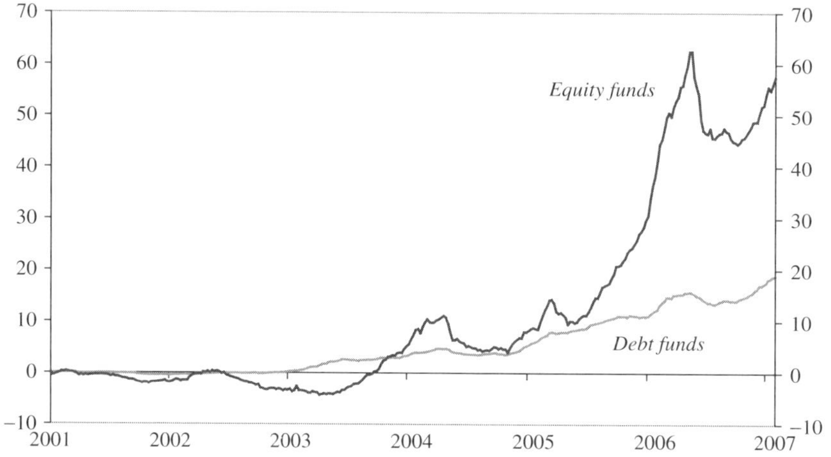

Source: IMF: Global Financial Stability Report, April 2007.

1975 that trust "is an important lubricant of a social system. It is extremely efficient; it saves a lot of trouble to have a fair degree of reliance on other people's word."[46] Fukuyama (1996) asserts that the general level of trust, an important component of social capital, was a strong explanatory factor in the economic performance of industrial countries; the high level of trust was reinforced in these societies by strong institutions.[47] A recent empirical paper by Guiso et al. (2005) demonstrates low trust as a crucial factor in explaining the low level of stock market participation; that is, the equity premium puzzle. Based on the analysis of cross-country data, the paper suggests that where the level of trust is relatively high, investment in equity, in general, and in the stock market, in particular, is also relatively high.

The turmoil in global financial markets that was ignited by the collapse of the subprime mortgage market in the United States—most pointedly the reluctance of banks to trust each other and resume normal lending activities—has demonstrated the importance of trust in financial markets as never before. The policy implication is to strengthen legal institutions, improve transparency, accountability, and governance—both in private and public sectors—and to provide the public with greater amounts of information on risk sharing, in general, and equity markets, in particular.

3.2 ISLAMIC FINANCE: BENEFITS AND CONDITIONS FOR PROGRESS

The central proposition of Islamic finance is the prohibition of a transaction in which a rent is collected as a percentage of an amount of principal, loaned for a specific time period, without the transfer of the property rights over the money loaned to the borrower, thus shifting the entire risk of the transaction to the borrower. The *Qur'an* simultaneously recommends an alternative in consonance with its systemic approach that as something is prohibited. The alternative to debt-based contract is *al-bay'* (البيع): a mutual exchange in which one bundle of property rights is exchanged for another; consequently, the risk of the transaction is shared. It is clear that the objective is to promote risk sharing. Why? Here, an economic hermeneutic of the relevant verses placed within the systemic context of the *Qur'an* strongly suggests that risk sharing, along with other prescribed behavior rules—for example, exhortation on cooperation (*Qur'an* 5:2)—serves to bring humans closer to unity which is itself a corollary of Islam's central axiom: the Unity of the Creation. An Islamic philosophic axiom declares that from *One Creator* only *one creation* can emerge. The *Qur'an* itself unambiguously declares: "*Neither your creation (was) nor your resurrection (will be) other than as one united soul*" (*Qur'an* 31:28). In a series of verses, the *Qur'an* exhorts humans to take individual and collective action to achieve social unity and cohesion and then strive to preserve and protect collectivity from all elements of disunity (for example, 6:153; 3:103). Unity and social cohesion are so central among the objectives of the *Qur'an* for humankind that all conducts prohibited may be regarded as those that cause disunity and, conversely, those prescribed to promote and protect social cohesion. It is a natural consequence of such a system to require risk sharing as an instrument of social integration. Therefore, promoting maximum risk sharing is, arguably, the ultimate objective of Islamic finance. It is for this reason that Muslim scholars consider profit–loss sharing and equity participation as the best instruments of risk sharing.[48] Indeed, there is some evidence that stock market and social interaction are related.[49]

One scholar that has recognized the full potential benefits of risk sharing for humankind is Shiller (2003). He points out that "massive risk sharing can carry with it benefits far beyond that of reducing poverty and diminishing income inequality. The reduction of risks on a greater scale would provide substantial impetus to human and economic progress." Arguably, the most meaningful human progress will be achieved when all distinctions among human beings on the basis of race, color, creed, income, and wealth are obliterated to the point where humanity truly views itself as one. The *Qur'an* (4:1) unambiguously calls attention to the fact that, despite all apparent multiplicity, humans are fundamentally of one kind, and rejects all bases for distinction between and among them except righteousness (*Qur'an* 49:13). This axiom applies to all dimensions of human existence on this planet, including the fields of economics and finance. The objective of the unity of humankind could well be promoted by financial globalization since it has the potential of being the great equalizer of our time. It can assess all risk/return to assets and the real rate of return, leading to greater risk sharing. It can do so across geographic, racial, national, religious, cultural, language, and time boundaries. In the process, it can level playing fields of finance and help remove barriers among people and nations. The same potential holds for Islamic finance if progress follows the trajectory envisioned by Islam.

Among the institutions prescribed by Islam are: property rights; contracts; trust; and governance. The word "property" is defined as a bundle of rights, duties, powers, and liabilities with respect to an asset. In the Western context, private property is considered the right of an individual to use and dispose of a property along with the right to exclude others from the use of that property. Even in the evolution of Western economies, this is a rather new conception of property that is thought to have accompanied the emergence of the market economy. Before that, however, while a grant of the property rights in land and other assets was the right to use and enjoy the asset, it did not include the right to dispose of it or exclude others from its use. For example, the right to use the revenues from a parcel of land, a corporate charter, or a monopoly granted by the state did not carry the right of disposing of the property. It is thought that the development of the market economy necessitated a revision of this conception of property since it was thought that the right not to be excluded from the use of assets owned by another individual was not marketable; it was deemed impossible to reconcile this particular right with a market economy. Hence, of the two earlier property rights principles—the right to exclude others and the right not to be excluded by others—the latter was abandoned and the new conception of property rights was narrowed to cover only the right to exclude others. In Islam, however, this right is retained without diminishing the role of the market as a resource allocation and impulse transmission mechanism within the framework; property ownership is ruled by a set of property rights and obligations.[50]

The first principle of Islamic property rights is that the Supreme Creator is the ultimate owner of all properties and assets, but in order that humans become materially able to perform duties and obligations prescribed by the Law Giver, they have been granted a conditional right of possession of property; this right is granted to the collectivity of humans. The second principle establishes the right of collectivity to the created resources. The third principle allows individuals to appropriate the products resulting from the combination of their labor of these resources, without the collectivity losing its original rights either to the resources or to the goods and services by individuals. The fourth principle recognizes only two ways in which individuals accrue rights to property: through their own creative labor and/or through transfers—via exchange, contracts, grants, or inheritance—from others who have gained property rights title to a property or an asset through their labor.

Fundamentally, therefore, work is the basis of acquisition of right to property. Work, however, is not only performed for the purpose of satisfaction of wants or needs, it is considered a duty and obligation required from everyone. Similarly, access and use of natural resources for producing goods and services is also everyone's right and obligation. So long as individuals are able, they have both the right and the obligation to apply their creative labor to natural resources to produce goods and services needed in the society. However, if individuals lack the ability, they no longer have an obligation to work and produce without losing their original right to resources. Therefore, an important principle called "immutability or invariance of ownership" constitutes the fifth principle of property rights in Islam.[51] The latter writes the duty of sharing into Islam's principles of property rights and obligations. Before any work is performed in conjunction with natural resources, all members of the society have equal right and opportunity to access these resources. When individuals apply their creative labor to resources, they gain a right of priority in the possession, use, or market exchange of the resulting product without nullifying the rights of the needy in the sale proceeds of the product. As a result, the sixth principle imposes the duty of sharing the monetary proceeds after the sale of the property. This principle regards private property ownership rights as a trust held to affect sharing. The seventh principle imposes limitation on the right of disposing of the property—presumably absolute in the Western concept of property rights. Individuals have a severely mandated obligation not to waste, destroy, squander, or use property for unlawful purposes. Once the specified property obligations are appropriately discharged, including that of sharing in the prescribed amount and manner, property rights are held inviolate and no one has a right to force appropriation or expropriation. This right is held so sacred that even in relatively modern times, a rule had to be developed to accommodate emergency cases; for example, exercise of eminent domain for expropriation of land for public utility development. It was called "*ikrah hukmi*,"; "unpleasant necessity," a legitimate violation.[52] Even in these unusual cases, action could be undertaken only after adequate compensation was paid to the owner.

While the above principles strongly affirm humankind's natural tendency to possess—particularly products resulting from individual creative labor—the concomitant private property obligations give rise to the interdependence among the members of the society. These principles, in effect, reject the notion that individuals do no harm if, as a result of effort, they are better off and others are no worse off. Private initiative, choice, and reward are recognized but not allowed to subvert the obligation of sharing. The inviolability of appropriately acquired private property rights in Islam deserves emphasis. As observed by a legal expert[53], given the divine origin of Islam:

> Its institutions, such as individual ownership, private rights, and contractual obligations, share its sacredness. To the authority of law, as it is understood in the West, is added the great weight of religion. Infringement of the property and rights of another person is not only a trespass against the law; it is also a sin against the religion and God. Private ownership and individual rights are gifts from God, and creative labor, inheritance, contract, and other lawful means of acquiring property or entitlement to rights are only channels of God's bounty and goodness to man.... All Muslim schools teach that private property and rights are inviolable in relations between individuals as well as in relations with the state.... It is not only by their divine origin that the Muslim institutions of private ownership and right differ from their counterpart in Western system of law; their content and range of application

> are more far-reaching... If absolutes can be compared, it can be safely said that the right of ownership in Muslim law is more absolute than it is in modern system of law. ... The Muslim concept of property and right is less restricted than is the modern concept of these institutions.

In a terse, unambiguous verse, the *Qur'an* exhorts the believers to "*be faithful to contracts*" (5:1). This command, buttressed by other verses (2:282, 288; 4:33; 6:151-153; 9:4; 16:91-94; 17:34-36; 23:1-8), establishes the observance and faithfulness to the terms of a contract as the central anchor of a complex relationship between: the Creator and His created order, including humans; the Creator and the human collectivities; individuals and the state, which represents the collectivity; human collectivities; and individuals. The concept of contracts in Islam transcends its usual conception as a legal institution "necessary for the satisfaction of legitimate human need." It is considered that the entire fabric of the Divine Law is contractual in its concept and content. A contract binds humans to the Creator, and binds them together. As Habachy (1962) suggests: "This is not only true of private law contacts, but also of public law contracts and international law treaties. Every public office in Islam, even the Imamate (temporal and spiritual leadership of the society), is regarded as a contract, an agreement (áqd) that defines the rights and obligations of the parties. Every contract entered into by the faithful must include a forthright intention to remain loyal to performing the obligations specified by the terms of contract." The fulfillment of contracts is exalted in the *Qur'an* to rank it with the highest achievements and noblest virtues (2:172).[54]

The divinely mandated adherence to the terms and conditions of contracts is undergirded by the equally strong and divinely originated institution of trust.[55] There is strong interdependence between contract and trust; without the latter, contracts will be difficult to enter into and costly to monitor and enforce. When and where trust is weak, laws and complex administrative apparatuses are needed to enforce contracts. Perhaps this is why so much emphasis is placed on trust: to make entering into and enforcing contracts less costly. Accordingly, the *Qur'an*, in a number of unambiguous verses (2:58, 283; 7:172; 8:58; 12:52; 16:93, 94; 17:34, 36; 23:1–8; 42:107, 125, 143, 162, 178, and 193; 48:10) proclaims trustworthiness as a sign of true belief and insists on remaining fully conscious of the obligation of ensuring that the intention to remain trustworthy in fulfilling the terms and conditions precedes promises or entering into contracts. Moreover, the *Qur'an* makes clear that fulfilling the obligations of a contract or a promise is mandatory. In short, the *Qur'an* makes trust and trustworthiness, as well as keeping faith with contracts and promises, obligatory and has rendered them inviolable, except in the event of an explicitly permissible justification (Iqbal and Mirakhor 2007; Habachy 1962). In addition, there are numerous prophetic sayings that supplement the Qur'anic verses on trust. For example, it is reported that the Prophet (صلى الله عليه وآله وسلم) was asked: who is a believer. He replied: "a believer is a person to whom people can trust their person and possession...".[56] It is also reported that he said: "the person who is not trustworthy has no faith, and the person who breaks his promise has no religion." Also, "keeping promises is a sign of faith," and "there are three (behavioral traits) if found in a person, then he is a hypocrite even if he fasts, prays, performs big and small pilgrimages, and declares 'I am a Muslim': when he speaks, he lies; when he promises, he breeches; and when trusted, he betrays."[57]

Other than what has been presented above, there are other individual and collective behavioral rules and norms that strengthen the governance structure—including transparency, accountability, voice, and representation—of the state and firms which will not be discussed here. Nevertheless, the three basic institutions—property rights, contracts, and trust—give a flavor of the strength of governance in Islam. The rule of Law governs the behavior of rulers no less stringently than those of ordinary individuals. As two Western legal experts (Anderson and Coulson 1958) observe: "Islam is the direct rule of God. His Law, the *Shari'ah*, is the sole criterion of behavior," and "the authority of the temporal ruler is both derived and defined by this law." Under the rule of Law, "the ruler is by no means a free agent in the determination of the public interest," and the decisions that the ruler makes "must not be arbitrary, but rather the result of conscientious reasoning on the basis of the general principles of the *Shari'ah* as enunciated in the authoritative texts." These legal experts also assert that, based on their consideration of Islamic legal texts, the command of faithfully observing contracts and covenants "apply to the ruler acting in a public capacity" just as severely as to individuals. "Indeed, when considerations of expediency and public interests are taken into account, they apply even with greater force to the actions of the ruler." Therefore, a breech of faith on the part of a ruler is much more heinous in its nature and serious in its consequence than of anyone else. Importantly, they observe that

> just as the ruler has no special prerogative or exemptions as regards the substantive law, so he has none regarding the application of the law through the courts. Ideally, the jurisdiction of the *qadi* (the judge), the only person qualified to apply the *Shari'ah*, is comprehensive and exclusive. The principle that no one can be judge in his own cause is firmly established in the legal texts, and when personally involved, the ruler should submit to the jurisdiction of the ordinary *qadis*' courts.... the ruler that breaks faith cannot shelter behind any claim of sovereignty from the dictates of the law which brooks no such plea.

The same principles of governance under which a ruler or a state should function also apply to firms. Iqbal and Mirakhor (2005) argue that within the Islamic framework a firm can be viewed as a "nexus of contracts" whose objective is to minimize transaction costs and maximize profits and returns to investors, subject to constraints that these objectives do not violate the property rights of any party whether it interacts with the firm directly or indirectly. In pursuit of these goals, the firm honors all implicit or explicit contractual obligations. As could be discerned from the discussions on contracts and trust, it is incumbent on individuals to preserve the sanctity of implicit contractual obligations no less than those of explicit contracts. By the same token, firms have to preserve the sanctity of implicit and explicit contractual obligations by recognizing and protecting the property rights of stakeholders, community, society, and state. Since the firm's behavior is shaped by that of its managers, it becomes their fiduciary duty to manage the firm as a trust for all stakeholders in ensuring that the behavior of the firm conforms to the rules and norms specified by the Law.[58]

Even from the above rather cursory consideration, it should become clear that, once fully implemented, Islamic institutional framework would support rapid financial development and encourage financial integration and globalization which, in turn, would promote risk sharing. The institutions ordained by Islam reduce uncertainty and ambiguity to ensure predictable behavior. Islam also prescribes rules regarding income and wealth sharing to promote income–consumption smoothing. Arguably, sharing of economic risks in the society is of great concern to Islam. This is evidenced by the strong position taken by the *Qur'an* on distributive justice through *Zakah*, an obligatory 2.5 percent of wealth, as well as additional exhortation for voluntary economic assistance to those less able; all of which are insurance against income risk. However, these institutions are exceptional by their absence in many, if not all, Muslim countries.[59] A number of Muslim countries, within and outside the Middle East and North Africa (MENA) region, have recently implemented macroeconomic and structural reform policies and have adopted international best-practice standards and codes. As a result, the economic performance of these countries has improved markedly, further supported by an increase in oil revenues. While adoption, implementation, and development of Islamic institutions may be slow, implementation of international best-practice of transparency and accountability plus development of an independent and effective judiciary and the reform of the legal system—to protect property, creditor, and investor rights and enforce contracts—and promotion of financial sector development would increase investment, employment, and income, leading to a reduction in poverty.

Islamic finance has experienced rapid growth,[60] especially over the last decade. Its growth is astonishing, given that its analytic underpinnings, in modern economic and financial terms, were explained just two decades ago.[61] There is no accurate estimate of the size of the market at present, but it is certain that it is nowhere near its potential. Just as is the case with financial globalization, Islamic finance has realized only an insignificant fraction of its risk-sharing capacity; of the 15 basic modes of available transactions, only a few have been used widely, and even then only a few instruments have been developed based on these transactions modes.[62] Nearly three decades ago, beginning with Ross (1996, 1978), the theory of finance showed that a basic instrument could be spanned into a large number.[63] The wide range of innovations of instruments has demonstrated the validity of this idea. Undoubtedly, the process of instrument design within the field of Islamic finance will gather momentum once it attracts the needed expertise. At the moment, this is the most important challenge of Islamic finance.[64] The lack of expertise has been the reason why, so far, financial engineering in designing new instruments has focused on fast-tracking a reverse-engineering process of redesigning some conventional vehicles. Not only the process of instrument design based on the approved transactions modes has to accelerate, but also inventions of new instruments paralleling Shiller's (2003) ideas on "macro markets" should start; and here the potential is great.

For example, virtually all government financing in Muslim countries is debt-based. To remedy this, Nadeem ul Haque and Mirakhor (1999) proposed an equity instrument to be sold by governments with its rate of return indexed to the domestic rate of return in Islamic countries and to the return in international-Islamic equity markets, each with specified weights (see chapter 7). The analytic arguments underpinning this proposal were explained by Choudhry and Mirakhor (1998). The reasons governments would want to raise funds are to supply social overhead capital, defense, health, and education. If the private sector was either unwilling or unable, it would fall on governments to undertake the needed investments and cover the related expenditure with usual government revenues. The shortfall would be covered by floating the equity instrument which would be, in essence, an instrument backed by assets represented by either earlier bundles of social overhead capital already completed or in train; for example, roads, dams, hospitals, and the like. Since these are lumpy investments and their public goods nature provides a higher social return than investments undertaken by the private sector, the rate of return to be paid must be at least as high as the rate of return to be paid by the private sector when raising equity in the stock market. But, since domestic markets may experience volatilities to which government finance should not be exposed, Nadeem ul Haque and Mirakhor suggested adding two other markets—the index of returns to all Islamic countries' stock returns and the index of returns to Islamic equity funds in the West—to the index of returns to the domestic equity market. There are obvious advantages to this instrument; one being a vehicle for integration of equity markets across the world while another would be globalization of this instrument forcing governments to compete for funds domestically, regionally, and globally, leading to efficiency gains.

How likely is the convergence of conventional and Islamic finance (as they go through the globalization process) and the likelihood that Islamic finance receives a boost from globalization? The answer would be *quite likely* if global finance would rely more extensively on equity or equity-like flows, on the one hand, and invent or innovate a wider spectrum of risk-sharing instruments, on the other. The same process of innovations in Islamic finance would allow an asymptotic convergence between the two. Nearly five decades ago, Modigliani and Miller (1958) showed that, in the absence of frictions, firms' financial structure would be indifferent between debt and equity. In the real world, there are a number of frictions that bias financial structures in favor of debt and debt-based contracts. The two most important are tax and information. The tax treatment of equity returns and interest in industrial countries, which dominate the world of finance and the present structure of capital flows, is heavily biased against equities. Informational problems (information asymmetry and the related problems of moral hazard and adverse selection) also bias financial transactions in favor of debt or debt-based contracts. Legal–financial systems in advanced countries are also structured, tilting in favor of debt and debt-based transactions. However, as financial market developments progress, legal and institutional developments across the world accelerate, and information technology advances, the informational problems diminish. Whether tax and legal treatment of equity versus debt will become less biased is a policy question. What is clear is that as informational problems decline, it will become increasingly difficult to maintain legal, institutional, and tax policy impediments to level the playing field between equity and debt. Consequently, it is not unreasonable to expect a process of decreasing dominance of the financial system by debt and debt-based instruments, which has not been without costs, including severe financial crises.

It is well known that the full-scale adoption of a fixed-interest-based financial system, with a fractional reserve banking sector at its core, has a major deficiency; the system is inherently fragile.[65] Toward the late 1970s and early 1980s, existence of financial intermediaries, in general, and banks, in particular, was justified due to their ability to reduce transaction and monitoring costs as well as to manage risk. However, minimal attention was paid to reasons why banks operated on the basis of fixed, predetermined interest-rate-based contracts—that is, on a fixed-interest basis—that rendered the system fragile and unstable, requiring a lender of last resort to regulate it. Generally, interest rate theories explain the rate as an equilibrating mechanism between supply of, and demand for, finance, which is a rate that prevails in the market as a spot price and not as a price determined *ex ante* and fixed, tied to the principal and the period covered by the debt contract. In an important paper, Bhattacharya (1982) argued that: "... with risk-neutral preferences, when the choice of risk level is unobservable, then any sacrifice of higher mean asset payoff constitutes an inefficient choice. The classical model of intermediaries existing to save on transactions/monitoring costs in asset choice does not explain why their liability structure should not be all equity." With the development and growth of information economics and agency literature, another explanation was added to the list of reasons for the existence of intermediaries. They served as delegated monitoring as well as signaling agents to solve the informational problems, including asymmetric information existing between principals and agents. Based on the findings of the developing field of information economics (see, in particular, Stiglitz and Weiss 1981), it has been argued that adverse selection and moral hazard effects in a banking system operating on the basis of fixed-fee contracts in the presence of asymmetric information—particularly in cases where this problem is acute—means that some groups will be excluded from the credit market even when the expected rate of return for these groups may be higher than for those with access to credit. Furthermore, when risk/return sharing contracts—for example, equity—are not subject to adverse selection and moral hazard effects, "the expected return to an equity investor would be exactly the same as the expected return of the project itself" (Cho 1986).

The fragility of a financial system operating on the basis of fixed, predetermined interest rates was underlined by Stiglitz (1988) who argued that an "interest rate is not like a conventional price. It is a promise to pay an amount in the future. Promises are often broken. If they were not, there would be no issue in determining creditworthiness. Raising interest rates may not increase the expected return to a loan; at higher interest rates one obtains a lower quality set of applicants (adverse selection effect) and each one's applicants undertakes greater risks (the adverse incentive effect). These effects are sufficiently strong that the net return may be lowered as banks increase the interest rates charged: it does not pay to charge higher interest rates." The findings of the new field of information economics strengthened the arguments of Minsky (1982) and others that a debt-based financial system with the fractional reserve banking—operating with a fixed, predetermined, interest-rate mechanism at its core—is inherently fragile and prone to periodic instability. Stiglitz's findings underlined Minsky's arguments that, as returns to banks decline, unable to raise interest rates on their loans, they enter a liability-management mode by increasing interest rates on their deposits. As this vicious circle continues to pick up momentum, the liability management transforms into Ponzi financing and eventually bank runs develop (Posen 2001). The last two decades of the twentieth century witnessed a number of global bouts of financial instability and debt crises, with devastating consequences for a large segment of humanity, thus raising consciousness regarding the vulnerability and fragility of the financial systems which are based, at their core, on fixed-price debt contracts. As previously emphasized, legal and institutional developments—along with good governance and the adoption of standards of best practice in transparency and accountability at the level of individuals, firms, and state, buttressed by information technology advances—will mitigate the informational problems, leading to lesser reliance on debt-based contracts.

3.3 SUMMARY AND CONCLUSIONS

We have addressed the question regarding the future of financial globalization, and of Islamic finance: will conventional finance, at the heart of the current financial globalization, and Islamic finance converge, and thus will Islamic finance receive a boost from the forces of globalization?

We began by considering the recent development and the future of financial globalization. There is evidence that financial globalization has not been as helpful as expected, given the potential of its benefits for growth of investment, employment, and income as well for reduction of income inequality and poverty. We argued that, ultimately, the success of globalization will depend on the spread and degree of risk sharing around the world. The greater the momentum, the deeper the markets, and the wider the spectrum of risk-sharing instruments, the greater will be shared ownership and participation by a larger number of people in finance. Faster, deeper, wider financial development has a symbiotic relationship with globalization as the feedback process between the two strengthens both. Evidence suggests that, thus far, the degree of risk sharing achieved by globalization is insignificant. We have presented reasons why that integration has been small. It is believed that the process of liberalization of economies, adoption of best international standards, and the development of good legal and/or institutional frameworks and practices explain why the degree of risk sharing is gathering momentum in many countries, as is the pace of innovation of financial instruments. We have suggested that parallel progress and challenges also characterize Islamic finance.

While it has experienced phenomenal success in the last two decades, Islamic finance still has a long way to go to achieve its objective of maximum risk sharing. We have argued that the institutional structures ordained, within which Islamic finance is to operate, are those that promote good state and corporate governance, trust, protection of rights, and contract enforcement. It was suggested that, in the case of Islamic finance, the progress achieved to date is a negligible fraction of the potential. The reasons are identical to those offered in financial globalization. It is suggested that financial, legal, and institutional developments, and a greater pace of instrumentalization of basic modes of transactions permitted, would accelerate the progress of Islamic finance. As it would appear that Islamic finance and financial globalization share a common objective of achieving maximum risk sharing, it is not too unrealistic to expect convergence and thus a significant boost to even more rapid growth of Islamic finance in the future.

It was also argued that legal and institutional developments as well as further advances in information technology will reduce informational problems and lead to growing trust, which is essential for risk sharing. The result will be the dominance of equity in financial structures and relationships. Recent data appear to suggest that global finance may be experiencing the early stage of return of dominance of equity and widespread risk sharing through the growth of Islamic financial techniques, as well as greater innovation of equity-based instruments of risk sharing within the conventional finance. And therein lies the seeds of convergence and rapid growth of Islamic finance.

ENDNOTES

1 Evans, M. and V. Hnatkovska, "International Capital Flows Returns and World Financial Integration," *NBER Working Paper 11701*, (Cambridge, Massachusetts: National Bureau of Economic Research, 2005).

2 Bekaert, G., "Emerging Equity Market and Economic Development," *NBER Working Paper 7763*, (Cambridge, Massachusetts: National Bureau of Economic Research, 2000); Bekaert (2006); Kose et al. "Financial Globalization: A Reappraisal," IMF Working Paper WP/06/189, (Washington, DC: International Monetary Fund, 2006); R. Albuquerque, "The Composition of International Capital Flows: Risk Sharing Through Foreign Direct Investment," *Journal of International Economics* 1, no. 2 (2003): 353–383; Alfaro et al. "How Does Foreign Direct Investment Promote Economic Growth? Exploring the Effects of Financial Markets on Linkages," *NBER Working Paper* no. 12522, (Cambridge, Massachusetts: National Bureau of Economic Research, 2005).

3 Levchenko, A. and P. Mauro, "Do Some Forms of Financial Flows Help Protect from Sudden Stops?" *IMF Occasional Paper* no. 202, (Washington, DC: International Monetary Fund, 2006).

4 Frankel, J. A. and A. K. Rose, "Currency Crashes in Emerging Markets: Empirical Indicators," *CEPR Discussion Papers* 1349 (1996).

5 Häusler, G., "The Globalization of Finance," *Finance and Development*, A compilation of Articles from Finance and Development, (Washington, DC: International Monetary Fund, 2007).

6 Levine, R., "Financial Development and Economic Growth," *Journal of Economic Literature* 35, (1997): 688–726; R. Levine and S. Zervos, "Stock

Market, Banks and Economic Growth," *American Economic Review* 88, (1998): 537–558.

7 Stulz, R., "International Portfolio Flows and Security Markets," *International Capital Flows*, ed. Martin Feldstein, (Chicago, IL: University Chicago Press, 1999a); R. Stulz, "Globalization, Corporate Finance, and the Cost of Capital," *Journal of Applied Corporate Finance* 12, no. 3, (1999b): 8–25.

8 Perotti, E. C. and P. van Oijen, "Privatization, Political Risk and Stock Market Development in Emerging Economies," *Journal of International Money and Finance* 20, (2001): 43–69; E. C. Perotti, "Credible Privatization," *American Economic Review* 85, (1995): 847–859.

9 Ayyagari, M., et al. "What Determines Protection of Property Rights? An Analysis of Direct and Indirect Effects," *Robert H. Smith School Research Paper* no. RHS 06-032, (2006); D. Acemoglu and V. Guerrieri, "Capital Deepening and Non-Balanced Economic Growth," *NBER Working Paper* no. 12475, (Cambridge, Massachusetts: National Bureau of Economic Research, 2006).

10 Honohan, P., "Financial Sector Policy and the Poor: Selected Findings and Issues," *World Bank Working Paper* no. 43, (Washington, DC: World Bank, 2006); A. Demirgüc-Kunt, T. Beck, and R. Levine, "Small and Medium Enterprises, Growth, and Poverty: Cross-Country Evidence," *World Bank Policy Research Working Paper* 3178, (Washington, DC: World Bank, 2006); T. Beck, A. Demirgüç-Kunt, and R. Levine, "Finance, Inequality and the Poor," *Journal of Economic Growth*, (2007); T. Beck and R. Levine, "Legal Institutions and Financial Development," *Handbook of New Institutional Economics*, eds. Claude Menard and Mary Shirley, (Dordrech: Kluwer, 2004); G. Batra, D. Kaufmann, and A. H. W. Stone, *Investment Climate Around the World*, (Washington, DC: World Bank, 2003); K. Watkins, "Making Globalization Work for the Poor: Point, Counterpoint," *Finance and Development*. A compilation of Articles from Finance and Development, (Washington, DC: International Monetary Fund, 2007); M. Ravallion, "Inequality is Bad for the Poor," *World Bank Policy Research Working Paper* 3677, (Washington, DC: World Bank, 2005); M. Ravallion, "Competing Concepts of Inequality in the Globalization Debate," *World Bank Policy Research Paper* 3243, (Washington, DC: World Bank, 2004); M. Ravallion and S. Chen, "How did the World's Poorest Fare in the 1990's?" *Review of Income and Wealth* Series 47, no. 3, (2001): 283–300; J. Aizenman and Y. Jinjarak, "Globalization and Developing Countries—A Shrinking Tax Base?" *NBER Working Paper* no. 11933, (Cambridge, Massachusetts: National Bureau of Economic Research, 2006); S. Claessens and E. Perotti, "The Links between Finance and Inequality: Channels and Evidence," Background paper for the *World Development Report 2006*, (Washington, DC: World Bank, 2006b); C. Goodhart, *Financial Development and Economic Growth, Explaining the Links*, British Association for the Advancement of Science Books, (New York: Palgrave Macmillan, 2004).

11 Clementi, G. L. and G. MacDonald, "Investor Protection, Optimal Incentives, and Economic Growth," *Journal of Economics*, (August 2004): 1131–1175.

12 Johnson, S., J. McMillan, and C. Woodruff, "Property Rights and Finance," *The American Economic Review*, 92, no. 5 (2002): 1335–1356.

13 Prasad, E., K. Rogoff, S. Wei, and M.A. Kose, "Effects of Financial Globalization on Developing Countries: Some Empirical Evidence," *IMF Occasional Paper* 220, (Washington, DC: International Monetary Fund, 2004).

14 Wei, S. J., "Domestic Crony Capitalism and International Fickle Capital: Is there a Connection?" *International Finance,* 4 (spring, 2001): 15–46; R. G. Gelos and S. J. Wei, "Transparency and International Investor Behavior," *NBER Working Paper No. 9260*, (Cambridge, Massachusetts: National Bureau of Economic Research, 2002); S. J. Wei and Y. Wu, "Negative Alchemy? Corruption, Composition of Capital Flows, and Currency Crises," *Preventing Currency Crises in Emerging Markets*, eds. Sebastian Edwards and Jeffrey Frankel, (University of Chicago Press, 2002a): 461–501; B. K. Smarzynska and S. J. Wei, "Corruption and the Composition of Foreign Direct Investment: Firm-Level Evidence," *NBER Working Paper* 7969, (Cambridge, Massachusetts: National Bureau of Economic Research, 2000); S. J. Wei, "How Taxing is Corruption on International Investors?" *Review of Economics and Statistics*, 82, (February, 2000a): 1–11; S. J. Wei, "Local Corruption and Global Capital Flows," *Brookings Papers on Economic Activity: 2* (Washington, DC: Brookings Institution, 2000b): 303–354; S. J. Wei, "Natural Openness and Good Government," *NBER Working Paper No. 7765*, (Cambridge, Massachusetts: National Bureau of Economic Research, 2000c); S. J. Wei, "Why is Corruption Much More Taxing than Tax? Arbitrariness Kills," *NBER Working Paper No. 6255*, (Cambridge, Massachusetts: National Bureau of Economic Research, 1997); D. Kaufman, A. Kraay, and M. Mastruzzi, "Governance Matters: Governance Indicators for 1996–2004," (Washington, DC: World Bank, 2005); G. T. Abed and S. Gupta, *Governance, Corruption and Economic Performance*, (Washington, DC: International Monetary Fund, 2002).

15 Carlson, Mark A. and Leonardo Hernández, "Determinants and Repercussions of the Composition of Capital Inflows," *IMF Working Paper* no. 02/86, (May 2002). Available at SSRN: http://ssrn.com/abstract=879 621.

16 Acemoglu, D., S. Johnson, and J. Robinson, "Institutions as the Fundamental Cause of Long-Run Growth," *NBER Working Paper* no. 10481, (Cambridge, Massachusetts: National Bureau of Economic Research, 2004); D. Acemoglu and S. Johnson, "Unbundling Institutions," *NBER Working Paper* no. 9934, (Cambridge, Massachusetts: National Bureau of Economic Research, 2003); B. Balgati, P. Demitriades, and S. H. Law, "Financial Openness and Institution: Evidence from Panel Data," paper presented at the Conference on New Perspective on Financial Globalization, sponsored by the Research Department (Washington, DC: International Monetary Fund, 2007).

17 Yartey, C. A., "The Stock Market and the Financing of Corporate Growth in Africa: The Case of Ghana," *IMF Occasional Paper* no. 201, (Washington, DC: International Monetary Fund, 2006).

18 Bekaert, G. and C. Lundblad, "Growth Volatility and Financial Liberalization," *Journal of International Money and Finance* 25 (2006): 370–403.

19 Prasad, E., K. Rogoff, S. Wei, and M.A. Kose, "Effects of Financial Globalization on Developing Countries: Some Empirical Evidence," *IMF Occasional Paper* 220 (Washington, DC: International Monetary Fund, 2004).

20 Wei, S. J., "Connecting Two Views on Financial Globalization: Can We Make Further Progress?" prepared for the 18th Annual TRIO Conference, organized by Shin-ichi Fukuda, Takeo Hoshi, Takatoshi Ito, and Andrew Rose, University of Tokyo, Japan (2005); J. Ju and S. J. Wei, "A Solution to Two Paradoxes of International Capital Flows," *IMF Occasional Paper* no. 178, (Washington, DC: International Monetary Fund, 2006); Andre Lince de Faria and Paolo Mauro, "Institutions and the External Capital Structure of Countries," *IMF Working Papers* 04/236 (Washington, DC: International Monetary Fund, 2005).

21 Atje, R. and B. Jovanovic, "Stock Markets and Development," *European Economic Review*, 37 (1993): 632–640; T. Beck, A. Demirgüç-Kunt, and R. Levine, "Finance, Inequality and the Poor," *Journal of Economic Growth* (2007); S. Claessens and E. Feijen, "Financial Sector Development and the Millennium Development," *World Bank Working Paper* no. 89, (Washington, DC: World Bank, 2006a); M. Ravallion and S. Chen, "How did the World's Poorest Fare in the 1990's?" *Review of Income and Wealth* Series 47, no. 3 (2001): 283–300; M. Ravallion, "Inequality is Bad for the Poor," *World Bank Policy Research Working Paper* 3677, (Washington, DC: World Bank, 2005); S. Claessens and E. Perotti, "The Links between Finance and Inequality: Channels and Evidence," Background paper for the *World Development Report 2006*, (Washington, DC: World Bank, 2006b); A. Harrison, "Globalization and Poverty," *NBER Working Paper* no. 12347, (Cambridge, Massachusetts: National Bureau of Economic Research, 2006).

22 Shiller, R. J., *The New Financial Order: Risk in the 21st Century*, (Princeton, NJ: Princeton University Press, 2003).

23 Obstfeld, M. and A. Taylor, *Global Capital Markets: Integration, Crisis and Growth*, (Cambridge: Cambridge University Press, 2003a).

24 Coval, J. D., "Home Bias at Home: Local Equity Preference in Domestic Portfolios," *The Journal of Finance,* 54, no. 6, (1999); L. L. Tesar, "Home Bias and High Turnover," *Journal of International Money and Finance,* 14, (August, 1995b): 467–492; K. R. French and J. M. Poterba, "Investor Diversification and International Equity Markets," *American Economic Review,* 81, no. 2, (1991): 222–226.

25 Aurelio, M. M., "Going Global: The Changing Pattern of U.S. Investment Abroad," *Federal Reserve Bank of Kansas Economic Review*, (third quarter, 2006).

26 Halaissos, M. and C. Bertaut, "Why do so Few Hold Stocks?" *The Economic Journal* 105, no. 432, (1995): 1110–1129.

27 Mehra, R., "The Equity Premium in India," *NBER Working Paper* no. 12434, (Cambridge, Massachusetts: National Bureau of Economic Research, 2006).

28 Stiglitz, J., *Making Globalization Work*, (New York: W. W. Norton, 2006); J. Stiglitz, *Globalization and its Discontents*, (New York: W.W. Norton, 2003); P. H. Lindert and J. G. Williamson, "Does Globalization Make the World More Unequal?" *NEBR Working Paper* 8228, (Cambridge, Massachusetts: National Bureau of Economic Research, 2001); A. Mody and Antu Panini Murshid, "Growing up with Capital Flows," *Journal of International Economics*, 65, (2005): 249–266; R. Ranciere, A. Tornell, and F. Westermann,"Decomposing the Effects of Financial Liberalization: Crises vs. Growth," *NBER Working* Paper

no. 12806, (Cambridge, Massachusetts: National Bureau of Economic Research, 2006); A. Tornell, F. Westermann, and L. Martinez, "The Positive Link Between Financial Liberalization, Growth, and Crises," *NBER Working Paper* no. 10 293, (Cambridge, Massachusetts: National Bureau of Economic Research, 2004); L. L. Tesar, "Evaluating the Gains from International Risk-Sharing," *Carnegie-Rochester Conference Series on Public Policy*, 42, (June, 1995a): 95–143; P. K. Goldberg and N. Pavcnik, "Distributional Effects of Globalization in Developing Countries," *NBER Working Paper* no. 12 885, (Cambridge, Massachusetts: National Bureau of Economic Research, 2007); G. Kaminsky and S. Schmuckler, "Short-Run Pain, Long-Run Gain: The Effects of Financial Liberalization", unpublished working paper (Washington, DC: International Monetary Fund, 2002); E. Van Wincoop, "How Big are Potential Welfare Gains from International Risk Sharing?" *Journal of International Economics* 47, (February, 1999): 109–235; E. Van Wincoop. "Welfare Gains from International Risk Sharing," *Journal of Monetary Economics* 34, (October, 1994): 175–200; S. J. Wei and Y. Wu, "The Life-and-Death Implications of Globalization," paper presented at the National Bureau of Economic Research Inter-American Seminar in Economics, Monterrey, Mexico, November, *IMF Working Paper*, (Washington, DC: International Monetary Fund, 2002b).

29 Aizenman, J., "Financial Opening: Evidence and Policy Options," *NBER Working Paper* no. 8900, (Cambridge, Massachusetts: National Bureau of Economic Research, 2002); A. Kose and M. Terrones, "How Does Financial Globalization Affect Risk Sharing? Patterns and Channels," IMF, Research Department, (Washington, DC: International Monetary Fund, 2007).

30 El-Erian, M. A., "Dealing with Global Fluidity," *Finance and Development.* A compilation of articles from *Finance and Development*, (Washington, DC: International Monetary Fund, 2007).

31 Ibid.

32 Shiller (2003).

33 Chinn, M. D. and H. Ito, "Capital Account Liberalization, Institutions and Financial Development: Cross Country Evidence," *NBER Working Paper* no. 8967, (Cambridge, Massachusetts: National Bureau of Economic Research, 2002); Francesco Caselli and Nicola Gennaioli, "Economics and Politics of Alternative Institutional Reforms," *NBER Working Papers* no. 12 833, (National Bureau of Economic Research, Inc., 2007). A. Kose and M. Terrones, "How Does Financial Globalization Affect Risk Sharing? Patterns and Channels," IMF, Research Department (Washington, DC: International Monetary Fund, 2007).

34 Stulz, R., "Financial Globalization, Corporate Governance, and Eastern Europe," *NBER Working Paper* no. 11 912, (Cambridge, Massachusetts: National Bureau of Economic Research, 2006).

35 Pinkowitz, L., R. M. Stulz, and R. Williamson, "Do Firms in Countries with Poor Protection of Investor Rights Hold More Cash?" NEBR unpublished working paper, (Cambridge, Massachusetts: National Bureau of Economic Research, 2004).

36 Antunes, A. R. and V. C. Tiago, "Corruption, Credit Market Imperfections, and Economic Development," *Working Paper 17-03*, (Banco de Portugal, Economic Research Department, 2003).

37 Chinn, M. D. and H. Ito, "Capital Account Liberalization, Institutions and Financial Development: Cross Country Evidence," *NBER Working Paper* no. 8967, (Cambridge, Massachusetts: National Bureau of Economic Research, 2002).

38 Doidge, C., A. G. Karolyi, and R. M. Stulz, "Why are Foreign Firms Listed in the U.S. Worth More?" *Journal of Financial Economics*, (2004): 205–238; H. J. Edison and F. E. Warnock, "Cross-Border Listings, Capital Controls, and Equity Flows to Emerging Markets," *NBER Working Paper* no. 12 589, (Cambridge, Massachusetts: National Bureau of Economic Research, 2006); A. G. Karolyi, "The Role of American Depositary Receipts in the Development of Emerging Equity Markets," *The Review of Economics and Statistics,* August, 86, no. 3, (2004): 670–690.

39 IMF: GFSR, April 2007; M. Dehesa et al. "Relative Price Stability, Creditor Rights, and Financial Deepening," *IMF Working Paper*, (Washington, DC: International Monetary Fund, 2007); also see Table 3.1 and Figures 3.1, 3.6, and 3.7.

40 Henderson, J. V., Z. Shalizi, and A. J. Venables, "Geography and Development," *Journal of Economic Geography*, 1, (2001): 81–106.

41 Ju, J. and S. J. Wei, "A Solution to Two Paradoxes of International Capital Flows," *IMF Occasional Paper* no. 178, (Washington, DC: International Monetary Fund, 2006).

42 IMF: GFSR, April 2007; J. Ammer, S. B. Holland, D. C. Smith, and F. E. Warnock, "Look at Me Now: What Attracts U.S. Shareholders?" *NBER Working Paper* no. 12500, (Cambridge, Massachusetts: National Bureau of Economic Research, 2006); M. M. Aurelio, "Going Global: The Changing Pattern of U.S. Investment Abroad," *Federal Reserve Bank of Kansas Economic Review*, (third quarter, 2006); B. C. Kho, R. M. Stulz, and F. E. Warnock, "Financial Globalization, Governance, and the Evolution of the Home Bias," *NBER Working Paper* no. 12389, (Cambridge, Massachusetts: National Bureau of Economic Research, 2006).

43 O'Hara, K., *Trust from Socrates to Spin*, (Duxford: Icon Books, 2004); E. Lorenz, "Trust, Contract and Economic Cooperation," *Cambridge Journal of Economics,* 23, (1999): 301–315; F. Lopez-de-Silanes, R. F. La Porta, A. Shleifer, and R. W. Vishny, "Trust in Large Organizations," *The American Economic Review*, 87. no. 2, Papers and Proceedings of the Hundred and Fourth Annual Meeting of the American Economic Association, (1997): 333–338; J. F. Helliwell and R. Putnam, "Economic Growth and Social Capital in Italy," *Eastern Economic Journal*, Summer, 21, no. 3, (1995): 295–307; J. Berg, D. John, and K. McCabe, "Trust, Reciprocity, and Social History," *Games and Economic Behavior*, 10, (1995): 122–142; N. Ashraf, B. Iris, and P. Nikita, "Decomposing Trust and Trustworthiness," *Working Paper*, (Harvard University: Department of Economics, 2005); P. Dasgupta and I. Serageldin, *Social Capital: A Multifaceted Perspective*, (Washington, DC: World Bank, 1999).

44 Calderon, C., A. Chong, and A. Galindo, "Development and Efficiency of the Financial Sector and Links with Trust: Cross-Country Evidence," *Economic Development and Cultural Change*, (University of Chicago, 2002): 189–204; L. Guiso, P. Sapienza, and L. Zingales, "The Role of Social Capital in Financial Development," *The American Economic Review* 94, no. 3, (2004).

45 Knack, S. and P. Keefer, "Does Social Capital Have an Economic Payoff? A Cross-Country Investigation," *The Quarterly Journal of Economics*, (November 1997): 1251–1288; Rafael La Porta, Florencio Lopez-de-Silanes, Andrei Shleifer, and Robert W. Vishny, "Agency Problems and Dividend Policies Around the World," *NBER Working Paper 6594*, (1998); E. L. Glaeser, "Measuring Trust," *The Quarterly Journal of Economics*, (August 2000): 811–846; Paul Zak and S. Knack, "Trust and Growth," *The Economic Journal,* 111, (April 2001): 295–321; Paul Zak, "The Neurobiology of Trust," article in Corante Tech News, (2003); S. Beugelsdijk, H. de Groot, and A. van Schaik, "Trust and Economic Growth: a Robustness Analysis," *Oxford Economic Papers* 56, (2004): 118–134.

46 Arrow, J. A., *The Limits of Organization*, (New York: W.W. Norton 1974).

47 Coleman, J. S., *Foundations of Social Theory*, (The Belknap Press of Harvard University Press, 1990); J. S. Coleman, "Social Capital in the Creation of Human Capital," *The American Journal of Sociology* Vol. 94 Supplement, (University of Chicago, 1988): 95–120; E. L. Glaeser, D. Laibson, J. A. Scheinkman, and C. L. Soutter, "What is Social Capital? The Determinants of Trust and Trustworthiness," *NBER Working Paper 7216*, (Cambridge, Massachusetts: National Bureau of Economic Research, 1999); A. Alesina and E. La Ferrara, "Who Trusts Others?" *Journal of Public Economics*, 85, (2002): 207–234.

48 Iqbal, Z. and A. Mirakhor, *An Introduction to Islamic Finance: Theory and Practice* (2007); A. Mirakhor and I. Zaidi, "Profit-and-loss Sharing Contracts in Islamic Finance" *Handbook of Islamic Banking*, eds. M. K. Hassan and M. K. Lewis, (Cheltenham, UK, and Northampton, U.S.: Edward Elgar, 2007): 49–63.

49 Hong, H., J. D. Kubik, and J. C. Stein, "Social Interaction and Stock-Market Participation," *The Journal of Finance,* 54, no. 1, (February 2004): 137–163; Gur Huberman, "Familiarity Breeds Investment," *The Review of Financial Studies*, 14, no. 3, (2001): 659–680.

50 Iqbal and Mirakhor (2007).

51 Ibid.

52 Ibid.

53 Habachy, S., "Property, Right, and Contract in Muslim Law," *Columbia Law Review I* 62, no. 3, (1962).

54 Ibid.

55 Iqbal and Mirakhor (2007); P. N. Kourides, "The Influence of Islamic Law on Contemporary Middle Eastern Legal System: the Foundation and Binding Force of Contracts," in *Columbia Journal of Transnational Law*, 9, no. 2, (1970): 384–435.

56 Habachy (1962).

57 Payandeh, A., *Nahjulfasahah: Collected Short Sayings of the Messenger*, (Tehran: Golestanian, 1984); Iqbal and Mirakhor (2007).

58 Iqbal, Zamir and Abbas Mirakhor, "A Stakeholders Model of Corporate Governance of Firm in Islamic Economic System," *Islamic Economic Studies*, 11, no. 2, (March 2005).

59 Chapra, M. U., "The Future of Economics," *The Islamic Foundation*, (UK, 2000).

60 See *Financial Times* reports: Islamic Finance, May 24, 2007, for estimates of growth, size, and potential of Islamic Finance.
61 Khan, M. and A. Mirakhor, "Islamic Interest-Free Banking: A Theoretical Analysis," *Theoretical Studies in Islamic Banking and Finance*, eds. Khan and Mirakhor, (Houston, TX: IRIS Books, 1987).
62 Iqbal, Zubair and Abbas Mirakhor, "Islamic Banking," Occasional Paper no. 49, (Washington, DC: International Monetary Fund, 1987).
63 Huberman, Gur and S. Kandel, "Mean-Variance Spanning," *The Journal of Finance*, 42, no. 4, (1987a): 873–888; Gur Huberman, S. Kandel, and R. F. Stambaugh, "Mimicking Portfolios and Exact Arbitrage Pricing," *The Journal of Finance*, 42, no. 1, (1987b): 1–9; G. Bekaert and M. S. Urias, "Diversification, Integration and Emerging Market Closed-End Funds," *The Journal of Finance* 51, no. 3, (1996): 835–869; W. E. Fearson, S. R. Foerster and D. B. Keim, "General Tests of Latent Variable Models and Mean-Variance Spanning," *The Journal of Finance*, 48, no. 1, (1993): 131–155.
64 Baldwin, K., "Risks Management in Islamic Banks," *Islamic Finance*, eds. S. Archer and Rifaat Ahmed Abdel Karim, (London: Euromoney, 2002); Z. Iqbal and A. Mirakhor, "Progress and Challenges of Islamic Banking," *Thunderbird International Business Review*, 41, nos. 4/5, (1999): 381–405.
65 Minsky, H., *Inflation, Recession and Economic Policy*, (London: Wheatsheaf Books, 1982); Mohsin Khan, *Islamic Interest-Free Banking: A Theoretical Analysis*, eds. Khan and Mirakhor *Theoretical Studies in Islamic Banking and Finance*, (Houston, TX: IRIS Books, 1987); A. S. Posen, "A Strategy to Prevent Future Crises: Safety Shrink the Banking Sector," *Peter G. Peterson Institute for International Economics*, (2001).

CHAPTER 4

Globalization and Its Implications for Muslim Countries

Globalization is akin to a process whereby numerous countries become one. This process proceeds when barriers (affecting the movement of goods, capital, technology, and labor) between countries are reduced. Globalization is the result of reduced information and transportation costs, and liberalization of trade, finance, investment, capital flows, and factor movements (O'Rourke 2001; Crafts 2004). It is a multifaceted and multidimensional process of growing interconnectedness among nations and peoples of the world. Its main dimensions are cultural, sociopolitical, and economic. Its cultural implications are the convergence of cultures. Its sociopolitical tendencies are convergence of ideas and norms. Its economic dimensions include growing a variety of flows: trade flows across countries; flows of capital and investment; flows of technology; and labor flows (both skilled and unskilled). This is accompanied by the standardization of processes, regulations, and institutions, all facilitated by the free flow of information and ideas.

Globalization is not unidirectional, as witnessed over the last century. Before the onset of hostilities in World War I, trade, capital, and labor flows across national borders had been increasing steadily. World War I and the Great Depression (accompanied by protectionism) reversed the process. It was not until after World War II that there was the will to reduce barriers. Even then, only trade barriers were slowly reduced, to be followed much later by a reduction to barriers limiting financial flows. Labor flows across most borders are highly restricted even today.

Globalization is today far from "complete." For instance, consider a country whose share of global gross domestic product (GDP) is 25 percent, its trade/GDP is 15 percent, share of global finance is 20 percent, and whose cross-border financial flows/total financing is 10 percent. Is globalization "complete" for such a country? The answer is clearly no. If its share of global GDP is 25 percent, for "complete" trade globalization its trade/GDP should be 75 percent, not 15 percent. If its share of global finance is 20 percent, for "complete" financial globalization its cross-border financial flows/total financing should be 80 percent, not 10 percent. It would have a long way to go to attain "complete" globalization! No country in the world comes close to meeting these targets for goods and capital flows. If countries today feel the pressures of globalization, they have seen nothing yet if the process of globalization continues unabated.

Numerous trade rounds under the General Agreement on Tariffs and Trade (GATT) reduced barriers to the movement of goods across national borders. The process, though not always smooth, is continuing under the World Trade Organization (WTO) with coverage extending to services.

In the area of financial flows, the last few decades have witnessed dramatic and rapid changes in the structure of financial markets and institutions across the world. Advances in financial theory, the rapid pace of innovation in the practice of finance, the revolution in information technology, deregulation, and institutional reforms have irreversibly changed the nature of financial relations and a "new finance" has emerged. As a result, "people can borrow greater amounts at cheaper rates than ever before, invest in a multitude of instruments catering to every possible profile of risk and return, and share risks with strangers from across the globe. ... These changes have altered the nature of the typical transaction in the financial sector, making it more arm's length and allowing broader participation. Financial markets have expanded and have become deeper. The broad participation has allowed risks to be more widely spread throughout the economy" (Rajan 2005). The new finance has an important role in leveling economic playing fields, thus becoming the great equalizer of our time: it requires no passport, and does not discriminate on the basis of color, creed, race, or national origin. It unwinds and unbundles, dissects, analyzes, and prices risk, and searches for the highest return. It explores all opportunities for risk/return sharing, in order to exploit the wedge between the real rate of return to assets and the real rate of interest, leading to greater reliance on risk sharing.

In this chapter we focus on three central questions. First, how will globalization affect the broad economic developments of countries that have adopted, or are adopting, Islamic economic principles? Second, how will continuing globalization affect the development of Islamic finance and Islamic financial markets? Third, what policies should Muslim countries adopt to benefit from globalization without sacrificing their Islamic heritage?

4.1 THE BROAD ECONOMIC AND FINANCIAL IMPACT OF GLOBALIZATION

Globalization, as with most things in life, has its fans and detractors. Some argue that globalization increases economic growth and prosperity no matter what, others respond that faster growth could come about only *if* countries are properly positioned to take advantage of it, and yet others say that globalization is bad for everyone. The danger for the future of globalization is that if enough countries or large constituencies within countries do not gain from globalization, the forces of protectionism will increase, as experienced in the early part of the twentieth century, with the pinnacle of protectionism during the Great Depression, a case of near autarchy where everyone was a loser.

In the case of Muslim countries, Islam advocates a number of important principles for the smooth functioning and long-term prosperity of an Islamic economy. The forces of globalization affect many of the economic prescriptions of Islam. If Muslim countries do not prepare for the onslaught from abroad when they open up their markets and borders, their Islamic economic and social fabric will deteriorate and political strife will increase.

First of all, globalization entails the lifting of barriers to economic flows and interactions between countries, resulting in increased competition from abroad. It is akin to the convergence of a number of countries into one big country, a process that takes time. The process of globalization is ever-changing and by some measures still has a long way to go.

Globalization is essentially the process of eliminating all barriers so that countries appear as if they are one integrated country. Barriers that inhibit economic interactions, or flows, between countries include those on: goods and services, capital (portfolio, foreign direct investment (FDI), and debt), technology, and labor (both skilled and unskilled). The lifting of barriers in turn leads to an enhanced level of competition. The manifestation of this competition from abroad is multidimensional:

- Increased flow of goods into the country at a lower price
- Increased flow of services (including banking and other forms of financial services) at a lower price

- Increased flow of capital (FDI, portfolio, and debt) at a lower cost
- Increased flow of technology
- Increased flow of labor (professional, skilled, and unskilled)

These flows, in turn, affect a number of critical economic indicators, including: real wage rates or the real rates of return to differing categories of labor (professional, skilled, and unskilled); real rates of return to capital; real incomes; income distribution (poverty alleviation); employment and unemployment; and economic growth. Before we look at the impact of globalization on these, we must stress one important point. In all instances there are numerous other forces, besides globalization, that affect these outcomes and there are more direct policy options, than globalization, for governments to affect these variables. For example, governments can affect income distribution through taxation. Globalization by itself does not determine any of these important economic developments.

Globalization is, in the first instance, advocated because of its presumed positive impact on overall economic growth. The classical argument in support of trade is quite appealing. Free trade and the unimpeded flows of labor, capital and technology, by moving from where they are plentiful to where they are scarce, increase global output and enhance the welfare-promoting movement of factors and goods. The presumption is that these forces allow a country to expand its production possibility frontier by taking advantage of efficiency gains afforded by a larger market, specialization, better technology through economies of scale, learning by doing, higher investment, and the like. A more recent argument (Balassa 1978; Krueger 1980) is that outward-oriented policies reflect a real exchange rate that promotes the development of exports whereas inward policies are accompanied by an overvalued real exchange rate, retarding the growth of exports; the clear presumption here is that the benefit of outward-oriented policies is from better exchange rate management. Thus it is presumed that economic growth can normally be expected to accelerate as a result of globalization. But this theoretical, positive association of globalization to economic growth and the indicated policy of opening up all markets may be questioned for a variety of reasons.

First, there is the standard infant industry argument against complete and indiscriminate liberalization—some industries, especially those where economies of scale and learning by doing are important, cannot develop, in the early stage of their existence, in the face of price competition from already established and advanced industries from abroad. Infant industry protection has clearly been a positive factor for growth and development in a number of countries, including Japan and South Korea (Ha-Joon Chang 2007). A country that does not protect its infant industries may inhibit their eventual development. While many countries, including Japan and South Korea, disavow this pro-protection argument today, they are forgetting their own path to development (Ha-Joon Chang 2007).

Second, whether trade liberalization may be unequivocally beneficial or not depends on the exact form of existing barriers in all countries and other factors that accelerate or decelerate growth. It is time (and environment) specific.

Third, it must be remembered that not all trade flows occur under perfect competitive market conditions. Foreign firms may resort to "dumping" to get their goods into a country's market. There are three motivations behind dumping: sporadic dumping (excess inventory, and so on), persistent dumping (to maximize profits if price elasticities vary across markets), and predatory dumping (to drive domestic firms out of business). Dumping can clearly impair growth and be otherwise detrimental. As a result, countries may need to monitor dumping and impose barriers when it occurs.

Fourth, the inflow of services, especially financial services, may have widespread effects. Foreign banks could drive out domestic banks, reducing competition, or they could drive out some domestic banks and render other domestic banks more efficient, increasing competition. Foreign financial institutions could stimulate capital inflows, forcing recipient countries to adopt better macroeconomic policies or be subject to heightened economic and financial volatility. Financial volatility and financial turmoil can be costly for economic growth and be especially harmful for the disadvantaged members of society. The net effect on economic growth and income distribution (poverty alleviation) will largely depend on the quality of regulatory oversight.

What is the net effect of globalization on economic growth? An unequivocal answer cannot be given. The net result is that the impact of globalization on growth is country, case, and time specific. Thus while we can say very little a priori about the net effect of globalization on economic growth for all countries, we can say more about individual countries if we are given their specific circumstances.

How does globalization affect real incomes and income distribution? The flow of goods and services directly affects the domestic price of goods and services, and in turn the real return to labor (different for each labor classification) and capital. The impact on the return to labor and capital is due to the fact that goods and services are essentially the embodiment of the inputs that are used to manufacture or deliver them. If a country—say, a capital-abundant country—imports labor-intensive goods and exports capital-intensive goods (as predicted in the Heckscher-Ohlin trade model—two countries, two goods, two factors of production which are mobile within countries but immobile across countries, diminishing marginal productivity of factors, constant returns to scale, zero transportation cost, and broadly similar consumption taste patterns), then real wage rates (assuming for the moment that all labor is the same) decline with more trade. This is because the import of labor-intensive goods is akin to importing more labor; in other words, similar to increasing the domestic labor supply and in turn reducing the return to labor. The opposite of reducing barriers to trade, namely the imposition of barriers to trade, is the famous Stolper-Samuelson Theorem. At the same time in the same country—that is, the capital-abundant country—the real rate of return to capital goes up as the demand for capital-intensive goods, and thus the demand for capital inputs, has effectively increased (from abroad). The decline in the real wage rate and the increase in the rate of return to capital will in turn affect the level of real income. Those who have only their labor to sell lose relative to those who own capital, resulting in a change in income distribution. The opposite is the case for the labor-abundant country. Globalization gives birth to winners as well as losers, and inevitably to conflict!

In order to examine the return to different labor categories, we can simply replace capital and labor inputs by skilled and unskilled labor (as the two factors of production) and apply the Heckscher-Ohlin model as before. Then in the unskilled-labor–abundant country (developing country) trade would increase the real return of unskilled labor and reduce the real return of skilled labor, in turn improving income distribution (reducing inequality between the two classes of labor). But in the skilled-labor–abundant country (advanced country), the return to skilled labor would increase while that to unskilled labor would decrease, adversely affecting the income distribution (higher inequality). Thus the impact on income distribution is country dependent; in some countries income distribution will improve and in others it will get worse.

Income distribution is also affected by the flow of technology across borders. To the extent that the flow of technology increases or decreases the relative demand for skilled labor (unskilled labor saving or unskilled labor dissaving), returns to different labor categories and thus income distribution will be affected. The presumption is that most technological change increases the relative demand for skilled labor (increasing its return relative to that of unskilled labor) and thus tends to increase income inequality (International Monetary Fund (IMF), *World Economic Outlook* 2007, p. 59), but this is an empirical issue and need not always be the case.

A further effect on income distribution is attributable to trade in noncompeting goods (goods that are not produced in the importing country), a possibility that is excluded in the standard Heckscher-Ohlin model. If tariffs on these goods are reduced, import prices for these goods decline and the imports of these goods increase. If these noncompeting goods are a significant part of the basket of goods consumed by unskilled workers, then income inequality will be reduced. It should be stressed that this reduction in income inequality can be expected to occur in both the advanced (skilled labor abundant) and the developing country as long as the countries are importers of such goods and they are a significant component of consumption.

Finally, if a critical assumption of the Heckscher-Ohlin model—immobility of factors (capital and labor) across countries—is relaxed, then the sharpness of the Stolper-Samuelson result is blunted. The flow of labor across countries may reduce inequality or increase it in both the advanced and developing country, depending on the category of labor flows and their destinations. If unskilled labor (the abundant category of labor in a developing country) flows from the developing country to the advanced country, then inequality can be expected to decline in the developing country and increase in the advanced country; but if skilled labor flows from the developing country, the inequality can be expected to increase in the developing country and decrease in the advanced country. Capital flows can have an adverse or positive effect on income equality depending on whether the capital flow increases the relative demand for skilled or unskilled labor. Moreover, in the case of capital flows there are additional effects. First, to what extent do capital flows enhance the financial access of the disadvantaged members of society? If the answer to this is that cross-border capital flows improve the relative access of the poor, then capital flows can be expected to improve income distribution. Second, capital flows may affect financial and exchange rate stability. This in turn may have a disproportionately adverse effect on the poor. If this is the case, then income inequality may increase.

Where does this all lead to concerning the impact on real incomes and income distribution? As can be seen, there are a number of opposing forces at work here. The net result clearly depends on the specifics of the country and the type of flows that are stimulated—in goods, labor, capital, and technology. Any conclusion has to be country specific. Similar considerations affect the impact of globalization on poverty alleviation. Whether globalization reduces global poverty will depend on the particular circumstances of individual countries. Thus the overall impact of globalization (liberalization of trade, labor, capital, and technology flows) on income equality and income distribution cannot be a priori and unequivocally stated for all countries. It is not a theoretical issue but an empirical one that has to be assessed on a case-by-case basis. Again, it must also be recalled that globalization is not the most direct policy instrument for addressing issues such as economic growth, income distribution, and poverty alleviation. Macroeconomic policies have a more direct and immediate impact. Globalization may also stimulate competition in a number of policy areas, such as labor standards and taxation, in turn affecting real incomes and income distribution.

In sum, we can say very little that is unequivocal about the theoretical impact of globalization on economic growth (and employment), real incomes, income distribution, and regulations in countries. Everything is country, case, and time specific. To benefit from globalization, while minimizing the adverse effects, governments should develop policies and institutions to address adverse effects on income growth and income equality in order to preserve economic prosperity and social cohesion (employment and income equality). For instance, if a segment of the labor force becomes unemployed, then better access to education and labor retraining will be needed to absorb displaced labor into new sectors of comparative advantage. If the demand for highly skilled and educated labor is expected to increase, then education and its accessibility should be promoted. If income equality is adversely affected, better opportunities for advancement—such as enhanced access to higher quality education, tax enforcement, or a revision of the tax code—may be necessary. If competition is impaired, regulatory oversight is needed to ensure that markets are competitive and function smoothly and that harmful dumping is recognized and addressed. It would appear that, in the face of adverse developments accompanying globalization (such as those described above), countries should not resort to isolation but should instead adopt policies to mitigate any adverse developments while capturing the benefits.

To benefit, governments need targeted policies, thoughtful regulations, and efficient institutions. This simplistic conclusion was probably obvious and expected at the outset of this discussion. Many forces besides globalization, both positive and negative, affect growth. Globalization itself embraces many elements, some having positive and some having negative effects on growth. It would, therefore, seem reasonable to assert that to benefit, countries need to adopt policies that minimize the negative and maximize the positive effects of globalization. While there are important theoretical indications that globalization would be growth-promoting, the conclusion must be that the net benefits of globalization are likely to be country, case, and time specific. Much the same can be said for real incomes, income distribution, and poverty alleviation. In conclusion, economic benefits, in particular welfare gains, from globalization are not guaranteed. Governments must adopt prudent policies to benefit.

The inflow of services, especially financial services, can cause even more widespread effects than the flow of goods. Financial deepening resulting from capital inflows and the appearance of foreign institutions can be expected to increase the liquidity of the local stock market and to reduce the cost of capital. Foreign financial institutions will introduce new financial products. Capital flows will force recipient countries to adopt better macroeconomic policies or be subject to heightened economic and financial volatility. To fully benefit from these changes, countries need a well-developed oversight structure. If regulatory oversight is not well developed, then foreign participation could be harmful to the real as well as the financial sector of the economy. Foreign banks could drive out domestic banks, reducing competition, or they could drive out some domestic banks and render other domestic banks more efficient, increasing competition. Capital flows could cause financial volatility. The outcome will depend on the quality of regulatory oversight.

In addition to affecting the rate of return to capital, the flow of capital also brings in foreign entities in the form of FDI. A multinational corporation (MNC) can invest in an existing firm or a new firm (greenfield). The appearance of MNCs could enhance or damage competition; it all depends on whether FDI increases or decreases the market power of individual firms. The MNC brings its own culture and management. Its business approach may, in turn, affect employment and working conditions. At the same time, the presence of foreign management will impact the salaries of local managers. Again regulation and oversight may be needed to address these and related issues in order to maximize benefits and minimize disruptions and costs.

Besides these potential results of globalization, there is a tendency for globalization to encourage competition in regulation, sometimes referred to as a "race to the bottom," or harmonization of regulations. On the one hand, in their quest to be competitive countries have an incentive to adopt legislation and regulations in the areas of labor, healthcare, and environment, among others, that will make it cheaper to manufacture goods and to deliver services. Such legislation is often to the detriment of the citizenry and may be in conflict with fundamental Islamic teachings on social and economic justice. On the other hand, countries may be pressured by other countries to harmonize their regulatory regimes to attract foreign MNCs.

After this brief summary of the major economic effects of globalization, a few things should be evident. Globalization has a long way to go to be "complete" but it is not monotonic and could be reversed. The impact of globalization is multidimensional. Some segments of society will gain while others will lose. If and when a large segment of society loses out and becomes disadvantaged, then the voices of protectionism in a country become loud, as was the case from around 1910 until the end of World War II. In fact, even today, by some measures (flow of FDI and labor mobility across national borders), globalization is less advanced than at the beginning of the previous century. The overall extent of potential benefits depends on how a country is organized, its competitiveness in global goods and services markets, on the flexibility of its markets, and on its policy and regulatory infrastructure. All countries have to develop the necessary economic and social policies, the appropriate regulatory environment, flexible markets, and the needed institutions to benefit from globalization, while guarding the economic welfare of *all* segments of society and preventing social and economic upheavals.

4.2 THE ISLAMIC ECONOMIC SYSTEM

It may be useful to repeat relevant Islamic teachings that may be affected by globalization. Islam was revealed to bring justice, particularly economic and social justice, to the people. The *Qur'an* states that *Allah* (*swt*) sent all the prophets and messengers to induce the people toward justice. The all inclusive and universal religion, Islam is here for the purpose of making the lives of the people better. Economic prosperity is encouraged in order to further this all-important goal.

The details of an Islamic economic system include but are not limited to: competition, taxation, government finances, the behavior of financial institutions, social and economic expenditures affecting poverty, income distribution, private ownership, rule of law and sanctity of contracts, land tenure, wage policy, natural resource management including depletable resources, and inheritance.[1]

The basic philosophy of Islamic economics can be summarized as capitalism (competition in business, private property rights with some limitations, economic gains through hard work and taking risk in investments, and the right to enjoy the fruits of labor and return on investment) and self-interest ("Islam, in fact, considers self interest a primary factor in its incentive-motivation system; it is a necessity in any organized society if the individual is to find it utility maximizing to follow behavioral rules prescribed by the system"[2]) *but* with some important qualifications.[3]

The first and foremost qualification is that the basic principles of capitalism are encouraged in Islam *as long as* they are in harmony with the basic goals of society, are consistent with Islamic social order and justice, and reinforce the social fabric. Thus if globalization is embraced in such a way that there are a significant number of people without adequate and equal economic opportunity (a level playing field for all, especially in education which receives special emphasis in Islam) or the basic human needs of food, shelter, and clothing, then society's needs must take precedence over the "efficient and most productive" practice of capitalism (and the rights of the wealthy).

Second, honest capitalism and the sanctity of contracts are stressed and are integral elements of an Islamic economic system:[4] "... when the Prophet was asked 'who is the believer?' He replied, 'A believer is a person in whom people can trust their person and possession.' He is also reported to having said, 'A person without trustworthiness is a person without religion.'"

Corruption in the pursuit of wealth is abhorred in the *Qur'an*:[5] "The *Qur'an* states: '*Seek with [the wealth] which God has bestowed on you the home of the Hereafter, nor forget your portion of this world; but do good [unto others] as God has been good to you; and seek not corruption on earth, for verily, God does not like the spreaders of corruption.*' (28:77)."

Third, while private ownership is endorsed in Islam, *absolute* ownership (as in Western capitalism) is not. In Islam, absolute ownership belongs to the Creator (the principle of *tawhid*). Man cannot own without any limitations what God created (raw land, water, mineral deposits, and so on) in the first place.

Fourth, there are clear laws and guidelines set out in Islam that govern economic policies and practices. These include, but are not limited to, economic development and growth, population policy, rule of law, labor, capital, public finance and taxation, interest, rent, wealth, inheritance, income distribution, education, social safety net, and natural resource management. Clearly, when it comes to the prescribed economic and financial behavior of individuals and society, Islam differs from other religions. In Islam, these accepted behaviors are spelled out in quite some detail.

Globalization, as described above, affects most, if not all, critical areas of the welfare of society. An Islamic government must monitor the differential affects of globalization on every segment of society and ensure that social and economic justice are preserved.

4.3 GLOBALIZATION, FINANCIAL MARKETS, AND FINANCIAL PRODUCTS

The impact of globalization on financial markets and the development of financial products can be best examined in two time frames—the long and the short. In the previous chapter, the longer term impact of globalization on Islamic finance was analyzed through the proposition that there could be a convergence of Islamic and conventional finance. Here we look at the short-term result by examining the more predictable and more mundane developments.

Continued financial integration will mean that capital mobility will increase, with investors seeking the highest return for a given level of risk and borrowers funding at the lowest cost. At the same time, globalization will mean that Western and other foreign financial institutions will enter the financial markets of Muslim countries while Muslim institutions expand their activities outside their own borders to seek profitable opportunities. Simultaneously, these developments will enable Muslim investors to select more diverse financial products—Islamic and non-Islamic—from both Islamic and non-Islamic institutions, while Muslim borrowers will be able to fund from similar, more diversified sources. These simple developments will have profound implications for Islamic financial institutions, for the development of Islamic finance, and for government policy.

The most noticeable result will be that competition will increase in the financial markets of all Muslim countries. Islamic institutions will have to offer a broad array of financial products to investors and borrowers. They will have to offer higher returns with commensurate risk, and lower risk with commensurate returns. They will have to innovate in order to stay relevant. They will need to provide Islamic products that mimic those offered by conventional institutions and more competitive Islamic products to compete with Islamic products offered by conventional institutions. As a result, if Islamic institutions rise to the challenge, one could expect a true renaissance of Islamic finance to compete with conventional financial products.

Since World War II, conventional institutions have expanded beyond their borders to seek profitable opportunities, to service their clients further afield, and to internalize the benefits of economies of scale. Islamic institutions will have to gear up to do the same. They have a ready market of Muslims in other Muslim countries and in Western countries, especially in Europe and the United States. As Muslim nonfinancial corporations become more global, they will need financial services in non-Muslim countries. In time, as non-Muslim corporations are exposed to the benefits of equity-based Islamic financial products for covering their funding needs (see the previous chapter for details), they can be expected to become clients. For Islamic institutions to become competitive and global, they will have to look beyond their borders and develop a truly global strategy.

Two important elements in the quest for Islamic institutions to expand globally are financial education and safety. Islamic financial products and the functioning of Islamic financial institutions are a mystery to non-Muslims, and even most Muslims in developing countries have at best a very rudimentary appreciation of these. A global Islamic entity that could benefit from economies of scale could undertake such a task. At the same time, investors will have to be convinced of the safety of their deposits with Islamic financial institutions. One major financial scandal or collapse will set Islamic finance back by years. There is a need for supervision that is standardized across countries and regulated internationally, much the same as the Basel Accords. If Islamic finance is to go global, expand faster than before, and achieve its true potential, there is a need for a well-designed global supervisory system.

Generally, institutions are weak in Muslim countries. The impact of weak institutions is felt beyond financial markets. The last decade of the twentieth century had already witnessed a large volume of empirical research that focused on the existence (or the lack) of strong institutions explaining cross-country differences in economic performance.

This literature had isolated two specific institutions—those that protect property rights and those that enforce contracts—as the most important in explaining why some economies performed well and others did not (Acemoglu and Johnson 2003).

Recently we have witnessed growing literature about the importance of trust to, inter alia, development of the financial system (Calderon et al. 2002; Guiso et al. 2004). This body of research demonstrated that since finance—particularly risk-sharing instruments such as equity—was trust intensive, high-trust societies exhibited more developed and deeper financial systems. In particular, this literature indicated that there is a high correlation between trust and the development of the financial sector. If the level of trust is high, people rely more on risky assets, such as equity, invest a larger share of their wealth in stocks, use more checks, and have access to a greater amount of credit than in low-trust countries. Importantly also, since the second half of the 1990s a number of researchers, using a variety of techniques, have attempted to demonstrate the impact of trust on economic performance (Knack and Keefer 1997; Glaeser 2000; Bengelsdijk et al. 2004).

In a paper, Luigi Guiso, Paola Sapienza, and Luigi Zingales (2005) assert that evidence suggests low trust as a crucial factor in explaining a low level of stock market participation. The authors define trust as "the subjective probability that individuals attribute to the possibility of being cheated." Their paper reports that, based on the analysis of cross-country data, where the level of trust is high, investment in equities, in general, and in the stock market, in particular, is also high. Moreover, the paper suggests that in low-trust countries, equity participation depends on observance of the rule of law and the existence of legal institutions that protect property and investor rights and those that enforce contracts. It suggests that in low-performing economies not only is the level of trust low, but property and investor rights are poorly protected, and legal contract enforcement weak. Consequently, in these countries corporations either do not form or, if they do, they resort to debt financing. Policy implications for these economies are to strengthen legal institutions, improve transparency, accountability, and governance—both in private and public sectors—and to provide the public with a greater amount of information and education on risk/reward-sharing finance, in general, and equity markets, in particular.

4.4 GLOBALIZATION AND POLICY IN MUSLIM COUNTRIES

Islam preaches the importance of: economic growth and prosperity; gainful employment for all who seek work; a level playing field to afford equal opportunities to all; a fair and just income distribution; and a comprehensive social safety net to take care of those who cannot work, who are aged, and who do not have the resources to acquire food, shelter, healthcare, and the other basic necessities of life. As we have seen from the above brief discussion of globalization, all of these critical variables and areas of economic and social concern are affected by globalization and more fully materialized through WTO membership. Whether globalization and WTO membership support a Muslim country's economic and social aspirations will largely depend on its competitiveness in the global market for goods and services, on the quality of a number of institutions, flexibility of markets, and policies in place. What are these policies and institutions?

First and foremost, it is important for Muslim governments to appreciate a simple fact: as a general rule most productive jobs are created by the private sector and not by governments. Unfortunately, a number of Muslim countries have neglected this simple proposition and have acted as employer of last resort when confronted by high unemployment rates. Globalization and WTO membership *can* enhance private sector job creation under the right circumstances. To increase the likelihood of job creation, there is a need for a vibrant private sector.

The foundations of a vibrant private sector are several for any country. Setting aside the sequencing of policies, countries need to relax economic controls, reduce the role of government, and create an environment where the private sector can thrive. This would entail:

- Elimination (or at least dramatic reduction) of explicit and implicit subsidies
- Effective privatization of state enterprises (including commercial banks and foundations)
- Elimination of price and financial controls
- Creation of an effective and equitable tax system
- A gradual reduction in tariffs and nontariff barriers to promote domestic competition
- Liberalization of labor laws and markets

- Improved education policies to promote quality education and technical and managerial skills
- A real crackdown on corruption
- A more favorable attitude toward FDI (including more personal freedoms for foreigners as well as citizens)
- A managed, flexible exchange rate
- A total commitment to upholding the rule of law and to developing the supporting institutional structure

At the same time, Muslim countries need to adopt more consistent macroeconomic policies to attract foreign investors and to avoid financial crises. These policies in combination should create a favorable business climate where investment, financed domestically and from abroad, will increase significantly and finance the needed growth. In the case of a number of Muslim countries these major structural and policy changes should motivate citizens living abroad to return home, bringing their needed skills and capital.

While many of the prescriptions need no further elaboration, a number of them should be emphasized. An equitable and effective tax system is an absolute necessity to address income distribution changes (recall the Prophetic saying that: "Nothing makes a poor man starve except that with which a rich person avails in luxury") and to afford the government the ability to address social needs that will be affected by globalization and to create a level playing field as prescribed in Islam. At the same time a tax system is needed to tax MNCs so that they pay taxes locally as opposed to in their home country. A sound tax system will afford government the flexibility to address a number of issues, such as adverse wage rate and real income changes for a segment of society that will come about because of globalization and WTO membership. At a minimum it will take ten years to establish an efficient and effective tax system if a country starts basically from scratch. As an integral component of creating a level playing field for citizens, a first-class system of education is indispensable for competing on a global level and increasing the real income of citizens. Also critical is an effective labor retraining program and flexible markets, because some jobs will be lost due to competition from abroad while on the other hand employment opportunities will emerge in areas of increased exports. To create new jobs, labor markets must be reformed to be more flexible. The government cannot ask the private sector to finance social needs but must instead raise taxes and develop policies and institutions to address such needs in a comprehensive manner. Such social needs include education, healthcare, shelter, food, and retirement; all of this will require a sound agency for social security. A transparent and effective judicial system must be established to give assurance to foreign companies and investors.

In the case of most Muslim countries a number of new institutions will be needed, not just in name, but also in fact. These institutions are: an office of trade representative; a competition authority to monitor competition; a securities and exchange commission; and a financial and banking regulatory commission, an agency with much wider responsibilities than currently exercised by most central banks. The need for these institutions and the importance of effectiveness and transparency require no elaboration. However, it must be noted that to set up these institutions and to staff them with the qualified personnel will take time and effort.

If Muslim countries do not adopt these preparations, policies, and institutions, then they will experience a disruptive shock to their economies as the pace of globalization continues and as they accede to WTO membership. Most Muslim countries do not produce goods and services that are competitive on the world scene. As globalization continues, competition from abroad will at least initially result in higher unemployment, economic and financial dislocations, social disruptions, and a political backlash.

4.5 CONCLUSION

Globalization for Muslim countries holds the promise of more rapid economic growth and prosperity. But it is only a promise. It is a promise that could also further undermine the implied Islamic social contract between those who govern and the general citizenry, which would become a social and economic nightmare. On the one hand, globalization affords Muslim countries yet another reason to restructure their economies, embrace social and economic justice, and face up to the challenge of upholding their Islamic contract with the citizenry. On the other hand, if the needed institutions and policies are not developed rapidly, the same globalization could exacerbate economic growth, at least in the short and medium terms, and magnify social and economic problems. If globalization results in the poor losing in the Muslim countries, then we could witness a broad backlash in the Muslim world against globalization and governments. There is little time to lose for the majority of Muslim countries to begin their economic restructuring, and develop viable institutions and flexible markets.

Our central thesis in the area of finance is that, as globalization proceeds, its main engines—the new finance and advances in information technology—will shift the methods and instruments of financing trade, investment, and production in favor of more risk spreading and sharing rather than risk shifting via fixed-price debt contracts. It follows that this is the result of financial innovations that are dissecting, analyzing, and pricing risk better, so that—combined with efficient availability of information and adoption of best international standards of transparency, accountability, and good governance in public and private sectors—the raison d'être of fixed-price debt contracts will erode. The rapid progress in development of risk-sharing techniques and asset-backed instruments is evidence of this shift; in particular, there is already a perceptible shift of household portfolios toward equity and shareholding in a number of industrial countries.

As Muslim societies continue the process of strengthening legal institutions, which some have already begun, their economic performance will improve. Efforts at reforming education with concentration on adherence to Islamic values, norms, and rules should strengthen the social capital—including, importantly, the level of trust—in these countries. One result of strengthening institutions and enhancing the general level of trust will be adoption of Islamic financial techniques of risk and reward sharing. Consequently, a global convergence process may be already at work toward risk sharing in the West and in the Islamic world. As the risks of globalization are shared more equitably, so will be its rewards, at least in terms of financial transactions and investment.

ENDNOTES

1 Cummings, John Thomas, Hossein Askari, and Ahmad Mustafa, "Islam and Modern Economic Change," *Islam and Development: Religion and Sociopolitical Change*, ed. John L. Esposito, (New York: Syracuse University Press, 1980).

2 Mirakhor, Abbas, "The General Characteristics of an Islamic Economic System", in B. Al-Hassani and A. Mirakhor, *Essays on Iqtisad*, (New York: Global Scholarly Publications, 2003).

3 This is also true of medieval Christian and Judaic debates on usury and, more importantly, and much more recently, the continuing Catholic problems with Western capitalism.

4 Mirakhor (2003).

5 Irfan Ul Haq, *Economic Doctrines of Islam: A Study in the Doctrines of Islam and Their Implications for Poverty, Employment, and Economic Growth*: 87.

CHAPTER 5

Expanding Financial Frontiers

Financial market efficiency and resilience are determined by market depth and breadth. Market depth is indicated by the volume and frequency of transactions, while breadth is measured by the array of financial instruments and services available in the market. The depth of Islamic financial markets is still relatively small when compared to conventional markets. A large share of Islamic financial markets is dominated by commercial banking activities, but even this is still less than 1 percent of total conventional banking. Although there is growth in other areas of finance, such as capital markets and insurance, the relative size of these is also very small. For example, the total size of outstanding *sukuk* as of 2007 was US$140 billon, which is only 0.47 percent of total outstanding debt of US$29,728 billion as of 2007 in U.S. markets.[1]

In terms of market breadth, Islamic financial markets offer limited products and services. Even when compared to an emerging market, the pace of growth and introduction of new products and services is very slow. There are several reasons for this, as discussed in Chapter 2. There are two observations that deserve mention here: the first is the quality of innovation, and the second is the process of innovation. In terms of the quality, most of the innovation at this time is being driven by increased demand for products and services compatible with *Shari'ah*, which in turn is putting undue pressure on the financial intermediaries to deliver. In addition, financial intermediaries—whether Islamic or conventional offering Islamic products—are rushing to capture the market without much transparency and due diligence in the design of the products. A good example of such rush to deliver is the introduction of those *sukuk* structures that are now questioned by AAOIFI, and are not considered to be fully compatible with *Shari'ah*.

Other than the quality, the process of introducing new products is worthy of scrutiny. The developments in the Islamic financial markets and the introduction of new products are prime examples of "reverse engineering," where a conventional product is being replicated to conform to *Shari'ah* or a conventional product is "wrapped" in a *Shari'ah*-compatible deliverable. This trend is troublesome as the process may not be strictly following *Shari'ah*. Furthermore, there is less emphasis on the development of infrastructure supporting the introduction of *Shari'ah*-compatible instruments, which are unique in risk/return profile. For example, as mentioned in Chapter 2, whereas *Shari'ah* encourages risk-sharing financial instruments and services, in reality there is a dearth of such instruments because the financial infrastructure conducive to such risk-sharing instruments is absent.

Both the quality and the process, of introducing new products and services need to be improved. If such measures are not taken, Islamic finance cannot maintain a healthy growth rate and sustain itself. The real danger is that due to low transparency, products will be introduced that are not fully compatible with *Shari'ah* and, therefore, become contaminated. The other danger is that working within current constraints and without building a sound infrastructure, Islamic finance will fail to provide practical solutions to the needs of individuals, firms, and the state, which will lead to loss of confidence in the system. If Islamic finance's full potential is to be realized, it is important that Islamic finance expand itself beyond commercial banking and venture into other financial frontiers that are currently unexplored. There is a need to develop a spectrum of products and services that will not only serve the demands of the markets but also help develop a sound foundation for building more complex products and services through financial engineering.

There are several areas where innovative solutions from Islamic finance are long overdue; this chapter briefly discusses some challenging areas while the other issues are discussed at length in the remaining chapters.

5.1 EXPLORING NEW FRONTIERS THROUGH FINANCIAL ENGINEERING[2]

Financial engineering and financial innovations are driving the global financial system toward greater economic efficiency by expanding the opportunities for sharing risk, lowering transaction costs, and reducing asymmetric information and agency costs. Financial engineering involves the design, development, and implementation of innovative financial instruments and processes, as well as the formulation of creative solutions. Financial engineering may lead to a new consumer-type financial instrument, a new security, a new process, or creative solution to corporate finance problems, such as the need to lower funding costs, manage risk better, or increase the return on investments.

For Islamic financial institutions, a financial engineering challenge is to introduce new *Shari'ah*-compatible products that develop much-needed money and capital markets and enhance liquidity, risk management, and portfolio diversification. Generally, attempts to apply financial engineering techniques to Islamic banking will require the commitment of a great deal of resources to understanding the risk/return characteristics of each building block of the system and build new products with different risk/return profiles that meet the demand of investors, financial intermediaries, and entrepreneurs for liquidity and safety. New financial innovations are also needed to satisfy the demand for instruments at both ends of the maturity structure: extremely short-term deposits and long-term investments. Money markets that are *Shari'ah*-compatible do not exist at present, and there is no equivalent of an Islamic interbank market where banks could place, say, overnight funds or could borrow to satisfy a need for short-term liquidity. Although securitization of a pool of lease portfolios could help to develop the interbank market, the volume of transactions offered by securitization may not be sufficient to meet the demand.

With increased globalization, integration and linkages with global financial markets have become critical to the success of any capital market. Such integration becomes seamless and transparent when a financial market offers a wide array of instruments with varying structures of maturity and opportunities for portfolio diversification and risk management. Financial engineering in Islamic finance will have to focus on the development of products that foster market integration and attract investors and entrepreneurs to the risk/return characteristics of the product rather than to the fact of the product being Islamic. As impressive as the record of growth of individual Islamic banks may be, so far they have served mostly as intermediaries between Muslim financial resources and major commercial banks in the West. It has been a one-way relationship. No major Islamic bank has been able to develop ways and means of intermediating between the supply of Western financial resources and the demand for them in Muslim countries. There is an urgent need to develop marketable *Shari'ah*-based instruments by which asset portfolios generated in Muslim countries can be marketed in the West.

Development of new products and financial engineering are resource-intensive activities. All major conventional banks have dedicated departments that conduct background market research, product development, and analytical modeling. These activities demand financial and human resources, which are costly. Conventional financial institutions can justify these costs because they are able to recover them, in most cases, from the volume of business generated as a result of the innovative product. Costs associated with the development of new products are rising due to the increasing complexity of the business environment as a result of regulatory or accounting and reporting standards.

Islamic financial institutions are, in general, of small size and cannot afford to invest substantial funds in research and development. They are unable to reap the benefits of economies of scale. Considering the importance of financial engineering, Islamic financial institutions should seriously consider making joint efforts to develop the basic infrastructure for introducing new products. Conducting basic research and development collectively may save some of the costs required to build this infrastructure individually. A good example of such collective effort would be to sponsor research into the development of analytical models, computer systems, and tools to analyze the risk and return on different instruments.

Financial engineering is an area where Islamic financial institutions could benefit from more-experienced Western institutions, which are more sophisticated in engineering and marketing the right product to the right client. Conventional investment banks, which have invested heavily in the infrastructure for developing new products, can work for or with Islamic financial institutions to develop *Shari'ah*-compliant products. Once a financial engineering shop is set up, they can develop different products with different risk and return profiles. In this respect, Islamic financial institutions would do well to develop synergies and collaborate with conventional institutions. Islamic financial institutions could outsource the development part to conventional institutions and keep the marketing part to themselves, a division of labor that could benefit both institutions.

It is also useful to make some observations on current practices of financial engineering. There is growing concern that the financial engineering is not taking place in a coordinated or systematic fashion. Financial institutions are very secretive about the structures they create and there is a sense of a lack of transparency with many products. Therefore, it is critical that a more organized and systematic approach is taken towards the process of innovation. Suwailem (2006) lays down four principles for financial engineering from an Islamic perspective. First, the "principle of balance" asks for an integrated and balanced approach where all aspects of economic and social values—such as justice inclusiveness, cooperation, and competition—are considered. Second, he advocates the "principle of acceptability," that all economic dealings are generally acceptable unless otherwise stated by *Shari'ah*. This principle linked to freedom of contract in Islam has been the cornerstone for innovation in Islamic history. Third, the "principle of integration" states that an integrated real and financial sector are essential for sustainable growth, and, therefore, any innovation's foremost objective should be to enhance integration between the two sectors. Finally, the "principle of consistency" states that the form and substance of Islamic products must be consistent with each other; that is, form should serve substance, and means should conform to ends.

During high-growth periods, there is real danger of introducing innovations under intense competition, which can expose the institution to the risk of introducing a product that is not in full compliance, and in some cases may even be opposite to the essence of the system. In such cases, introducing a new product defeats the whole objective and the purpose of Islamic finance, and can also lead to serious costs in terms of reputational risks. In order to avoid such a scenario, it is important that:

- Underlying principles of financial engineering in Islam are followed
- Serious efforts are made to introduce products with distinct risk/return characteristics, rather than trying to "reverse engineer" a conventional financial product
- Prudent behavior by *Shari'ah* scholars is exhibited after careful review of the legal and economic consequences of a product
- Time and effort to introduce new products is minimized
- Steps are taken to develop infrastructure and institutions to promote financial engineering and innovation

5.2 EXPANDING FINANCIAL INTERMEDIATION

A financial intermediary transforms savings into investment and, in the process, creates additional value by reducing search, monitoring, and transaction costs, as well as diversification and/or hedging risks, thereby allowing more efficient utilization of resources. A financial intermediary performs these functions through the design and utilization of instruments or products intended to achieve a specific objective. A financial intermediary in the Islamic financial system is expected to play a critical role. The nature of financial intermediation in Islamic finance is distinct from conventional finance in several ways, but one distinction is critical. Unlike a conventional financial intermediary, which takes on a well-defined and narrow function, a financial intermediary in the Islamic financial system plays multiple roles. Whereas organized markets—such as money, capital, and derivative markets—complement the role of a financial intermediary in the conventional system, a financial intermediary in the Islamic financial system is expected to undertake some of the functions provided by these organized markets. In other words, an Islamic financial system has more common features with a "bank-centered" financial system, such as those of Japan and Germany, as opposed to a "market-centered" financial system such as those of the U.S. and the UK (Iqbal 2005; Iqbal and Mirakhor 2007).

At present, financial intermediation in Islamic financial markets is very restricted. It is limited mainly to commercial banking activities, with the gradual introduction of investment banking activities. Within commercial banking, there is more emphasis on trade financing and some leasing-based assets that are of short-term maturity and often illiquid. In the case of investment banking, the menu of products and services is even more limited and is often targeted at high-net-worth individuals. There are several areas where there are clear gaps when compared to products and services offered by conventional financial intermediaries.

Islamic financial institutions have to expand the scope of their activities to provide a wider range of products and services in the areas of corporate finance, risk management, small- and medium-size enterprises (SME) financing, and wealth management. Research has shown that during the early phases of development where capital markets are not well developed, financial intermediaries play a critical role in providing financial services to the corporate sector. In the absence of liquid Islamic capital markets, financial intermediaries will have to become the main source of financing. Furthermore, the simple availability of financing will not serve this purpose; the mode of the service will have to be improved. The financing would have to be cost-effective, flexible, and client-oriented. Financial intermediaries must understand the needs of corporate-sector clients to develop custom solutions that can make them competitive in the market.

Major structural changes in the role of financial intermediaries are required in the area of risk management. The emergence of a new form of financial intermediary, with an expanded role, is the key to successful risk management in Islamic finance. Their role in developing a risk-management infrastructure should be twofold; first, to develop and apply risk-management techniques for their own portfolios, and second to offer risk-management services to their clients. Risk-management tools expand the role of a financial intermediary that can offer innovative products and risk-management services to the client, and can also manage its own exposure more efficiently and in a cost-effective manner. Management of financial risk also creates profitable opportunities for financial intermediaries in several ways. First, a bank's risk experts are likely to provide more effective advice to clients and more effectively differentiate their products. Second, fees associated with supplying risk-management transactions can be an important source of revenue. And finally, since risk-management transactions increase the intermediary's customers' profits by lowering their customer's probability of financial distress, these transactions indirectly lower that intermediary's loss exposure.[3] Risk management is discussed further later in this chapter.

Consumer and retail banking is another area where there are gaps. The question is often raised about the potential for developing financing instruments for consumers that are not based on a tangible asset; for example, a financial instrument to provide financial assistance for student loans. Education loans do not create any tangible asset and do not have any collateral other than personal guarantees. Another case is the area of consumer services, such as credit cards. An original purchase on a credit card may not have any conflict with *Shari'ah* principles, but once the purchase becomes an interest-bearing loan, the same transaction is in conflict with *Shari'ah*. In such cases, Islamic financial intermediaries will have to become innovative and find solutions to such problems. Islamic financial institutions cannot provide selective services—they need to provide a complete set of services for the clients. If such services are not provided, consumers wishing to comply with *Shari'ah* will be at a disadvantage, as they will not have access to the full array of options.

Another area requiring attention from Islamic financial intermediaries is financial products and services for SMEs. A vibrant SME sector plays a critical role in the economic development of any country. Proponents of Islamic finance advocate that it encourages it grassroots entrepreneurship. However, in reality the majority of Islamic financial institutions do not have any systematic program to promote SMEs. Discussion on SMEs is undertaken later in the chapter.

Advancement in information technology and financial engineering innovations have made it possible for financial instruments disseminated over the Internet to obviate the need for "bricks and mortar" banking and financial markets. As Bill Gates once remarked, "banking is essential, banks are not." Now consumer and mortgage financing, corporate credit, all depository asset management, and investment banking services—which not long ago would have required considerable physical infrastructural investment to provide—are offered by means of global e-commerce trading systems that can easily accommodate different languages across borders. Importantly, these systems are defined by their product rather than by their geographic location. Islamic financial institutions are scattered over different geographical regions and, therefore, are overexposed to credit and market risk in domestic markets and regions. Availability of services through the Internet will expand the client base of Islamic financial intermediaries and will help them diversify their portfolios.

5.3 WEALTH MANAGEMENT

Wealth management entails offering financial planning and management to high-net-worth individuals and private and public institutions with the goal of sustaining long-term wealth. With the current wave of petrodollars earned by Gulf Cooperation Council (GCC) countries, several public sector institutions are bound to increase the demand for the management of such accumulated funds. Table 1.11 in Chapter 1 lists major sovereign wealth funds (SWFs) which include several Muslim countries. Although a number of GCC countries are currently using conventional investment vehicles, given the increasing demand for *Shari'ah*-compatible products, whole or some portions of this wealth may be available for Islamic financial markets. This will also depend on how successfully Islamic financial markets provide such services. Similarly, there are increased numbers of institutional investors who will be interested in *Shari'ah*-compatible wealth management. These include the excess foreign exchange reserves of the central banks, funds maintained by state pension funds, future funds such as oil funds established by some countries, and sovereign wealth managers.

It is worth mentioning that several prominent economists, such as Larry Summers, have argued that at the current high levels of foreign exchange reserves held by the central banks and some sovereign wealth managers, such institutions should consider investing some portion of these reserves in riskier assets such as the equity markets. This should be encouraging for Islamic finance, which is based on the principle of risk sharing and is friendly to equity-sharing investments.

Given the current state of affairs, offering robust wealth management in Islamic finance faces serious challenges. Any wealth management process begins with defining investment objectives and goals. Defining the objectives is followed by a rigorous strategic asset allocation (SAA) process which determines the optimal mix of asset classes to achieve the desired goals and objectives. In conventional finance, the SAA process has become a science, with the aid of sophisticated statistical and quantitative models. The analysis is well supported by considerable historical data for each asset class to help understand past behavior and to forecast the performance in the future. Such models are driven by comparable benchmarks, arbitrage-free strategies, hedging mechanisms, and—most importantly—reference points for returns of different maturity structures in the debt market. With these tools, the SAA process helps in constructing an optimal portfolio of different asset classes to achieve target investment objectives at acceptable levels of risk.

Constructing a meaningful SAA framework in Islamic finance is a challenge. First, a fixed-income debt market—other than the limited and illiquid *sukuk* market—does not exist. Therefore, the SAA framework will resort to using proxies from conventional debt markets, which may not be an ideal situation. Second, there are no *Shari'ah*-compliant benchmarks against which an SAA strategy can be devised. Although a number of *Shari'ah*-compliant benchmarks are available in the equity asset-class space, similar benchmarks in fixed-income markets are limited or may not be efficient. Third, given the prohibition of interest and consequent prohibition of pure debt security, an SAA framework will have to work with other asset classes with distinct risk/return profiles. For example, it would require development of models for *mudarabah* arrangements where the manager can deploy funds in a customized fashion, which are hard to model. The highly customized nature of financial assets adds to the complexity of modeling.

All the abovementioned factors mean that the SAA framework will require a more complex design and, therefore, extensive quantitative modeling. In the absence of a meaningful SAA framework, the investor will be exposed to unknown risks, and, as the result of inappropriate asset allocation, may not be successful in achieving long-term goals.

The concern over the lack of liquidity in Islamic financial markets cannot be overemphasized. An effective portfolio diversification plan cannot be implemented in the absence of a liquid interbank, money, and capital market. Liquidity has always been a problem for Islamic financial institutions because of the limited number of instruments that could be termed liquid. Further, financing based on partnership contract could be highly customized and hard to transfer or negotiate.

Apart from Islamic funds, the liquidity of other financial instruments provides great exposure for the investor. A lack of liquidity-enhancing financial products, such as securitization, forces the fund manager to operate in short-term maturity instruments which may not be optimal to achieve the investor's medium- to long-term goals and objectives. The other extreme is to have a buy-and-hold strategy which exposes investors to liquidity risk in case of the unexpected need to dispose of the asset. For example, some *sukuk* (Islamic bonds) do not trade frequently in the market, and those that do trade are subject to large bid–ask spreads. A buy-and-hold strategy may not achieve desirable results, and selling a large bid–ask spread will result in additional transaction costs. Another serious issue with the lack of liquidity is the restrictions imposed on portfolio managers in the construction of portfolios. In cases where a portfolio is constructed to replicate a benchmark, portfolios require periodic rebalancing to align the risk/return profiles with the risk/return profile of the benchmark. In an illiquid market, both the portfolio and the benchmark are subject to less frequent updates, which will lead to unexpected mismatches and undue exposure for the investor.

5.4 RISK MANAGEMENT

The increasing complexity of domestic and international financial markets has led to greater awareness and realization of the critical role of risk and risk management in modern finance. Whereas financial innovations dominated the markets during the past three decades, most of the innovations were demand-driven and were in the area of risk management to combat high volatilities in financial markets.

Financial markets are more integrated and interdependent than ever, thus increasing the probability of expeditious contagion effects without leaving much room for swift measures against unexpected risk. As elegantly expressed by Merton (1996), insufficient understanding of the new environment can create a sense of greater risk even if the objective level of risk in the system is unchanged or reduced.

The absence of a developed risk-management framework in Islamic finance has a significant impact on the current and future growth of the market because:

- A *Shari'ah*-compliant firm will lose its business competitiveness due to its inability to handle variability in its cost, revenues, and profitability through active hedging of financial risk.
- A firm without active risk management will be perceived as a high-risk firm and thus will be subject to higher funding costs and to a higher expected rate of return.
- There will be fewer optimal investment and diversification opportunities.
- The firm will be subject to a high risk of financial distress.
- A firm will be exposed to higher risk during a system-wide financial crisis.
- All of the abovementioned factors will lead to increased riskiness for the investors and their wealth.

The current wave of capital market liberalizations and globalization is bound to prompt the need for enhanced risk-management measures, especially for the developing economies and the emerging markets, such as Islamic financial markets. Risk management is an area where Islamic financial markets are lagging, particularly in innovating instruments to share, transfer, and mitigate market risk. Historically, the Islamic finance industry has grown out of commercial banking activities where Islamic banks act as deposit-taking institutions and invest in trade-financing activities. With the growth of the markets and the recent surge in demand, investment-banking activities are growing fast. New institutions are emerging that are providing more sophisticated financial services, including accessing capital markets, a wider range of investment vehicles, insurance functionality, and wealth management. In addition, investors are offered more choices in terms of different asset classes and more diversification opportunities.

Shiller (2004) argues that, at present, the practice of risk management through pooling, diversification, and hedging by today's institutions is unable to satisfy the needs of risk reduction in certain areas.

He suggests that risk management "be extended far beyond its former realm, covering important new *classes* of risks. This is innovation that changes the assumptions about what can be insured, hedged or diversified, and that has major impact on human welfare." He identifies new areas such as risk management for individuals, their livelihood, and protection of their most valuable asset (the home) as the new frontiers. Islamic financial institutions need to explore new frontiers and offer Islamic solutions to risk management along these lines.

Risk management is a two-step process. Risk management can only be as good as our understanding and assessment of risk. The development of good risk and pricing models is extremely critical to risk management because if one cannot quantify the risk, one cannot hedge it. Although extensive research has been carried out in conventional financial markets on understanding risk/return profiles for different financial products, similar exercises in Islamic financial markets are sparse. Even where risk-management techniques in conventional finance are applicable to Islamic products, the implementation of risk management—especially in hedging market, price, FX, and commodity risks—is problematic (van Greuning and Iqbal 2007).

Although conventional and Islamic markets share similar risks, the level of risk is different and certainly higher in the case of today's Islamic financial markets. This can be attributed mainly to two reasons; first, the lack of risk-management tools and the absence of institutional arrangements and infrastructure, and second, the lack of risk culture in financial institutions offering *Shari'ah*-compatible products and services. There is debate among scholars on the usage and applicability of derivative products. Some scholars have rejected derivatives outright on the basis of the possible usage of derivatives for speculative purposes, while others have argued that such rejection of derivatives should be based on careful review of the products on a case-by-case basis. Nevertheless, in today's volatile markets there is a need to develop hedging mechanisms that are *Shari'ah*-compliant. Such hedging tools could be in the form of derivatives or in the form of other arrangements such as collective risk bearing, insurance, or solidarity funds. Development of these are essential to transfer and share financial risks. See Suweilum (2007) for further discussion on hedging in Islamic finance.

Institutions providing *Shari'ah*-compliant products and services are often acting as universal banks, providing both commercial- and investment-banking services. The nature of the risk and the risk management is different for each service type and, therefore, requires extensive infrastructure to measure and monitor risk. During the high-growth periods, institutions often fail to pay due attention to risk management. However, risk control is a management problem, and financial debacles such as Barings Bank, Daiwa Bank, and Société Générale are not random events. Studies suggest that management failure rather than misfortune, errors, or complexity are the major sources of these financial problems. Risk management must take these facts into account. Although the academic literature in Islamic finance has focused on market risk and credit risk, it has ignored operational risk, a term that includes, inter alia, problems with information systems, operational problems, and breaches in internal control, fraud, or unforeseen catastrophes.[4] Many Islamic financial houses are too small to afford the costs of developing and maintaining risk control and management systems.

Risk-management strategies can be classified into three broad categories: risk sharing through transfer of risks or maintenance of reserves; diversification of nonsystematic risks; and insurance either through options or re-insurance.[5] Risk sharing or risk transfer can be facilitated through structured products with embedded optionalities, pooling or securitization of dormant assets, or trading derivatives. Although some form of securitization is available through *sukuk*, derivatives or their substitutes need to be developed to implement a robust risk-management framework.

Developing risk-management tools and practices is one of the biggest challenges for Islamic financial institutions. This challenge also offers some opportunities to develop unique solutions to age-old problems. If Islamic financial institutions are unable to meet the challenge, their further growth will be seriously hampered.

5.5 DEVELOPMENT OF NON-BANK FINANCIAL INSTITUTIONS

The emergence of Islamic finance in modern history began with non-bank financial institutions such as Tabung Haji in Malaysia, and Mitghamr and Nasser Social Bank in Egypt. The objective of these institutions was to fill the gap left by conventional banking institutions. Research over the last couple of decades shows how significant are the contributions of non-bank financial institutions that complement the activities of banks by providing various services to different segments of the economy. Research also documents the diversification benefits of non-bank financial institutions adding to the stability of the financial services.

Non-banking financial institutions in the conventional financial system have grown to cover a wide range of activities such as private equity, joint venture, credit unions, advisory services, and specialized finance houses. In addition to the abovementioned services, specialized forms of financing are in practice as well. These include trust finance, endowment funds, and cooperatives. Such non-banking financial institutions have special relevance to Islamic finance. For example, today's trust financing or endowment funds have their roots in the Islamic institution of *waqf*, which has made enormous contributions to the economic development of Muslim societies throughout their history. In addition, the Islamic financial system offers unique instruments that do not have any direct comparison in conventional finance. One such example is the institution of *qard-ul-hassan* (interest-free loans) which has been proved to be an effective means of economic development and poverty alleviation.

The objectives of socioeconomic justice and equitable distribution of wealth separate Islamic economic principles from others. The *Qur'an* places great emphasis on the redistribution of income and wealth, and legislates institutions for this purpose, the most important of which are the institutions of inheritance, *sadaqat* (charity), *Zakah*, *waqf* and *qard-ul-hassan*, which all have wide-ranging economic development implications and, therefore, are needed for the welfare of the society. These instruments are vehicles for ensuring just conduct and maintaining a healthy level of wealth distribution. A major reason for the lack of a sufficient level of economic growth and prosperity, as well as the existence of widespread poverty, in many Muslim societies is noncompliance with the rules of just conduct in the economic sphere, as specified by Islam. It is also clear that this state of affairs, in turn, stems from a general lack of familiarity with these rules among Muslims.

In an Islamic economic system, various levies are imposed on production or income, to redeem property rights accrued by different members of the society. It is important to realize that in no way are these levies to be considered charity, as often misunderstood by laymen and scholars alike. The fact that the general Qur'anic terms for these levies, such as *Zakah* or *sadaqat*, are translated into "charity" is an indication of this general misunderstanding. In fact, *Zakah* indicates a cleansing of the resulting production or income from the rights of others in them; that is, *Zakah* purifies the production or income resulting from an economic activity from the rights of others in the surplus, others being those that, for one reason or another, have been unable to partake in the act of production or exchange. Consider, for example, the categories of the *Zakah* receivers named in the *Qur'an* (see, for example, 2:177 or 8:41); most are those who have not been able to participate in these processes, or if they have, for a variety of reasons have been unable to generate enough surplus to satisfy a minimum level of living (Mirakhor 2004).

Sadaqat are a very important redistributive institution in Islam for two reasons: first, they operationalize the truthfulness of one's belief in *Allah* (*swt*) in the voluntarily giving of one's income and wealth. Second, the importance of this institution derives from the fact that the receiver is not the person to whom *sadaqat* is given, but *Allah* (*swt*).[6] *Allah* (*swt*) has also created an incentive structure in which there is a promise of multiple returns for *sadaqat*. In fact, the *Qur'an* promises the return to *sadaqat* from *Allah* (*swt*) in an increasing rate (see verses 2:265, 276). Development of this institution has the potential of mobilizing considerable financial resources.

Zakah is considered a component of *sadaqat*, but it has been given a special status in the *Qur'an* because it is ordained with obligatory prayer in at least 20 verses (see, for example, 2:110). In some Muslim countries, *Zakah* is paid directly to the government; in others, when and if paid, it is locally collected and distributed. Assuming there is a globally reputable Islamic financial institution with a network of branches and correspondents that could develop financial instruments on both sides of its balance sheet, it could issue an instrument to the *Zakah* payers that would facilitate collection and could issue instruments according to uses and locations of mobilized resources. It is not difficult to calculate quickly the size and magnitude of potential financial resources that could be mobilized through *Zakah* from the population of Muslims around the world. Again, information technology and the Internet obviates the need for physical or massive bureaucratic resources for this purpose, as every dimension of the process of operationalization and instrumentalization of this institution can be done electronically, effectively, and efficiently.

According to some estimates, the assets of the non-bank financial sector will make up around 8–10 percent of total Islamic assets.[7] Given the size of the Muslim population and GDP of Islamic countries, this estimate appears to be on the low side. Actual potential is much more, as these institutions have to be expanded to cover wider segments of the society.

The following steps are suggested to strengthen this sector:

- Develop institutions to formalize the implementation of redistributive instruments of Islam. Formal institutions to channel these flows in the most effective fashion need to be developed. These could be dedicated institutions specializing in the distribution of funds in the most cost-effective manner which also has the most development impact. If there are well-functioning Islamic financial intermediaries, these can become a distribution channel and provide these social welfare services as part of their customer services. A reputation of positive contributions to social welfare could serve as an asset for the financial institution which can use this to attract or retain customers.
- Develop a legal framework to encourage and to protect non-banking financial institutions so that such institutions can operate in a friendly environment.
- It is necessary to have a prudent regulatory and policy framework for a broad-based and efficient, non-bank, financial segment. Some regulatory overview may also be needed, not only to instill confidence and protect stakeholders, but also to ensure the healthy growth of the industry. Furthermore, tax neutrality can play an important role in further growth of this sector.[8]

5.6 FINANCIAL INTEGRATION

To date, the main customers of the Islamic financial industry have been Muslims who wish to comply with *Shari'ah*. Growth in demand for *Shari'ah*-compliant products and services is dominated by Muslims who want to see this market succeed. With the current wave of globalization, a financial product does not have local presence only but can reach clients anywhere in the world who demand the product. The reasons for the demand for these products could be purely religious or ethical, or due to their financial characteristics, or a combination of both. There is no reason that a financial product would not be attractive to an investor on the basis of its return/risk profile if the investor is indifferent to its *Shari'ah*-compliant feature. In other words, the Islamic financial industry is yet to tap that class of investors, or entrepreneurs seeking funding.

Currently, the number of Islamic products marketed to conventional investors is very small relative to Muslim investors. *Sukuk* is one product that has been embraced by conventional borrowers as well as investors. In the case of investors, their decision-making is determined by yield level and the credit standing of the issuer. In the case of floating-rate *sukuk*, the spread above the London Interbank Offered Rate (LIBOR) drives the investors' decision because they do not distinguish between a *sukuk* and a bond. This also indicates that the investor does not view *sukuk* as an asset-backed or asset-based security as it is evident that the pricing of *sukuk* is a function of discounting future coupons without any adjustment of it being asset-based or for the embedded optionality. In the case of conventional borrowers, they consider the *sukuk* market as a means to raise funds at lower cost than what they could raise in the conventional markets. Nevertheless, a conventional client is attracted to the product based on the features of the product and will certainly be interested in products that satisfy their needs irrespective of whether they are *Shari'ah*-compliant.

The Islamic financial industry needs to tap into this potential market as well. They need to develop products that are attractive to conventional clients but still comply with *Shari'ah*. This can offer several benefits. First, investment by conventional investors can provide the funding for economic development, such as infrastructure projects as well as for the corporate sector. Second, demand for borrowing funds can create investment opportunities for Islamic investors to enhance their yields. Third, the introduction of conventional customers will increase competition in the market and will force the financial intermediaries to enhance efficiency. Finally, this may lead to commoditization of Islamic products just like any other products in the market, enhancing overall market efficiency.

Attracting conventional customers is not going to be easy. In the light of financial crises in emerging markets and the most recent crisis in the subprime market, the task does not become easier. In both cases, the issues of regulation and governance play critical roles. Conventional customers would be extremely concerned about the regulatory and governance issues in this market. The Islamic financial industry needs to take serious steps to enhance the governance of financial institutions and markets, to enhance the transparency in the market, to implement comprehensive risk-management policies and procedures, and, finally, to introduce the standardization of contracts and accounting standards.

The Islamic Financial Services Board (IFSB) has been active in all of the abovementioned areas, but needs partners to work with. Therefore, it is highly desirable that policymakers form partnerships with organizations such as IFSB and the conventional organizations such as International Accounting Standards Board (IASB) or International Organization of Securities Commissions (IOSCO) to provide a level playing field to Islamic financial institutions and to conventional institutions that may be interested in entering the market. A seamless integration of Islamic and conventional markets can benefit all customers—Islamic and non-Islamic.

5.7 CONCLUSION

For Islamic finance to achieve its potential there is an urgent need to enhance the supply and demand of Islamic financial products. On the supply side, institutions offering Islamic financial products must expand beyond commercial banking and venture into other financial markets. There is a need to develop a much wider spectrum of products and services to satisfy the demand of the market in banking and non-banking areas. This effort should also support the development of a sound foundation for building more complex products and services through financial engineering in the future. For this to occur there is a need for a concerted program of research and product development on the part of a public entity, as Islamic institutions may be too small in size to invest in such an effort. At the same time these efforts must be supported by the global supervision of Islamic financial markets and institutions. Simultaneously, on the demand side, Muslims should be educated on the array of *Shari'ah*-compatible products that may be able to satisfy their financial needs to replace the conventional financial products that they have used in the past. It must also be recognized that because these efforts may take some time, it would be a mistake to push through products that may not be *Shari'ah*-compatible in order to preserve a façade of Islamic finance.

One of the positive developments of Islamic finance is the area of regulation and standards. In this respect, the IFSB has played an exemplary role and has been a leader in promoting Islamic finance and supporting its growth. The IFSB's performance in a short period of time is remarkable, and its model of operation should be adopted by other institutions. The Islamic Development Bank (IDB) has been working on the promotion of Islamic finance since 1975, but its efforts have not been as effective as hoped. There are several reasons for this.

First, the institution has taken several initiatives, all of which are steps in the right direction, but the implementation of several initiatives has been below par. Second, given the resources and the size of the institution, it has taken on more initiatives than it can effectively handle. Finally, the institution has a limited capital base and has not developed the means to access capital markets on a regular basis. The research arm of the institution has done well despite limited resources.

The IDB should play a leading role in the innovation of products on both the demand and the supply side. The institution has to expand its sources of capital by accessing capital markets to provide cost-effective financing to member countries. Frequent access to the capital markets will help develop liquidity in the market and will promote the development of a benchmark which can be used in the primary and secondary markets. With a wider capital base, the IDB will be able to expand services to member countries to help alleviate poverty and also provide capital to support and strengthen Islamic capital markets. Similarly, the IDB needs to develop institutions in member countries to promote SMEs and Islamic financial concepts such as *Zakah*, *sadaqat*, and *waqf*. In short, the IDB has to play active and leading role in developing institutions to promote long-term growth of Islamic finance.

ENDNOTES

1 U.S. debt includes U.S. Treasury, mortgage-related, corporate, and agency debt. Source: Securities Industry and Financial Markets Association (SIFMA), http://www.sifma.org

2 For details see: Iqbal, Zamir, "Financial Engineering in Islamic Finance", *Thunderbird International Business Review*, 41, (1999): 541–559; Iqbal, Zamir and Abbas Mirakhor, *Introduction to Islamic Finance: Theory and Practice*, (Singapore: John Wiley & Sons (Asia), 2007); Al-Suwailem, Sami *Hedging in Islamic Finance*, Occasional Paper no. 10, (Jeddah: IRTI, 2006).

3 Clifford, W. Smith, Jr., "Risk Management in Banking," in *Advanced Strategies in Financial Risk Management*, eds. Robert J. Schwartz and Clifford W. Smith, Jr., (New York: New York Institute of Finance, 1993): 147–162.

4 Tschoegl, Adrian E., "The Key to Risk Management: Management," Working Paper, (Philadelphia, PA: The Wharton Financial Institutions Center, 2000).

5 Scholes, M., Key Note Address, Risk 2000 Conference, Boston, MA, USA, June 13–14, 2000.

6 In two verses of the Chapter of Repentance, it is noted that:
(103): "*of their goods (wealth) take* sadaqah, *so that you might purify and sanctify them; and pray on their behalf. Indeed, your prayers are a source of security for them: and* Allah (swt) *is One Who Hears and Knows.*"

(104): "*Do they not know that* Allah (swt) *accepts repentance from His servants and Receives their* sadaqat, *and that* Allah (swt) *is indeed He, the Oft-Returning, Most Merciful.*"

7 IRTI and IF, *Islamic Financial Services Industry Development: Ten-Year Framework and Strategies, Islamic Research and Training Institution* (IRTI), (Jeddah, Saudi Arabia: Islamic Development Bank, 2006).

8 IRTI and IFSB, Islamic Financial Services Industry Development: Ten-Year Framework And Strategies, (Jeddah: Islamic Research and Training Institution (IRTI), Islamic Development Bank, 2006).

CHAPTER 6

Reputational Risk for the Islamic Financial Industry

"It takes 20 years to build a reputation and five minutes to destroy it."[1]

Reputational risk is increasingly gaining the attention of researchers, policymakers, and managers in financial institutions due to the significant impact it can have on the future of institutions. Reputational risk has special relevance to financial institutions and services because the activities of financial institutions are different from those of other economic agents. Financial intermediation comes with special fiduciary responsibilities, and failure of fiduciary responsibilities can lead to serious external costs. Financial institutions see reputational risk as a difficult challenge, and, therefore, financial service companies have pushed risk management further up the corporate agenda. In a survey of more than 130 senior executives in financial institutions worldwide, 82 percent agreed that awareness of risk is now more pervasive in their organization than it was two years ago.[2] Another survey conducted by PricewaterhouseCooper (PwC), in early 2004, showed that of the 1,400 CEOs taking part in the study, 35 percent identified reputational risk as either "one of the biggest threats" (10 percent) or "a significant threat" (25 percent) to their business growth prospects.[3]

Despite high growth rates, the issue of reputational risk has not received necessary attention in the Islamic financial industry or by the institutions offering financial products and services compatible with Islamic Law. This does not mean that the Islamic financial industry is immune to such risk, but that, despite the high growth rate, exposure to this risk has not received due attention. The relevance of reputational risk pertains to the Islamic financial industry for three reasons. The first and most critical reason is the maintenance of clients' expectations, clients who have placed their trust in Islamic financial institutions to fulfill operations according to their religious commitment. Second, with the increasing growth of Islamic finance, good reputation can be an asset in establishing a conventional client base. And finally, the post-9/11 environment necessitates the attention of financial institutions to reputational risk due to the increased scrutiny and regulations dealing with financial institutions, anti-money laundering (AML), and the finance of terrorism (CFT).[4]

6.1 WHAT IS REPUTATIONAL RISK?

Reputational risk has often been considered a subset of operational risk; however, convincing arguments have been put forth over time to distinguish reputational risk from operational risk and to highlight the sole significance of reputational risk. According to the Basel II Accords, operational risks are associated with people (internal fraud, clients, product and business practices, employment practices, and workplace safety), internal processes and systems, and external events (external fraud, damage or loss of assets), while reputational risk is subtler and may result in permanent damage to a firm's long-term relationships. Even though it is difficult to quantify reputational risk, some researchers have advanced the idea of "reputational capital" as part of a financial institution's economic capital representing the component of capital that is employed in absorbing unexpected shocks caused by negative information regarding the company.[5]

Reputational risk is more subtle than operational risk because it deals with intangible assets such as brand equity, intellectual capital, goodwill, trust, and relationships, which have high replacement costs compared to a tangible asset. According to Alan Greenspan, the former chairman of the U.S. Federal Reserve Board, the proportion of gross domestic product(GDP) that results from the use of conceptual, as distinct from physical, assets has been growing, and whereas physical assets retain a good portion of their value, even if the reputation of management is destroyed, intangible assets may lose value more rapidly.[6] This increased realization is forcing large, high-profile, and established companies to pay attention to the exposures and vulnerabilities of intangible assets such as reputation. It is often observed that firms with strong positive reputations attract better people, are perceived as providing more value, and have more loyal customers. Furthermore, since the market believes that such companies will deliver sustained earnings and future growth, these firms have lower costs of capital and higher price-earnings multiples and market values.[7]

In addition, increased interest in reputational risk is attributed to two other factors. First, increased awareness and a shift from a shareholder-centered governance model to a stakeholder-centered model is expanding the role and commitment of stakeholders. For example, a business's reputation can influence the consumers' willingness to buy the product or service, the suppliers' willingness to partner with the business, the regulators' attitude towards the firm, or the stakeholders' willingness to give the firm the benefit of the doubt when a problem or crisis occurs.[8] Second, with increased globalization and competition, reputation often becomes a distinguishing factor in giving an edge to a product or service.

In identifying reputation as a set of external and internal factors affecting the company and comprising its image, it is important to define what causes and constitutes an exposure to such a reputation. A simple definition of reputational risk is failure to meet stakeholders' reasonable expectations of an organization's performance and behavior.[9] In a broad sense, the concept of reputational risk covers the range of risks that rise from: the company's relationships, its brand name, operational failures in products and services; a failure to comply with relevant laws; and damage to the organization's credibility and reputation which threatens long-term trust with the stakeholders such as customers, employees, shareholders, the regulatory bodies, and suppliers.[10] For a service organization, it can mean failure of delivering its service commitments, including inadequately meeting customer needs or expectations, unreliable or inefficient delivery systems, untimely responses to customer inquiries, or violation of customer privacy.[11]

In the case of the financial services industry, reputation is considered a zero tolerance risk because trust and confidence are the basis of a firm's reputation.[12] Reputation is very much interlocked with issues such as ethics, values, corporate governance, leadership, behavior, commitment, relationships, the social context, and how stakeholders' attitudes, experiences, feelings and expectations ultimately affect the corporate reputation.

Corporate reputation has certain features that distinguish it from other corporate assets. Rayner (2003) discusses seven drivers of corporate reputations:

- Financial performance and long-term investment value
- Corporate governance and leadership
- Regulatory compliance
- Delivering customer promise

- Workplace talent and culture
- Corporate social responsibility
- Communications and crisis management

There are other features of corporate reputation which are worth noting, such as those listed below.

6.1.1 Reputation Develops Over Time Through Repeated Interactions

Reputation is closely linked with the perception of past and present experiences of the stakeholders in terms of their expectations and the corporate response to such expectations. Reputation also depends on the consistency and quality of the product and the service over a period of time. A company's overall reputation is a function of its reputation among its various stakeholders (investors, customers, suppliers, employees, regulators, politicians, nongovernmental organizations, the communities in which the firm operates) in specific categories (product quality, corporate governance, employee relations, customer service, intellectual capital, financial performance, handling of environmental and social issues). A strong positive reputation among stakeholders across multiple categories will result in a strong positive reputation for the company overall.[13]

6.1.2 The Customer is Central to Understanding Reputation

Among all the stakeholders, customers matter the most for corporate reputation and are central to understanding reputation and managing reputational risk. Reputation is directly related to the customers' perceptions, feelings, memories, attitudes, and expectations—both positive and negative. In the long term, image and brand are sustained by things such as empathy with customers' needs, reliability, and quality, which help to make the overall relationship experience something to be valued.[14]

6.1.3 Exposure to Reputation is Often Triggered by an Externality

Reputation is often regarded as a secondary effect because it is considered only after certain events occur. For example, lack of a prompt response or ill-management of a crisis situation can lead to long-term damage to reputation. Similarly, slow response to corporate social responsibility, unfair employment practices, lapses in governance, or a breach of security can lead to the formation of an unfriendly image or perceptions.[15]

6.1.4 Reputation is Driven by "Reputational Agents"[16]

According to the World Bank, key stakeholders serve as "reputational agents" who keep an eye on the companies. Such reputational agents include accounting and auditing professionals, lawyers, investment bankers and analysts, credit-rating agencies, customer activists, environmentalists, and the media. Observing corporate performance and insider behavior, these reputational agents can exert pressure on companies to disclose relevant information, improve human capital, recognize the interests of outsiders, and otherwise behave as good corporate citizens. They can also put pressure on government through their influence over public opinion.

6.1.5 Corporate Reputation is Socially Determined[17]

Reputations are often built and communicated throughout social networks. These social networks consist of loosely connected members who share common values, objectives, and interests. Corporate reputation can be destroyed by a social group's activism when the corporate behavior violates their expected behavior or breaches the trust developed between the corporation and the group.

Since reputation is linked with expectations and social values, reputational risk arises when there is a gap between the corporate behavior and the expectations of the stakeholders. The larger this gap is, the larger the exposure is to reputational risk. Some businesses may be more sensitive to social expectations, identified as appropriate and inappropriate actions, which, in turn, are driven by values imbedded in society. Basic values dealing with lying, cheating, stealing, trust, honor, and what is "right" and what is "wrong" are universally acceptable. These are the *ultimate* benchmarks against which conduct is measured and can be the origins of key reputational losses.[18]

Out of all the values that contribute to building reputation, trust is the most significant, especially for institutions offering financial products and services. Given the critical role the notion of trust plays in reputation building, it is important to further understand the link between trust and reputation. First, trust is concerned with stakeholder expectations about how a business will behave in the future (that is, expectations about a business honoring its implicit and explicit commitments). Second, once trust is established, it ensures that the stakeholder will neither be coerced nor taken advantage of. Third, during a crisis the business will communicate openly, honestly, transparently, and in a timely manner. Fourth, negative (trust-destroying) events such as errors and mismanagement are more visible and noticeable than positive (trust-building) events which are usually vague. Unfortunately, the sources of negative (trust-destroying) publicity tend to be seen as more credible than sources of positive publicity. Finally, trust between a corporation and its stakeholders is built gradually over a long period of time, and once established ensures the dependability and reliability of the relationship. Conversely, distrust tends to reinforce and perpetuate itself because it inhibits the factors necessary to build trust (that is, personal contacts and experiences).[19]

Reputation and trust are built upon a form of "social capital"—an emerging idea that is also considered as a key building block in understanding reputational risk.[20] Social capital is a web of social networks that influences individual behavior and is embedded in the relationships that the company has established with its stakeholders. Reputation reflects social capital because it mobilizes others to act. The size of social networks is also important in relaying and spreading recognition about a firm's reputation.

6.2 WHY IT MATTERS FOR THE ISLAMIC FINANCIAL INDUSTRY

Reputation is an especially valuable asset for the Islamic financial industry due to the specialized nature of its undertakings to attract customers and stakeholders. Not only is the management of an institution engaged in providing *Shari'ah*-compliant financial products and services subject to similar fiduciary responsibilities as its conventional counterpart, but they also carry additional responsibilities as defined by *Shari'ah*. There is a sense of sacredness to this responsibility which needs to be preserved. For example, a depositor in an Islamic bank not only expects that his or her funds are protected and earn prevailing market returns, but he or she also expects that the institution does so in a manner which also fulfills his or her religious duty through the preservation of the principles and tenets of Islam. An explicit or implicit commitment by the institution to preserve the values dear to the customer brings additional responsibilities upon the management, and any distortion to this commitment is a source of irreversible reputation risk.

Another distinct feature of reputation for the Islamic financial industry is that the reputation of the whole industry is at stake due to the reputation of any member of the industry. Increased globalization and competition, a financial landscape sensitive to good governance standards, a high degree of integration in financial systems, and greater efforts to attract conventional borrowers and investors magnify reputational damages. These damages are devastating because they do not solely destroy a single institution but can bring the whole industry into disrepute, which could be devastating for an industry that is still trying to establish itself at a global level.

Given that the reputation of an institution is directly linked to the "expected behavior" of an institution in relation to its stakeholders, such expected behavior can be best understood in the light of Islam's principles on contracts, property rights, trust, and the principles of governance. These principles will determine the true character of an institution, and any deviation from these principles will expose the institution and the industry to reputational risk.

6.2.1 Sanctity of Contracts

Islam places great importance on contracts and expects the believers to make strong commitments to contracts. In several verses, the believers are asked to be faithful to contracts (5:1; 2:282, 288; 4:33; 6:151–153; 9:4; 16:91–94; 17:34–36; 23:1–8). The *Qur'an* puts the fulfilment of contracts close to the highest achievements and noblest virtues of a believer (2:172). The notion of the observance and faithfulness to the terms of contract lays the foundation for defining a complex but a balanced relationship between the Creator and His created order, individuals, community, society and the state. This foundation further defines the framework to determine the rights and obligations of economic agents and the stakeholders and thus leads to the development of a theory of governance. By understanding the significance of the sanctity of contracts, one can define the framework of expected behavior of managers, employees, rulers, and other stakeholders. When each party entering into the contract exhibits explicitly or implicitly a forthright intention to remain loyal to performing the obligations specified by the terms of contract, it leads to an element of trust which minimizes the possibility of willful misconduct and negligence. With strong commitment to contracts, a sound governance framework is put in place where the managers are fully conscious of their obligations and commitments to their contracts. Same principles of contracts and governance are applicable to public law contracts and international law treaties.

6.2.2 The Preservation of Property Rights

Shari'ah offers a comprehensive framework to identify, recognize, respect, and protect the rights of every individual in creation, community, society, and the state. The importance of being conscious and mindful of the rights of others (including stakeholders—human or non-human) and the significance of discharging the responsibilities associated with such rights is reflected by the following saying of the Prophet (pbuh):[21]

> So give to everyone who possesses a right his right (*kull dhi haqin haquhu*).

The term right (*haq*) denotes something that can be justly claimed, or the interests and claims that people may have been granted by *Shari'ah*. The majority of *Shari'ah* scholars and jurists hold that rights are a property (*al mal*) because—like physical property, which has beneficial uses and can be possessed—rights have beneficial uses and are regarded as capable of being possessed.[22] Rules defining property rights in Islam deal with the rights of ownership, acquisition, usage, and disposition of property. Any violation of these rules is considered a transgression and leads to the disruption of social order. Finally, inclusion (or exclusion) and recognition (or denial) of the rights of stakeholders in an Islamic economic system are based on a foundation of rules and laws, which do not need justification merely on the grounds of morality, but are derived from principles aimed at creating a balance in the economic and social system.

Concomitant with property rights, the *Shari'ah* imposes responsibilities, among which are the obligations—severely incumbent upon the individual—not to waste, destroy, squander, or to use the property for purposes not permitted by the *Shari'ah*.[23] To do so would be to transgress the limits set on one's right and an encroachment on the rights of others. The right of the collectivity to the property is further protected by the *Shari'ah* through the limitations imposed on the right of disposition of the property by the person who has gained priority in the use and enjoyment of that property. Hence, while the right of use and enjoyment of the property is affirmed by the *Shari'ah*, the exclusive and absolute right of disposition of the property is rejected.[24]

The prohibition of *israf* (waste) and *tabdhir* (squandering) in all areas applies to property as well. The individual may not make an alteration in his property that may harm his neighbor. If the property owner proves his inability to use the property properly (within boundaries defined by the *Shari'ah*), he forfeits his ownership rights. Under such conditions, the legitimate authority is fully justified in withdrawing the rights of usage of that property in order to protect it from the misuses by the owner.[25] This position of the *Shari'ah* is in conformity with the Islamic conception of justice (*al-adl* and *al-ihsan*) and the rights and responsibilities of the individual and the community.

6.2.3 Trust

The *Qur'an* establishes human beings as the *khalifah* or trustees of God on earth, and life is a test of the worth of men in the eyes of God (67:2). The divinely mandated command of faithfulness to the terms and conditions of contracts and abiding by their obligations is undergirded by the equally strong and divinely originated institution of trust.[26] There is strong interdependence between contract and trust; without the latter, contracts become difficult to enter into and costly to monitor and enforce. Laws and expensive administrative apparatuses are needed to enforce contracts when and where trust is weak. Perhaps trust is emphasized to make entering into and enforcing contracts less costly. Accordingly, numerous verses in the *Qur'an* proclaim trustworthiness as a sign of true belief. These verses insist that human beings remain fully conscious of the obligation of ensuring trust in fulfilling the terms and conditions of contracts before entering into them. Conversely untrustworthiness and betrayal of trust are considered a clear sign of disbelief.[27]

Several verses of the *Qur'an* directly and indirectly emphasize the significance of honoring trust. For example, in verses 4:58 ("*BEHOLD, God bids you to deliver all that you have been entrusted with unto those who are entitled thereto, and whenever you judge between people, to judge with justice.*") "*God commands you to deliver trust back to their owners and, humans*" are reminded that trust belongs to the owner and justice requires that the trust is delivered back to the owner as a sacred duty. In verse 8:27 ("*... O you who have attained to faith, do not be false to God and the Apostle, and do not knowingly be false to the trust that has been reposed in you ...*"), believers are reminded that the one who believes should be watchful not to knowingly act in a manner that can betray the trust reposed in him or her. This is further reinforced by verses 22:38 ("... *verily, God does not love anyone who betrays his trust and is bereft of gratitude* ...") and 12:52 ("*God does not bless with His guidance the artful schemes of those who betray their trust*") where a stern warning is given that betrayal of trust amounts to losing God's favors. Finally, verses 23:8 ("... *and who are faithful to their trusts and to their pledges* ...") and 70:32 ("... *and who are faithful to their trusts and to their pledges* ...") define the characteristics of true believers (*al-mu'minun*) as trustworthy and people who make strong commitments to their promises and pledges.

Moreover, the *Qur'an* makes clear that fulfilling the obligations of a contract or a promise is mandatory. In short, the *Qur'an* makes trust and trustworthiness, as well as keeping faith with contracts and promises, obligatory and has rendered them inviolable except in the event of an explicitly permissible justification.[28] In addition, there are numerous prophetic sayings that supplement the Qur'anic verses on trust. For example, it is reported that the Prophet (pbuh) was asked: who is a believer? He replied: "a believer is a person to whom people can trust their person and possession."[29] It is also reported that he said: "the person who is not trustworthy has no faith, and the person who breaks his promise has no religion." Also, "keeping promises is a sign of faith."

6.2.4 High Standards of Ethics and a Code of Conduct

Islam demands high standards of ethical behavior from everyone in society, but stresses these standards on those who govern or represent others in society. Within the framework of economic justice, emphasis is placed on being mindful of giving full measure and weight in all business transactions. When this principle is understood in the light of principles of property rights, it establishes an important business rule that full measure and weight is not limited to physical quantities but is equally applicable to measuring intangible rights and obligations. In other words, it is the responsibility of the one who is in charge of others property—tangible or intangible, financial or nonfinancial, explicit or implicit—to ensure that all obligations are accounted for with great care and all claims and rights are returned in full to the one who deserves it.

The verses 83:1–3 ("*Woe unto those who give short measure, those who, when they are to receive their due from [other] people, demand that it be given in full but when they have to measure or weigh whatever they owe to others, give less than what is due!*") remind individuals against any negligence or cheating in determining what one owes to others. These verses refer not only to commercial dealings but encompass every aspect of social relations, both practical and moral, applying to every individual's rights and obligations no less than to his physical possessions.[30]

Allah (*swt*) considers those who keep their promises pious and commands all to be true to their promises. Verses 2:177 ("... *and [truly pious are] they who keep their promises whenever they promise* ...") and 17:34 ("... *And be true to every promise* ...") testify to the significance of keeping promises. The *Qur'an* stresses the importance of one's promises and pledges when *Allah* (*swt*) warns people that any gain earned at the cost of not fulfilling promises will be of no value in His eyes. Verses 3:77 ("*Behold, those who barter away their bond with God and their own pledges for a trifling gain—they shall not partake in the blessings of the life to come; and God will neither speak unto them nor look upon them on the Day of Resurrection, nor will He cleanse them of their sins;*") and 16:95 ("*Hence, do not barter away your bond with God for a trifling gain! Verily, that which is with God is by far the best for you, if you but knew it:*") testify grave consequences of not being faithful to one's promises and pledges.

The reputation of an entity—individual or corporation—is determined by the expectations of the stakeholders. These expectations are, in turn, formed on the basis of past experiences and the perception of that entity's commitment to its promises. Any agent or manager who makes false promises or is unable to keep his or her promises will certainly deviate from the expected behavior of a believer. This notion places high responsibility on managers to take all measures to ensure that through their conduct and behavior they fully comply with their promises and expectations of their stakeholders.

6.2.5 Stakeholder-Oriented Governance

Other than the above, there are other individual and collective behavioral rules and norms that strengthen the governance structure of the state and firms, including transparency, accountability, voice, and representation. Nevertheless, the three basic institutions—property rights, contracts, and trust—give a flavor of the strength of governance in Islam. The rule of Qur'anic Law governs the behavior of state rulers no less stringently than those of individuals. These legal experts also assert that, based on their consideration of Islamic legal texts, the command of observing contracts and covenants faithfully "apply to the ruler acting in a public capacity" just as severely as to individuals. "Indeed, when considerations of expediency and public interests are taken into account, they apply even with greater force to the actions of the ruler." Therefore, a breech of faith on the part of a ruler is more heinous in its nature and serious in its consequence than of individuals.

The same principles of governance under which a ruler or a state should function apply also to firms. Iqbal and Mirakhor (2005) argue that within the Islamic framework a firm can be viewed as a "nexus of contracts" whose objective is to minimize transaction costs and maximize profits and returns to investors, subject to the constraints that these objectives do not violate the property rights of any party whether it interacts with the firm directly or indirectly. In pursuit of these goals, the firm honors all implicit or explicit contractual obligations. As could be discerned from the discussions on contracts and trust, it is incumbent on individuals to preserve the sanctity of implicit contractual obligations no less than those of explicit contracts. By the same token, firms have to preserve the sanctity of implicit and explicit contractual obligations by recognizing and protecting the property rights of stakeholders, community, society, and state. Since the firm's behavior is shaped by that of its managers, it becomes their fiduciary duty to manage the firm as a trust for all stakeholders in ensuring that the behavior of the firm conforms to the rules and norms specified by the Law.[31]

The aforementioned principles define the social norms in Islam which determine the expected behavior of individuals and institutions and establish a set of socially approved values. While the values and respective expectations in a given society may shift or change with the passage of time, Islamic values are inviolable at all times. Therefore, these values set a benchmark against which the behavior of individuals and institutions will be expected and judged.

To summarize, the reputation of a financial institution in the Islamic system will be at stake if it fails to meet the expectations of the stakeholders because:

- The financial institution has entered into a contract with its stakeholders that it will conduct its business according to the spirit of *Shari'ah* and will, therefore, be required to fulfill its obligation to the best of its abilities. In addition, the institution has made an implicit contract to ensure that no violation of

Shari'ah principles occurs. Anytime the institution fails to meet this explicit and implicit contractual obligation, or is guilty of breach of contract, the stakeholder will refuse to continue doing business with it.

- The financial institution is subject to higher standards of preserving the property rights of the stakeholders and makes sure that it does not withhold anyone's rights, willingly or unwillingly. For example, if an institution is engaged in a practice where the rights of one stakeholder, such as depositors, are violated to benefit another stakeholder, such as the owner, the institution would be guilty of failing to preserve rights and, therefore, will be subject to risking its reputation.
- By conducting business with the financial institutions, a stakeholder—especially the customer—has placed a *sacred trust* in the institution and expects the institution to be faithful to this trust and its promises. A breach of this trust or violation of this trust will greatly affect the image of the institution and therefore the reputation.

6.3 CASE STUDIES

Although there has not been a major failure of an Islamic bank in more than 30 years of history, there have been instances of failures of financial institutions claiming to offer Islamic financial products. A review of the causes leading to their failure can shed light on how such failure impacted on other institutions offering similar products and services, could have been avoided, and can be used to learn lessons for other institutions.

6.3.1 Ihlas Finans of Turkey[32]

Ihlas Finans was a Turkish institution that behaved similarly to a deposit-taking bank offering *Shari'ah*-compliant financial services. These financial houses were not recognized as part of the regular banking sector but were given the status of Special Finance Houses (SFHs) as they were considered to be offering nonconventional and specialized services. SFHs constituted only 3.1 percent of the total banking sector deposits, and their investment allocations were only 4.7 percent of the total banking sector investment allocations. Due to being SFHs, these institutions were not subject to the same regulations as other institutions in the banking sector.

During early 2000, the Turkish financial sector went through a macroeconomic and financial crisis which impacted the entire banking sector, including SFHs. As a result, some conventional banks failed, but among five SFHs engaged in Islamic finance, Ihlas Finans was the only one that could not survive. Ihlas Finans was a subsidiary of Ihlas Holding, established in the 1970s as a social-oriented business organization and eventually growing into a large holding company with its core business in construction, healthcare, and education, and having a number of subsidiary businesses ranging from manufacturers of household appliances, to news media, to financial services and insurance of various kinds. Ihlas Finans was one of its subsidiaries, started in 1995 with the objective of providing interest-free investment opportunities to investors and small savers. Registered under the category of Special Finance House with the Central Bank of Turkey, it grew into the largest of its class. The size of its balance sheet assets had grown from US$17 million in 1995 to US$1,173 million by 1999.[33] Ihlas Finans held a majority market share (40 percent) among all SFHs offering Islamic products.

Ihlas Finans faced a run on its deposits in the wake of the banking crisis that developed in Turkey between the last quarter of 2000 and early 2001. The Banking Regulation and Supervision Agency (BRSA) intervened and cancelled the license of Ihlas Finans on February 10, 2001. The 200,000 depositors of Ihlas Finans were reportedly "wandering hopelessly" outside of the firm's branches in various parts of the country, unsure what had become of their deposits. The BRSA cited several reasons for this action. First, the BRSA announced that Ihlas Finans had irregularly appropriated almost US$1 billion (practically the entire value of the deposits) through connected lending to shareholders.[34] Second, BSRA considered Ihlas Finans unable to keep its promises and obligations to the public and, therefore, to be in violation of banking rules. Third, there were irregularities as Ihlas had made substantial investments in its subsidiaries and with the agents of its subsidiaries.

A detailed analysis of the case of Ihlas Finans—as conducted by Salman S. Ali (2007)—highlights several factors for the failure of the institution and holds several stakeholders and deteriorating market conditions responsible for this failure. There was clear evidence of carelessness from the regulators and supervisors, who were unable to detect the warning signs in time. However, for the sake of our subject of reputation, we will primarily focus on those factors where the management of Ihlas Finans was directly responsible for the negligence and where the *trust* of the stakeholders was breached through misrepresentation. It is important to understand the implications of these factors since they were the source of considerable concern for the depositors of other SFHs and to the reputation of the industry in the country. These factors are summarized below.[35]

6.3.1.1 Weak Governance Structure

It appears that Ihlas Finans was not following the best practices in corporate governance. For example, it is reported that the members of the Board of Directors showed a lax attitude towards governance and some members appointed to the board did not have the requisite experience. Since Ihlas Finans was a subsidiary of a large holding company, some of its board members represented multiple boards, which resulted in a conflict of interests.

6.3.1.2 Fraudulent Practices

It appears that Ihlas Finans tried to conceal its financial and managerial failures by indulging in fraudulent practices. For example, it was discovered that some of the agency (*mudarabah*) financing was done in the name of fictitious parties while the funds were in fact used for concealing internal financial problems.

6.3.1.3 Lack of Risk-Management Culture

There were serious flaws in the risk-management framework of Ihlas Finans. Credit was extended to finance other businesses in sibling holding companies and some of the clients became heavily dependent on Ihlas as a source of funding, thus increasing exposure to credit risk. The depositors' funds were used to finance several businesses of Ihlas Holding which in turn placed the funds in highly illiquid projects such as construction. Even though these projects were profitable ventures, they led to increased liquidity risk for Ihlas Finans and are cited as one of the primary reasons for its failure. It is evident that Ihlas Finans lacked a crisis management plan, and decision-making during the crisis was ad hoc and uncoordinated internally and externally.

6.3.1.4 Management Failure

It appears that the management of Ihlas Finans did not follow the best practices in management and did not act in good faith. A serious allegation was that Ihlas Finans was ignorant in the hiring and selection process and hired a senior executive from a previously failed bank who came under scrutiny by BRSA in connection with a then ongoing investigation of the failed bank. During the financial crisis, this news further fuelled customers' concerns and damaged their confidence. Furthermore, the management was slow in responding to the changing legal and regulatory environment. Finally, the management demonstrated poor judgment during the crisis by ignoring the severity of the problem during the early phases of the crisis. For example, while other SFHs were able to convince the depositors to hold on to their withdrawal requests to avoid the liquidity crunch, Ihlas Finans lost more than US$200 million worth of the most liquid assets by paying for the depositors' demands before hitting the liquidity crunch. As a result, withdrawal requests increased, which ultimately placed pressure on the BSRA to close down the institution.

The closure of Ihlas Finans put immediate pressure on the other SFHs, and the reputation of other SFHs was put at stake. The depositors immediately became concerned with Ihlas Finans's tainted reputation and became suspicious of the credibility and authenticity of other SFHs. Although there were valid reasons for the depositors to be concerned about the safety of their funds in the SFHs, their sense of urgency for withdrawing their money was unwarranted and was caused by the poor reputation of Ihlas Finans. But as details of the case against Ihlas Finans were released, it became clear that it had committed substantial wrongdoing and the problem was isolated to this institution.

The deteriorating reputation of Ihlas Finans immediately forced other SFHs to proactively repair the reputation of the whole industry. The Association of Special Finance Houses highlighted that the troubles of Ihlas Finans were the result of its irregular and illegal use of funds, and that no such charges had been leveled against any of the other houses. The remaining houses took out newspaper advertisements emphasizing that the situation of Ihlas Finans in no way reflected their own circumstances. It was also stressed that the Special Finance Houses had always met their obligations, without help from the state, even in the heavy withdrawals of the 2000 liquidity crunch.[36]

6.3.2 The Islamic Bank of South Africa

The Islamic Bank of South Africa (IBSA) failed in November 1997 with debts of between R50 million and R70 million. The primary depositor base of IBSA consisted of small depositors, mostly Muslims who saw the IBSA as a community bank and deposited their money to make the *Hajj* pilgrimage to Mecca. Okeahalam (1998) conducted an analysis of its failure and the role of the supervisors, and concluded that bad management and improper accounting and management systems caused the bank to fail. Allegedly, a large amount of insider unsecured lending took place, which resulted in a large proportion of nonperforming assets in the balance sheet. The study found that the management of IBSA hid behind the self-regulatory position accorded to true Islamic banks but IBSA abused this special trust. The regulators should have been more cautious.[37]

Further details of the causes of failure are found in van Greuning (2005), who makes the following observations:

- IBSA claimed to share profits and losses with ratios of 66 percent for the investor and 33 percent for the bank. However, as opposed to this agreement, the bank paid 11–13 percent return regardless of actual profits or losses, which created a false image about the health of the institution to the potential investors. The bank was to provide a monthly P&L statement, something that was never done. Distribution of profits and losses was at the discretion of the CEO with no records to back up.
- It was discovered that numerous loans were made to the directors. There was evidence of connected lending, self-dealing, and insider lending through an overextension of credit to directors and large shareholders, or to their interests. Forty percent of nonperforming loans had never paid anything since the origination of the loan. Twenty-seven percent of loans were to insiders.
- Shareholders did not pay in their capital (capital was immediately lent back to the shareholders), so the "cash" received was converted into a loan. Accordingly, there was a negative impact for depositors since they had no "buffer" against their losses. One shareholder had more than 15 percent control and hid his stake through front companies.
- There were no risk committees to assist the board; thus, management and decision-making were performed within an extremely informal framework. Banking law was also breached because audit committees and internal audits did not exist. Banking law also required directors to be "fit and proper"

and understand the "business of banking and banking risks"; however, the liquidator did not find this to be true as there were no risk-management systems in existence. Furthermore, credit information was incomplete since the purpose of borrowing and the intended plan and source of repayment were not specified.

- Since the CEO had to approve all communications to others, the quality of information to the board and to the supervisory authority was not only poor but was also fraudulent. The bank reported profits to the supervisors while there were only losses.
- There was a lack of adequate supervision of familiar borrowers, dependence on oral information rather than reliable and complete financial data, and ignorance of warning signs regarding the borrowers, economy, region, and industry. IBSA also lacked knowledge about borrowers' affairs over the lifetime of their loans and lacked the technical ability to analyze financial statements and obtain and evaluate pertinent credit information.
- IBSA included debit balances in deposits, which contravened banking regulations and understated liabilities to the public, thus misleading the public as well as the authorities.

The case study of IBSA clearly shows that the bank was not following the practices of basic banking. The management was guilty of misrepresentation and indulging in unethical practices, which resulted in distortion of information and lack of transparency. Assuming that the bank would impose the discipline of self-regulation, the regulators trusted the management of the bank and did not prudently supervise. Consequently, this trust was breached when detailed investigation revealed the wrongdoing of the institution. This resulted in a tainted reputation for not only IBSA, but also strengthened the regulators' suspicion and prejudice towards other Islamic institutions.

6.3.3 Islamic Investment Companies of Egypt[38]

Some investment companies caught the attention of regulators and the media in Egypt in the years 1985 to 1988. These investment companies began operations in the 1980s and were based on a profit-sharing principle (*sharikat tawzif al-amwal*), accepting deposits from the public and investing funds in *Shari'ah*-compatible modes. During 1985 and 1986 these companies attracted the attention of investors when they started to offer high rates of returns (20–30 percent), claimed as profits. By the end of 1986, there were 190 registered companies concerning private investment and operations, and 90 nonregistered companies. These investment companies were able to attract a large number of depositors from all walks of life and, according to some estimates, by 1988 they managed about half a million customers with deposits of between 4.5 and 8 billion Egyptian pounds.

The rate of return offered was so attractive that money flew out of the banking sectors, and in some cases investors created arbitrage by borrowing from banks and investing in these companies. However, these companies were not subject to any regulation and supervision, and the operations of the companies lacked transparency. These investment companies were exposed in 1988 when the government decided to regulate the sector by fully disclosing accounts and the activities of investment companies. This regulation triggered the failure of several companies, resulting in the closure of a majority of investment companies. Here is a summary of the issues pertaining to this case study:

- It appears that the investment companies were not following *Shari'ah*-approved modes of investment, despite their claims. In some cases, companies were paying high returns by drawing on a continuing high level of deposits as opposed to actual profits.
- It was reported that investments were made in international currencies and financial markets which were of a speculative nature. When the prices collapsed in international markets in 1987, many investment companies suffered losses. A major portion of funds were invested in illiquid sectors of construction, tourism, housing, and book publications (mostly Islamic publications). Several investment companies maintained close business partnerships with other trading companies and managed a number of subsidiaries. In short, funds were used to internally finance businesses of subsidiaries and partner trading companies.
- In 1988, legislation was introduced to regulate these investment companies. This triggered a public debate, with the companies and their defenders vehemently opposed to any proposals for

regulation. With the introduction of the regulation, several companies froze payments to investors and many announced plans for liquidation which led to public confusion, loss of public confidence, and increased withdrawals. As a result, most of the investment companies were shut down.

- Official audit reports discovered many irregularities and funds unaccounted for, partly in complex transactions with subsidiaries. Authorities began the investigation of select investment companies for criminal charges.
- This episode of failed investment companies became a very interesting social issue as it sparked a debate between the defenders of investment companies who thought that the legislation was intended to discourage the spread of Islamic financial institutions and the Islamic economic ideas. On the other hand, the critics of investment companies took this opportunity to accuse Islamist factions in society. The result was a political struggle of ideas, without realizing that it was a simple case of bad governance and supervision, and lack of regulation.
- In short, the failure of investment companies in Egypt caused a considerable reputational risk to Islamic finance, and for several years this episode was quoted in discussions of Islamic finance. It clearly breached the trust of the investors who were cheated in the name of *Shari'ah*-compatible investments and damaged the reputation of Islamic finance for decades to come.

Several lessons can be learnt from these three case studies. First, the main cause of the failure in all three cases was irresponsible management and bad supervision and governance. Second, there were regulation and supervision lapses. There were improper regulatory frameworks, and in all cases the regulator failed to anticipate the trouble in time. Third, these financial institutions were clearly engaged in activities that were against the basic teachings of Islam on contracts, property rights, justice, trust, and honoring commitments. Fourth, in all cases, none of the Islamic financial instruments were questioned or were the cause of any concern. Finally, in all three cases, *significant reputational risk resulted and the stakeholders' confidence was seriously damaged.* The public's trust was broken, regulators became more suspicious and cautious, and opponent forces were given valid excuses to criticize even a legitimate effort to establish a financial institution compliant with *Shari'ah*.

6.4 MITIGATING REPUTATIONAL RISK

Given recent corporate scandals and executive misconduct, companies have become more sensitive to their reputation and thus to their reputational risk. More and more companies are realizing that once a company's reputation has been damaged or tainted, restoring public confidence is extremely challenging.[39] Although the concept of reputational risk is becoming the center of attention for most corporate executives, the concept is not easy to distinguish from other risks because of its complexity, which results from multiple sources across all business functions. As a result, corporate executives face the dilemma of identifying reputational risk as a separate risk requiring its own management or to assign it as a component of operational risk. Furthermore, most organizations currently do not manage their reputational risk in a manner that is systematic, effective, or allows them to form an overall assessment of the gross risk faced.[40]

Since reputational risk cannot be insured against, it needs to be tackled on multiple fronts, some of which are discussed below.

6.4.1 Corporate Behavior

Turnbull remains the most considered view on reputational risk within the policy arena.[41] Turnbull points out reputation as being all about corporate behavior. Companies need to acknowledge that risk assurance starts and ends with corporate behavior. A stakeholder-oriented society promoting corporate social responsibility (CSR) is forcing corporations to identify their key stakeholders and their respective needs. Therefore, it is critical that corporations maintain a relationship with all key stakeholders and exhibit mutual respect and trust to ensure that their expectations are understood, and that the company's objectives, strategy, plans, and performance are kept in alignment with the reasonable expectations of stakeholders.

Even if a corporation recognizes the importance of cultivating ethical behavior and monitoring and maintaining expectations, its implementation is more challenging. It is observed that corporations often have the tendency to overlook or, at best, minimally meet these requirements. There are many examples of companies where formal behavioral codes have been produced but there have been no serious attempts made to ensure compliance with them, nor to ensure that the underlying culture is consistent with the code.[42] Therefore, it is essential that the issue of reputational risk is taken up at the corporate level with serious steps to follow up.

6.4.2 A Framework and Process for Confronting Reputational Risk

Corporations need to develop a comprehensive framework for confronting reputational risk and need to design robust processes to manage this risk. As with any risk, one does not manage the risk itself, but takes measures to prevent the occurrences of events that can taint or damage the reputation. As the first step, a corporation needs to understand its reputation and make a realistic assessment of what is at stake and how serious this stake is. Since reputation is a function of the perception of corporate behavior by the stakeholders, an assessment of the "reputation reality gap" is necessary.[43]

Although it is difficult to quantify the exposure to reputational risk, a corporation can make subjective judgments with respect to the potential impact of such risk. Once an assessment is made, the reputational risk management process can be implemented in three steps. The first step is to identify the risks that have potential implications for the reputation. The second step is to determine the strategy to mitigate and manage if an event occurs. The strategy to manage reputational risk should be proactive rather than passive. Finally, it is necessary for the corporation to design an action plan. An action plan is a detailed timeline of sequential steps describing the response to a prospective threat to a company's reputation.[44]

6.4.3 Governance Framework

The importance of good governance, as evident from the case studies above, cannot be overemphasized. It is often argued that principles of good governance should be a component of every corporation's DNA. Effective governance is based on well-conceived bylaws and board policies, especially dealing with conflict-of-interest statements, which guide and restrict board members in ways that reduce the likelihood of such conflicts. Effective internal controls and procedures are essential for accurate and transparent financial reporting. The board should assume greater responsibility to monitor and prevent fraud. Audit committees have primary responsibility for reviewing and monitoring procedures transactions with trustees and employees, including conflicts of interest and transactions with affiliated entities.[45]

The quality of management is vital in the success or failure of any institution. The key role played by poor management in crises has also been highlighted by various academic studies. A sample of 24 systemic banking crises in emerging-market and developed countries found that deficient bank management and controls (in conjunction with other factors such as macroeconomic shocks) were responsible in all cases.[46] Similar observations can be made from the case studies where incompetent management failed to foresee problems and was actively involved in misconduct.

Implementation of a well-designed control and compliance framework is critical for any financial institution, and without first-class compliance financial institutions become vulnerable to reputational damage. Making compliance part of the enterprise-wide, risk-management framework is critical to success and the elimination of reputational risk. Therefore, it is essential that corporations establish a standard process for responding to allegations or suspicions of fraud or misconduct.[47]

6.4.4 The Role of the Regulators

Reputational risk has not been part of any systemic efforts by regulators and policymakers. For example, in 2004 the Committee of Sponsoring Organizations of the Treadway Commission (COSO) (a group of professional associations of U.S. accountants and financial executives that issues guidelines for internal controls) proposed a 135-page framework for enterprise risk management (ERM), which mentioned virtually every imaginable risk except for reputational risk. The Basel II international accord for regulating capital requirements for large international banks also failed to acknowledge reputational risk.[48]

One reason for regulators' disregard of reputational risk is the severity of the challenge it poses. First, it is highly subjective and difficult to quantify reputational risk. Second, compliance with an increasingly complex regulatory environment is a major undertaking requiring constant attention and expert resources. Nevertheless, it does not solve the problem and regulators still need to pay more attention to fraud and misconduct in financial institutions. Others have also argued that a market-discipline oriented solution should be also explored, which could be a complementary solution to regulation. It is argued that even in the absence of regulatory constraints, actions that are widely considered to be "unfair" or "unethical" will tend to be subject to market discipline through reputational impacts. Moreover, just as market discipline can reinforce the effectiveness of regulation, it can also serve as a precursor of sensible regulatory change.[49]

6.4.5 The Role of Stakeholders

Stakeholders' perceptions and expectations are key to reputational risk Therefore, careful management of such perceptions and expectations is necessary. Among stakeholders of financial institutions, customers are the most vital. Customers react very strongly to any perception of being cheated, sold a "false promise," misled, misrepresented, overcharged, or taken for granted. When one looks at some of the highest profile losses of reputation in recent years they reveal certain basic customer expectations that were not satisfied.[50]

Similarly, other stakeholders—including employees, business partners, suppliers, and auditors—need assurance that all dealings are done transparently, fairly, and without any exploitation. The customers expect the company to manage its partnership relationships properly, and in the event of failure the management will ultimately be held responsible for not performing their duty. On their part, the stakeholders need to act as reputation agents and keep a close eye on the corporation's actions, relationships, and dealings through formal and informal checks. An early warning can prevent a greater loss of reputation and subsequently financial loss.

6.5 POLICY RECOMMENDATIONS FOR THE ISLAMIC FINANCIAL INDUSTRY

The Islamic financial industry is relatively young but is growing at a fast pace. During high-growth periods, financial institutions often pay less attention to subtle risks such as reputational risk. Islamic financial institutions need to take this risk more seriously, because of the special nature of their business that carries a sacred trust between them and their clients to comply with religious beliefs. Our case studies have shown how misconduct by a few institutions taints the image of the entire industry and has a long-lasting impact on the function of fellow institutions. The following policy recommendations are made to mitigate reputational risk.

6.5.1 Develop Awareness at Macro- and Micro-Level

In the case of Islamic financial institutions, reputational risk is not a matter of any one institution but should be viewed as a risk exposing all institutions offering similar products and services. Therefore, it is necessary that collective action be taken by the stakeholders to assess, avoid, mitigate, and manage reputational risk at the institution and at the industry level. This requires the development of a mutual and self-regulatory style support system. It is often said that reputational risk should not be managed but should be treated as a case of crisis management. The Islamic financial industry needs to develop plans for such crises management in case their reputation is put at stake as the result of the misconduct of a few institutions. An ongoing reputational risk assessment can ensure that an institution's good name is not only protected, but is enhanced.[51]

6.5.2 Understand What Your Reputation is Worth

Islamic financial institutions—both individually and collectively—need to make a realistic assessment of the value of their reputation. Instead of quantifying the exposure, efforts should be made to understand the sources, causes, and implications of risks both in financial and nonfinancial terms. A better understanding of the nature of the risk will help in combating the risk and in designing a mitigating strategy. Given the nature of the risk, this assessment should be on a pre-emptive basis rather than an after-the-fact exercise. Responsibility for the reputational risk management process must be clearly assigned to a competent senior executive who is accountable for establishing a plan.

6.5.3 Strengthen Good Governance

There is no substitute for good governance. Starting from the selection of board members to the design of effective control procedures to financial reporting and transparent disclosure, the design of sound governance should be given priority.[52] The quality of management should be kept high through hiring competent and skilled managers. Given that a corporation is a legal entity, the conduct and behavior of the managers represents the behavior of the intangible personality of the corporation. In Islam, individual responsibility replaces corporate responsibility, and as such Muslims do not look to companies to act in a responsible way but rather to the individuals who comprise the company.[53] Therefore, the management should follow the best practices to ensure that they fulfill the important duty of carrying the "trust" placed in the corporation by the depositors and other stakeholders.

In addition to following good governance principles applicable to all financial institutions irrespective of being conventional or Islamic, Islamic financial institutions need to pay special attention to a certain area.[54] Islamic financial institutions are often characterized with a low degree of financial and fiscal transparency. Since open access to financial operations fosters the trust and confidence of stakeholders, efforts should be made to enhance reports and disclosures of financial statements. This transparency is especially relevant in matters relating to the determination and the distribution of profits and losses to investors (depositors). Similarly, Islamic financial institutions are often perceived as having a high level of operational risk. Therefore, attention should be paid in implementing robust key controls and monitoring mechanisms, including the enhanced role of internal auditors, proper documentation, segregation of duties, and appropriate fraud prevention and detection controls.

6.5.4 The Role of *Shari'ah* Boards

Shari'ah boards play a critical role in ensuring that the institution's behavior is in accordance with the principles of Islam and that the institution does not engage in any activity, product, or service that is in violation of the spirit of *Shari'ah*. This is an enormous undertaking and requires active and vigilant involvement. In this respect, the *Shari'ah* board should pay careful attention not only to the contracts and the design of a product but to its actual implementation as well. Several suggestions have been made to enhance the effectiveness of *Shari'ah* boards. For example, it is suggested that the quality of an institution's compliance with the *Shari'ah* should be rated by independent agencies similar to credit-rating agencies. Additionally, *Shari'ah* audits should be established to audit the operations of *Shari'ah* boards. These ideas should be given serious consideration since these measures will enhance the transparency of *Shari'ah* boards, minimize any errors or misconducts, and increase the trust of stakeholders, thus reducing the reputational risk of the institution.

6.5.5 The Role of Stakeholders

Due to the nature of financial intermediation by Islamic financial institutions, partnerships with entrepreneurs are formed on the asset side. By design, the system encourages profit-and-loss-sharing contracts such as *mudarabah* and *musharakah* partnerships to invest depositors' funds. This exposes the institution to the reputation of business partners. For example, if an Islamic bank forms a partnership with a business partner who is found to be involved in unethical practices, the reputation of the financial institution will be at stake. Similar situations can occur with other stakeholders, and it is, therefore, important that financial institutions undertake additional steps to screen business partners before engaging with them. However, the responsibility of the financial institution does not end at this screening stage; the management should devise proper procedures to monitor the ongoing conduct of its business partners.

Employees of a financial institution are critical stakeholders and their conduct and practices can expose the institution to reputational risk. Employees committed to the cause and mission of the institution develop a positive image of the institution and, therefore, decrease reputational risk. The management of Islamic financial institutions should focus on developing training for the employees to understand the sensitivities of the stakeholders. The management should also encourage open and transparent work environment policies such as implementing a whistleblower policy and creating a system conducive to upward feedback.

6.5.6 Proactive Risk Management

One important lesson from the case studies is that the failed institutions did not follow good practices of risk mitigation and risk management. Advancement in risk-management techniques, especially of operational risk in conventional financial markets, is equally applicable to Islamic financial institutions' risk management.[55] For example, liquidity management is one area of concern for Islamic financial institutions due to the lack of *Shari'ah*-compatible marketable securities and the limited role of a lender of last resort. Liquidity often becomes the first issue that raises a red flag with the depositors of institutions at risk. In addition, existence of effective compliance monitoring is mandatory to mitigate any risk before it gets out of hand and it is too late to repair the damage.[56]

Islamic financial institutions should be proactive in designing and implementing an enterprise-wide, risk-management framework that also incorporates plans for combating reputational risk. It is observed that many companies rely too much on retrospective action—that is, post-event crisis management and damage limitation, such as through public relations—rather than seeking to prevent reputational damage in the first place. A proactive risk management approach should involve identifying reputational risk issues before they occur.[57]

6.5.7 The Importance of Clear Communications

Communication with all stakeholders who are affected by the way a company performs is vital. Communication with customers, employees, and shareholders needs to be seen as inherently dynamic, constantly evolving, and visibly built on mutual respect and trust. Nothing less will do.

ENDNOTES

1 This statement is attributed to Warren Buffett as quoted in Rayner. Rayner, Jenny, *Managing Reputational Risk: Curbing Threats, Leveraging Opportunities*, Institute of Internal Auditors Risk Management Series, (Chichester: John Wiley & Sons, 2003).
2 Continuity Central. "Financial Institutions see Reputational Risk as the Greatest Threat," (2004) http://www.continuitycentral.com/news01427.htm.
3 Godwin, Michael and Irma Freese, "Banks Zero in on Reputational Risk," *CA Magazines*, (2005). http://www.camagazine.com/2/7/6/1/0/index1.shtml.
4 It's worth noting that—to date—no major Islamic bank has been conclusively linked to terrorists or terrorist activities; Mahmoud Kassem and Anita Greil, Dow Jones Newswires, "Islamic Banking Reputation Suffers in Wake of Sept. 11," *WSJ*, (November 6, 2001).
5 Kovářík, and Tomáš Pavel Nevický, *Reputational Risk Management and Reputational Capital*, (DTTI, 2007). http://www.deloitte.com/dtt/article/0,1002, sid=11629&cid=141087,00.html?list=gfsi-risk.
6 Zaman, Arif, *Reputational Risk: How to Manage for Value Creation*, (London: Financial Times/Prentice Hall, 2003).
7 Eccles, Robert G., Scott C. Newquist, and Roland Schatz, "Reputation and Its Risks: Identify, quantify, and manage the risks to your company's reputation long before a problem or crisis strikes," *Harvard Business Review*, (February 2007).
8 Rayner (2002).
9 Atkins, Derek, Ian Bates, and Lynn Drennan, *Reputational Risk: A Question of Trust*, (UK: Financial World Publications, 2006).
10 Zaman (2003).
11 Ibid.
12 Godwin and Freese (2005).
13 Eccles, Newquist, and Schatz (2007).
14 Zaman (2003).
15 Louisot, Jean-Paul, "Managing Reputation Risks," *Risk Management: An International Journal* 6, no. 3, (2004): 35–50.
16 http://www.worldbank.org/html/fpd/privatesector/cg/aboutus.htm.
17 Zaman (2003).
18 Walter, Ingo, "Reputational Risk and Conflicts of Interest in Banking and Finance: The Evidence So Far," *Social Science Research Network*, December 20, 2006. http://ssrn.com/abstract=952 682.
19 Zaman (2003).
20 Ibid.

21 Al-Husayn, Ali ibn, Imam Zayn al-Abidin, Risalat Al-Huquq, trans., William C. Chittick, *The Treatise on Rights*, (Qum: Foundation of Islamic Cultural Propagation in the World, 1990).

22 Islam, Muhammad W., "Al-Mal: The Concept of Property in Islamic Legal Thought", *Arab Law Quarterly*, (1999): 361–368. The term *mal* and its derivatives have been mentioned in the *Qur'an* in more than 90 verses and in numerous sayings of the Prophet (pbuh).

23 These rules are supported by various verses in the *Qur'an*, such as the following: "*And do not eat up your property among yourselves for vanities, nor use it as bait for the judges, with intent that ye may eat up wrongfully and knowingly a little of (other) people's property.*" (2:188).
"Those who when they spend are not extravagant and not niggardly, but hold a just (balance) between those (extremes)." (25:67).
"Behold, the squanderers are, indeed, of the ilk of the satans ... " (17:27).

24 The concept that man has an unrestricted handling authority over his wealth is unacceptable. *Allah* (*swt*) has condemned the people of Shuayb for adopting such an attitude. See the *Qur'an* (11:87). Ahmad, Mushtaq, *Business Ethics in Islam*, (Islamabad: The International Institute of Islamic Thought, 1995).

25 Bashir (1999) argues that Islam attaches great importance on protecting people from harm caused by others. The Prophet (pbuh) is reported to have said "to cause harm to others is not allowed in Islam." Abdel-Hameed M. Bashir, "Property Rights in Islam," Conference Proceedings of the Third Harvard University Forum on Islamic Finance (Cambridge, MA: Harvard University, 1999): 71–82.

26 Iqbal, Z. and A. Mirakhor, *An Introduction to Islamic Finance: Theory and Practice*, (Singapore: John Wiley & Sons (Asia), 2007). P. N. Kourides, "The Influence of Islamic Law on Contemporary Middle Eastern Legal System: the Foundation and Binding Force of Contracts," *Columbia Journal of Transnational Law*, (1970): 384–435.

27 Verses of the *Qur'an* dealing with trust are: 2:27; 2:40; 2:80; 2:177; 2:282–83; 3:161; 4:107; 4:155; 6:153; 7:85; 8:27; 8:58; 9:12; 9:75; 9:111; 11:85; 13:20; 16:91; 16:94; 16:95; 17:34; and 23:8.

28 Iqbal and Mirakhor (2007); Habachy (1962).

29 Habachy (1962).

30 Asad, Mohammad, *The Message of the Qur'an*, (USA: The Book Foundation, 2004). http://www.thebook.org/

31 Iqbal, Z. and A. Mirakhor "Stakeholders Model of Corporate Governance of Firms in Islamic Economic System," *Islamic Economic Studies*, 11, no. 2, (March 2004).

32 For a very detailed analysis of failure of Ihlas Finans, see Salman S. Ali, "Financial Distress and Bank Failure: Lessons from Ihlas Finans Turkey," *Islamic Economic Studies*, 14, no. 2, (January 2007): 1–52.

33 Ali (2007).

34 Shares of Ihlas Holding were suspended from trading, driving the stock market down 4.9 percent in one day; Martha A. Starr and Rasim Yilmaz. "Bank Runs in Emerging-Market Countries: The Experience of Turkey's Islamic Banks in the 2001 Crisis", Working Papers 2006–08, American University, Department of Economics, (Washington, DC: USA, 2006).

35 Ali. (2007).

36 Simsek, Yalcin, "Special Finance Institutions Urge Ihlas Holding Savings Holders: No Need for Panic," *Turkish Daily News*, (February 14, 2001), as reported in Starr and Yilmaz (2006).
37 Okeahalam, Charles C., "The Political Economy of Bank Failure and Supervision in the Republic of South Africa," *African Journal of Political Science* 3 no. 2, (1998): 29–48.
38 Zuhaida, Sami, "The Politics of the Islamic Investment Companies in Egypt" *Bulletion of the British Society for Middle Eastern Studies*, 17, no. 2, (1990): 152–161.
39 Godwin and Freese (2005).
40 Atkins, Bates, and Drennan (2006).
41 Turnbull, Nigel Internal Control: Guidance for Directors on the Combined Code (the Turnbull Report), The Institute of Chartered Accountants in England & Wales, London, UK, 1999.
42 Atkins, Bates, and Drennan (2006).
43 Eccles, Newquist, and Schatz (2007).
44 Kovářík and Nevický (2007).
45 Kurre, Frank, "Assessing Reputational Risk," http://www.nacubo.org/x8958.xml?ss=pf.
46 Dziobek, C., and C. Pazarbasioglu, "Lessons from Systemic Bank Restructuring: a Survey of 24 Countries," IMF Working Paper 97/161, (Washington, DC: 1997).
47 Godwin and Freese (2005).
48 Eccles, Newquist, and Schatz (2007).
49 Walter (2006).
50 Atkins, Bates, and Drennan (2006).
51 Kurre (2007).
52 Ibid. Kurre suggests requiring that board members sign a conflict-of-interest statement which will clarify that members must always act in the best interests of the institution and refrain from actions that promote self-benefit.
53 Williams, Geoffrey Alan and John Zinkin, "Doing Business with Islam: Can Corporate Social Responsibility be a Bridge between Civilisations?" (October 2005). Available at SSRN: http://ssrn.com/abstract=905 184
54 For discussion of governance issues of Islamic financial institutions, see Wafik Grais and Zamir Iqbal, "Corporate Governance Challenges of Islamic Financial Institutions," 7th Harvard Forum on Islamic Finance, Boston, USA, April 22–23, 2006.
55 For further discussion, see Hennie van Greuning and Zamir Iqbal, "Risk Analysis for Islamic Banks," (Washington, DC: World Bank, 2007).
56 Godwin and Freese (2005) argue that critical components of a first-class, enterprise-wide compliance program should include an effective antifraud program, guidelines to ensure adherence to laws and regulations, and a code of conduct for the board, management, and employees.
57 Atkins, Bates, and Drennan (2006).

CHAPTER 7

The Design of Benchmarks for Asset Pricing[1]

Benchmarks serve a critical role in today's financial markets and serve multiple purposes. First and foremost, the purpose of a benchmark is to serve as a point of reference for pricing the riskiness of a financial security, and this, ultimately, is an essential element for the pricing of any security. The second purpose of a benchmark is to indicate the relative value or opportunity cost of capital in the financial markets, and, finally, the third purpose is to serve as a yardstick for the relative performance of a portfolio. The existence of a transparent, observable, liquid, easy-to-compute and nonmanipulative benchmark is vital for efficient financial markets. In conventional financial markets, the interest rate on sovereign debt serves as the most popular benchmark and is often referred to as the risk-free rate. Similarly, in the swap market the London Interbank Offered Rate (LIBOR) serves as a benchmark and reference point to price securities. In the case of Islamic finance, where by virtue of prohibition of interest debt security is eliminated from the system, benchmarks from conventional financial markets cannot be used.

Despite more than 30 years of practice, Islamic finance has yet to develop appropriate benchmarks. Unfortunately, the common practice is to use LIBOR as the reference benchmark in determining expected rate of return in *Shari'ah*-compliant securities. The practice started in the absence of a *Shari'ah*-compliant benchmark and was considered as an exception allowed by *Shari'ah* scholars under the law of necessity.[2] This exception has become a general rule and the practice is so prevalent that most practitioners often do not even question it. The practice of using LIBOR as a benchmark has its proponents and opponents. The proponents of the practice argue that it is simply a reference point of the current capital market indicating the opportunity cost of capital, which should not be different in global markets where Islamic and conventional markets coexist. If the opportunity cost of capital is not the same, arbitrage opportunities will arise. It is also argued that using a non-*Shari'ah*-compliant reference point does not invalidate a *Shari'ah*-compliant transaction.

The opponents of this practice argue that in an Islamic economic system, the rate of return on a financial asset should be derived from the rate of return in the real sector and using LIBOR as a benchmark does precisely the opposite and thus violates the foundation of an Islamic financial system. There is, in our opinion, a need to develop benchmarks which are *Shari'ah*-compatible and can serve as benchmarks for pricing securities and their risk, starting with a benchmark which represents the risk-free rate in an Islamic economy. Ul Haque and Mirakhor (1998) suggested an innovative way of developing benchmarks and instruments for public finance. This chapter is a reproduction of that paper.

7.1 INTRODUCTION

The religious edict against fixed-income securities limits the use of conventional treasury instruments in Islamic economies. Equity-based, floating-rate securities, which pay a rate equivalent to the observed rate of return obtained in the private sector and adjusted for risk premiums, are much needed policy instruments in these countries. The key difficulty lies in obtaining a rate of return based on profit-sharing derived from private sector activity. In conventional economies, such a rate is the market interest rate. In an Islamic economy, the rate must be derived from observation of private sector activity.

This is a first attempt to identify alternative methodologies to estimate such a rate and derive from it the rate that prospective issues of government paper in Islamic economies could offer. It discusses several approaches, ranging from simple ratios to more complicated broad market indices. We recommend filtering out from the private sector rate of return derived for this purpose: expectations of future earnings, which is an important element of stock market prices; speculative elements that may at times grip the private sector; and seasonal variation. Additionally, to derive the rate of return on government paper, it is necessary to remove an estimate of risk premium that may relate to private defaults.

Government financing on a noninterest basis has presented a dilemma as there has been no generally acceptable method that meets the requirements of Islamic Law. Simply stated, in an Islamic system all rates of return in the financial sector are determined by activities in the real sector. This requirement causes difficulties for governments used to conventional debt financing of expenditure without the need to justify financially the operations being undertaken or, as is often the case, to compete with the private sector for financial resources. Our purpose is to suggest a noninterest-based method of mobilizing resources to finance government infrastructural and development projects through issuance of a national participation paper (NPP) that can also serve as an instrument of monetary management. The plan of this chapter is as follows: we will discuss various conceptual issues underpinning the introduction of such an instrument and methods of calculating a corresponding rate of return; we will examine issues relating to risk premium; then we will address maturity and the cost and trading characteristics of the proposed paper; and then outline techniques for developing primary and secondary markets for NPPs. We conclude with a summary of our main findings.

7.2 CONCEPTUAL ISSUES

There is now a consensus view that, in the absence of a predetermined rate of interest, the economy's financial system becomes predominantly equity-based, and the stock of physical capital is valued in the market for equities. The significance of a system that operates without the central authority's intervention, as is the case in an interest-based regime, is that it allows the pricing system, via a market-determined rate of return driven by real sector activities, to function freely and to ensure the efficient rationing of scarce financial resources.

While in such a system private-sector financing can be arranged on an equity basis, difficult issues arise when governments need to mobilize funds for their operations. Presumably, the nature of government operations does not permit equity participation by private agents. But, while current government expenditure may not allow assignment of individual equity claims, public expenditure on infrastructural and development projects—often a major element of governments' budget—can be financed via equity participation. This approach bifurcates government expenditure into asset-creating and non-asset-creating expenditure. The former is financed via equity participation. The latter is financed through taxation.

Islam recognizes public and joint ownership of assets as legitimate even when they are indivisible, as long as ownership claims can be priced in the market so that, in the event of dissolving partnerships, equity holders can monetize their claims. Therefore, capital expenditure can be financed via equity participation, provided that a market exists for trading shares. The issue then becomes one of determining a rate of return that compensates shareholders of assets created by the government when there are no benchmarks, such as a fixed and predetermined interest rate in reference to which market participants can make a decision, as is the case in a conventional financial system.

In an Islamic system, the rate of return of financial assets is determined by the rate of return of the real sector of the economy that serves as a benchmark for investment decisions (Khan and Mirakhor 1988). In Mirakhor (1996), it is also shown that such a reference rate can be approximated by calculating a cost of capital using Tobin's q against which expected rates of return to private and public projects can be measured.

It can also be argued that since the expected earnings of holders of securities are derived from the expected dividends, the discounted value of the stream of expected earnings at the prevailing rate of return is the market value of a security and the supply price of capital. In the case of government securities, this would also constitute the demand side of the market for these instruments. Moreover, the face value of securities, the length of maturity, and the expected dividend constitute the supply side of the market for government securities.

The expectations of equity holders and government provide the necessary input for the market to determine the volume and the market-clearing price for government securities in which the social rate of return to public investment projects serves as the discount rate. At equilibrium, the social rate of return is such that the marginal social benefit from public investment projects is equal to the opportunity cost of the provision of the services from these projects. But, because of the public good nature of these projects, the marginal social benefits may not be truly measurable.

It can be argued, however, that precisely because of this characteristic of infrastructural and developmental projects, their social rate of return must be greater than, or at least equal to, the rate of return in the private sector; otherwise, there is no justification for governments to undertake these projects on financial grounds (Choudhry and Mirakhor 1997). Based on this reasoning, the coupon on noninterest-based government securities can be issued and traded in equity markets that promise on maturity to pay a rate of return proxied by an average rate of return on the underlying assets that is equal to the rate of return in the private sector. In addition to financing new projects, this method can be used to retire government debt to the central bank that has financed previous projects since this debt can be securitized, providing the basis for the flotation of an NPP that is to be traded on the stock markets.

These government securities are considered to be in consonance with Islamic Law. Indeed, a recent ruling by an eminent religious authority has permitted the Central Bank of Iran to issue securities based on a portfolio of completed infrastructural and developmental projects whose source of financing was direct central bank credit to the government.

The ruling authorizes the central bank to apply the proceeds from the sale of these securities to the write-down of government debt to the bank. These securities provide a powerful instrument of indirect monetary policy in the absence of conventional Treasury bills (Choudhry and Mirakhor 1997).

7.3 DERIVING A RATE OF RETURN TO NPPs

Since the rate of return to NPPs is to be proxied by the rate of return to the real sector of the economy, it is necessary to ensure that speculative behavior and other windfall gains arising from private sector financial markets do not distort the rate of return on NPPs. In view of this consideration, it is reasonable to assume that the private sector rate of return, though unknown at any given moment, is on average stable over time. In a statistical sense, we expect the rate of return to be drawn from a stationary distribution. Therefore, the rate of return quoted on such papers would be fairly stable over time and reflective of the investment climate in the country. With such a coupon rate, the instrument could be widely tradable and hence useful as a monetary policy instrument.

The natural place to look for a measure of the private sector rate of return is the stock market. However, stock market prices contain three elements that would have to be considered separately to obtain the signal of the true private sector rate of return:

- Expectation of future earnings, which is an important element of stock market prices
- Speculative elements that may at times grip the market
- Seasonal variation

If stock prices were to be used, they would have to be appropriately filtered through statistical techniques to extract the appropriate signal of a rate of return. A search could be conducted to allow the required index to replicate closely past movement in growth of nominal grass domestic protect (GDP), given that this growth closely proxies the expected growth of private-sector output. In addition, the use of stock prices and/or indices should be based on a determination of the degree of competition and efficiency of the market. In case the market is shallow and does not allow for complete arbitrage through competition, it may be difficult to obtain information on the rate of return from stock market data since the process of price discovery may be distorted.

7.3.1 The Difficulties of Nascent Financial Markets

Given the relatively limited state of development of financial markets in Muslim countries, the average rate of return in the private sector is difficult to determine. It is still harder to obtain the sort of return that is required for NPPs, given the likelihood of distortions and speculative behavior in nascent markets.

Ideally, such a rate of return should be obtained on two markets—the stock market and the participation paper market—as and when they begin to function at a reasonably advanced stage. Although the stock market has been functioning in many Muslim countries, preliminary tests suggest that the hypothesis of market efficiency is not confirmed.[3] Moreover, there is little or no development of the corporate paper market along Islamic lines. Basing the index on domestic stock market prices alone will have the following disadvantages:

- The government paper and the stock market will have closely related rates of return[4]
- The stock market is too small to infer a market rate of return
- The government, the central bank, and commercial banks will have an incentive to intervene in the stock market for consideration relating to the NPP market
- Speculators will have the incentive to use the stock market for manipulating returns on the NPPs.

To compensate for these factors, the inclusion of an international index could be considered as it has the clear advantage of being exogenous to the economy, easily monitorable, and representing the external financial environment. Therefore, an appropriately chosen index could enhance the credibility of the NPP and make it more desirable. Moreover, given the globalization and convergence in international capital markets, it is reasonable to assume that rates prevailing in Muslim countries must reflect the scarcity price of capital worldwide. However, inclusion of an international index in the calculation of a rate of return on NPPs may have the disadvantage of not being fully representative of domestic market conditions. But, if the choice of the index is such that it is stable and somewhat representative of local conditions, the discount on the secondary market will establish the rate of return that is more representative of domestic considerations.[5] Unfortunately, there is no adequate regional index available for the Middle East that could be used. The available ones are broader in regional coverage such as Morgan Stanley's World Index.

A search for indices should be made and their properties should be examined for the choice of the most suitable. In conducting this search and investigation, the applicable criteria are to find an index that is: easily monitorable and available; relatively stable; and broadly in line with the domestic economy.[6] Rates of return in the private sector need not only be inferred from the index of broader market performance. Many Muslim countries may have markets that are not developed enough to derive an appropriate estimate. At least three different rates of return that guide investment decisions can be used to obtain an estimate more readily usable even in situations of limited market developments: earnings per share; the price-earnings ratio; and the return on shareholders' equity.

7.3.1.1 Earnings per Share

The earnings per share is typically used to compare an individual company's financial performance over time. It is of little relevance for intercompany comparisons or for aggregative indices comprising different companies. For example, individual companies of the same capital base can issue any number of shares, each with a different par value. This means that two companies with the same financial performance can have very different earnings per share. At the same time, earnings per share can be affected by stock splits and mergers in ways that have little relevance to underlying performance.

7.3.1.2 The Price-Earnings Ratio and Dividend Yields

The price-earnings ratio relates a company's net revenues per share to the market price of its shares. As such, the price-earnings ratio provides a measure of the return that investors receive from the company's equity at current stock market prices. This ratio also provides a useful measure of appropriateness of current stock prices, but is limited as a measure of the current underlying economic return. For example, price-earnings on the stock market are forward looking as they incorporate the evaluation of a company's ability to earn returns. Moreover, what is required for NPPs is a measure of return that focuses on the present. The price-earnings ratio can also be very volatile and can deviate from its underlying value in a market environment where trading is thin, as is the case in many Muslim countries. Concerns similar to those relating to price-earnings argue against the use of dividend yields.

7.3.1.3 Return on Shareholders' Equity

Return on shareholders' equity (ROE) is a premier measure of current financial performance that relates a company's current after-tax and after-interest earnings to current shareholders' equity. Shareholders' equity is the initial capital provided to the company through the initial offering, plus additional equity issues, plus accumulated retained earnings. Essentially, ROE measures the value extracted by management from the capital that owners have invested. As such, ROE is fungible and suitable for intertemporal, intercompany, and intersectoral comparisons.

7.3.2 A General Index

In its most general form, the rate of return on the private sector may be written as follows:

$$I = w_1 WI + w_2 PPI + w_3 LSI + w_4 ROG$$

Where:

I = the index growth of which will determine the uncertain (or the nonguaranteed) rate of return on the NPP

WI = an international stock market index like the Morgan Stanley World Index

LSI = a measure of market performance index in the country in which paper is being issued (stock index, EPS, dividends, ROE, average q for the economy)

PPI = a weighted average of returns in the commercial participation paper market as it develops

ROG = measure of the rate of return on government investments that underlie the NPP
EPS = earnings per share
ROE = return on equity
$w_1, \ldots, w_4$ = weights that need to be determined

Using this general formulation, the following suggestions should be considered and investigated:

- *ROG only* ($w_1, \ldots, w_3 = 0$, $w_4 = 1$). If the ROG could be estimated and reported by the central bank, this would be a simple solution.
- *LSI only (stock index based)* (w_1, w_2, $w_4 = 0$, $w_3 = 1$). Here, it should be borne in mind that the stock market is subject to speculative and other pressures. These should be excluded from the rate of return applied to the NPP.
- *LSI only (EPS, dividend or ROE based)* (w_1, w_2, $w_4 = 0$, $w_3 = 1$). Given the difficulties with the stock market development, proxies of economy-wide rates of return can be derived from estimates of EPS, dividend yields, and ROEs.
- *PPI only* (w_1, w_3, $w_4 = 0$, $w_2 = 1$). A weighted average of NPP returns could be a useful indicator for the future when the NPP market develops.
- *A more general index*. Weights can be derived for any and all $w_i (i = 1 \ldots 4)$. However, this will require considerable investigation and maintenance work. If desired, investigative efforts should be exerted to derive and maintain the appropriate index.

Experimentation with weights and variables mentioned in the expression for "I" above will allow a stable and realistic indicator to be developed for the rate of return.

7.3.2.1 The Choice of Weights

The choice of weights should be dictated to a large extent by the need to derive a stable measure of the rate of return for the private sector. When the local markets—the stock market and the participation paper market—are developed adequately, they should be given due weight in the index. Until then, their weight should be limited. The appropriate determination weights should be determined through empirical investigation, and then kept under constant review, although the weights should be changed only at discreet preannounced intervals. A preannounced formula for weights is as follows:

$$w_i = f(\text{turnover, number of new issues, market capitalization/GDP});$$
$$i = 2, 3, 4$$ [7]

This means that some formulae are adopted that allow the share of the stock market index and the weighted average to increase as these markets expand. Growth in turnover in secondary trading, rapid expansion in new issues, and an increase in market capitalization are indicators of market development.

7.3.3 Institutional Requirements for Developing a More General Index

Since flotation of the NPP will represent a longer term government intention to develop this market, we suggest that the authorities concerned keep the index under review and development. The index, in its most general form, will require considerable research to foster its development and quotation on a market basis, which, in turn, will promote expansion of the market for commercial and government paper in Muslim countries.

7.4 THE RETURN ON GOVERNMENT PAPER: THE ELIMINATION OF RISK PREMIUM

Because of market volatility, asymmetric information, and the possibility of speculative behavior, stock prices as well as market indices include a risk premium that risk-averse investors require to hold risky assets. In most markets, government paper represents the most secured asset (often considered as the "risk-free asset") and its rate of return is used as a benchmark for comparing all investments.[8] In equilibrium, the rate of return on government domestic paper would be equal to the rate of return on the stock market after adjustment for the risk premium. The index, derived from using the techniques discussed, represents the rate of return to the private sector. Therefore, a risk premium should be subtracted from the private sector rate of return to obtain the rate of return that should be applied to government paper that is relatively free of market-based risk. The difficulty lies in finding an appropriate measure of rate of return on assets that are similar in character to the government's to allow the system to start. Any available bank deposit or loan rate (for example, adjusted foreign rate, exchange rate, or rate on equity-based domestic transactions) would be a candidate if it were determined on market considerations. Any other reference rate that allows the establishment of a risk-free rate could also be used. This rate could be derived from any borrowing on a government project or a rate of return that has been obtained from such a project. When the NPP system is developed, its rates of return in the immediately preceding period could be used to estimate the risk premium. In this sense, the risk premium, like the index, will be updated on a regular basis. Using this rate, we can derive the risk premium as follows:

$$RP = \mu^{I} - R^{country}$$

Where:

RP = risk premium

μ^{I} = mean of the index I that has been derived above

$R^{country}$ = rate of return on bank deposits or government project

The risk premium can be calculated by applying data from the immediate past period. This formula, as well as the risk premium itself, can be revised periodically. But, given that the stability of preferences has been observed around the world and through different time periods, there is little reason to assume large changes in this variable.

Payment on the NPP coupon will be made according to the growth of the "I" during the term of the paper. This RP should be subtracted from the growth of "I" to determine the final rate of return:

$$R_f = R_s - RP$$

where R_f is the final rate of return to be paid, and R_s is the rate of growth of "I" that has been suitably smoothed to correct for speculative and other behavior.

7.4.1 Maturity and Cost

NPPs should be offered with a term-to-maturity that best meets market demand and provides an opportunity to quickly develop an environment where outstanding volumes are sufficient to be useful in the conduct of monetary policy. As a general rule, the terms-to-maturity should be one year or less as shorter dated instruments provide a smaller potential for realized capital loss. At the same time, focus on a limited set of maturities increases market depth and, correspondingly, liquidity. This can be achieved by limiting issues to a relatively few terms-to-maturity and by reopening issues on a frequent basis.

The question of who issues NPPs is also an important consideration. In most countries, such a paper is issued by the government with the central bank as its agent. More importantly, the cost is directly borne by the government for two reasons: the central bank conducts monetary policy on behalf of the government, and the central bank's capital has been protected. It is recommended that the generally accepted practice of the cost being borne by the government be followed in Muslim countries as well.

7.5 THE TRADING CHARACTERISTICS OF THE NPP

Like most financial instruments, the proposed NPP can be regarded as a composite instrument. Basically, it is a combination of two underlying instruments:

- A futures contract on the items in index "I"
- A zero coupon bond on the face value of the instrument

To the extent that due diligence has been applied to derive a smooth, stable, and stationary rate of return using the index, the futures contract value should be relatively stable reflecting market sentiment regarding the performance of the underlying real assets. In this case, secondary market trading should impact on the zero coupon part of the instrument. Consequently, variation in this trading will reflect domestic market sentiment. This is exactly the way it should be for domestic monetary policy.

7.6 DEVELOPING PRIMARY AND SECONDARY MARKETS FOR THE NPP

Considerable international experience is available to assist in developing new national markets for government securities. There is, however, little experience in doing so under the Islamic code. Nevertheless, if a stable and smooth path could be derived for the *ex ante* return on NPPs, the menu of practices, techniques, and trade-offs, generally available elsewhere, should largely apply to Muslim countries. However, this conclusion will require practical confirmation in an Islamic environment, and the central bank must remain ready to adjust its practices and techniques as required. At the same time, market design cannot be sketched in isolation. It must adapt its detail to fit the existing institutional, market, and instrument structures unique to every country, and it must accommodate their ongoing evolution. In brief, while the government security market considered here must meet basic economic and financial criteria, there is considerable room for Muslim countries to exercise their own preferences. The following recommendations should be evaluated in this light.

7.6.1 Developing a Primary Market for NPPs

7.6.1.1 The Auction Technique

It is recommended that the central bank sells NPPs through an auction. The rationale for an auction, which is internationally a standard practice, is twofold: first, it provides information to the central bank about current market conditions and trends, and, second, it provides insurance against failure due to mispricing by the central bank[9]; failure could be very costly to a young market.

There are two types of auction techniques, both involving sealed bids: *uniform price auctions* and *multiple price auctions*. For both, bid prices are arranged in order and auctioneers move down from the highest price until all offered instruments are sold. In the uniform price auction, all successful bidders pay the lowest winning price. In the multiple price auctions, each successful bidder pays his or her own bid price. There is no clear theoretical case for preference of either method, particularly when collusion, cornering, and risk aversion are considered. As a practical matter, virtually all countries use the multiple price technique. It is recommended that a multiple price auction technique be adopted for NPPs.

7.6.1.2 No Redemption

Agents wishing to liquidate their holdings have to approach the secondary market. Making the NPPs redeemable at face value at any time is difficult to justify on various grounds. First, in the event of a change in market conditions, the investor has a no-cost bailout option. Additionally, through this approach, investors lose the right to the cumulative return above the minimum yield generated by the underlying infrastructure or productive investment. In case NPPs are used as a monetary instrument, an early repurchase feature will reduce the information available from the auction and weaken the central bank's control over its own balance sheet. It is recommended that the central bank advise purchasers that the NPP will not be repurchased before maturity. However, owners will be permitted to transfer their participation bonds in the secondary market where the market mechanism will allow the appropriate discount for sale or purchase for the remaining term to maturity.

7.6.1.3 Participation

Some countries limit auction participation to banks and other financial institutions. Limited participation reduces administrative costs and fosters the development of a secondary market. At the same time, primary dealers often assume obligations, such as a commitment to participate frequently in scheduled auctions and to maintain an inventory of the auctioned instruments for secondary market trading. Open participation allows all interested investors to bid, though usually subject to a minimum bid size. The advantage of open bidding is that it increases competition and narrows the spread between prices on the primary and secondary markets.

7.6.1.4 Limits on Competitive Bids

A few countries limit the number of bids from a single bidder, and others limit the size of any issue that can be won by any single bidder. While circumstances can easily be conceived where such limitations improve competition, the opposite is also true. These limits on competitive bids constitute a complication and should be avoided.

7.6.1.5 Noncompetitive Bids

Many countries allow noncompetitive bids where buyers purchase the instrument at the weighted average auction price. noncompetitive bids allow investors with uncertain or unformed expectations to buy at market rates. Large investors may make competitive and noncompetitive bids simultaneously as a hedging strategy. In some markets, noncompetitive bids are subject to a cap to prevent large investors from using the facility and/or subject to a floor to avoid a large number of small bids.

7.6.1.6 Minimum Price Rule

In some countries, bids are subject to a minimum price rule for each individual auction; that is, bids below a certain preannounced price are not accepted. The innovative nature of NPPs, as well as the opportunity provided to discover investor expectations, suggest that a minimum bid price should not be imposed.

7.6.1.7 Auction Announcement, Schedule, and Other Details

Auction procedures and details should be transparent to ensure that all information is available to all investors at roughly the same time. As in most countries, the central bank in Muslim countries should announce well in advance auction dates, the amounts to be auctioned, and all other terms and details, and should hold auctions at regular intervals.

7.6.2 Developing a Secondary Market for NPPs

Secondary markets broaden and deepen primary markets by offering liquidity, transparency, and ongoing price discovery. As emphasized above, the central bank should advise purchasers of the NPPs that no repurchase will be permitted before maturity. It is also recommended that NPPs should have a fixed term with no early repurchase, and that the private-sector issuers should be encouraged to follow the same practice. However, participation bonds will be transferable and the central bank should take supportive steps to encourage the formation of a corresponding secondary market.

7.6.2.1 Market Structure

Secondary markets can take various forms. *Call secondary markets* bring buyers and sellers together periodically to establish a uniform market clearing price. *Continuous markets* may be either auction markets or dealer markets. Auction markets bring buyers and sellers together on an ongoing basis and effect transactions immediately whenever sellers' offered price and the purchasers' bid price come together. A dealer market consists of traders (dealers) who hold inventories and continuously post buy–sell prices, and trading occurs both between dealers and between dealers and clients.

In countries with well-developed financial markets, continuous markets predominate. However, for countries with young financial markets, a call secondary market may be the preferable approach until such time that trading volumes warrant a switch. For example, while continuous markets allow the rapid incorporation of all new economic and other information into price, they require a sufficient flow of buy–sell orders to ensure smooth price adjustments.

Call secondary markets are well-suited for securities that are thinly traded because they allow an accumulation of buy–sell orders. Call markets also provide a uniform clearing price and low cost. Call markets do not generally accommodate quick trades on the basis of immediate information. However, a continuous secondary market in many Muslim countries that do allow such trades could in likelihood be volatile. The resolution of this trade-off between timeliness and volatility is a question likely best handled through experience in the coming years of many Muslim countries' financial development. It is recommended at present that these countries adopt a call secondary market for participation bonds.

7.6.2.2 Call Market Procedure

Call markets are held in a single location on a periodic and regular basis. During the call auction for each instrument and maturity, the auctioneer sets an opening price. Traders act on their own behalf or on a client's expressed interest in buying or selling at that price. The auctioneer then adjusts the price downward or upward until excess supply or demand is eliminated. All transactions are completed at this equilibrium market clearing price.

7.7 CONCLUSION

The religious edict against fixed-income securities limits the use of conventional treasury instruments in Islamic economies. Equity-based, floating-rate securities, which will pay a rate equivalent to the observed rate of return obtained in the private sector and adjusted for risk premiums, is a much-needed policy instrument in these countries. The key difficulty lies in obtaining a rate of return in an economy based on profit sharing. In conventional economies, such a rate is given by the market interest rate. In this chapter we make a first attempt at identifying alternative methodologies to estimate such a rate and derive from it the rate that prospective issues of government paper in Islamic economies could offer.

Several approaches, ranging from simple ratios to more complicated broad market indices, are discussed. This range of measures will hopefully allow countries at different stages of development in the diverse Islamic group of countries to choose a method suited for their level of market development. While proposing this approach, we remain conscious of, and emphasize the need for, further study of the proposed indices and measures. This should be done at the international as well as at the country-specific level. Even after the issue of NPP, these measures will have to remain under some form of surveillance and development. Therefore, we recommend that a country wishing to adopt this approach take the following steps to prepare for the development of the NPP market:

1. It is important that some department or institution assumes ownership of the index that is being used and to monitor it; after all, whichever index is adopted, it will have to be compiled and reported to the public on a regular basis. Wherever possible, perhaps the stock exchange could undertake this responsibility since it compiles market indices. Furthermore, the stock exchange, as well as the central bank research and banking supervision departments, could be made responsible for reviewing developments in the index and for checking that speculative and other pressures do not contaminate the signal of the current rate of return in the private sector. Through experience and continuous investigation, the index will improve over time.
2. While noting the lack of adequate data for a detailed study in most of the concerned countries, we believe that ratios, such as gross profit/total assets or return on equity discussed here, could serve as the index of the rate of return in the private sector. These measures have an advantage over the price of equity as they are a pure measure of current earnings; the latter also include a component of expected developments in the private sector. Consequently, obtaining these ratios for a defined group of companies (say the ten largest companies) over the past few years will allow the appropriate index to be constructed relatively quickly.
3. Once an index is computed, no matter how crude, further work could be initiated to widen it. Considerations, similar to the ones raised above, would argue in favor of making room

in the development of such a measure for an international index, which, in combination with the domestic index, will reflect a certain weight of external market conditions facing the country, as well as a certain element in the index that is not endogenous to domestic events. The weights can be determined as suggested above.

4. Once the index has finally been computed, the instrument can be floated and the primary and secondary markets developed through the use of the techniques outlined above.

In conclusion, we must emphasize that the use of risk-free interest obtained from conventional finance is not, in our opinion, appropriate for Islamic finance. Any modern financial system needs such a benchmark. There is thus a need to derive a risk-free rate that is compatible with Islamic economic and financial doctrines. In this chapter we have outlined the first steps in this quest.

ENDNOTES

1 This chapter is based on Ul-Haque, Nadeem and Abbas Mirakhor, "The Design of Instruments for Government Finance in an Islamic Economy," International Monetary Fund (IMF) Working Paper no. WP/98/54 (Washington, DC: International Monetary Fund, 1998).

2 It is ironic that the latest debate in conventional finance is questioning the usefulness of LIBOR and if it is indeed a good benchmark.

3 El-Erian, Mohamed and Kumar Monmohan, "Emerging Equity Markets in the Middle Eastern Countries," Working Paper No. 94/103, (Washington, DC: International Monetary Fund, 1994).

4 Strictly speaking, the two rates of return will differ by a factor since the NPP will be discounted given that government paper is riskfree while private investment is not.

5 To the extent possible, the World or regional index and the domestic stock index should include dividends for the stocks that pay dividends.

6 The last of these is likely to be quite difficult and hence perhaps not something that should delay the development of the instrument.

7 i = 1 is excluded as it will be determined by the constraint $\sum_{i=1}^{4} w_i = 1$

8 In particular, government, unlike private firms, is considered to be free of default risk.

9 In the case of the NPP, the return is *ex ante* undetermined but known as *ex post* based on independent market criteria. Accordingly, it may be argued that a price equal to the face value of the NPP is appropriate. However, the NPP's *ex post* return is based on a complex formula designed to approximate the ongoing return on investment in an Islamic country and may not accurately capture market expectations. In this case, an auction approach will be required to establish the market clearing price.

CHAPTER 8

Qard-ul-Hassan-based Microfinance[1]

The growth of microfinance (MF) institutions in the last two decades has been impressive. Recently, the Nobel Prize awarded to Dr. Mohammed Yunis of Bangladesh has renewed interest in the subject of MF, which is mainly targeted towards the poor or the "non-banked" segment of a society. While MF institutions have been successful in the conventional markets, there are limited cases of such institutions that are operating on the principles of Islamic finance. However, in view of the fact that MF is focused on the poor and Islam emphasizes socioeconomic justice and support for the poorer segment of society, MF and Islamic finance clearly share a similar social objective. In an Islamic economic and financial system, instruments such as *qard-ul-hassan*[2], *sadaqah*, and *Zakah* can play a vital role in serving the poor. Through these investment vehicles, the all-important objectives of economic prosperity and economic equity can be partially addressed. As such, these instruments could play an ever-increasing role in the field of Islamic finance. In this chapter we focus specifically on *qard-ul-hassan* and argue that this instrument can serve as a vehicle for successful MF activities in empowering the poor and leading to sustainable economic development in Muslim societies. As this instrument has been most widely used in the Islamic Republic of Iran, we present some data covering the Iranian experience.

8.1 A REVIEW OF CONVENTIONAL MF

As it is well known, within the present dominant economic system there are a number of serious market failures that cannot be resolved without external intervention. One such failure is the inability of the prevailing credit system to satisfy loan demands from segments of the population that cannot access formal credit channels or do not have sufficient collateral against which they can borrow. These groups—commonly referred to as "non-banked" or "non-bankable"—not only include the poor but also the would-be entrepreneurs with projects or ideas with potentially high rates of return.

A solution to this market failure came in the form of Grameen Bank, which has been a phenomenal success since its beginning in the mid-1970s. Information economics, developed by Joseph Stiglitz, another Nobel Prize winner, explains that informational problems underlie many failures of the market system. In particular, the credit-market failures are due to the fact that information collection and analysis is a high-cost activity for financial intermediaries (such as banks), making it expensive to collect and analyze the necessary information and to decide whether to extend a loan, and then monitor the behavior of the borrower to ensure compliance with the loan's terms and conditions as well as its repayment. If information costs are too high, banks extend loans only to those clients with a good credit record and/or high-valued collateral to make defaults costly. Underlying this is the notion of asymmetric information, that the borrower may have information regarding the project's purpose and chances of success that the lender lacks. This, in turn, leads to problems of adverse selection (the lender may decide to extend loans to risky borrowers willing to pay high interest rates) or moral hazard problems (the borrower will use the proceeds for purposes other than stated or with intention of defaulting).

MF gets around these problems by resorting to group lending. In its original conception (Grameen Bank I), no collateral is required and only the poor can borrow, but each client has to be a member of a five-person group that, in turn, belongs to an eight-group (a total of 40) "center" within a village. While the loans would be granted to individuals within the group for their own independent projects, failure to repay the loan would lead to collective punishment: the entire five-member group loses its membership in the bank. While there is no explicit requirement for the group to pay off a loan defaulted by one of its members, implicitly there is a strong incentive for the group to do so if it wants to regain its membership. MF banks' interest rates have been in the order of 20 to 30 percent.

This approach of lending to a close-knit group of borrowers resolves both informational problems of adverse selection and moral hazard by shifting the cost of *ex ante* selection of the right borrowers (those with low probability of default) and the responsibility for monitoring the borrower's behavior to the group. The track record of high repayment rates documents the success of this approach.

While Grameen II has modified some of the features of Grameen I, the basic structure of the earlier version of MF is retained in that reliance is still placed on the reputation of borrowers with group familiarity with each client, interest rates are still as high as 30 percent, and the eventual aim of these institutions is to become successful profit-making banks. As explained below, the Islamic solution—*qard-ul-hassan*—to the credit system's market failure to serve the target groups is substantially different from the prevailing MF approach.

8.2 THE ISLAMIC SOLUTION: *QARD-UL-HASSAN*

Qard-ul-hassan (*QH*) is a voluntary loan without the lender's expectation of any return on the principal. Additionally, while the debtor is obligated to return the principal, the lender is urged, according to a number of the sayings of the Prophet (pbuh), not to press the debtor if he or she is unable to repay at the specified deadline. There are at least six verses of the *Qur'an* addressing the subject (see Figure 8.1), but before dealing with these verses it would be useful to consider the etymology of the two words *qard* and *hassan*. The first is a noun signifying the act of tearing something apart with one's teeth, perhaps suggesting the act of tearing away a part of one's wealth in the form of a loan (suggesting a painful process). *Hassan* means splendid or

Figure 8.1 References to *qard-ul-hassan* in the *Qur'an*

(2:245)	*who is he that will lend* Allah *a* qard-ul-hassan *so that He will multiply it for him (the lender) many times over … ?*
(5:12)	*And certainly* Allah *took a covenant from the children of Israel and we raised up amongst them twelve captains, and* Allah *said "verily, I am with you if you keep up* Salat, *pay* Zakat, *believe in my messengers and support them, and lend* Allah *a* qard-ul-hassan. *I will certainly wipe off your sins and I will certainly cause you to enter the gardens in which rivers flow … "*
(11:57)	*Who is it that will lend* Allah *a* qard-ul-hassan *which He will multiply for him (the lender) many times and for him shall be a generous recompense?*
(18:57)	*Verily charity-giving men and women who loan* Allah *a* qard-ul-hassan, *shall have it multiplied for them and they will receive a generous recompense.*
(17:64)	*If you lend* Allah *a* qard-ul-hassan, *He will multiply it for you.* Allah *is the most appreciating, the most forbearing.*
(20:73)	*… so recite from it* (the Quran) *as you can easily, and establish* Salat *and pay* Zakat *and loan* Allah *a* qard-ul-hassan. *What so ever good you send for yourself beforehand, you will find it with* Allah. *This is the best and the greatest reward.*

beautiful. The two words together mean a "beautiful loan," perhaps because the *Qur'an* asserts that these loans are made to *Allah* (*swt*) rather than to the borrower, intending to ease the pain of "tearing away" part of one's wealth and parting with it to lend to someone in need. *Hassan* and *ihsan* belong to the constellation of the same root. There is a famous saying of the Prophet (pbuh) that when asked what *ihsan* means, he replied that it means "to adore *Allah* (*swt*) as if you see Him and know that (even) if you do not, He sees you." Perhaps the word *hassan*, understood in the context of *ihsan*, is meant to imply that only when a person is making a loan to someone in need, without expecting anything in return and only in order to please *Allah* (*swt*) will the transaction be possible. The difference between *QH* and *sadaqah* (charity)—another Islamic act of parting with one's wealth to help the needy—is that *QH* has to be repaid, although only the borrower specifies the time of repayment, while *sadaqah* is pure charity. It is reported from the Prophet (pbuh) that the reward by *Allah* (*swt*) for *sadaqah* is tenfold and that of *QH* is 18-fold, thus underlying the importance of *QH* by placing its rewards higher than *sadaqah* even if the principal of *QH* has to be repaid, which is not the case for charity.

In the *Qur'an*, that *Allah* (*swt*) places great emphasis on *QH* can be gleaned from many verses which indicate that:

- When a person grants a *QH* to someone in need without expecting any return over and above the principal, which the borrower is obligated to repay, *Allah* (*swt*) promises a reward multiple of that amount. Additionally, *Allah* (*swt*) adds that the person (the lender) will receive "*Ajr-un-Kareem*," a generous recompense, beyond imagination.
- Verse 18:57 indicates that *QH* is other than *sadaqah* (charity) and verses 5:12 and 20:73 indicate that *QH* is also different from *Zakah*. These verses also reveal the extraordinary importance *Allah* (*swt*) attaches to *QH* since He places it at the same level as the mandatory *Salah* and *Zakah*.
- There is no indication in any of the above verses that the rewards promised by *Allah* (*swt*) are limited to the hereafter only.
- There is no interest payment involved.
- The *Qur'an* creates a strong incentive structure for the funding of *QH*.

8.2.1 Comparison of MF and *QHMF*

The conventional MF industry has been growing at a pace of 13 percent annually since 1999, and today there are more than 320 sustainable institutions operating under the banner of MF. This phenomenal success has even forced the private investors to show a great deal of interest in it as a potential and viable asset class. Unlike conventional MF institutions, there is very limited information on MF institutions operating under Islamic finance. There is a relatively small operation of interest-free loans in Pakistan and small-scale micro/rural banks in Indonesia. However, there are no organized institutions operating on the basis of *QH* except in the Islamic Republic of Iran, where the institution of *QH* has been utilized effectively to provide finance for the needy and where these institutions are widespread throughout the country (see below).

While *QH* funds have been functioning in Iran for a long time, they have had a phenomenal growth and success track record since the Islamic Revolution in 1979. In the case of Iran, *QH* funds, by and large, provide small consumer and producer loans and, in some cases, engage in profit-sharing activities with small producers and firms, thus supplementing the capital of the fund. These funds are usually associated in each locality with mosques or other religious organizations and, at times, with guilds or professional group associations. The capital is contributed by the more well-to-do, who are at liberty to withdraw their funds at any time. These funds operate with reasonably low administrative costs since most are managed through volunteer service contributed by the people within the group.

A *QH* fund has the following characteristics:

- It is flexible with respect to collateral; usually, no physical collateral is required—a cosignature for the loan by capital contributors is, more often than not, a substitute for physical collateral.
- Documentary procedures are usually very simple.
- Loans are usually small in size, approval procedures rapid, and disbursement quick.
- There are no interest charges involved. However, some funds charge as much as 1 percent to cover administrative costs.
- The fund has easy accessibility to capital contributors, borrowers, and cosigners because of their local proximity.

- The fund managers, from among capital contributors, are fully accountable.

MF and *QH*MF have major similarities, and differences. They target the same groups and are, for the most part, effective ways of avoiding informational problems by relying on peer monitoring, in the case of MF, and familiarity with the borrower and his or her reputation. Moreover, collateral is not the primary requirement for a loan in either MF or *QH*MF. Among the differences, two are crucial: unlike *QH*MF, MF charges interest, an abomination from an Islamic perspective; and, whereas in the case of MF there is a collective punishment for the group if one of its members defaults on a loan, in the case of *QH*MF there is no such requirement. In the case of a *QH*MF, a capital contributor has to introduce the borrower and, at times, cosign for the loan. However, if there is a default, there is no requirement that the cosigner has to withdraw from the fund.

8.3 THE IRANIAN EXPERIENCE WITH *QH*

Qard-ul-hassan funds (*QH*Fs) are the oldest form of Islamic financial institution in Iran, and were established long before the Iranian Revolution. These institutions have grown both in number and in the spectrum of financial services that they offer. Their versatile and growing activities compelled the Central Bank of Iran to submit an Act to the Iranian parliament for its approval to supervise *QH*F's along with other financial institutions such as banks, credit institutions, and other monetary organizations.

Prior to the Islamic Revolution in Iran, these funds were voluntary and were established in mosques, among families, or among employees of an organization. Thus, they did not need a business location and did not need to be registered as a charity or non-governmental organization. For this reason it is difficult to trace the date of their establishment. However, the first known fund was registered in Tehran in 1969 with a capital of 140 thousand rials (almost US$2,000). It then extended activity by collecting deposits and facilitating zero-interest-bearing loans (Askari 1992; Komijani and Askari 1991; Mohajerani and Askari 2002). This fund has survived to become a well-developed and active fund today. It took four years until the third fund was registered in Tehran with capital of 1.2 million rials (US$17,143) and 120 shareholders (Askari 1992; Komijani and Askari 1991; Mohajerani and Askari 2002). This new fund was registered as a financial (commercial) entity and was eligible to collect deposits and extend non-interest-bearing loans. Before the Islamic Revolution all banks in Iran were interest-based institutions, so this new fund served as a model for an Islamic financial institution, and others were established on the same model (Askari 1992; Komijani and Askari 1991). Two types of *QH* organizations were developed prior to the revolution; first there were the voluntary funds collecting *QH* deposits and extending loans, and second there were the non-interest-bearing financial organizations. In fact, one of the latter was called "Islamic Bank." The total number of both types had reached at least 200 by 1979 (Komijani and Askari 1991; Mohajerani and Askari 2002).

After the revolution, the number of funds started growing, both in cities and villages. According to one source, out of 1,200 units surveyed, 59 percent were located in cities, 16 percent in counties, and 25 percent in villages (Mohajerani and Askari 2002). Their total number exceeded 1,250 by 1986 (Mohajerani and Askari 2002). The reason for this rapid growth was religious motives and the ambiguous nature of the banking system before the implementation of interest-free banking laws in 1984. Although the Interior Ministry could register *QH*Fs as nonprofit organizations, few of them opted to be registered. Therefore, today the total number is unknown. As banks were nationalized after the revolution, this decision took away the opportunity for any new private financial institutions to be established. One available avenue was the establishment of *QH*Fs (Tayyebi and Hertmani 2004). This necessitated the Central Bank of Iran to gain supervisory authority over the *QH*Fs in 1989. The central bank's efforts led to a proposal of the "Unstructured Money Market" Act, and its approval by the Parliament in 2005.

In some Iranian provinces, *QH*Fs have formed a regional unit in which they deposit their excess funds and borrow from the regional unit at times of a liquidity crunch. These regional *QH*Fs are also voluntary financial units and their membership is optional for the local units. Other than these two central and regional organizations, no other financial body monitors the financial activities of *QH*Fs.

As stated earlier, the organizational form of *QH*Fs in Iran varies according to their purpose and location. Those that are formed among families and employees of an organization have no specific structure, and the form of the rest varies according to their size. Mostly the latter type—those that are located in an organization or workshop—have a constituent assembly, board of directors, general manager, inspectors, and employees (Mohajerani and Askari 2002). Each fund also has a board of trustees, which are mostly selected from local well-known and trustworthy persons, among whom the board of directors will be chosen. Some employees are paid and some are volunteers (Mohajerani and Askari 2002).

The general requirements for the eligibility of applicants are as follows:

- The application should be for a legitimate purpose.
- The borrower should be qualified and in real need of the loan.
- He or she should have a deposit account in the fund or open an account.
- The applicant should be introduced by one of the directors.
- The applicant should offer adequate guarantee for repayment of the loan according to the terms set by the fund.
- Someone should guarantee the repayment of the loan by the borrower.
- The applicant should be located within the fund's service area.

The funds provide loans for the following purposes:

- Marriage
- Home repairs
- Residential rents and mortgages
- Hospital and illness expenses
- Business working capital
- Education
- Agricultural activities, including farming, animals, and poultry production
- Small industries
- Home appliances
- Rehabilitation of damages caused by natural disasters
- Pilgrimage
- Supporting other *QH*Fs
- Supporting private and state organizations
- Repairs of mosques and shrines, and library construction
- Others

As indicated before, the exact number of *QH*Fs is unknown. There were at least 2,250 units in 1986 (Statistical Center of Iran, 2001). But according to Mohajerani and Askari (2002), the number has been estimated to have grown to 5,500 units by 2000. The Statistical Center of Iran published the results of a sample survey of *QH*Fs in 2000. This center has reported the performance of 1,229 *QH*Fs, which are situated in small workshops. Some of their statistical results are reproduced in the following tables.

The average size of the 1,229 locations surveyed was 95 square meters. Fifty-four percent of them were privately owned, 25 percent were rented, 14 percent were religiously endowed (*waqf*), and 6 percent had other types of proprietorship. Almost all of them covered their expenses from their revenues, and only 42 units were dependent on donations.

It can be seen from Table 8.1 that the number of deposits in all *QH*Fs in 2000 was more than 6.48 million accounts and that of loans was more than 1.7 million. Since the size of individual deposits is on average small and that of loans much larger, the number of deposits is a multiple of the number of loans.

Table 8.1 Deposits and loans

Number of deposits	6,480,237
Number of loans	1,777,583
Total value of deposits (million rials)	2,109,914
Total value of loans (million rials)	1,572,959
Total outstanding (million rials)	620,368

As shown in Table 8.2, the total value of output or revenues of *QH*Fs was 70,443 million rials; they used 8,884 million rials of intermediate products and inputs, to produce 61,560 million rials of value added in 2000. The ratio of total output to input value was 12.6.

Table 8.2 Value added

	(million rials)
Output value (revenues)	70,443
Intermediate goods and inputs	8,884
Value added	61,560

Therefore, *QH*Fs contribute significantly to the value added to the Iranian economy and play an outstanding role in its financial sector.

What are the sources of revenues of *QH*Fs? The answer is provided in Table 8.3. Almost 71 percent of total revenue is derived from

Table 8.3 Revenues (million rials)

Loans service charges	62,587
Commodities sold	10,791
Communication	67
Renting residential buildings	363
Rental income of nonresidential buildings	1,000
Government grants and subsidies	104
Individuals and nongovernment donations	10,382
Others	3,201
Total	**88,495**

charges on loan services. This rate differs among fund units since their cost of operation is different. Some have voluntary employees and others have paid workers. Some pay the rent on their working place and some have it free. Some funds charge a fixed amount for each loan serviced, others charge a percentage of the loan principal. But the overall rate is about 1 percent of the principal, regardless of maturity of the loan. It should be added that since each borrower is fully interviewed and evaluated before receiving a loan, some of the poor applicants are exempted from charges.

Many funds provide home appliances, durable consumer goods, and production inputs in rural areas. The rental income of residential and nonresidential buildings is the next category. Other sources of income are donations and contributions from individuals, governments, and nongovernment organizations. Since some of these funds are established and operated by employees of government organizations, they sometimes receive support from their organizations.

The expenses of *QH*Fs are listed in Table 8.4. The major items are labor and capital input outlays. Although some workers are not paid by *QH*Fs, still the total employees' compensation, redemption, and missions is 37,579 million rials. If this figure is added to accounting and legal services, the sum comes out to 38,128 million rials or 40 percent of total fund expenses. The capital tools and building expenses include rental charge on workplace, total instruments and buildings repair, and purchase of office tools. All together they amount to 3,090 million rials or 3 percent of total expenses. If purchase of goods for sale is added to this figure, it comprises 12 percent of the total. Other than the operating cost—that is, utilities and fuel—the other important item is transfer payments (449), which includes poor and needy borrowers who are exempted from repayment of their loans.

Table 8.4 Outlays and expenses (million rials)

Employees' compensation	37,352
Employees' redemption	162
Cost of accounting and legal services	549
Out of town missions	65
Purchase of sold commodities	8,301
Rental charge of workplace	908
Repair of tools and instruments	346
Repair of cars	130
Repair of buildings	596
Office tools and machines	1,110
Cleaning materials	178
Communications	533
Insurance	415
Water	200
Electricity	613
Fuel and energy	457
Depreciation	2,697
Taxes	667
Transfer payments	449
Repayment of loans	35,479
Banking services	154
Payment to depositors	312
Others	2,831
Total	**94,504**

Table 8.5 Fixed capital formation (million rials)

	Purchase order	Construction	Reconstruction and repair
Equipments and instruments	1,364	2	23
Office furniture and tools	2,357	34	147
Cars	255	—	27
Buildings	2,613	345	864
Computer software	1,110	10	1
Others	256	—	—
Total (9,408)	7,955	391	1,062

Table 8.5 shows the total fixed capital formation of 9,408 million rials and its various components. As expected, investment in buildings has the highest share, and office material and tools has the next highest share. Another interesting item is computer software, indicating that

Table 8.6 Employee information

Paid full time	3,489
Men	3,439
Women	50
Paid part time	
Men	1,136
Women	16
Unpaid	
Men	1,490
Women	19
Literate	6,106
Male	6,021
Female	85
Illiterate	43
Male	43
Female	0
Total	6,149

some *QH*Fs are adopting computer technology to become efficient service providers.

Information on employees is presented in Table 8.6. Although there are funds operating with one worker, the average number per fund is five persons. The proportion of paid, part-time paid and unpaid employees are 57, 19, and 24 percent, respectively. It is noticeable that almost one-fifth of *QH*F employees work on a voluntary basis. Less than 1 percent of total workers are illiterate.

8.4 THE FUTURE OF *QHMF*

As important as *QH* is, it is difficult to explain why it is ignored as a means of helping the needy in Muslim countries. The explanation requires some effort by sociologists and economists to investigate the causes of the underutilization of this very important contribution to investment that also embodies a critical element of poverty alleviation. The following suggestions can be made to exploit the use of *QH* to its full potential.

8.4.1 Building Institutions

The Islamic economics system is a rule-based system, which comprises a network of institutions each specialized in achieving a specific objective. The system operates efficiently in the presence of an effective enforcement mechanism. Institution building is generally a cumulative process, with several changes in different areas building up to complement and support one another. A growing body of research links institutional success (and failure) to development over time and across countries. For example, the success of access to financial services and the sophistication of financial markets reflect how institutions protect the property rights of borrowers and lenders. Successful implementation of *QH*MF will require the existence of supporting institutions and markets.

8.4.2 Instrumentalization of *QH*

In many well-to-do Muslim countries, in addition to weak institutions there may be a concern about the safety and the security of the principal contribution associated with *QH*. This concern could be alleviated by developing a formal financial instrument based on *QH* that addresses the questions of exposure to capital. For example, a credible existing Islamic financial institution can issue a financial instrument that would provide safety and security to a *QH* capital contributor. The Islamic financial institution can also instrumentalize the asset side of its balance sheet and provide additional resources to a *QH* or safety and liquidity to its capital contributors. Furthermore, it could provide *QH* resources to existing MF institutions to reduce the burden of their interest rate charges on their borrowers. But, how would such an Islamic financial institution cover its administrative costs? There are two possibilities: through investing a fraction of the mobilized resources and/or undertaking profit-sharing arrangements investing in productive projects of young entrepreneurs that have no access to formal credit markets.

8.4.3 Distribution Channels

Any trusted local establishments, such as post offices or mosques and madras, that exist in each and every corner of an Islamic country can serve as a distribution channel and banking agent.[3] Using these channels will reduce the overheads for the operation of *QH*MF and will maximize the utilization.

8.4.4 *QH*MF and Empowerment

Both public and private sector financial institutions can benefit from *QH*MF. With collective efforts, *QH*MF can be targeted to provide training, education, knowledge-sharing, and skills-building to the non-banked segment of the society. This empowerment will help them in the transition from a "non-banked" to "bankable" segment of society.

Economic and social justice is at the heart of Islam. In a truly Islamic economic system every member of society must be afforded the same opportunity to be productive and to advance. While equal access to education and health receive the most publicity, equity in other areas helpful for economic advancement, such as equality before the law and access to financing, are also critical. *QH*, and more specifically *QH*MF, provide Muslim societies with the needed vehicle to support the poorer segments of society to reach their economic potential. Their success will increase economic prosperity, reduce poverty, and in turn marginally improve income distribution, an often-neglected factor in most Muslim countries. *QH*MF can thus make a significant contribution, especially in less developed Muslim societies.

ENDNOTES

1 The authors are thankful to Professor Kazem Sadr for sharing his empirical research with us. For full details of the empirical study, see: Kazem Sadr and Gharzul-Hasaneh, "Financing and Institutions," paper presented at the First International Conference on Inclusive Islamic Financial Sector Development: Enhancing Islamic Financial Services for Micro and Medium Sized Enterprises (MMEs), held April 17–19, 2007 in Negara Brunei Darussalam.

2 *Qard-ul-hassan* is often referred to as "*Gharzul-hasaneh*" in Persian literature.

3 For example, in Brazil, local agents known as *correspondentes bancarios* are delivering reliable financial services to the previously "unbanked" communities.

CHAPTER 9

Developing the Theoretical Foundations of Economics in Islam[1]

The fields of conventional finance and economics have a symbiotic relationship and are almost inseparable, if not indistinguishable. The rules of behavior are the same in both fields. Many of the major historical advances in the field of finance can be attributed to economists such as Modigliani, Miller, Samuelson, Tobin, Markowitz, Sharpe, Merton, Ross, Shiller, and others. Islam is a rule-based religion and the fundamental rules for economics and finance are the same. Moreover, technical progress in Islamic finance has been much faster than intellectual progress in Islamic economics, creating considerable cognitive dissonance regarding Islamic financial instruments. If historical progress in conventional finance serves as a guide, intellectual advances in Islamic economic thought will only serve the development of Islamic finance. Further advances in Islamic finance will, in large part, depend on advances in Islamic economics as the two are inseparable. As a result, one of the major challenges facing the development of Islamic finance is the limited progress in Islamic economic thought.

9.1 INTRODUCTION

The problem facing all economic systems is what is taught on the first day of all economics classes in all parts of the world: *what* goods and services to produce, *how* to produce them using factors of production, and *for whom* should these be produced? The reason why all economies have to tackle these questions is that resources are scarce—everything cannot be produced to satisfy all members of a society. Different economic systems address these central questions differently. In a market-based, Western economic system, the underlying assumptions are: consumers are rational individuals who buy goods and services at the lowest available price to maximize their individual utility; firms or producers produce what is demanded at the lowest cost in order to maximize their profit; and in a perfectly competitive market setting the interaction of these different independent agents (consumers and producers) produces an "optimal solution" to the economic questions facing any society. Minimal government intervention may be required when there are externalities associated with economic activity. This optimal solution embodies no judgment on the relative welfare of individual members of society, does not take into account the welfare of future generations, and essentially assumes perfect accord between the interest of individuals and that of society. As a result, though consumption and production may be close to the envisaged optimum, the welfare of future generations may be compromised to the benefit of the present, and a significant amount of people in society are destitute and have little or no economic opportunity. The Western economic model focuses on a narrowly defined economic efficiency, accepts the selfish nature of man, and abstains from any value judgment.

In the former Soviet Union, the Western economic system was dismissed as unfair to broad members of society and the progress of society at large. The state told producers what to produce, how to produce it, and decided how economic spoils would be divided. The predictable result was economic inefficiencies that produced unacceptable rates of economic growth, goods and services that were not desired by consumers, a state that extinguished individual motivation and drive, and universal economic deprivation. The Soviet approach endeavored to address socioeconomic justice and to promote societal goals (through the enhanced role of the state), but its efforts produced economic collapse.

Islamic societies face the same three economic problems of all societies; however, they have the additional task of integrating Islamic values into solving these economic questions. The Islamic goal, as proscribed in the *Qur'an* and the *sunnah*, is not consumption maximization. Economic solutions must be in conformity with the spiritual needs of humankind and thus with Islamic values. The central values of Islam are the welfare of society and socioeconomic justice. All members of an Islamic society must be given the same opportunities to advance; in other words, a level playing field. All members of society must be afforded the minimum required for a dignified life: shelter, food, and healthcare. The rights of future generations must be respected and preserved. Whereas the basis of Western economics is to accept selfish utility-maximizing individuals and profit-maximizing firms, Islam does not accept such behavior but advocates a behavior that conforms to Islamic teachings. Thus Islam advocates an environment where behavior is molded to support the goals of an Islamic society: societal welfare and socioeconomic justice. In the words of Chapra[2]:

> Unlike the secularist market paradigm, human well-being is not considered to be dependent primarily on maximizing wealth and consumption; it requires a balanced satisfaction of both the material and the spiritual needs of the human personality. The spiritual need is not satisfied merely by offering prayers; it also requires the molding of individual and social behavior in accordance with the *Shari'ah*, which is designed to ensure the realization of the *maqasid al-Shari'ah* (the goals of the *Shari'ah*, hereafter referred to as the *maqasid*), two of the most important of which are socioeconomic justice and the well-being of all God's creatures. Negligence of either the spiritual or the material needs would frustrate the realization of true well-being and exacerbate the symptoms of anomie, such as frustration, crime, alcoholism, drug addiction, divorce, mental illness and suicide, all indicating lack of inner contentment in the life of individuals.

And continuing with the words of Chapra, Islamic economics may be defined as[3]:

> ... that branch of knowledge which helps realize human well-being through an allocation and distribution of scarce resources that is in conformity with Islamic teachings without unduly curbing individual freedom or creating continued macroeconomic and ecological imbalances.

Thus it appears that there are two distinct approaches to the systematic development of Islamic economic theory. One approach is to start with the Western approach to consumer theory and the theory of the firm and then proceed with the analysis by imposing a series of Islamic constraints on the solution. A second approach is to ignore Western assumptions regarding consumer and firm behavior and assume behavior that would be compatible with Islamic doctrines, not accepting man as he is but as he should be. In this case society must, over time, mold human behavior to conform to the norms of human behavior advocated in the *Qur'an* and the *sunnah*, behavior that is in the interests of society as well as that of the individual and the firm. A good start in the first approach would be an elaboration of the constraints, and in the second approach an elaboration of the desired consumer and producer behavior coupled with the role of government policy. An interesting question is whether either approach—additional constraints or molded Islamic behavior—would result in solutions that yield lower individual utility? The answer is that it depends. If Islamic behavior motivates man more than before, then it is possible that firm output will increase, individual utility will rise, and societal welfare will be enhanced, even though there may be some loss of selfish motivation as assumed by conventional economic analysis.

9.2 THE DEVELOPMENT OF ISLAMIC ECONOMICS

Systematic thinking about Islam and economics by professional economists has a short history compared to the atrophy that followed an earlier remarkable period of fervent scholarship in the sciences and humanities in the Muslim world. This "hibernation," as Chapra calls it,[4] occurred after achievements in all areas of thought by Muslim scholars and the dynamic economic growth of Muslim societies, and after the contributions, discoveries, and intermediation of Islamic sciences helped kick off the development and growth in Western societies and economies. From present day perspectives, however, and especially when judged against the first three decades of development of other disciplines, the published writings on Islamic economics in various languages give a sense of a vibrant and energetic birth and infancy of a discipline. These efforts are directed toward the development of a coherent and rigorous explanation of how Islam proposes to organize an economic system by answering the fundamental questions of what should be produced, how and for whom, how decisions should be made and by whom, and, finally, how Islamic institutions could be revived to address modern societies' problems. However, such efforts to formulate a coherent foundation for Islamic economics have been disputed by two groups of thinkers: the first group expresses dissatisfaction with the pace and direction of progress made thus far in Islamic economics and disagrees with the concept, methodology, and objective of the discipline.[5] The second group expresses a strident New Weberian critique of Islam, in general, and Islamic economics, in particular, and views Islamic institutions and thought as contrary to the growth and development of Muslim societies.[6]

Neither of these critiques should come as a surprise to those engaged in serious scholarship and who follow developments in the Muslim world. The first group is a feature of the natural development of disciplines; such debates have intrinsicly existed within traditional economics. For professionals to be self-critical in any discipline only helps to sow the seeds for further inquiry, thereby providing the potential, if not the impetus, for new ideas. The second current is also natural, given the highly intense, charged, and noisy background of political developments of the last three decades. It is not surprising that this background would provide opportunities that, unfortunately, help to sustain particular phobias. Expressions of the detrimental effects of Islam and its institutions are not new; moreover, their most recent articulations are based on mere conjecture, or simple, spurious relationships and distortions designed to serve certain priorities. On the other hand, there have been views rejecting the New Weberian thesis as, indeed, there were counterarguments against the "Old" critique. The preliminary results of recent empirical research on the relationship between religion and economic growth seem to question the building blocks of this thesis; at least one recent systematic and methodologically defensible empirical study concludes that "Islam promotes growth."[7] Neither the New Weberian thesis nor the outrageous charge that the proponents of Islamic economics are basically anti-Western and that their writings feed into a presumed "clash of civilizations" could, or should, deter the progress of Islamic economics. Criticism encourages presentation of views in the marketplace of ideas, particularly if they are forcefully challenged. However, it will not just rest there, but rather continue to contribute to the further development of the discipline.

The need to tap deeply into the legacy of the wealth of information in Islamic sources—the *Qur'an*, *sunnah*, scholarly writings, *fiqh*, ethics, philosophy, history of Muslim societies, and history of thought—for the development of Islamic economics calls for patience with the pace of progress of the discipline. Sciences and disciplines grow in stages, and agreement among scholars regarding the analytical framework of any discipline provides a platform for progress. The outline of such a framework is emerging for Islamic economics, but clarification of the content of the framework and the specific details on a range of issues are just beginning to appear in the literature. Systematic and rigorous specification of the characteristics of the ideal economic system and of economic behavior that is consistent with Islamic injunctions would provide a benchmark for policies to bring reality closer to the ideal, which has to be an essential element of the content of the framework of Islamic economics. Any progress that results in a clear specification of the ideal, and which could command consensus among scholars, would depend in no small measure on the degree of precision and clarity embedded in the language of discourse proposed for the discipline. Scholars need a common language with agreed definitions of words, terms, and concepts, including a clear specification of the institutions that define the ideal Islamic economic system, and the individual and collective behavior expected in such a system. Islamic economics would then be in a position to analyze the reality in Muslim societies, compare it to the ideal, and suggest ways and means of either strengthening Islamic institutions where they exist or where they have not yet developed. Policies could be also recommended on how to establish them to achieve the objectives of the system, and how to correct the structure of existing institutions if they contradict or conflict with Islamic injunctions.

9.3 THE ISLAMIC ECONOMIC PARADIGM

9.3.1 The Basis of the Islamic Economic Paradigm

- Islam has a view on how to organize political, social, and economic systems based on a set of ontological and epistemological propositions regarding individuals and their collectivities.
- Defining an economic system as a collection of institutions dealing with production, exchange, distribution, and redistribution, and defining institutions à la North as rules and norms, Islam proposes a distinct economic system that differs in many important respects from those recommended by other schools of thought regarding how an economy is to be organized.[8]
- The behavioral rules and norms of an Islamic system—once clearly, rigorously, and analytically articulated in a way intelligible to economists—could yield empirically testable propositions, which, in turn, could lead to policy analysis and recommendation on solutions to the problems of modern societies.
- At present, the most important function of Islamic economics, as a discipline, is to develop a language with enough precision that can lead to a consensus among researchers regarding the meaning and function of terms, ideas, rules, and norms.

Given the large number of terms and concepts needed for proper analysis in the field, this may seem to be a daunting challenge.[9]

9.3.2 Reaching a Consensus

9.3.2.1 Forming an Islamic Economic Vocabulary

Considering that this discipline is rather new, it is perhaps natural that a general sense of ambiguity permeates discourse on Islamic economics. If, for example, authors are native Arabic speakers, but also write on the subject in English, French, or German, it is not unusual to find different degrees of imprecision surrounding the same term translated into these languages. There are also writings on Islamic economics in Turkish, Malay, Persian, and Urdu—as well as in other languages—that further complicate the task. Part of this difficulty is inherent in translation, as pointed out by Ali Khan (1991).[10] This, however, does not absolve the present generation of researchers from the necessity of reaching a consensus in developing a reasonably precise language for Islamic economics. In this context, it is useful to consider the progress of Islamic banking.

At present, a consensus exists among scholars on two fundamental propositions: interest is *riba*, and risk- and profit-sharing is the Islamic alternative. Early establishment of these propositions allowed progress in the theory and empirics of Islamic banking. This was first conducted through systematic efforts that established economic understanding of Islamic ideas and, second, through derivation of analytic implications from the two consensus-based propositions. The establishment of such vocabulary has helped to clarify and develop the field. It thus follows that similar approaches in different areas of the field will be fruitful as Islamic economics passes from infancy into adolescence and maturity. This would be within the framework of Ali Khan's "grid of enquiry," which "simultaneously involves history, theory, and culture if the answers that we seek are to have a depth of understanding ... a historically-and-theoretically-informed understanding." Each of the eight propositions (questions) posed by Ali Khan at the end of his important contribution constitutes a challenge, in response to which his own "grid of enquiry" is indispensable, particularly in the "articulation of an Islamic ethos."[11]

A survey of literature on Islamic economics over the past few decades reveals a reasonable degree of agreement on at least two important and fundamental issues: "Justice and Equity" as "the focus of the prophetic message," and the *Qur'an*, *hadith*, and *fiqh* as sources of Islamic Law.[12]

9.3.2.2 Justice and Equity

Siddiqi suggests that "Justice and Equity" are the focus of the prophetic message:[13]

> Islam is primarily about a spiritual view of life and a moral approach to life's problems, including the economic problem. The contentment Islam promised man is rooted in this spiritual and moral framework. ... It is time to demonstrate how modern man can live a peaceful, satisfying life by shifting to the Islamic paradigm that values human relations above material possessions.[14]

Such a "paradigm," in Siddiqi's conception, also shared by other scholars, is specified in its juxtaposition to another "paradigm," which contains three features:

- It is focused on the individual, society, or community, and appears as a mere aggregate having no independent significance.
- The individual is motivated by self-interest and focused on private gain.
- Maximization is the norm in this individual's pursuit of profit in enterprise and/or satisfaction in consumption.

9.3.2.3 The Qur'an, Hadith, and Fiqh

There is also a reasonable basis for agreement that the sources for specification of the characteristics of the "Islamic paradigm" are: the *Qur'an*, the *hadith* of the Messenger (pbuh), and *fiqh*. In developing this "paradigm," however, Siddiqi suggests that the most important source of ideas is the *Qur'an*, then the *hadith* of the Messenger (pbuh) and his behavior "as a consumer, as head of household, a producer of wealth through trade, as Head of State looking after the welfare of his people by guiding them in their economic activities, supervising and sometimes regulating their market, managing public property, etc ... These *sunnah*, are best understood as conduct and policy directed at realization of the objective and values in the *Qur'an* ... " It is in the use of *fiqh* that Siddiqi not only parts company with some other scholars' emphasis, but also suggests that too strong a focus on *fiqh* has hindered the progress of Islamic economics: "For many, if not most of the scholars, *fiqh* came first and the contemporary reality came next." He recommends that after consideration of the *Qur'an* and the *sunnah*, the "next thing to focus on is the contemporary reality, the current environment ... How to realize the economic values and achieve the Islamic ends in economic life in our times? That is the question we have to answer. It is in answering this question that we consult *fiqh*. It is a great help, an indispensable source, but not the only one. When it comes to identifying the appropriate means for realization of a certain end, [the] current state of human knowledge and technology may have things to offer no old treasure possibly could." So the "state of human knowledge and technology" would seem to suggest the last source of ideas that can inform the process of formation of the "Islamic paradigm."

9.3.3 Creating an Islamic Economic Paradigm

While there is a basis for consensus on the objective of Islam for the economy, on the sources, and on the idea that Islamic economics is capable of providing a "paradigm" different from traditional economics, there is no general agreement how such a paradigm would emerge. As suggested by Siddiqi, it has been difficult for scholars to think themselves out of the twin boxes of *fiqh* and traditional economics, both of which have led to disagreement on a number of issues, including the name and the definition of Islamic economics.

There are some who suggest that if Islamic economics is a science, it makes little sense to attach it to Islam. This view considers science as value-free—and, therefore, unattachable to a system of ethics, ideology, or religion—and has a narrow perspective even as applied to traditional economics as a science.[15] There is a considerable body of work not only questioning this judgment, but going further to show that science, in general, and "economic science," in particular, cannot be norm- or value-free. The latter view suggests that economics, as a social science, deals with economic behavior that is embedded in the culture as the economy itself is embedded in the society, and culture is shaped by the beliefs, mores, and values of the people that form society. Therefore, economics is by necessity culture-bound, and while it is possible to develop a set of propositions tautologically derived from a priori concepts, its usefulness in solving society's problems is questionable.

There are also those who hold the view that precisely because traditional economics grew out of a different historical–social–cultural experience than in Muslim societies, it is incompatible with Islam. Therefore, there is nothing useful to be gained in terms of finding solutions to the problems of Muslim societies through a marriage of Islam and economics.

There is a third view that seems to consider "economics" in what Polanyi calls its "substantive" rather than its "formal" meaning.[16] This view, which seems to be aware of the limitations implied by the "formal" notion of economics, suggests that Islamic economics could well situate itself, analytically at least, within the general field of economic enquiry.[17]

9.3.3.1 Is the "Means–Ends" Characterization Applicable?

Along with disagreements on what to name the emerging discipline is the question of how to define it. There have been a number of definitions of Islamic economics, but none seem to command a general consensus. Scholars within Islamic economics raise legitimate questions—as has been the case in general economics—as to whether the "means–ends" characterization is a satisfactory anchor for a definition of the discipline. Some writings suggest that this definition, with minor modifications, provides an appropriate framework for defining Islamic economics. Others, however, relying on various verses of the *Qur'an*, suggest the unacceptability of the notion of "scarcity" in the definition. This view holds that *Allah* (*swt*) has provided resources "in exact measure" for man to carry out his responsibilities, and that poverty emerges as a result of maldistribution and shirking responsible behavior. There is no question that there are verses in the *Qur'an* indicating clearly that the assumption of scarcity cannot hold in the aggregate and that maldistribution and shirking in redistributive responsibilities are causes of poverty. On the other hand, scarcity at the micro level is acknowledged in the *Qur'an*, with strong emphasis on the need for redistribution.[18]

There are those who suggest that economics, in its formal "means–ends" meaning, is applicable to "the study of any behavior since all behavior requires the expenditure of resources."[19] Nonetheless, it is important to acknowledge a substantial criticism of "means–ends" characterization that should be brought to bear on attempts to forge a definition for Islamic economics that could command consensus. In this effort, it is critical that the words of Ali Khan

(1991) are heeded that "... in the phrase Islamic economics one cannot give meaning to the noun without understanding the adjective and that such understanding can never be final and complete for any generation of scholars." This should not be interpreted that there are no immutable propositions, principles, rules, and norms in Islam relating to economic behavior, but that any generation's understanding of them should not be assumed final.

Consider the behavioral rule of prohibition of "إسراف" (overspending or extravagant spending) which, in any generation, will depend on the relativities of the economic ground realities defined by the conditions of each society. Therefore, what the present generation could do is to record its understanding of the adjective and pass it on to the next. In this effort, the present generation will need to clearly position its understanding of Islam as it pertains to the economic (in its substantive meaning) behavior as well as on the applicability of formal economics and its methods as they relate to that understanding. The present efforts to forge a consensus-based name or definition for Islamic economics, however, should not deter research in understanding Islam in its relation to economic behavior awaiting a consensus on a clear definition, which will emerge in due course.

9.3.3.2 Humanity and Islamic Economics

There is no avoiding the fact that in Islam all behavior is rules-based, that ethical values underlie the rules, and that the source of the rules is *Allah* (*swt*). Humanity knows the presence and force of these rules and the ethical values from the revelation—either directly from the *Qur'an*, or indirectly from the actions and sayings of the behavior that represented the most perfect implementation of the rules of the *Qur'an*: that of the Messenger (pbuh). Humanity also possesses the faculty of reason to understand the ethical propositions and the prescribed rules, and can apply the same faculty to deliberate when faced with a decision. To the extent that humanity uses this process of deliberation and reasoning to understand the ethical propositions and the rules contained in the Guidance of the Creator, and to arrive at decisions, it is rational.[20] Not only does the *Qur'an* rely strongly on reasoning, but it also prescribes and specifies the domain of observation, intellection, and reasoning for humanity, which begins from the depth of the individual's self (*nafs*) to the depth of the universe.

Neoclassical economics, relying on the "means–ends" definition and the "self-interest" hypothesis, postulates that the individual's behavior is rational in the sense that, faced with a choice, the decision-maker prefers more to less. The individual is the source of ontology and epistemology; all the needed knowledge is there for consumers to maximize utility, producers their profits, and society its welfare. The strong assumptions in neoclassical economics—the self-interest hypothesis and the rationality postulate—as well as the theorems of welfare economics have received considerable criticism from a variety of viewpoints. Over the last four decades, a number of new fields of enquiry have developed within economics to deal with the shortcomings of the neoclassical economics. These include, inter alia, the fields of "bounded-rationality," "information economics," "contract theory," "behavioral economics," "experimental economics," "noncooperative game theory," "new institutional economics," and "cognitive science."[21]

9.3.3.3 Behavioral and Experimental Economics

Intellectual developments in each of the abovementioned areas should hold considerable interest for Islamic economics. It would certainly be helpful to the development of the discipline if there were agreement among the scholars that there was no need to reinvent wheels. For example, very little effort is made at the present to understand empirically the behavior of Muslims, including the observed dissonance between rules and behavior or ideal and reality. In this regard, methodological progress in the field of behavioral and experimental economics could be helpful.

9.3.3.4 Bounded Rationality

Developments in the field of "bounded rationality" would be worth studying to see if useful results could be obtained by extending the present understanding of this field in terms of cognitive constraints on rational behavior to constraints originating from the behavioral rules of Islam.

9.3.3.5 New Institutional Economics

Recent efforts to explain the wide income differentials among countries, or why some economies grow and others stagnate, have brought much attention to the role of institutions. In particular, two sets of institutions have been identified as crucially important: institutions that protect property rights and those that enforce contracts.

New Institutional Economics—particularly as it has been extended to understand ideology—seems to hold promises of fruitful investigation for Islamic economics since Islam is rules-based and New Institutional Economics defines institutions in terms of rules and norms. Research work in this area could be extended to understand Islamic economic institutions and to analyze the extent or even existence of these institutions and their operation at present in Muslim societies. To create an incentive structure for the establishment of new institutions compatible with Islamic objectives would be another fruitful line of inquiry.

9.3.3.6 Contract Theory

Developments in the field of contract theory seem to provide a fertile ground for investigation as the institution of contracts is of primary importance within the constellation of behavioral rules of Islam. A potentially useful area of inquiry is investigation of applicability of the concept of "incentive compatibility" in structuring contracts as well as organizing new institutions compatible with Islam. Similarly, the closely related concepts of "trust," "commitment," and "reciprocity," which are being investigated in a variety of settings, could provide useful grounds for operationalizing the understanding of interpersonal relationships in Muslim societies which play a key role in the fostering of institutions.

9.3.3.7 Information Economics

Information economics has yielded important results, applicable mainly to situations where there are limitations and constraints on the availability of information. While the findings of information economics have already played a useful role in Islamic finance, a more general application of these insights in other areas of Islamic economics would be no doubt productive.[22]

9.4 HERMENEUTICS AND ISLAMIC ECONOMICS

The Islamic economic "paradigm" will be successfully constructed, and solutions proposed to society's problems—such as what is to be done about distorted income distribution, external diseconomies accompanying growth, unemployment and poverty, environmental problems, and the like—only when a clear and analytically rigorous language of discourse is developed. In addition to forming an Islamic economic vocabulary, two other sources are useful in developing such a common language: history of thought and economic hermeneutics.

The history of thought consists of a rich field of research and serves as a source of ideas. Preliminary research suggests considerable contribution from Muslims to the development of economics, particularly in the early stage of the formation of the discipline, which the profession has been slow to recognize and acknowledge. Further in-depth research in this area is important for a variety of reasons.

First, it would show that ideas developed anywhere belong to humanity as a whole, and that borrowing of the results of investigations of one segment of humanity from another is a normal course of evolution of ideas. It is, therefore, the right of those interested in the development of Islamic economics to borrow any useful ideas in this regard, just as it was the practice of the European scholars in the Middle Ages to borrow from Muslims.

Second, moral philosophy gave birth to political economy, out of which grew the present discipline of economics. And moral philosophy from the Middle Ages to the time of Adam Smith was influenced by the scholarship of Muslims. While the historians of economic thought generally ignore Muslim contributions, they emphasize the Aristotelian thought of the Middle Ages. However, the latter arrived in Europe already influenced by Muslim intermediation and was as Aristotelian as present day neoclassical economics is classical.[23]

Studies of the contributions of Muslim scholars up to the time of Adam Smith could provide an opportunity for the present generation of scholars to splice present Islamic thinking about economics with pre-Smith thought and, thus, accelerate the recovery from centuries of atrophy in thinking about Islamic economic behavior. Moreover, such scholarship may well provide the appropriate response to the question of why Muslim scholarship did not continue the tradition of Ibn Rushd and develop an analytic discipline to deal with economic matters. Research has demonstrated that, in his commentary on Aristotle's Nichomachean Ethics, Ibn Rushd had developed an initial expression of the law of demand.[24] It is important to investigate why Muslim scholars who followed Ibn Rushd did not pursue this line of thought.

Third, the relationship between moral philosophy and political economy is now receiving fresh attention in new exegetical research in reinterpreting Adam Smith and other classical economists. Scholarship by those interested in Islamic economics may contribute to a reconstruction of a political economy based on moral philosophy, and serve to provide a common ground for analysis of all behavior. A simple example of research into the contribution of Muslims to the history of thought may be helpful.

Hicks (1986) attributes the rationality assumption to historic mercantile dealings:

> ... each transaction is separate ... undertaken for its own sake, without reference to the possibility that the terms on which it is made may influence the terms on which it will be possible to make further transactions ... There can be no question of the rationality of the proceeding ... The merchant—the pure merchant, who confines himself to such market-oriented dealings—is the original economic man. His behavior is so rational, so clearly rational, that we (economists) can readily reason from it; our reasoning from it is the start of economics ... It may be objected that in the work of what we reckon to be the first great school of economists, the classical economics of Smith and Ricardo, the merchant does not so obviously occupy a leading place ... I believe however that the picture looks different if one goes further back ... It was many centuries earlier, in fifteenth-century Florence, that merchants began to study how to keep accounts ... The appearance of the practice of keeping accounts, which first appears among merchants, is a clear indication that the business is being conducted rationally, with one eye to profit ... During the centuries that elapsed between the invention of accounting and the time of Adam Smith, the practice of bookkeeping must have spread quite widely ... Thus it was natural to assume that non-merchants, or many of them, would be behaving more or less like merchants. Though it was a simplification to treat them as Economic Men, they would be moving in that direction. That was all the classical economics needed, for their use of profit motive.[25]

It is interesting that Hicks suggests in the same article that the classical economics did not need the assumption of utility maximization:

> It is notable that the classical economists did not treat the consumer as an Economic Man; they had no need to do

so. That comes in with Jevons, with Marginal Utility. The producer was making money, so his goal could be set in monetary terms. The consumer is spending money, so his goal must be defined in a different manner. 'Utility' had to be invented in order to give him something in which to do his maximizing ... To treat consumption, or spending, as a maximization against constraints is so appealing, mathematically, that it was bound to carry all before it. But, is it any more than a convenient assumption? There can be no question of the service it has performed in fitting statistics into a pattern; but that is just convenience—it does not show that people do act in the way the theory describes.

9.4.1 The Implications of Hick's Model of Mercantile Behavior

Hicks has been quoted here extensively for two reasons: first, according to him, it was the practice of bookkeeping that suggested the "rationality" concept and the profit motive to the classical economists. Now, from the eighth century AD onwards, Muslims succeeded in developing international trade and commerce on a scale that surpassed anything known before. The greatest contribution of the Muslim world to the medieval economic life was arguably the development of commercial methods based on writing and recording. Scholarship has demonstrated that the system of commercial arithmetic and accounting was first introduced to Europe in the book *Liber Abaci* by Leonardo Fibonacci or Leonardo Pisano in 1202, who had learned the system from Muslims at Bougie in North Africa.[26] If Bernardelli is correct to suggest that *Liber Abaci* should be considered as the beginning of economic analysis, then the discipline, at least in part, owes its origin to Muslim scholarship.[27] Second, Hícks suggests that classical economics only needed the rationality assumption in terms of "self-interest" and the profit motive to develop the corpus of its ideas.

Recent scholarship has questioned the "pure selfishness" attributed to Adam Smith's understanding of the "self-interest" motive. Given the broad-based philosophical views of Adam Smith and, in particular, the depth of thinking in the *Theory of Moral Sentiments*, the economic man, with pure selfishness as his mover, seems too narrow and too one-dimensional to correspond to the understanding of the ethical and moral concerns of Adam Smith, which are so apparent in his writings and lectures. Moreover, it appears, even from the passages quoted from Hicks, that there is no need to interpret "self-interest" as "pure selfishness" to justify the profit motive. Careful reading of the *Theory of Moral Sentiments* and *The Wealth of Nations* seems to indicate that Smith's views are based and focused on two characteristics that he postulated for human nature: self-interest and the need for social cooperation, both of which he needs to explain the workings of the market. A "pure selfishness" seems an unnecessarily strong assumption for a theorist such as Adam Smith with a moral/ethical orientation, on the one hand, and belief in parsimony and Occam's Razor, on the other.[28]

Considering Hick's very simple model of mercantile behavior, what motive could be attributed to agents operating in an Islamic market? By the latter, it is meant a market in which merchants have internalized Islamic injunctions and behave according to the rules specified by the *Shari'ah*. An understanding of these rules of behavior suggests that they are intended to ensure a level playing field for all participants. A present-day understanding of these rules suggests that this is done by prohibiting barriers to entry and exit and by encouraging the flow of free and full information accomplished, in part, through prohibition of deliberate creation of asymmetric information.[29]

Assuming merchants observe all the rules of market behavior, would there be any prohibition on the profit motive? While a Muslim merchant may have other motives, there is no evidence—from the sacred sources, the economic history of Medina during the lifetime of the Messenger (pbuh), or the writings of Muslim scholars and *fuqaha'*—to suggest that, provided the rules prescribed for market operations are observed, the profit motive should be ruled out. The Islamic vision of how markets are organized, operate, and clear is different from that of other systems: the physical analogue of that vision existed in remarkable uniformity in the Muslim world for centuries. These markets were physically structured to facilitate the workings of the Islamic rules governing market operations. Each product had its own specialized market; for example, clothing, jewelry, housewares, food products, and raw materials. This concentration allowed the efficient flow of information, realization of economies of agglomeration, ease of supervision, and quality control by guilds (أصناف) and *muhtasibs*.[30]

However, it is important to note that, while markets exist and, indeed, are encouraged, an Islamic economy is not a market economy in the sense of neoclassical economic theory. Even though the Fundamental Theorems of the neoclassical economics allowed a limited role for the government to correct market failure, it is, by and large, the price system that rules the market economy. Through its rules of behavior for market participants, and without negating the signaling function of the price system in the market, the *Shari'ah* assigns a significant role to nonmarket decisions to ensure economic and social justice. This seems to be true in cases of all pre- and post-market activities in terms of preproduction principles of property rights, in the case of the former, and through redistributive institutions, in the case of the latter.

If there is any validity in what has been said so far, investigations in the history of thought of Muslim and non-Muslim scholars, up to the time of the marginalist schools on the ontological and epistemological foundations of economic behavior, could be fruitful. This effort could provide, in turn, a rigorous foundation for analytic thinking in Islamic economics. Investigation in this area ties well with another field of research that can also prove a fertile ground for contribution to the development of Islamic economics: hermeneutics.

In the Islamic context, hermeneutics is a systematic, rigorous, and analytic economic interpretation of sources of Islam, the *Qur'an*, the *sunnah* of the Messenger (pbuh), the economic history of early Islam, and the writings of scholars and *fuqaha'*. Because of the extreme sensitivity of this issue, particularly as it relates to the *Qur'an* and the *sunnah*, it is essential to differentiate between what is meant here by hermeneutics and the generally understood notion of *tafseer*.[31] Hermeneutics, as used here, does not mean *tafseer*—that is, the first order interpretation of the sacred sources which is a highly specialized field—but rather the process of extracting economic meaning from the first order interpretation.

9.4.1.1 Differentiating Tafseer from Hermeneutics

A simple example of what is meant by hermeneutics in the present context may help to clarify the difference. The *Qur'an*'s declaration in verse 276 of Chapter 2 that "... يمحق الله الربا ويربي الصدقات ..." (that *Allah* (*swt*) destroys *riba* and (but) makes transfer to the needy grow at a compound rate) has a first order interpretation (*tafseer*) which is primarily the responsibility of those specialized in the science of interpretation. However, an economist could understand this verse by relating the two future verbs "يمحق" (destroys) and "يربي" (makes grow at compound rate) to the differential impact of "الربا" (interest) and "الصدقات" (transfer to the needy) in the economy by noting who is at the giving end and who at the receiving end of these transactions. The economist could then model—say in a simple Keynesian framework with computed marginal propensities to save and consume—the differential impact.[32] He could even empirically test the results against actual observations.

The existing literature on Islamic economics contains other examples of economic hermeneutics. One example is Ali Khan's efforts to understand various concepts that play key roles in the ontological and epistemological foundations of Islamic economics. Chapra's important book *The Future of Economics* contains many illustrations of economic hermeneutics. Another example is the recent effort by Tajeddin in explaining the Qur'anic rules of inheritance; it is a good beginning. Additional economic insights and meaning could be gained from analyzing these rules within an intergenerational, intertemporal framework. Yet another example is the papers by Braima in which a Qur'anic model of the economy is presented. The impressive papers of Rafic Al-Misri are also worthy of mention.

9.4.1.2 Relating Hermeneutics to Rationality, Self-Interest, and Human Traits

Efforts in arriving at rigorous and analytic economic insights into Islamic views of such elemental concepts as rationality, self-interest, and human traits through hermeneutics seem essential. For example, it was suggested earlier that, provided the rules of market behavior are observed, profit motive—as a guide to behavior in the market—cannot be ruled out. This, however, does neither necessitate an assumption of pure selfishness in the market, nor a narrow conception of self-interest for behavior, in general. For example, it is possible to argue that the notion of self-interest is an essential Islamic behavioral postulate, provided account is taken of the fact of an infinite planning horizon for the individual and the collectivity in concordance with the Islamic belief in the Hereafter (الآخرة). The *Qur'an*, in a number of verses, insists that whatever the result of the behavior, it is "for" or "against" the nafs of the actor; that is, *"If you do good, you will do good for your own souls, and if you do evil, it shall be for them."* 17:7, meaning that if you act beautifully you are doing so for your own self and if you behave ugly you also do so to your own self. Moreover, there are a number of other verses in which rules prescribed are coupled with; "it is better for you."

Considering the notion of "the self" (*nafs*), there are some economists who have considered this concept in more than a single dimension.[33] Economic hermeneutics of the *Qur'an*'s concept of the *nafs*, the explanations provided by the *hadith* of the Messenger (pbuh), and the writings of Muslim scholars on this subject could be immensely valuable here. These sources seem to view the *nafs*, which motivates behavior, as dynamically moving: positively toward perfection, or negatively toward a position "worse than" animals. This is one area where Muslim philosophers have advanced crucial ideas based on the sacred sources. Since changes in the *nafs* affect tastes and preferences, the insights gained from a study of the works of these scholars will have implications for economic behavior.[34]

9.4.1.3 Relating Hermeneutics to Islamic Institutions

Applying economic hermeneutics to important Islamic concepts—such as covenant, contract, trust, commitment, *iman*, *taqwa*, and other essential notions—is imperative for a clear and rigorous articulation of Islam's views on economics, the economy, finance, market structure, poverty, and economic development and growth. For example, hermeneutics of Islam's position on contracts and insights into the incentive structure for observance of their stipulation and breech remedies would be enormously helpful for understanding this important institution within the Islamic economic system. Similarly, extracting economic meaning as to what the sources consider important conditions for economic development and growth, as well as the institutions that must exist in the society for these conditions to be met, would seem crucial to formulating policy recommendations based on economic analysis. For example, verse 96 of Chapter 7 of the *Qur'an* "*And if the people of towns had believed and had* taqwa (*ever-awareness and consciousness of* Allah), *We would have opened for them blessings from the heavens and from the earth; but they belied so We seized them for what they achieved.*"—suggests conditions under which societies can develop and grow as well as reasons why they do not. The verse specifies *iman* and *taqwa* as conditions (necessary and sufficient?) for growth. If this understanding turns out to be consistent with first order interpretation (*tafseer*), an economist could seek behavioral traits and characteristics that define these conditions in order to develop a Qur'anic theory of growth. This would mean an investigation of sources to reach a clear specification of behavioral rules, the collective observation of which would define these conditions. An economic hermeneutical understanding of each of these rules can yield a matrix of elements that define the conditions. For example, first verse of the fifth chapter of the *Qur'an* declares: "O you who believe! fulfill the obligations." This is a behavioral rule emphasized in the sayings and actions of the Messenger (pbuh) and commented upon in Islamic philosophical, ethical, *fiqhi*, and judicial scholarship. An economist's understanding of this rule would also tap into areas such as information economics, law and economics, transaction cost economics, institutional economics, and contract theory to have a clear understanding of the economic implications of observance, or otherwise, of this rule and draw operational inferences for empirical verification. The order to the believers to be faithful to their contracts, with far-reaching implications for contract negotiations, enforcement, and breech remedies, is only one among the rules that define *iman*. A matrix of the rules for both *iman* and *taqwa* could well define the Islamic theory of economic growth and development.

9.4.1.4 Relating Hermeneutics to the Islamic Economic History

The economic history of Muslim societies, especially in the earliest period, particularly during the time of the Messenger (pbuh), is another rich source for economic hermeneutics. An excellent example is Sadr's work on the early Islamic period, which, through hermeneutics, draws implications for fiscal, monetary, development, and environmental policies. Hasanuz Zaman's book *The Economic Functions of the Early Islamic State* [International Islamic Publishers, Karachi (1981)], published over 20 years ago, also focuses on the economics of the early period of Islam. For centuries and before the beginning of the discipline of economics, Muslim societies managed their economic affairs. It is, therefore, natural to expect that an understanding of the economic history of these societies would yield valuable insights into the workings of Islamic economic institutions, based on which an understanding could be gained into the reasons why some of these institutions did not evolve. Investigation into the historical evolution of markets in Muslim societies, beginning with the first market established by the Messsenger (pbuh) in Medina, could yield valuable insights into their operations in terms of observance of the rules of *Shari'ah*, instruments of supervision and regulation of these markets, and the role of the prices and the equilibrium process.

Hermeneutics of this historical evolution could yield insights into how markets could be structured and organized in consonance with the rules of *Shari'ah*. As Siddiqi has suggested in his presentation quoted earlier, in many of the published works of the recent years on Islamic economics references to *fiqh* have been prominent. *Fiqh* literature is a valuable legacy for ideas regarding economic behavior.[35]

9.4.1.5 Relating Hermeneutics to an Islamic Definition of Justice

One area in which economic hermeneutics of all sources could be of great help is efforts to elucidate a concrete economic definition of Islam's view on justice. There is a consensus among scholars of Islamic economics that social justice is the most important objective of an Islamic economy and abstract models have been proposed based on the desiderata of justice and beneficence. However, no clear sense of what these concepts mean, analytically and operationally, has been provided. Without such a definition, it is difficult to see how economic analysis and policy recommendations can be made on ways to achieve social justice. The history of scholarship in traditional economics demonstrates the complexities of arriving at a consensus on a criterion by which a particular pattern of economic distribution can be judged as being just. Hermeneutics of various concepts of justice related to economic behavior, whether on individual or aggregate levels, in the Islamic sources to arrive at consensus regarding an analytic definition and criteria of justice would be a major contribution.[36]

Even a cursory look at Islamic sources suggests a comprehensive conception of justice that permeates throughout individual and community life.[37] Every dimension of individual behavior affecting the individual and social interactions is subject to some conception of justice. Each conception of justice, as applied in the *Qur'an*, refers to a specific dimension of individual and collective behavior. Associated with each conception is a term and a context. Economic hermeneutics of these terms and their associated context pose a major challenge. A simple example should illustrate the task.

One of the miracles of the *Qur'an* is the economy and parsimony of its language concomitant with its precision. Yet, sometimes the *Qur'an* uses two or more words to indicate what appears to be the same term or the same process. The precision of the *Qur'an* would suggest that there have to be deeper reasons for this phenomenon. In the case of "justice" terms such as "حق" (right), "ميزان" (scale),"قسط" (interrelational justice), "عدل" (justice) and others are used in various contexts. Based on the already available literature, conception of justice plays a major role in the initial allocation of resources, production, exchange, market, distribution, and redistribution. The economic hermeneutics of dimensions and meaning of these terms, particularly as used in the *Qur'an* and *hadith* of the Messenger (pbuh), in the writings of scholars and philosophers would seem indispensable to building a rigorous foundation of Islamic economic analyses, if indeed achieving justice is the major objective of an Islamic economy.

9.5 CONCLUSION

Whether Islamic economics is considered to be an entirely different discipline from traditional economics—a position justified by its world view, its view of rationality, its view on humanity's nature, its emphasis on the need for correspondence between behavior and the prescribed rules as well as its other specific dimensions—or as a special subfield within that discipline, it has made considerable progress since its revival a little over three decades ago. This is remarkable, given that there is virtually no organized support for this effort, in sharp contrast to the multitude of private and public foundations providing financial support to research in traditional economics. Despite the wealth of resources available in many Muslim societies, there is lamentably little support for scholarship in Islamic economics. Moreover, even the academic recognition of research activities in this field is, by and large, lacking, and there is a dearth of incentives for scholars to pursue their interest in furthering contemporary thinking in the discipline. Nevertheless, the personal dedication of scholars has produced a credible corpus of work that provides a sense of optimism regarding the future of Islamic economics.

There is no reason to doubt that scholarly activities in this field will continue, or to think that, at some point in the future, it will not develop a rigorous analytic foundation for policy analysis and prescription to achieve the objectives of Islam for the economy. Learning from the historical development of traditional economics—both its successes and failures—research in Islamic economics should anchor its progress on an interdisciplinary approach, paying due attention to the historical, philosophical, psychological, and sociological dimensions of what Islam intends for individual and collective economic behavior. The immense scholarly works of Muslim philosophers, *fuqaha'*, historians, and social critics provide a valuable legacy that should be extremely helpful in this process. Developments in traditional economics are also a fertile field for researchers in Islamic economics to harvest as a source of ideas. In this chapter, while the economic history of Muslim societies and thoughts has been emphasized as a major source of ideas, special attention has also been directed at developing a proper "language" of discourse in Islamic economics with the hope of the emergence of consensus-based, analytic, and operational definitions and descriptions of major concepts that scholars would need to further refine ideas and generate new insights. A common language, with its own "grammar," of Islamic economics is fundamentally important; as Ali Khan suggests: " ... the choice of language has epistemological implications."

For this reason, there is a critical need for the development of a coherent, comprehensive, and systematic economic hermeneutics as a foundational structure that would support research, dialogue, and debate in Islamic economics, as well as in building the future edifice of theoretical, empirical, and policy structure of this discipline. The present generation of researchers is in a position to make an important contribution by focusing on activities that can draw economic meanings and inferences from terms, ideas, and concepts expounded in the sources of Islam. The hope would be that at some point in time a collection similar to Palgrave's *Dictionary of Economics* could be developed for Islamic economics. The momentum of these efforts would be much accelerated if financial resources, similar to those provided to investigations in traditional economics by major foundations, could be mobilized in Muslim societies to support such activities.

ENDNOTES

1 This chapter is based on the lecture delivered by Abbas Mirakhor at the acceptance of the Islamic Development Bank's award in recognition of his contribution to Islamic economics in April 2005.

2 See Chapra, M. U., "What Is Islamic Economics," Islamic Development Bank Winner's Lecture Series no. 9, (Jeddah, Saudi Arabia, 1996): 25–26.

3 Ibid.: 33.

4 See Chapra, M. U., *The Future of Economics*, The Islamic Foundation (2000). This is a valuable book, a valiant effort in framing the past, present, and future of the discipline. Nevertheless, the appeal here for the development of a common language of discourse for Islamic economics that can command consensus among practitioners remains valid. Meeting the challenging task of removing, or at least reducing, the present fuzziness is still an imperative for the acceleration of development and growth of the discipline.

5 See, for example, the discussions in the Round Table organized by the Islamic Research and Training Institute (IRTI) of the Islamic Development Bank on May 26–27, 2004, in cooperation with the Kuwait-based Arab Planning Institute (API).

6 Ali Khan in his "Globalization" paper—*Islamic Economic Studies*, 8, no. 1: 52—suggests that "there seems to be a tremendous anxiety about Islamic economics and how it may have an adverse effect on globalization." Timur Kuran, in all his writings on Islamic economics, displays such anxiety. An example is, "Islam and Under-Development: An Old Puzzle Revisited," *Journal of Institutional and Theoretical Economics*, 153 (1997): 41–71. Despite pretensions of "dispassionate analysis," the content of this paper and the position taken in others of his published works on the subject belie the claim. Superficial understanding of Islam, lack of familiarity with the canonical texts, Islamic history, and history of thought and strong priors lead to "a very distorted image of Islam," as Ebrahim and Safadi indicate in their paper "Behavioral Norms in the Islamic Doctrine of Economics: A Comment," *Journal of Economic Behavior and Organization*, 27 (1995). Distortion by selectivity is rather transparent in Kuran's paper, "The Discontents of Islamic Morality" in *American Economic Review*, 86, no. 2 (May 1996): 438–42, in which Islamic economics is passionately criticized and a profoundly absurd claim is made that, " . . . the main purpose of Islamic economics is not to improve economic performance . . . its real purpose is to help prevent Muslims from assimilating into the emerging global culture whose core elements have a Western pedigree . . . Its chief instrument for fighting assimilation is the guilt that it fosters by characterizing certain universal economic practices as un-Islamic . . . From Maududi onwards, the moral discourse of Islamic economics has cultivated the view that the behavioral standards of Islam are fundamentally at odds with those of the West." Kuran then continues his delusional claim that "the civilizational clash that Islamic economics is fueling is often misconstrued as a collision of old and new . . . In trying to strengthen the Islamic identity of Muslim communities as a means of breaking their nonreligious solidarity patterns, today's Islamic fundamentalists are attempting, then, to perform a task at which the earliest Muslims failed" (p. 440). Nowhere in the paper is an attempt made to demonstrate the existence of the "nonreligious solidarity" of today's Muslim communities which Islamic economics is presumed to be trying to break. The selective reading of Islamic sources, history, and history of thought and unwarranted inferences in Kuran's criticism take much more space to address than is available here, nevertheless one point is worth noting: Kuran does not seem to be aware of the universality of the message of Islam. The fact is that the unity of humankind and of the creation is so emphasized in the *Qur'an* and *ahadith* that Muslim philosophers consider the Unity of Creation as a corollary to the axiom of *tawheed* (the Unity of the Creator); as the *Qur'an* states: "*Neither your creation (was) nor your resurrection (will be) except as one united soul.*" (31:28). Moreover, the position of the *Qur'an* and the *sunnah* on inducing efforts at integration and unity of humankind is so strong that all the moral and ethical rules can be interpreted as being addressed to this objective; see A. A. Sakr: "Individual and Social Responsibility in Islamic Thought," PhD dissertation (New York University, 1966): 167–175. Also see Tariq Ramadan, *Western Muslims and the Future of Islam*, (New York: Oxford University Press, 2004.) All the "dos" relate to behavior that promotes integration

of the humanity and all the "don'ts" are those that lead to disintegration. It is a misjudgment to accuse the scholars named in Kuran's article as attempting to prevent assimilation of Muslims "into the emerging global culture."

7 See Marcus Noland, "Religion, Culture, and Economic Performance," *Institute for International Economics* (2004). Other recent empirical research into religion and economics includes: Luigi Guiso, Paola Sapienza, and Luigi Zingales "People's Opium: Religion and economic attitudes," *Journal of Monetary Economics*, 50 (2003): 225–282. This paper concludes that "on average, religious beliefs are associated with 'good' economic attitudes," and that "Christian religions are more positively associated with attitudes conducive to economic growth." But, see their sample and questions on pp. 234–37. The second recent empirical paper is by Robert J. Barro and Rachel McCleary, "Religion and Political Economy in an International Panel," *Working Paper No. 8931*, National Bureau of Economic Research, May 2002. The paper finds that "growth responds positively to enhanced religious beliefs ... " but also see their sample and regression results.

8 For an attempt at a definition of such a system, see A. Mirakhor, "Outline of an Islamic economic system," Zahid Husain Memorial, Lecture Series, no. 11 (22 March 1995), State Bank of Pakistan, in which the system is defined as a collection of institutions and these are defined, in the tradition of North, as rules and norms of behavior. Present understanding of Islamic economics, based on published writings, is that there are rules (قواعد) and value norms (قيم) which underlie all economic behavior, individual and collective. These rules and norms need to be analytically and rigorously defined in terms of their economic meaning and systematically catalogued. This effort would help not only the present and future generations of economists working in the discipline of Islamic economic but also others, as Yosri suggests (pp. 23–24), and also as suggested by Rafik Younis Al-Misri in his paper "Definition of Islamic Economics" in the *Review of Islamic Economics*, 4, no. 1 (1995): 36. See also Mohsin Khan and Abbas Mirakhor: "Islam and the Economic System," *Review of Islamic Economics*, 2, no. 1 (1992): 1–30.

9 Ali Khan has emphasized this point in a number of his articles. See M. Ali Khan "Review: Journal of King Abdul Aziz University," *Islamic Economics*, 3 (1991): 97–177: " ... what I am trying to emphasize is that we, as scholars, need to make explicit, the order of the language we use ... we would be better served if we are clear as to the domain of discourse we work in, clear as to which body or style of knowledge we address." He also points to the need to discuss issues from "differing vantage points from which to grope toward the subject of Islamic Economics ... I would submit that we keep firmly at the back of our minds the fact that political economy is a mutant of moral philosophy and that in an avoidance of a static conception of the subject, we engage in wide-ranging conversations, much as the Apostle himself did in his lifetime" (p. 116). See also his paper "On Trust as a Commodity and on the Grammar of Trust," in *Journal of Banking and Finance* Vol. 26, (2002): 1719–66, in which he points to the epistemological dimensions of language. See also Rashid, who echoes the sentiments of Ali Khan, ("An Agenda for Muslim Economists: A Historico-Inductive Approach," *Journal of King Abdul Aziz University*, 3 (1991): 45–55), and suggests insights can be gained from studying economics in its relation to its Christian values. For the Old Testament views on issues of justice, morality, and economic order see Meir

Tamari "With All Your Possessions: Jewish Ethics and Economic Life," *The Free Press*, (New York, 1987).

10 See his Review in *Journal of King Abdul Aziz University*, 3, (1991): 97–177. Perhaps a simple example could help illustrate. One of the most important ontological terms, which serves as a cornerstone of the behavior of man, is the notion of *khilafa* (خلافة) or vice regency, a Qur'anic concept employed by most writers on Islamic economics. The recent debate on the proper understanding of what this term means points to the difficulty of "minding one's language," as repeatedly emphasized by Ali Khan. Could economists working in the field reach a consensus that this very important principle be defined in terms of *agency*? Could they also agree then on the domain of this agency?

11 Herms, Eilert, "Religion, ethics, the economy and economics," *JITE*, Vol. 153, 1997, (pp. 182-206) defines "ethos" to be "conceived as a system of interaction covering the whole range of the essential functions of a society and shaped from within by convictions concerning the origin, the constitution and the destiny of reality and of human life within it."

12 See Chapra's book *The Future of Economics* as well as a paper by Abdel-Rahman Yosri Ahmed, presented in the recent Round Table, for a survey of literature on Islamic economics.

13 See his keynote presentation to the Round Table.

14 It should be noted that long before Siddiqi and others who bemoan the lack of moral values in economics, there were economists sharply critical of economics on the same grounds; for example, Wilhelm Röpke (in his book *A Humane Economy: The Logical Framework of the Free Market*, first published in German in 1958, translated into English and published in 1960 and reprinted in 1971 by Henry Regnery Company, Chicago, Illinois).

15 For an example of differing views on this issue, see the discussions of the Round Table. On various definitions of Islamic economics, see Chapra's book *The Future of Economics*, footnote 14 (p. 141) for seven different definitions. His own definition is given on page 125.

16 See *Primitive, Archaic, and Modern Economics: Essays of Karl Polanyi*, edited by George Dalton (1971): "and if choice there be, it need not be induced by the limiting effect of a 'scarcity' of the means . . . " (p. 140).

17 Aside from the fact that the development of economics is culture-bound, the discipline itself has developed its own culture; see Melvin W. Reder, *Economics: The Culture of a Controversial Science,* (Chicago: The University of Chicago Press, 1999). Especially useful is the discussion of the development of the paradigm that dominates economics—the resource allocation paradigm—and the role of the rationality assumption, in Chapter 3 of the book.

18 Over two decades ago, Hasanuz Zaman pointed to the problem of defining Islamic economics within a traditional "means–ends" framework and provided an alternative definition (see S. M. Hasanuz Zaman, "Definition of Islamic Economics," *Journal of Research in Islamic Economics*, 1, no. 2 (winter 1984): 55–60). In this paper, the author refers to the *Qur'an* 41:10 and suggests that *Allah* (*swt*) "has created sufficient resources for His creatures. Therefore, scarcity may be either due to lack of proper utilization of natural endowments or an imbalanced distribution" (p. 55). This paper also draws on the main features of

the difference between Islamic and traditional economics. Shaheed Al-Sadr—in his classic book *Our Economics*, published by The House of Knowledge for Publication, Beirut—maintains the view that resources are not scarce, but in contrast see K. Sadr ("Sustainable development" *Name Mofid* No. 17 (1999): 9–28), in which he suggests (p. 11) that Shaheed Al-Sadr in ""اقتصادنا" (Economics)" holds the view that the scarcity assumption does not apply in the Islamic world view because *Allah* (*swt*) has provided enough resources to meet the needs of human society. Sadr, however, interprets this position as referring to "the long run" and that Shaheed did not mean that at micro level individuals are not faced with the scarcity problem. In this article, Sadr presents an economic understanding of Islamic conditions for sustainable development. See M. B. As Sadr, *Our Philosophy*, translated by Sham S. C. Inati (London: Muhammadi Trust, 1987).

19 See Khalil, Elias L., "On the Scope of Economics: What is the Question?", Finnish Economic Papers, 8, no. 1, (Spring 1995): 40–55, for a useful discussion of "means–ends" definition of economics. In a curious and cryptic footnote 2 (p. 42), he says: "Ironically, the etymology of the English word 'economics' in Greek: '*oikonomikos*' (literally: house management) does not concur with Robbin's meaning of the word. Incidentally, the Arabic word for economics, '*iktisad*', squarely fits Robbins's sense." It is difficult to see how an etymology of *iqtisad* could possibly square with the definition of economics by Robbins. The derivatives of this term from the root '*qasada*' appears in the *Qur'an*, and in its own form, *iqtisad*, appears in the earliest sources, including in the *ahadith* of the Messenger (pbuh) and refers to a much deeper and more complex constellation of behavioral rules and norms. It is so desirable, as a mode of behavior, that it is made a subject of prayer and supplication (see note 2 above).

20 Arrow, Kenneth J., "Economic Theory and the Hypothesis of Rationality," *The World of Economics*, (p. 198) J. C. Harasanyi "Morality and the Theory of Rational Behavior," *Social Research* 44 (pp. 623–56). On rationality, see the collection of essays in *Rationality in Economics: Alternative Perspectives*, edited by Kenneth Dennis (Kluwer Academic Publishers, 1998). On the criticism of neoclassical assumptions from the perspective of methodology of subjectivism, see *Subjectivism, Intelligibility and Economic Understanding*, (New York University Press). It is a collection of 24 essays in honor of Ludwig M. Lachman, nearly all of which constitute criticism of the assumptions of neoclassical economics, including rationality, perfect information and perfect foresight, and the competitive equilibrium. The volume includes ideas useful to the development of Islamic economics, including a paper by Don Lavoie on Hermeneutics, and another by Willie Meyer on "Beyond Choice." The list of references of the papers in this volume is also useful.

Joan Robinson—in her paper "What are the Questions?" in *Journal of Economic Literature*, 15, no. 4, (December 1977): 1318–39—raises a number of questions for which economics has no answers, including "the greatest of all economic questions, but one that in fact is never asked: what is growth for?" (p. 1337). It is important for Islamic economics to address this and other fundamental questions for which there are clear Islamic answers. As Robinson also suggests, " ... the neoclassicists conceived the subject of production to be provision for consumption. But consumption by whom, of what?" (p. 1337). In this context, a recent multidisciplinary study asks "Are We Consuming Too Much?" by Kenneth Arrow et al. in *The Journal of Economic Perspective*, 18, no. 3 (summer 2004):

147–72, and reports on interesting results and insights. See M. B. As Sadr, *Our Philosophy*, translated by Sham S. C. Inati (London: Muhammadi Trust, 1987). See also Joseph E. Stiglitz, *Whither Socialism?* (The MIT Press, 1996), on the shortcomings of the neoclassical economics, particularly the Fundamental Theorems of welfare economics and on the fact that these theorems were shared by socialism, which Stiglitz believes was a major reason for its downfall.

21 On the New Institutional Economics, see the collection of papers edited by Richard Langlois, *Economics as a Process: Essays in the New Institutional Economics,* (Chicago: The University of Chicago Press, 1986). On institutions see Douglass C. North's Nobel Lecture published in *The American Economic Review*, as "Economic Performance Through Time," 84, (June 1994): 359–68. Also see "Institutions and Governance of Economic Reform" by Oliver E. Williamson in *Proceedings of the World Bank Annual Conference on Development Economics*, (1994): 171–97, and "Comment" by Robert D. Putnam, as well as the paper by Jon Elser "The Impact of Constitutions on Economic Performance" (pp. 209–26), and another "Comment" by Adam Przeworski in the same Proceedings.

A recent paper by Hall and Jones—"Why do Some Countries Produce so Much More Output per Worker than Others?" in *Quarterly Journal of Economics*, 114, no. 1, (February 1999): 83–116—reports that countries with a better institutional environment have a much higher level of productivity. The paper explains that there is enough exogenous variation in structural policies and institutions to identify a causal link from institutional quality to productivity. What are the features of good institutions? The answer depends on the perceptions about the protection of property rights, absence of corruption in the public sector, and respect for the rule of law. These perceptions reflect institutions themselves as well as structural policies, including an independent and effective judiciary, quality of bureaucracy, constitutional features that guarantee basic political and civic rights, and checks and balances on the executive. In this regard, an important paper is "Unbundling Institutions" by Acemoglu and Johnson, *NBER Working Paper* No. 9934 (2003), which shows that two sets of institutions—property rights institutions and contractual institutions—are crucial. The former are defined as technologies for avoiding expropriation of property, and the latter as technologies for enforcing contracts. See *Economic Behavior and Institutions* by Thranin Eggertsson (Cambridge: Cambridge University Press, 1990). The author utilizes the New Institutional Economics to explain the workings of the economy and how institutions, specifically property rights and rules that deal with transaction costs, organize collective behavior. In an interesting paper, B. F. Jones and B. A. Olken ("Do Leaders Matter?" *NBER*, July 2004) suggest that leaders can play a crucial role in economic growth through their influence on economic institutions.

22 On trust, see P. Dasgupta; "Trust as a Commodity," *Economic Theory Discussion Paper*, no. 101, (University of Cambridge, April 1986). See also Ali Khan' s paper "On Trust as a Commodity and on the Grammar of Trust," in *Journal of Banking and Finance*, 26 (2002): 1719–66. On trustworthiness see "Evolutionary Norm Enforcement" by Werner Güth and Axel Ockenfels, *Journal of Institutional and Theoretical Economics,* 156 (2000): 335–47. On commitments, promising, and trust see Michael H. Robins, *Promising, Intending, and Moral Autonomy*, (Cambridge University Press, 1984). On reciprocity, see "Fairness and Retaliation:

The Economics of Reciprocity" by Ernst Fehr and Simon Gächter in the *Journal of Economic Perspective*, 14, no. 3, (summer 2000): 159–81, in which they argue that " ... a sizable portion of economic actors act on considerations of reciprocity," and also provide evidence that "strongly suggests that reciprocity substantially contributes to the enforcement of contracts" (p. 170).

On property rights, see the collection of papers on the *Economic Foundation of Property Law*, edited by Bruce A. Ackerman, published by Little, Brown and Company (Boston, 1975). See also Louis De Alessi, "Property Rights, Transaction Costs, and X-Efficiency: An Essay in Economic Theory," *American Economic Review,* 73 (March 1983): 64–81, and also Harvey Leibenstein, "Property Rights and X-Efficiency: Comment," *American Economic Review,* 73 (September 1983): 831–45. For the importance of property rights, see "Establishing property rights" by Andrei Shleifer in *Proceedings of the World Bank Annual Conference on Development Economics*, 1994, published by the World Bank in 1995, which discusses establishing property rights in East European transition economies but is relevant to Muslim societies with poorly defined property rights.

23 See Mirakhor, Abbas, "Muslim Contribution to Economics," first presented at the *Midwest Economic Association Meeting*, April 7–9, 1983, and reprinted in *Essays on Iqtisad* by Al-Hassani and Mirakhor (New York, NY: Global Scholarly Publications). The list of references to this paper provides sources of information on Muslim scholars' contributions to Medieval thought.

24 See Odd Langholm, who also says: "it is easy now to forget that those who laid the foundation of modern economics in the eighteenth century were as familiar with the accumulated knowledge of scholastic analysis as the average twentieth century economist is ignorant of it. Vital elements of new theories, on which these authors did not elaborate because they took them for granted, were inheritances from the medieval schools" (p. 11), in Odd Langholm, *Price and Value in the Aristotelian Tradition*, published by the Norwegian Research Council for Science and the Humanities, 1979, distributed by Columbia University Press—a most valuable book on the beginning stage in the process of tracing the influence of Muslim scholars on economics. Langholm asserts that "if a certain general moral code is to find expression in consistent rules of conduct in a specific area, for instance in terms of economic variables, the working of the economic system on which these variables operate must be to some extent understood. The ethical motive then reverts to the immediate intellectual need of all positive analysis ..." (p. 27); also see G.F. Hourani, "Two Theories of Value in Medieval Islam," *The Muslim World,* XLIX (1959): 269–78.

25 Hicks, John, "Rational Behavior—Observation or Assumption?", in *Subjectivism, Intelligibility and Economic Understanding*, edited by Israel M. Kirzner (New York: New York University Press, 1986).

26 On Liber Abaci, see C. Singer, "East and West in Retrospect", in *A History of Technology*, edited by Singer et al. (Oxford, 1956). See also G. E. M. de Ste Croix, "Greek and Roman Accounting," in *Studies in the History of Accounting*, edited by A. C. Littleton and B. S. Yamey (1956).

27 See Bernardelli, H., "The Origins of Modern Economic Theory," *Economic Record*, 37 (1961): 320–38.

28 For examples of efforts at reinterpreting Adam Smith, see David Lieberman; "Adam Smith on Justice, Rights, and Law," *Boalt Working Papers in Public Law*,

no. 67, (Berkeley: University of California), (1999). Also, see Elias L. Khalil, "Is Justice the Primary Feature of the State? Adam Smith Critique of Social Contract Theory," *European Journal of Law and Economics*, 6, no. 3, (November 1988): 215–30. Also see his paper "Beyond Self-Interest and Altruism" in *Economics and Philosophy*, 6, no. 1, (April 1990): 255–73, on Adam Smith's views on human nature.

29 On rules of market behavior in Islam see Mabid Ali Al-Jarhi, "A Short Discourse on Markets in an Islamic Economic System," draft paper presented to the Round Table on Islamic Economics (May 26–27, 2004). See also Muhammad Lawal Ahmad Bashar, "Price Control in an Islamic Economy," *Journal of King Abdul Aziz University: Islamic Economics*, 9 (1997): 29–52.

30 On history, see *History of Monetary Systems in Various States*, by Alexander Del Mar (New York: Angustus M. Kelly): 163–99.

31 A contribution to the hermeneutic or interpretive approach to economics is Donald McClosky, *The Rhetoric of Economics* (University of Wisconsin Press, 1985). By hermeneutics in the present note it is meant drawing economic meaning from the Islamic sources. It is worth noting its difference with the new field of investigation that attempts to marry rational choice and hermeneutics in the Austrian tradition of Von Mises, Weber, Shutz, Hayek, and the subjectivist school. On this latter see *Economics and Hermeneutics*, ed. Don Lavoie, (London: Routledge, 1991); also *Individuals, Institutions, Interpretations: Hermeneutics Applied to Economics*, edited by David L. Prychitko (Aldershot: Avebury Publishing, 1995). There are also three useful papers: Bruce Coldwell, "Does Methodology Matter? How Should it be Practiced?"; D. Wade Hands, "Thirteen Theses on Progress in Economic Methodology"; and Uskali Mäki, "Methodology of Economics: Complaints and Guidelines," *Finnish Economic Papers*, 3, no. 1, (1990).

32 Nearly two decades ago, Fahim Khan developed a "Macro Consumption Function in an Islamic Framework," (see the *Journal of Research in Islamic Economics*, 1, no. 1), which employs the ideas here as part of his analysis.

33 On studies on the self see Richard H. Thaler and H. M. Sherfin, "An Economic Theory of Self-Control," *Journal of Political Economy*, 89, no. 2 (1981): 392–406, which develops a "two-self" model within the neoclassical tradition. See also the various writings of Serge Christopher Kolm on the subject; for example, "The Buddhist Theory of 'No Self'" in an interesting volume *The Multiple Self*, edited by Jon Elster (Cambridge University Press: 233–63). There are other interesting papers in this volume, including: the introductory paper by Jon Elster; "The Mind as a Consuming Organ" by Thomas Schelling; and "Goethe's Faust, Arrow's Possibility Theorem and the Individual Decision-Taker" by Ian Steedman and Ulrich Krause. See also Charles Taylor, *Sources of Self* (Cambridge University Press, 1989). On self-interest, and interests in general, see Albert O. Hirshman "Interests" in *World of Economics* (pp. 349–60); also "Self-Interest" by D. H. Monroe (pp. 640–45), in the same volume.

34 Note that in an Islamic view, tastes and preferences change not only due to the dynamism of the economy—a view held by the subjectivists—but also because the self is always in a dynamic inner motion.

35 While, thus far, *fiqh* has generally been used as a source of explanation of behavioral rules of participation in exchange and markets, it is also fertile ground for generating ideas that could be applied in different contexts. In studies of

early Islamic history, among early sources deserving of attention by economists is the document referred to as the "Constitution of Medina" showing how the Messenger (pbuh) organized a multireligion and multicultural society in Medina. For a brief paper on the subject, see "The Constitution of Medina" by R.B. Serjeant in *Islamic Quarterly*, 8–9 (1964–65): 3–16.

36 See Edmond Phelps on "Distributive Justice" in the *World of Economics*, (The McMillan Press, 1991), pp. 164–67. On justice, see R. Vaitheswaran, "The Evolution of Economic Theory of Justice from Sidgwick to Rawls and Hayak," paper presented at the Midwest Economic Association Meetings, April 7–9, 1983. *Equality, Moral Incentives, and the Market* by Joseph M. Carens (Chicago and London: The University of Chicago Press, 1981) discusses the conditions under which moral incentives, combined with "a private-property market" can yield an egalitarian system. See also W. W. Baldwin, *Social Justice* (Oxford: Pergamon Press, 1966). A paper by Amartaya Sen—"Well-Being, Agency and Freedom," *The Journal of Philosophy* LXXXII, no. 4 (April 1985): 169–221—contains ideas on agency freedom, well-being, and its definition problem of interpersonal comparison of utility and the notion of welfare. See John Arthur and William H. Shaw, eds., *Justice and Economic Distribution* (Prentice Hall, Second edition, 1990). This is a collection of essays discussing economic justice from contractarian, libertarian, and utilitarian points of view. It is interesting to note that in all these approaches, justice is considered as a part of morality, in contrast to Islamic thought that considers to act morally in accordance with the rules prescribed by the Law Giver is to be just. Further, on economic justice, see Samuel T. Phillips, "Some Economic Implications of John Rawl's Theory of Justice" in *Public Finance Quarterly*, 3, no. 1 (January 1975). It is a useful economic hermeneutics of Rawl's theory and interprets Rawl's position as falling "some where between those of egalitarianism and meritocracy, the exact degree of egalitarianism depending on the impact of just institutions" (p. 84).

37 It is important to compare and contrast the discussion of justice in the economic discipline and in Islam. Whereas the former looks at various dimensions and concepts of justice as a systemic phenomena—that is, allocations, exchange, market, distribution system—the latter considers them to be first and foremost as part and parcel of an individual's adherence to and implementation of the "rights" of others. There is a specific right for every dimension of an individual's behavior. As a member of a family, as an employer/employee, as a member of a community, there are rights for the individual and there are rights for all those with whom the individual interacts. One of the earliest sources of Islam in which these rights are systematically catalogued and defined is the "book of Rights" of Imam Zain ul Abedeen who lists 47 rights (see note 2 above).

CHAPTER 10

Islam and Economic Development[1]

In Islam there are clear indications that economic prosperity is essential for the survival of the *Ummah*. Unfortunately, all Islamic countries are still in the category of developing or emerging countries. While some Islamic countries have performed well, such as Malaysia, and others are rich because of oil and gas resources, such as Kuwait, Qatar, and the UAE, the broad economic performance, in real per capita income growth, of Islamic countries has been subpar in the last 30–40 years; and economic equity has not been addressed. Unfortunately, based on these facts, a number of uninformed pundits have drawn the simplistic conclusion that Islam and economic progress are incompatible. Given the facts, Islamic countries need to tackle economic growth and development, and the related issues of economic and social justice with the same strong emphasis that is advocated in the *Qur'an* and supported in the *ahadith*.

In some quarters, economic and social malaise in Muslim countries, especially in the oil-exporting countries of the Middle East, is without justification attributed to Islam. Many Muslim countries have not performed well economically and socially since World War II; therefore, these observers conclude that Islam must be hostile to economic, financial, and social progress! That is more or less the sophistication level of the attack on Islam promulgated in the popular Western media. Ironically, the opposite assertion would be more accurate: economic, financial, and social malaise may be attributed to the fact that Muslim countries do *not* follow Islamic tenets of social and economic justice (in part because most Muslims do *not* have a solid grasp of these tenets). If countries followed Islamic teachings, their economic, social, and political performance would likely be far superior. What these countries need is more real Islam and less false Islam.

To analyze and assess from primary sources (the *Qur'an*, namely, the revelations of *Allah* (*swt*) to the Prophet Mohammad over a period of about 23 years, and the *sunnah*, namely, the teachings of the

Prophet (pbuh)) the potential contributions of Islamic teachings to economic development, economic growth, fiscal affairs, the role of the state, economic justice, an economic safety net, and so on would require a lifetime and numerous volumes. Our goal here is infinitely more manageable: to summarize the major teachings, the foundation and themes (with modest reference to a few critical primary sources) that might be helpful in explaining recent achievement in the arena of economic development—that is, economic and financial performance—in Muslim countries. In this endeavor we will try, subject to an acceptable level of human biases and shortcomings, to present the conventional interpretations. The *Qur'an* and the *sunnah* provide only basic principles and rules for establishing an Islamic society. In order to understand a verse in the *Qur'an* or a teaching of the Prophet (pbuh) it must be interpreted in the context of other relevant verses; that is, it must be seen as a whole. Moreover, while these fundamental principles and laws are the basis of an Islamic society and are thus broadly independent of time, other actions and decisions attributed to the Prophet (pbuh) were made at a special time and place and are thus subject to different interpretations as circumstances change.

10.1 BROAD TENETS

The principal aim of Islam is to establish a just, moral, and viable society.[2] The two principle themes in the *Qur'an* are submission to *Allah* (*swt*) (propagation of the Faith) and the institution of social and economic justice. The essence of the Islamic system is that it is a rules-based system centering on the concept of justice. All issues faced by government and by those who govern fall within this central axiom. This, in turn, is derived from the central axiom of *tawhid*: Uniticity of the Creator and of His Creation. In the *Qur'an* there is a clear sense that one cannot believe in the first without believing in the second. *Allah* (*swt*) is the Creator and each person (His Creation) is brother to other people.

In Islam, rules are critical in developing and preserving the community. Rule compliance promotes and preserves the unity of humanity and noncompliance leads to discord and disunity. Every rule is designed to pull humankind together. The basic message for economic doctrine is economic progress, cooperation, equality, and justice. As a result, harmful actions such as corruption, bad governance, mismanagement, theft, bribery, and neglect of education, of economic development, of healthcare, and the suppression of human freedom (as manifested in dictatorships) can all be viewed as causing discord and disunity and are, therefore, *haram*—that is, forbidden—in Islam. Immediately it is evident that Islam preaches practices that would support economic development and progress.

Contrary to popular Western beliefs, Islam does not condone dictatorships and the suppression of freedom; it strictly forbids them. It is up to *Ummah* (the Muslim community or fraternity) to determine what governmental structure is appropriate at a particular point in time. Governments and the collective Islamic community must create a society where every individual can realize his or her full potential. *Allah* (*swt*) created all humankind as equals and no individual can be favored over another. Specifically, everyone is equal before the Law and is free to pursue their dreams as long as they do not violate the right of others and those of the community at large. For the preservation, cohesion, and well-being of society there is a need for authority.[3] The political authorities must, however, conform to the principles of Islam and must always keep the interests of society in mind. As a result, governments must uphold Islamic principles, and to the extent that they do so they earn legitimacy. The community should change governments that do not uphold these principles.

Justice is at the foundation of an Islamic society, and the unity of religion and justice (law) must be implemented in practice.[4] For this to happen, the individual must be aware of the limits of his or her actions and the government must at all times make sure that laws are faithfully implemented and all members in the community receive equal treatment. In turn, the Islamic economic system (including permissible economic behavior) is based on the Islamic concept of justice and ownership. While private ownership is allowed, it is not an absolute concept in Islam; humankind must know that it is not the Creator and cannot exert unequivocal ownership over *Allah's* (*swt*) Creation.

10.2 ISLAM, PLURALISM, AND GOVERNANCE

The Islamic treatments of the conscience, free will, and tolerance toward other religions have preoccupied many scholars. Before proceeding to their place in Islam, it may be instructive to begin with one summary of the Western perspective on these topics:[5]

> . . . [Human beings] are purposeful and deliberative rather than simply passive, externally determined creatures. It is to believe that the right to religious freedom and conscience

> rests upon the deep conviction that human beings are fulfilled in being guided by "reasons" and by persuasion, rather than by external "causes" and controls. In short, to conceive of human beings in terms of an indefeasible "right to freedom of thought, conscience, religion and belief...

As for the Islamic perspective on this topic, the same authors conclude:[6]

> ...the *Qur'an* posits, or contains evidence for, a kind of universal guidance which, in its availability to all humanity seems parallel to the Western-Christian idea of a natural moral law. Similarly, careful study of the *Qur'an* seems to indicate that several notions combine to suggest a personal capacity to know and act on the good that is analogous to Western-Christian conscience.
>
> ...[the *Qur'an*] implies the personal, inward nature of faith, or of the choosing of faith, which in the hands of some Christian theologians has produced the doctrine of religious liberty. This idea, made explicit in such Qur'anic verses as 'There is no compulsion in religion' (2:256), would seem to be at the heart of Qur'anic teaching on the relation between God and humanity. It would also seem to have important implications for any Islamic polity; it certainly suggests a number of possibilities for the discussion of human rights in relation to the cultures of the West and Islam.

And in comparing the two religions:[7]

> And thus Christianity presents us with problems as well as possibilities for human rights discussion no less, it seems, than does Islam.

The basic Islamic doctrine that forms the foundation of religious and democratic pluralism is that humankind is but a single community. This assertion is best illustrated by quoting Sachedina on the subject:[8]

> In the citation that introduces this chapter (Q. 2:213), three facets emerge: the unity of humankind under One God; the particularity of religions brought by the prophets; and the role of revelation (the Book) in resolving the differences

> that touch communities of faith. All three are fundamental to the Qur'anic conception of religious pluralism. On the one hand, it does not deny the specificity of various religions and the contradictions that might exist among them in matters touching on correct belief and practice; on the other, it emphasizes the need to recognize the oneness of humanity in creation and to work toward better understanding among peoples of faith.
>
> The major argument for religious pluralism in the *Qur'an* is based on the relationship between private faith and its public projection in the Islamic polity. Whereas in matters of private faith, the position of the *Qur'an* is non-interventionist (i.e., human authority in any form must defer to the individual's internal convictions), in the public projection of that faith the Qur'anic stance is based on the principle of coexistence, the willingness of a dominant community to recognize self-governing communities free to run their internal affairs and coexist with Muslims.

Sachedina further elaborates:[9]

> Instead of regarding this diversity as a source of inevitable tensions, the *Qur'an* suggests that human variety is indispensable for a particular tradition to define its common beliefs, values, and the traditions for its community life:
>
> *O humankind, We have created you male and female, and appointed you races and tribes, that you may know one another*. (Q. 49:14)

And:[10]

> Instead of denying the validity of other human experiences of transcendence, Islam recognizes and even confirms its salvific efficacy within the wider boundaries of monotheism:
>
> *Surely they that believe, and those of Jewry, and the Christians, and those Sabaeans, whoso believes in God and the Last Day, and works righteousness—their wage awaits them with their Lord and no fear shall be on them, neither shall they sorrow*. (Q. 2:62)

And as Sachedina rightly concludes:[11]

> The unique characteristic of Islam is its conviction that belief in the oneness of God unites the Muslim community with all humanity because God is the creator of all humans, irrespective of their religious traditions.

Islam, if practiced as written in the *Qur'an*, is an *inclusive* and not an exclusive religion. Pluralism is at the root of Islam. Yet today and throughout recent history, Muslim fundamentalists, both those who rule and those who aspire to rule, have adopted a posture that is antipluralistic and, thus, in our view anti-Islamic. As Sachedina points out, Muslims must embrace the principle of Qur'anic coexistence if they are to realize the civil society that was encouraged by the Prophet (pbuh). Moreover, as the *Qur'an* clearly places God–human relations on a footing of accountability to God in contrast to inter-human relations, which are governed by personal responsibility and social accountability, there is a clear sense that in practice there can be a separation of church and state. These teachings confirm such a separation, although some religious rulers say otherwise in order to rule and to gain legitimacy for their rule.

The *Qur'an* stresses that all members of the human race, regardless of any differences in gender, religion, and ethnicity, share the same essence (*nafs*)[12] and are considered by God to be inherently identical.[13] Any form of discrimination against members of the Muslim community or *Ummah*—including any non-Muslims living within it—is, therefore, strongly condemned and prohibited by Islamic Law.[14] Non-Muslim communities living within the *Ummah* have the *same* social, economic, and religious rights as Muslims. They may adhere to their own religious laws and customs, and can set up their own religious institutions.[15] No individual is required to practice or convert to the Islamic faith if he or she is living under the auspices of a predominantly Muslim state.[16] The *Ummah* must uphold the safety and security of its non-Muslim communities, and is expected to confer and cooperate with them on public policy issues.[17] Thus culturally, ethnically, and religiously distinct communities may live freely within an Islamic state and have the same economic and social rights as the Muslim *Ummah*.

The *Qur'an* grants men and women equal religious, social, and economic rights. Both sexes are expected to adhere to Islamic ethical standards,[18] participate in civil society, and play a role in the formation of public policy.[19] Men and women may both own property, and must be granted equal access to education and social benefits. Both sexes must strive to enhance their intellectual capacity, maintain their health, and contribute to the social and economic development of the state.[20] They are both expected to work—and are permitted by Islam to work in virtually every field of work—and have the right to become financially independent.[21]

There is little disagreement when it comes to the role of the state in Islam. For example, in Ul Haq's words the message is:[22]

> The purpose of the Islamic political order or the objectives of the Islamic state can be summarized as follows: to prevent injustice and to establish all-encompassing justice—legal, social, economic, and political; to ensure freedom, dignity and equality of all; to enable all Muslim men and women to realize the ethical goals of Islam, not only in their beliefs, but also in the practical spheres of their lives; to ensure to all non-Muslim citizens complete physical security as well as complete freedom of religion, of culture, and of social development; to defend the country against internal subversion and external aggression; and to create an environment conducive to the teaching and the preaching of Islam.

No matter which school of thought one subscribes to, rulers in many instances are responsible for failure in Muslim societies. Rulers and governments earn legitimacy to the extent that they uphold Islamic principles. For Islam to succeed, there is the presumption of justice and ethical order on earth. There is a clear sense that rulers should be chosen by the people. But there is no detailed, clear-cut prescription as to how this should be done. For instance, it would be perfectly permissible in Islam to have a democratic vote as in the U.S., United Kingdom, or French systems. And yes, women should have a vote and should be eligible for any public office. A modern-day example of the importance of choosing rulers was the insistence of Grand Ayatollah Ali al-Sistani for direct elections in Iraq in 2005. Elections in Iran, for example, present the following problem: in that country it is argued that candidates who do not possess proper Islamic credentials should be excluded from candidacy. The practical problem with this interpretation of Islam is that it is open to human corruption. Moreover, an educated electorate (an Islamic requirement of the state) could decide for itself on the qualification of candidates.

While these serious questions of representation do exist, Islam in its purest form dictates that the people should choose their rulers.

Although governments should be chosen by the people and rules obeyed in Islam, there is clearly room for dissent. Ul Haq provides a good summary in this regard:[23]

> The limits of allegiance to a government have also been given by the Prophet. He states: "No obedience is due in sinful matters; behold obedience is due only in the way of righteousness" and "No obedience is due to him who does not obey God" For such situations as outright immoral and illegal behavior or unjust policies on the part of government, the Prophet has made it virtually obligatory for Muslims to speak up and stand up for justice: "The highest kind of self-exertion (*jihad*) is to speak the truth in the face of a government that deviates from the right path.

There is a difference of degree between Shia and Sunni schools of thought as to what to do if confronted by an unjust ruler or government. For the Shia, Islam is based on five axioms: *tawhid, nubuwwah, adl, imama*, and *maad*. For the Sunnis, there are only three axioms: *tawhid, nubuwwah*, and *maad*. The Shia sect *insists* on the justice of a ruler, whereas for Sunnis the overriding goal is communal harmony. For the Shia, while the peace of the community is also of paramount importance, Justice of God (*adl*) and the rule of just individuals (*imama*) are critical; a ruler must be just. By definition, the 12 Imams of Shia are just. A Shia should not extend loyalty to an unjust ruler; cooperation with an unjust ruler is *haram*; that is, forbidden. In fact, according to some interpretations, disobedience to unjust rulers is seen as obedience to God.[24] In Islam, and particularly in Shia Islam, all of these admonitions follow from the general obligation of "enjoining the good and forbidding the evil."[25]

Economic and social justice have particular importance in Islam. The role of the state is critical in ensuring both equal opportunities (education, skills, access to technology)[26] for all citizens and the eradication of poverty (second in importance to the propagation of the faith in Islam). The role of the state can be summarized:[27]

> ... first to ensuring that everyone has equal liberty or access to natural resources and means of livelihood. Second, to ensure that each individual has equal opportunity including education, skills and technology—to utilize these

> resources. Third, to ensure that markets are supervised such that catalectic justice can be attained. Fourth, to ensure that transfer takes place from those more able to those less able ... And, finally, that distributive justice is ensured for the next generation through the laws of inheritance. The state is then empowered to design any specific economic policy that is required in order to guarantee the attainment of these objectives.

As Islam preaches coexistence of different races and religions, so it also advocates peaceful resolution of differences. In Islam, war is seen as an illness and the worst thing known to mankind.[28] Similarly, the killing of innocent people and violence are antithetical to Islam. The taking of innocent hostages as pawns and terrorist attacks on innocent civilians are clearly forbidden in Islam. Conflicts are always to be resolved through dialogue and peaceful means, not through hostilities and war. Only peace and the pursuit of peace are great achievements to be praised and rewarded.

10.3 THE FUNDAMENTALS OF AN ISLAMIC ECONOMIC SYSTEM

Western thinkers advocate the separation of church and state in all aspects of governance. In the case of Islam, this is somewhat problematic because Islam, unlike other major religions, gives Muslims detailed guidelines for an economic (and social) system. The details of an Islamic economic system are outlined through a number of channels—the *Qur'an*, the *sunnah*, the *ijma*, (the consensus of religious scholars known as *mujtahids*), and *qiyas* (opinions based on religious doctrine and analogy); Shia Muslims make use of only the first three sources.[29] These details include but are not limited to: competition, taxation, government finances, the behavior of financial institutions, social and economic expenditures affecting poverty, income distribution and the like, private ownership, rule of law and sanctity of contracts, land tenure, wage policy, natural resource management including depletable resources, and inheritance.

The basic philosophy of Islamic economics can be summarized as capitalism (competition in business, private property rights with some limitations, economic gains through hard work and taking risk in investments, and the right to enjoy the fruits of labor and return on investment) and self-interest ("Islam, in fact, considers self interest a primary factor in its incentive-motivation system; it is a necessity in any organized society if the individual is to find it utility maximizing to follow behavioral rules prescribed by the system"[30]) *but* with some important qualifications.[31]

The first and foremost qualification is that the basic principles of capitalism are encouraged in Islam as long as they are in harmony with the basic goals of society, are consistent with Islamic social order and justice, and reinforce the social fabric. Thus, if capitalism is adopted in such a way that there are a significant number of people without adequate and equal economic opportunity (a level playing field for all, especially in education which receives special emphasis in Islam) or the basic human needs of food, shelter, and clothing, then society's needs must take precedence over the "efficient and most productive" practice of capitalism (and the rights of the wealthy). In other words, in an Islamic economic system there are clear "maximums and minimums;" clear limits to the extent that capitalism can be adopted in Islam. Mirakhor has stated this succinctly:[32]

> Islam asserts unambiguously that poverty is neither caused by scarcity and paucity of natural resources, nor is due to the lack of proper synchronization between the mode of production and the relation of distribution, but as a result of waste, opulence, extravagance and nonpayment of what rightfully belongs to the less able segments of the society. This position is illustrated by the Prophetic saying that: "Nothing makes a poor man starve except that with which a rich person avails in luxury."

And Mirakhor goes on to add:[33]

> Eradication of poverty is undoubtedly one of the most important of all duties made incumbent upon the state, second only to the preservation and propagation of faith whose very existence is considered threatened by poverty.

Second, honest capitalism and the sanctity of contracts are stressed and are integral elements of an Islamic economic system:[34]

> ...when the Prophet was asked "who is the believer?" He replied, "A believer is a person in whom people can trust their person and possession." He is also reported to having said that "a person without trustworthiness is a person without religion."

Corruption in the pursuit of wealth is abhorred in the *Qur'an*:[35]

> *Seek with [the wealth] which God has bestowed on you the home of the Hereafter, nor forget your portion of this world; but do good [unto others] as God has been good to you; and seek not corruption on earth, for verily, God does not like the spreaders of corruption.* (28:77).

Third, while private ownership is endorsed in Islam, *absolute* ownership (as in Western capitalism) is not. In Islam, absolute ownership belongs to the Creator (the principle of *tawhid*). Man cannot own without any limitations what God created (raw land, water, mineral deposits, and so on) in the first place. This has critical implications for the sale of raw land, for the management of minerals, and the like. As Mirakhor notes:[36]

> The relationship between laboring and owning is central in Islam which recognizes two ways in which an individual can obtain rights to property: (i) through his own creative labor and/or (ii) through transfer—via exchange, contract, grants, or inheritance—of property rights from another individual who has gained title to the property or asset through his own labor.

Work and investment (and inheritance) are the only legitimate methods of acquiring property rights. A clear implication of this is that an individual may enjoy raw land (in its God-created state) but cannot sell it for a price if no improvement or investment has been made. Moreover, ownership in Islam carries with it social responsibilities.

Fourth, there are clear laws and guidelines set out in Islam that govern economic policies and practices. These include, but are not limited to, economic development and growth, population policy, rule of law, labor, capital, public finance and taxation, interest, rent, wealth, inheritance, income distribution, education, social safety net, and natural resource management. Clearly, when it comes to the prescribed economic and financial behavior of individuals and society, Islam differs from other religions. In Islam, these accepted behaviors are spelled out in quite some detail. This is an important reason why the separation of church and state is somewhat problematic in Islam.

It may be appropriate, however, to briefly address here the two aspects of an Islamic financial system that have received the most attention in the non-Islamic world: the prohibition of interest and its impact on the financial sector, on the conduct of monetary policy, and on economic growth and development; and Islamic charity tax or *Zakah*.

The fundamental reason for the prohibition of interest in Islam is that the investor should not profit unduly from the hard work and risk-bearing of others. To a Western-trained economist, a competitively determined market interest rate serves an indispensable function in a market economy. Interest rates affect savings and investment and efficiently allocate capital from where it is plentiful to where it is scarce. In competitive markets this allocation of capital is achieved most efficiently; namely, capital is attracted to where it will earn the highest rate of return. Moreover, interest rates offer policymakers an important instrument for macroeconomic management. Although Islam prohibits interest (*riba*), it encourages profit and return from investment where the investor takes calculated risk. Thus, financial institutions can offer an investor a share of their annual profits (and losses) in proportion to the investor's deposit (the share of an individual's deposit relative to total assets of the bank). This rate of return to the investor is different from interest in two important ways: a priori its size is unknown (there are no guarantees), and the investor has to take more of a risk (in a Western system the depositor takes less of a risk because the capital of the financial institution's stockholders is first at risk before the capital of the depositors).

Clearly institutions that are better managed will develop a better track record, offer historically higher returns, and thus attract capital before institutions that are not managed as well. Thus, profit rates of Islamic institutions can serve the same function as Western interest rates in attracting savings and allocating capital efficiently. In the case of macroeconomic management, policymakers can look at rates of return of financial institutions as an indicator of financial liquidity and can issue "participation" bonds (carrying no fixed rate of interest but an average of private sector rates of return) to finance budgetary shortfalls.

An individual who earns more than what he or she consumes must pay *Zakah*, which is calculated according to his or her level of net worth (essentially a wealth tax). Business capital and housing are exempt from *Zakah* taxation in order to promote investment in capital and construction and to encourage home ownership.[37] It is important to note that *Zakah*, discussed in more detail in Chapter 11, is *not* a substitute for taxation by the state, which may institute other forms of taxation to finance additional social, economic, infrastructural, and related programs to attain social and economic goals.[38]

Poverty exists, Islam reasons, not because economic resources are scarce, but because they are misallocated, inefficiently managed, unproductively hoarded, and unevenly distributed.[39] Independent social spending, according to Islam, is the best possible way for members of the Islamic social order to promote a more equitable distribution of wealth and resources. Muslims with the financial capacity to donate beyond their *Zakah* requirements are therefore strongly encouraged to further invest in *infaq* and *sadaqah*.[40] Islam does not require social institutions built through *infaq* and *sadaqah* to register with or be approved by a central political authority.[41] Thus by advocating extensive popular participation in the development of society, Islam reduces the need for an authority to intervene on behalf of the socioeconomic interests of the community.[42]

But before leaving this brief treatment of Islamic economics, it may be useful to conclude by addressing the broader and often-asked question of whether Islam discourages economic progress. This may be largely answered by a quote:[43]

> ...we have cited considerable evidence that Islam not only does not rule out economic progress, but that it clearly endorses several of the basic factors cited frequently by Western commentators as essential in historic economic transformation—private property, recognition of the profit incentive, a tradition of hard work, a link between economic success and eternal reward. Thus Islam seems unlikely to rule out rapid economic growth or even the construction of a strong system more or less capitalist in essence. On the other hand, Islamic principles cannot readily, if at all, be reconciled with economic "progress" that is contradicted by blatant economic and social injustice in the context of general social welfare.

But even this quote needs important additions. Islam also endorses and encourages competition, institutions, the rule of law, and a level playing field, all increasingly seen as the critical foundations for sustained economic growth and prosperity. Moreover, hard work (not subsidies) is given special attention in Islam:[44]

> Work, however, is not only performed for the purpose of satisfaction of needs and wants, but it is considered a duty and an obligation required of all members of society.

10.4 ISLAM AND ECONOMIC DEVELOPMENT

How have their economies performed? Have they followed Islamic prescriptions? Is their success or failure attributable to the fact that they have or have not followed the path of Islam? Where has Islam hurt economic performance and where could it have helped?

Sustained economic development and growth can come about in a society if:

- There is a clear national commitment to economic growth and development, and to the creation of wealth.
- Individual initiative is encouraged and government develops and pursues thoughtful and consistent policies to support sustained development and wealth creation.
- There is effective governance, and institutions are supportive of the economic growth and development.

As indicated earlier, Islam advocates the importance of economic prosperity and wealth creation for the survival of the religion and society. But it does so subject to the constraint of socioeconomic justice. Economic policies advocated in Islam support economic development and growth. Islam endorses wealth accumulation and the sanctity of private property as long as it does not impinge on the rights of others. Islam stresses the need to afford incentives to all members of society by creating a level playing field. Islam stresses numerous aspects of good governance and institutions. It abhors corruption, it upholds the sanctity of contracts, and it advocates the rule of law. Ironically, many Islamic teachings that pertain to economic development—such as poverty alleviation, good governance and institutions, and the rule of law—have been only recently discovered in Western economic thought.

Islamic finance is also supportive of economic development. As explained in Chapter 3, an equity-based, as opposed to debt-based, system of finance results in more widespread sharing of risk and would thus in turn promote investment and growth. As explained in Chapter 8, in an Islamic system, instruments such as *qard-ul-hassan, sadaqah*, and *Zakah* can play a vital role in serving the poor and promoting growth.

10.5 CONCLUSION

Islam was revealed to bring justice, particularly economic and social justice, to the people. The *Qur'an* states that *Allah* (*swt*) sent all the prophets and messengers to induce the people toward justice. The all-inclusive and universal religion that is Islam is here for the purpose of making the lives of the people better. *The religion is for the people and not the other way round.* Governments are there to facilitate the functioning of the institutions that Islam promulgates. Therefore, governments are for the religion, and the religion is for the people. The problem is that in Muslim countries governments use the religion to sustain themselves, and often what they practice bears no resemblance to true Islamic teachings. Islam preaches the importance of economic development and prosperity in the context of a just socioeconomic system. Islam preaches the importance of good governance and institutions. Islamic finance is supportive of risk sharing, investment, and growth. None of these principles are in practice in most Muslim countries.

Subpar economic performance in Muslim countries is not because of Islamic teachings; instead it is because governments and rulers in Muslim countries do not adhere to Islamic teachings. Corruption is all-pervasive in a number of countries. Markets do not function well. Institutions are inefficient. Expenditures on the military are high. Conflicts have been costly. Policies have been shortsighted and inconsistent. And rapid population growth has been encouraged without sufficient attention to the needs of citizens.

ENDNOTES

1 An earlier version of this paper appeared as a chapter in Hossein Askari, *The Middle East Oil Exporters: What Happened to Economic Development?* Foreword by Robert M. Solow (Edward Elgar Publishing, Cheltenham: UK, December 2006, and Northampton: US, February 2007).

2 Mirakhor, Abbas, "The General Characteristics of an Islamic Economic System," in *Essays on Iqtisad, the Islamic Approach to Economic Problems*, edited by Dr. Baqir Al-Hasani and Dr. Abbas Mirakhor, (Nur Corporation, 1989). On this point there is universal agreement by all Islamic scholars. Irfan Ul Haq gives a slight variant in *Economic Doctrines of Islam: A Study in the Doctrines of Islam and Their Implications for Poverty, Employment, and Economic*

Growth. Virginia, The International Institute of Islamic Thought, 1996: 65: "[Man's] task is to create an ethical social order on earth that is just and humanitarian."

3 Mirakhor, "The General Characteristics of an Islamic Economic System."

4 Ibid.

5 Little, David, John Kelsey, and Abdulaziz Sachedina, *Human Rights and the Conflicts of Culture: Western and Islamic Perspectives on Religious Liberty*, (South Carolina: University of South Carolina Press, 1988): 26.

6 Ibid., 91–92.

7 Ibid., 94.

8 Sachedina, Abdulaziz, *The Islamic Roots of Democratic Pluralism*, (New York: Oxford University Press, 2001): 23–24.

9 Ibid., 27

10 Ibid., 27–28

11 Ibid., 28.

12 *Nafs* may also be defined as: *self; person; soul; life*. See: Ibid.

13 Mirakhor, Abbas, "Outline of an Islamic Economic System," *Zahid Husain Memorial Lecture Series—No. 11* (March 22, 1995). Verses supporting this assertion: *Qur'an* 49:13: "*Behold, We have created you all out of a male and a female, and have made you into nations and tribes, so that you might come to know one another.*"

Also see the Prophetic saying (*hadith*): "We are all children of Adam and Adam was of dust." Source: Irfan Ul Haq, *Economic Doctrines of Islam: A Study in the Doctrines of Islam and Their Implications for Poverty, Employment, and Economic Growth*.

14 The Prophet (pbuh) is reported to have said: "Those who commit an act of aggression against a member of the non-Muslims, who usurp his rights, who make any demand upon him which is beyond his capacity to fulfill, or who forcibly obtain anything from him against his wishes, I will be his [that is, the oppressed's] advocate on the Day of Judgment."

He is also reported to have said: "He who harms a non-Muslim harms me, and he who harms me, harms God." Source: Irfan Ul Haq, *Economic Doctrines of Islam: A Study in the Doctrines of Islam and Their Implications for Poverty, Employment, and Economic Growth*.

See also: *Qur'an* 29:46: "*And do not argue with the followers of earlier revelation otherwise than in a most kindly manner—unless it be such of them as are bent on evildoing—and say: 'We believe in that which has been bestowed upon you: for our God and your God is one and the same, and it is unto Him that We [all] surrender ourselves.*'"

The Prophet (pbuh) is also reported to have said: "He who kills a man from the People of the Dhimma [non-Muslims living under the protection of an Islamic system of government] will be forbidden Paradise the perfume of which can be smelled at a distance of twelve years traveling."

See *Qur'an* 6:108: "*But do not revile those [beings] whom they invoke instead of God, lest they revile God out of spite, and in ignorance …* " Source: Imam Muhammad Shirazi, *War, Peace, and Non-Violence: An Islamic Perspective*, (2004).

See *Qur'an* 2:12: "*Nay, but whosoever submits his will to God, while being a good-doer, his wage is with the Lord, and no fear shall be on them, neither shall they sorrow.*" Source: Abdulaziz A. Sachedina, *The Just Ruler in Sh'ite Islam*, (New York: Oxford University Press, Inc., 1988).

See *Qur'an* 2:23: "*And if you doubt any part of what We have bestowed from on high, step by step, upon Our servant [Muhammad], then produce a* surah *of similar merit, and call upon any other than God to bear witness for you—if what you say is true!*" This verse can literally be translated as: "*Come forward with a* surah *like it, and call upon your witnesses other than God ... to attest that your hypothetical literary effort could be deemed equal to any part of the* Qur'an."

15 Support in the *sunnah*: The Prophet (pbuh) granted the Jewish community autonomous status while drafting the constitution of the Islamic state of Medina, and did the same for the Christian community when it came under Islamic dominion. Future Muslim caliphs followed this precedent. Source: Irfan Ul Haq, *Economic Doctrines of Islam: A Study in the Doctrines of Islam and Their Implications for Poverty, Employment, and Economic Growth.*

16 See *Qur'an*: 2:256: "*There shall be no coercion in matters of faith.*"

See *Qur'an* 9:1: "*Disavowal by God and His Apostle [is herewith announced] unto those who describe divinity to aught beside God, [and] with whom you [O believers] have made a covenant.*" *Disavowal* in this context means *immunity*. (Background: The majority of the Meccan population remained Polytheistic after Mecca became a Muslim state. The Prophet (pbuh) did not pressure them to convert; they were allowed to live as a religiously autonomous unit within the Muslim community). Source: Imam Muhammad Shirazi, *War, Peace, and Non-Violence: An Islamic Perspective*, (2004).

17 Ul Haq, Irfan, *Economic Doctrines of Islam: A Study in the Doctrines of Islam and Their Implications for Poverty, Employment, and Economic Growth.*

18 See *Qur'an* 4:124: "*... anyone—be it man or woman—who does [whatever he can] of good deeds and is a believer withal, shall enter paradise, and shall not be wronged by as much as [would fill] the groove of a date-stone.*"

See also *Qur'an* 40:40; 16:97; 9:71: "*And [as for] the believers, both men and women—they are friends and protectors of one another: they [all] enjoin the doing of what is right and forbid the doing of what is wrong, and are constant in prayer, and render the purifying dues* [Zakah], *and pay heed unto God and His Apostle.*" Source: Irfan Ul Haq, *Economic Doctrines of Islam: A Study in the Doctrines of Islam and Their Implications for Poverty, Employment, and Economic Growth.*

19 See *Qur'an* 3:195: "*I shall not lose sight of the labor of any of you who labors [in My way], be it man or woman: you are all members of one and the same human race, and therefore equal to one another.*" (Literal interpretation.)

In the *sunnah* it is reported that Muslim women played an active role in the administration of community life during the early Islamic period in Medina. Source: Ibid.

20 The Prophet (pbuh) deemed "striving after knowledge" to be "a religious duty of *all Muslims.*" Source: Ibid.

21 See *Qur'an* 4:32: "*Men shall have a benefit from what they earn, and women shall have a benefit from what they earn.*" No Qur'anic verses speak against women working, earning a living, or becoming financially independent; Islam has left it up to society to determine what types of work and training promote growth and development during a specific time period and within a particular socioeconomic context. Source: Ibid.

22 Ul Haq, Irfan, *Economic Doctrines of Islam: A Study in the Doctrines of Islam and Their Implications for Poverty, Employment, and Economic Growth*: 69.
23 Ibid., 73.
24 Sachedina, Abdulaziz A., *The Just Ruler in Sh'ite Islam*: 99.
25 Ibid., 101.
26 See Mirakhor, "The General Characteristics of an Islamic Economic System."
27 Ibid., 28–29.
28 Imam Muhammad Shirazi, *War, Peace and Non-Violence: An Islamic Perspective*.
29 Cummings, John Thomas, Hossein Askari, and Ahmad Mustafa, "Islam and Modern Economic Change," *Islam and Development: Religion and Sociopolitical Change*, ed. John L. Esposito, (New York: Syracuse University Press, 1980).
30 Mirakhor, "The General Characteristics of an Islamic Economic System": 12.
31 This is also true of medieval Christian and Judaic debates on usury and—more importantly, and much more recently—the continuing Catholic problems with Western capitalism.
32 Mirakhor. "The General Characteristics of an Islamic Economic System": 25.
33 Ibid., 28.
34 Ibid., 16.
35 Ul Haq, Irfan *Economic Doctrines of Islam: A Study in the Doctrines of Islam and Their Implications for Poverty, Employment, and Economic Growth*: 87.
36 Mirakhor, "The General Characteristics of an Islamic Economic System": 14.
37 Ul Haq, Irfan, *Economic Doctrines of Islam: A Study in the Doctrines of Islam and Their Implications for Poverty, Employment, and Economic Growth*.
38 Askari, Hossein, John Thomas Cummings, and Michael Glover, *Taxation and Tax Policies in the Middle East*, (United Kingdom: Butterworth Publishers, 1982).
39 The Prophet (pbuh) is reported to have said: "Nothing makes a poor man starve except that which a rich person avails in luxury." See: Abbas Mirakhor, *General Characteristics of an Islamic Economic System*.

See *Qur'an* in 20:118–119, Adam is told: "*Behold, it is provided for thee that thou shalt not hunger here nor feel naked, and that thou shalt not thirst here or suffer from the heat of the sun.*"

The Prophet (pbuh) is reported to have said: "He is not a faithful who eats his fill while his neighbor [or fellowman] remains hungry by his side." Source: Ibid.

40 See *Qur'an* 30:39: "*And [remember]: whatever you may give out in usury so that it might increase through [other] people's possessions will bring [you] no increase in the sight of God—whereas all that you give out in charity, seeking God's countenance, [will be blessed by Him:] for it is they, they [who thus seek His countenance] that shall have their recompense multiplied!*

See *Qur'an*: 3:92: "*[But as for you, O believers,] never shall you attain true piety unless you spend on others out of what you cherish yourselves; and whatever you spend—verily, God has full knowledge thereof.*"

See *Qur'an* 2:276: "*Allah . . . will give increase for goods of charity.*"

Source: Ed. Munawar. Iqbal, *Distributive Justice and Need Fulfillment in an Islamic Economy* (Islamabad, International Institute of Islamic Economics, International Islamic University, 1986).

See *Qur'an* 2:177: "*True piety does not consist in turning your faces towards the east or the west—but truly pious is he who believes in God, and the Last Day, and the angels, and revelation, and the prophets, and* spends his substance—*however much he himself may cherish it—upon his near of kin, and the orphans, and the needy, and the wayfarer, and the beggars, and for the freeing of human beings from bondage; and is constant in prayer, and* renders their purifying dues (zakah) . . . *it is they that have proved themselves true, and it is they, they who are conscious of God.*"

41 Ed. Munawar Iqbal, *Distributive Justice and Need Fulfillment in an Islamic Economy.*

42 Mirakhor, Abbas, "General Characteristics of an Islamic Economic System."

43 Ibid., 45–46.

44 Ibid., 14.

CHAPTER 11

Taxation and Public Expenditure in Islam[1]

In any economic system, the state needs revenues to support its expenditure and to address inequities in income and wealth. The main source of financing for government expenditure is taxation, principally an income tax, followed by sales tax (or a value added tax), wealth tax, real estate tax and custom duties); such taxation may be accompanied by two temporary sources—public borrowing and revenues from publicly held assets, such as oil and gas reserves. In many Islamic countries, however, tax systems are not fully developed, compliance is not effective, and in a number of countries income taxes do not even exist. *Zakah*, the Islamic wealth tax, is not a substitute for government revenues for a number of reasons, including its size, enforcement, its distribution, and the fact that it does not adequately address income and wealth inequity. There is an urgent need for many Islamic countries to develop a comprehensive tax system that enables the state to fulfill its duties in an Islamic context. In this chapter, we explore the broad range of Islamic taxes and address the need for comprehensive taxation, with a special consideration of public finances in countries that rely on natural resource (oil and gas) depletion for revenues.

Taxation and a public sector role in economic and social development is a distinct feature of Islamic governance. In Islam, two tax structures are laid down, one for Muslims and one for non-Muslims. While some taxation details are spelled out, the clear intention is that the specifics of taxation should and must be adjusted to fit the changing needs and circumstances of the Muslim community. Besides taxation, governments may resort to borrowing. At the same time the economic and social responsibilities of the government, with clear implications for public expenditures, are clearly spelled out in the *Qur'an* and in the *sunnah*. What are the appropriate forms of Islamic taxation? How and why might taxes be modified to meet the needs of the Muslim community today? What is the goal of taxation and how should revenues be used? How can Muslim governments borrow to finance revenue shortfalls? What programs and expenditure are delineated for the public sector? For countries that rely on oil and gas revenues to finance government coffers, is this the appropriate course of action?

11.1 ISLAMIC TAXATION

The specific forms of taxation in Islam are *Zakah* (wealth tax), *ushr* and *kharaj* (land taxes), *jizyah* (poll tax), and tax on natural resources (*khums*).

The principal tax on Muslims is *Zakah*. The rendering of *Zakah* is a divinely revealed requirement for those who want to achieve eternal salvation. As such, it ranks with the Old Testament Decalogue and New Testament Beatitudes in religious significance. As Islam's traditions have evolved, *Zakah* has been accorded central status as one of the five pillars of Islam. While Islam recognizes that some have been endowed with more worldly goods than others, it also creates mechanisms for redistribution, *Zakah*, calling on believers to engage in economic justice. *Zakah* is more than a simple tax:

> ... it is not only the end which is important, but also the means. This is why Islam provides for *Zakah*, a voluntary wealth tax which Muslims pay in recognition of their social responsibilities. This fosters good behavior by the more prosperous, by giving them a choice through its voluntary nature ... thus helps both rich and poor, and has a moral as well as material dimension ...[2]

The meanings attributed to the word *Zakah* itself go a long way towards indicating the problems of considering it merely as a tax, or as a conventional source of government revenue. Its obligations are founded in the Qur'anic injunctions which praise those who "*expend of that We have provided them, secretly and in public, and who avert evil with good—theirs should be the ultimate abode*,"[3] and "*those in whose wealth is a right known for the beggar and the outcast.*"[4] Obviously, in theory *Zakah* is to be given willingly, not to be paid grudgingly, if Divine Law is to be fulfilled. Its obligations are to the community as a whole: they are to be made specifically and directly to the community's less fortunate members, neither to an impersonalized government nor to its revenue-collecting agencies.

The etymological derivation of this important word has been traced to verbs that in English translate most closely as "to be pure" or "to be pious."[5] *Zakah* also signifies virtue in general, as well as—in the *Qur'an*—giving and the pious gift.[6] Thus, *Zakah* is seen as an act of purification for one's errors, a means of reducing selfishness and expiation of blame for past selfishness, thus, leading to self-improvement.[7] Others have emphasized its link to the verbs "to grow" and "to increase,"[8] and have interpreted the giving of *Zakah* as leading to a significant increase of blessings, both of material property in this world and of spiritual merit for the next. Whatever interpretation is adopted, *Zakah* is primarily a voluntary act of piety, and a far cry from what most modern-day taxpayers experience when confronted with increased income levies or complicated regulations.

According to the *Qur'an*, poverty and denial of assistance to the needy is forbidden. The *Qur'an* goes on to explain that material inequalities are not a manifestation of spiritual inequalities. Rather, such inequalities should be overcome through human effort and are thus meant to foster brotherhood, again stressing the importance of *Zakah*.

Although the term has been used in many different ways, there are three major situations in which *Zakah* is applicable: the ownership of animals, of gold, silver and articles of trade, and of the produce of the land. In theory *Zakah* is linked to all assets that produce an economic return. Thus, in essence, *Zakah* should be viewed as a generalized wealth tax.

An individual who earns more than he or she consumes must pay *Zakah*, which is calculated according to his or her level of net worth. Business capital and housing are exempt from *Zakah* taxation in order to promote investment in capital and construction and to encourage home ownership.[9] It is important to note that *Zakah* is not a substitute for taxation by the state, which may institute other forms of taxation to finance additional social, economic, infrastructural, and related programs to attain social and economic goals.[10]

While Islam encourages people to save their earnings after consumption, it calls for the investment of savings. The hoarding and accumulation of idle wealth are *haram*. Taxation is viewed as a mode of social investment.[11] Islam reasons that God bestowed natural resources to the entire human population, thus all people are entitled to a share of world production. Those who are impoverished, unemployed, underemployed, or lack the ability to work are the primary beneficiaries of *Zakah* payments.[12] Individuals who are employed but underpaid may receive *Zakah* payments so that they can earn a living wage, and those with refugee status may receive *Zakah* as well.

Surplus *Zakah* funds may be saved, invested in infrastructure and development, or donated to impoverished countries.[13] Islam holds that the payment and distribution of *Zakah* promotes a more equitable income distribution that ultimately enables those on a lower income scale to begin saving as their standard of living improves.[14] Evading this obligation, according to Islam, will cause an inequitable distribution of income and encourage an increase in poverty.[15] Again, it must be stressed that *Zakah* is not a substitute for taxation by the state to address the broad social and economic needs of society.

Islam instituted compulsory *Zakah* payments because every capable member of the *Ummah* is required to contribute to the development of a learned and economically prosperous social order. *Zakah* is a major component of *infaq* and *sadaqah*, compulsory and voluntary social expenditures made for the creation of nonprofit and nongovernmental institutions such as schools, health clinics, hospitals, and libraries.[16] Poverty exists, Islam reasons, not because economic resources are scarce, but because they are misallocated, inefficiently managed, unproductively hoarded, and unevenly distributed.[17] Independent social spending, according to Islam, is the best possible way for members of the Islamic social order to promote a more equitable distribution of wealth and resources. Muslims with the financial capacity to donate beyond their *Zakah* requirements are therefore strongly encouraged to further invest in *infaq* and *sadaqah*.[18] Islam does not require social institutions built through *infaq* and *sadaqah* to register with or be approved by a central political authority.[19] Thus by advocating extensive popular participation in the development of society, Islam reduces the need for an authority to intervene on behalf of the socioeconomic interests of the community.[20]

On the one hand, Muslim-held assets subject to *Zakah* were not spelled out specifically in the *Qur'an*; therefore, they have been much discussed by interpreters of Islamic Law. On the other hand, the *Qur'an* is specific as to those who are eligible to receive the alms distributed under *Zakah* provisions: "*The free will offerings are for the poor and the needy, those who work to collect them, those whose hearts are brought together, the ransoming of slaves, debtors, in God's way, and the traveler: so God ordains.*"[21] In short, in the time of the Prophet Mohammad (pbuh), virtually all of those who might experience economic need had a valid claim on the beneficence of the entire Islamic community.

The manner in which *Zakah* is to be collected has also been a subject of some dispute among legal scholars, the principal point of disagreement being what constitutes *apparent* property (on which *Zakah* is generally collected by representatives of the state or community) as opposed to *nonapparent* property (on which it is distributed directly by the owners).[22] Others have argued that, to ensure proper distribution among the needy, the state should oversee all *Zakah*, and should establish the right to collect it by force when Muslims ignore their obligations, or when the needs of one area in *Dar al-Islam* exceeds the ability of that particular region to collect enough *Zakah* from those that reside there.

The state in Islam is clearly authorized to collect additional taxes if *Zakah* is not sufficient to meet the needs of those with claims to assistance. For example, the state can always impose other forms of taxation for particular needs and programs. On the one hand, *Zakah* was not intended to be used by the state for purposes and recipients other than those stated above, but on the other hand, it was specifically recognized that legitimate claims for community revenues were not limited to *Zakah*. While this issue has been, and continues to be, debated by Islamic scholars, the basis for supporting additional taxation by the state is clear. God is the ultimate owner of everything; that is, ownership in Islam is not absolute. Thus the distribution of income and wealth must be *just* (as indicated by principles laid down in the *Qur'an* and manifested in the life of the Prophet (pbuh)). Economic and social justice and the development of a just society are at the heart of Islam. Humankind has been given natural resources and other wealth to create economic prosperity and enjoy the fruits of their investment and hard work; but adverse activities such as hoarding, corruption, and extravagance are great sins. The state must do all it can to promote economic prosperity and economic and social justice; this surely includes a just distribution of wealth and income, a level playing field for all Muslims to achieve their potential, and support for those who cannot provide for themselves. Taxation is one of the instruments that the state has to use in order to achieve these noble results. Although taxation beyond and above *Zakah* is indicated, its form and extent is much more open to interpretation and debate.

Dues on land, *ushr*, were due when and only when there is an actual output. The due was normally dependent on the quality of the land and was applied on gross output.

The other land tax, *kharaj*, was assessed on both Muslims and non-Muslims. Unlike *Zakah, kharaj* is a form of tax that can be changed by Islamic state as it is not ordained in the *Qur'an*. The provisions of *kharaj* are based on *ijma'*. This tax was divided into two parts—the fixed and the proportional. The fixed component was collected from all land that was suitable for cultivation, and was assessed in kind, so much per unit of land or per tree. The second Caliph Omar decreed the rates for several crops. For land not planted with these crops, the rates were based on the quality of the soil, the crops grown on it, and on the method of irrigation, with rates varying from 20 to 50 percent of the output.

The poll tax, *jizyah*, was imposed only on non-Muslims. The origin of this tax is in the *Qur'an*.[23] On the one hand, non-Muslims were liable for this tax because it guaranteed their security. On the other hand, it was also a levy due instead of military service, to which all Muslim males were at least theoretically obliged. Women and children, who of course did not fight, were exempted from this tax. The amount of this tax was prescribed in a number of ways, by treaty as non-Muslims acceded to Muslim rule or imposed by Muslim leaders. The rates were not made explicit in the *Qur'an*, were based on *ijma*, and were generally progressive, in proportion to the ability to pay.

Still another source of revenue was the tax on mines. Originally, *khums* was a tax levied on the spoils of war (at the rate of 20 percent). Later this was extended to mines and anything extracted on and off shore; the Shia see *khums* as even more inclusive, namely that income and uninvested wealth are also subject to *khums*. But basic disagreements on the type of levies on such property being present among various schools of law meant that the Shafi School included such wealth within the provision of *Zakah*, while the Hanafi School did not.[24] Accordingly to the latter, no matter who owned the mine, one-fifth of the deposit was due as tax to the state. However, only certain types of mineral deposits were subject to taxation. For example, ores that could be refined into pure metals (gold, silver, lead, and the like) were taxable; other deposits (coal, water, and the like) were not. One tradition attributes to the Prophet (pbuh) the dictum that all Muslims are partners in "grass, water and fire"—these were the only apparent God-given natural resources in the Arabia of 1400 years ago. Certainly, this would explain the exemptions for coal and for well water. This *hadith* could be used to justify an oil policy that exempted from taxation of the owners of land on which oil was found (as with the owners of water wells), or conversely, for invoking the guideline of universal partnership, in order to keep such land (or at least the mineral rights below it) totally within the public domain. But to us the intention of this *hadith* is clear. Private ownership in Islam is not absolute. For instance, to receive rent on virgin land or untapped resources is prohibited. However, if the owner has improved the land or the resources, through labor/or capital investment, rent can be levied in proportion to the improvements that have been made. All Muslims have an equal right to God's creation. Exhaustible resources are intended for the benefit of all generations and must thus be used in a way that benefits all generations, and all individuals within a generation, equally.

Before concluding this summary of Islamic taxation, we should note that there are three economic issues that also have important implications for taxation: interest (and its relation to profits), rent, and inheritance. Each of these represents an important form of income or wealth that is subject to taxation in the developed economies and about which much of the economic literature on taxation has been written.

11.2 TAX RECEIPTS IN MUSLIM COUNTRIES

Given the importance of economic and social justice in Islam, the expectation would be that the minimum economic needs of all members of society would be met in Muslim countries. The basic needs of the less fortunate can be achieved through direct or indirect (channeled through the government) *Zakah* payments. If this is insufficient, then the government can impose taxes to meet the basic needs (food, shelter, education, and healthcare) of all. Thus, on the one hand, our expectation would be that tax rates may be lower in Muslim countries as the strict payment of *Zakah* should meet much of the social needs of the less fortunate. On the other hand, tax rates may be higher in Muslim countries if the countries are poor or if *Zakah* payments are insufficient to meet these basic needs as mandated in Islam. Additionally, in the rich, oil-exporting countries one might expect a reluctance to impose taxes as readily available oil revenues provide governments with a source of income, income that should be used to benefit all members of society (current and future generations) equally but may be misused. However, taxes also afford governments the means to achieve economic equity. The Prophet (pbuh) emphasized the fact that if some members of society are deprived it must be that other members are living in luxury.

When it comes to government expenditure in a Muslim country, public expenditure should be focused on providing a level playing field where all citizens have the means and an equal chance to be productive and to improve themselves. Public expenditure must uphold the Islamic sense of social and economic justice. This means a concentration of expenditure on social and physical infrastructure, including world-class education, healthcare, and access to housing.

Unfortunately, data limitations do not afford us the opportunity to assess whether governments in Islamic countries are fulfilling their Islamic duties; that is, taxation and expenditure policies to attain social and economic equity and provide the basic needs of all members of society. In Table 11.1 we provide rudimentary data on tax revenues, education expenditure, and health expenditure as a percentage of gross domestic product (GDP). As expected, tax rates in some Islamic countries are very low or nonexistent, while in some countries they are comparable to industrial countries. It is very difficult, if not impossible, for these countries to achieve economic and social justice without taxation or large direct cash payments to all members of society (current and future) from oil and gas revenues (see section 11.2.2 below). At the same time, the data show that Islamic countries spend a much smaller share of GDP on education and healthcare than do industrial countries; again, a shortcoming in fulfilling their Islamic mission of social and economic justice.

11.2.1 Public Borrowing in Muslim Countries

Conventional public finance relies heavily on public borrowing (deficit financing) to finance government expenditure. In turn public borrowing, through the sales of government bonds, deepens capital markets and affords public institutions (central banks) an important instrument for affecting monetary policy. How can a Muslim country achieve the same results and be Islamically compliant?

Some Muslim governments have borrowed and have issued bonds with a fixed and predetermined rate of interest. Such bonds may or may not be sold to the public. They may or may not be publicly traded. They have not significantly deepened the capital markets of any Muslim country where they have been issued.

In an attempt to ameliorate government financing and to be Islamically compliant, Iran has issued two types of paper. In 1998, government participation papers (GPP) were issued for the first time, essentially, to finance government infrastructure projects. Basically, the government promises to pay a return that is equivalent to the return on the underlying asset. However, the coupon rate is fixed at issuance. The contribution of GPP to overall government finances has been modest at best, and it has done almost nothing to stimulate the development of capital markets. In 2001, the

Table 11.1 Comparative tax revenues and health and education expenditure

Selected OIC countries	Tax revenue (% of GDP) 2005	Health expenditure, total (% of GDP) 2005	Public spending on education, total (% of GDP) 2000
Afghanistan	..	5.20	..
Algeria	31.19	3.50	..
Bahrain	4.42	3.80	..
Bangladesh	..	2.80	2.38
Chad	..	3.70	..
Egypt	14.07	6.10	..
Indonesia	..	2.10	1.36
Iran	7.85	7.80	4.38
Iraq	..	4.10	..
Jordan	24.37	10.50	..
Kazakhstan	20.58	3.90	3.26
Kuwait	0.98	2.20	..
Kyrgyzstan	..	6.10	2.94
Lebanon	..	8.70	2.00
Libya	..	3.20	..
Malaysia	..	4.20	6.20
Mali	15.66	5.80	..
Middle East and North Africa	16.82	5.79	..
Morocco	21.65	5.30	6.40
Mozambique	..	4.30	..
Niger	..	3.80	..
Nigeria	..	3.90	..
Oman	..	2.50	3.14
Pakistan	9.60	2.10	1.84
Qatar	21.33	4.10	..
Saudi Arabia	..	3.40	5.94
Senegal	..	5.40	3.38
Sudan	..	3.80	..
Syria	..	4.20	..
Tunisia	21.25	5.50	6.85
Turkey	..	7.60	3.46
United Arab Emirates	..	2.60	1.98

Table 11.1 *(continued)*

	Tax revenue (% of GDP)	Health expenditure, total (% of GDP)	Public spending on education, total (% of GDP)
	2005	2005	2000
Selected developed countries			
Australia	23.72	8.80	4.68
Canada	14.30	9.70	5.65
China	8.73	4.70	..
France	22.42	11.10	5.67
Germany	11.07	10.70	4.46
Italy	21.30	8.90	4.47
Russian Federation	16.61	5.20	2.94
Spain	12.34	8.20	4.28
United Kingdom	27.92	8.20	4.63
United States	11.19	15.90	..

Source: World Development Indicators, World Bank.

central bank of Iran issued central bank participation papers (CBPP), another security deemed to be Islamically compliant. These are bearer securities with a predetermined rate of return, a range of maturities of up to one year, and a quarterly coupon payment. CBPP are backed by completed infrastructure projects that were financed by central bank credit extended to the government. Thus, the backing of CBPP is central bank credit to the government. The public buys participation bonds to take part in financing the government's major development projects. The government had hoped that this new instrument would add a needed tool for monetary control (to control inflation) by the central bank and to the development of the interbank money market. They have been sold in the primary market to non-bank entities. Commercial banks must rediscount them in the secondary market at par and guarantee the predetermined yield to maturity. As a result, in the secondary market they must be traded at par.

Whether paper issued by Iran or by other Muslim countries is Islamically compliant and well designed is not our central concern. The issue is can governments issue an Islamically compliant paper that can be used to finance revenue shortfalls, afford central banks an important policy instrument, and deepen and stimulate Islamic capital markets? We believe that the answer is in the affirmative. However, in our view, the rate of return should *not* be predetermined and should be related to a readily measurable market indicator. For instance, the coupon rate could be related to the nominal growth of GDP, the return to a national stock index, to an average of private sector return on equity, and in the case of an oil exporter to the price oil. The paper should be readily tradable on the secondary market. And as with all securities trading, prudent supervision is always a must. In this instance, as in others, Muslim countries must show flexibility and adapt to changing needs and circumstances while preserving their Islamic heritage.

11.2.2 Public Revenues from Oil and Gas Sales (Mineral Deposit Depletion in Islam)

In addition to taxation and public borrowing, revenues from the depletion of natural resources can provide governments with the needed income. The basis for this is two often-quoted principles in Islam—ownership is not absolute, and that economic activities, including taxation and the distribution of wealth, must be just.

In a number of Muslim countries, especially in the Middle East and North Africa, oil and gas revenues contribute the lion's share of government revenues. What are the economic implications of oil and gas depletion? What does Islam have to say about the use of oil and gas revenues to finance government expenditure?

In an oil-based economy, if the income from oil is consumed—and, as is the practice, if oil output is counted as a part of net national product (NNP)—then NNP declines as oil reserves are depleted.[25] So at least a part of current oil revenues must be saved and invested, domestically or abroad, to even out NNP and thus to avoid a decline in national output in the future.[26] Put differently, the normally or conventionally measured NNP in an oil-producing country diverges from the "theoretically correct" measure of NNP for a country that has no depleting resource such as oil. The higher the return on investments—that is, the more compensation made for resource depletion—and the longer the resource will last at the current rate of extraction, the closer (more comparable) are the conventionally measured and theoretically correct NNP.

While production and export diversification away from oil are necessary, so is government revenue stabilization and diversification. In most Middle Eastern oil-exporting countries oil (gas) provides the lion's share of revenues and it has fluctuated considerably from year to year. Relatively stable fiscal revenues are essential for macroeconomic management and in turn for sustained economic growth. Countries that achieve sustained long-term growth on average experienced less volatility in growth.[27] To stabilize oil revenues, countries can, and have, adopted some form of an oil stabilization fund. A portion of revenues are placed into the fund in a year of above a calculated average (moving or otherwise) expected oil revenues/prices and can be "theoretically" drawn down when revenues/prices fall below the average. Alternatively an oil-exporting country could hedge its exposure to oil price volatility through the futures market. While such funds and hedging may be used to stabilize available oil revenues from year to year, they do not diversify the basic source of government revenues.[28] Government revenue diversification ultimately requires a healthy and growing economy with an effective income tax system.

The issue of equity and social justice is another important consideration for countries with large oil and gas resources. Economists have addressed the issue before. Robert Solow in his famous article concluded by saying:[29]

> The finite pool of resources (I have excluded full recycling) should be used up optimally according to the general rules that govern the optimal use of reproducible assets. In particular, earlier generations are entitled to draw down the pool (optimally, of course!) so long as they add (optimally, of course!) to the stock of reproducible capital.

What if they cannot, or will not, optimally add to the stock of reproducible capital? The clear need is to find an alternative to Solow's prescribed optimal draw down and optimal addition to reproducible capital; this can be achieved by taking oil revenues away from the government and creating a fund to address issues of equity.

For any proposition regarding the management of exhaustible resources to be effective in Muslim countries, it must be compatible with basic Islamic teachings on the ownership and extraction of depletable resources. When it comes to depletable resources, Islam is unambiguous. Anything underground belongs to society at large; that is, all citizens should have an equal share in what is under the land. This incorporates both *current* and *all future* generations. Thus, Solow's prescription is essentially that which should be followed in these countries.

The task for these governments is clear but difficult. First, governments must take control of all minerals. Second, governments must make sure that they do not waste depleting mineral resources, because they are the birthright of all citizens and must be used productively. Third, as minerals are depleted, governments must make sure that they use their revenues in such a way that all citizens today, and for all future time, receive similar real benefits. Oil should benefit all members of the current generation equally (with optimal depletion and optimal compensation for depletion), with the implication of relatively even distribution of income given the overwhelming role of oil (as opposed to hard work and sound productive investments) in these economies.

Many countries and states (within countries) have adopted funds for future generations. These funds generally take but a *small* percentage of revenues of exhaustible resource depletion; their operations are generally opaque; and in some cases there are no rules for the portion to be saved, and in cases where there are rules, the rules for the portion to be saved, its management, and/or its distribution are highly imprecise. These funds do not follow Solow's prescription of intergenerational equity, as they do not replace all of the drawn down resource with future sources of output. In a number of oil-exporting countries, ruling families, or the elite, take a significant portion of the revenue, even *before* it becomes available for public expenditure or for placement in any sort of a fund, whether the fund be for revenue stabilization or for future generations.[30]

The *de-linking* of oil revenues from government coffers may avoid other problems normally associated with the exploitation of depletable natural resources, such as a high level of military expenditure.[31] Military expenditure, in turn, could be associated with a number of other adverse developments. Civil wars and conflict are more likely if military expenditure are high, and the risk of civil war is higher if natural resource endowment is double the average.[32] Civil wars in turn lead to higher military expenditure, capital flight, loss of social capital, slower economic growth, and more poverty and refugees, an almost impenetrable vicious circle. While some advocate an " ... international template for the acceptable governance of natural resource revenues to which a government with significant revenues could chose to subscribe,"[33] we believe that a fund that takes all revenues away from the government should be an integral and primary component of any template.

Table 11.2 Decadal medians of Gini coefficients for income distribution

	1960s	1970s	1980s	1990s
Middle East and North Africa	0.419	0.436	0.408	0.397
Sub-Saharan Africa	0.499	0.485	0.396	0.423
East Asia and Pacific	0.346	0.344	0.344	0.348
South Asia	0.317	0.323	0.322	0.316
OECD and high income	0.329	0.330	0.322	0.316

Source: Klaus Deininger, Lyn Squire, "New Ways of Looking at Old Issues: Inequality and Growth," *Journal of Development Economics*, Vol. 57, 1998.

Since equity is one of our central preoccupations, we should say a little more about it. In terms of income distribution, it is evident that the majority of people in oil-exporting countries have not benefited from the massive inflow of oil revenues. The 2002 United Nations Human Development Report verifies the growth of inequality. In Iran, the value of the Gini coefficient[34] was 0.443 in the mid-1980s and 0.430 in 1998. In Iraq, the value of the Gini coefficient increased from 0.370 in 1993 to 0.508 in 1998. As shown in Table 11.2, the Gini coefficients of the Middle East and North Africa regions, with the exception of the Sub-Saharan African region, lags consistently behind those of the comparator groups. Oil and gas reserves, the birthright of all citizens and generations, have not only not improved equity but may have instead affected it adversely.

Suppose there is "no" oil, then the government would develop economic policies with no oil revenues. Essentially, taking oil revenues away from governments would be a "forcing mechanism" to adopt and implement development policies just like other countries without oil would do, and many have done so very successfully. For our Oil Fund for All Generations (the "Fund"), 100 percent of the oil revenue will be placed into the Fund and proceeds will be distributed to all eligible citizens in the form of an annual payout that maintains the same real purchasing power. The detailed derivation of the payout is as follows.

Let's assume that the Fund, *F*, were established and proceeds from the Fund were distributed to every citizen immediately (starting at time 0). The inflow to the Fund would be current oil revenue and the outflow from the Fund would be an annuity payout to every citizen in the country. There would be a positive balance in the Fund if there were more oil revenues than the total payout in the first year.

Therefore, the Fund at the end of the first period, F_o, would be:

$$F_o = R_o - Y_o = R_o - P_oZ \qquad (1)$$

Where:

F_o: Oil Fund at time 0
R_o: Oil revenue at time 0
Y_0: Total annual payout to citizens at time 0
P_0: Population at time 0
Z: Real annual payout per citizen, assumed constant over time

At the end of the first year the size of the Fund, F_1, would be the oil revenues minus the payout to citizens plus the balance carried over from the previous year (year 0), if any, grown by appropriate reinvestment rate i. Therefore, we can write F_1 as:

$$F_1 = R_1 - Y_1 + F_oe^i \qquad (2)$$

Alternatively, equation 2 can be rewritten as:

$$F_1 = R_oe^r - P_oe^gZ + (R_0 - P_oZ)e^i \qquad (3)$$

Where:

i: Annual real return on Fund investments, assumed a constant
g: Annual population growth rate, assumed a constant
r: Annual real growth rate in oil revenues, assumed a constant

In year two, the year-end balance of the Fund would be oil revenues from year two minus payout to citizens plus any residual balance from the previous two years. Therefore, the Fund in year two or F_2 would be:

$$F_2 = R_2 - Y_2 + F_1e^i \qquad (4)$$

Equation 4 can be rewritten as:

$$F_2 = R_0e^{2r} - P_oe^{2g}Z + (R_0e^r - P_oe^gZ)e^i + (R_o - P_oZ)e^{2i} \qquad (5)$$

Accordingly, the Fund in any given year n would be a summation of oil revenues from year n or R_0e^{nr}, minus the payout to the citizens, $P_oe^{ng}Z$, and accumulation of reinvested Fund resources from previous years: $R_0 \sum_{k=o}^{n-1} e^{kr} e^{(n-k)i} - \sum_{k=o}^{n-1} P_0 e^{kg} e^{(n-k)i}$. In other words, F_n can be expressed as:

$$F_n = R_0 e^{nr} - P_o e^{ng} Z + R_0 \sum_{k=o}^{n-1} e^{kr} e^{(n-k)i} - \sum_{k=o}^{n-1} P_0 e^{kg} e^{(n-k)i} Z \qquad (6)$$

When there is no inflow of oil revenues, oil reserve is depleted, and the payout Z will simply be made from the accumulated balance from previous years. We can derive Z by rearranging equation 6:

$$Z \leq \frac{R_0}{P_0} \left[\frac{e^{nr} + \sum_{k=o}^{n-1} e^{kr} e^{(n-k)i}}{e^{ng} + \sum_{k=o}^{n-1} e^{kg} e^{(n-k)i}} \right] \Rightarrow Z \leq \frac{R_0}{P_0} \left[\frac{\sum_{k=o}^{n} e^{kr} e^{(n-k)i}}{\sum_{k=o}^{n} e^{kg} e^{(n-k)i}} \right] \qquad (7)$$

Where:

$F_n > 0$

It can be shown that equation 7 can be simplified using geometric algebra as follows:

$$\sum_{k=o}^{n-1} e^{kc} e^{(n-k)i} = e^{ni} \left[\frac{1 - e^{(c-i)n}}{1 - e^{(c-i)}} \right] \qquad (8)$$

Where c is a constant.

Using (8), and substituting c for r and g, respectively, equation 7 becomes:

$$Z \leq \frac{R_0}{P_o} \left\{ \frac{e^{ni} \left[\frac{1 - e^{(r-i)n+1}}{1 - e^{(r-i)}} \right]}{e^{ni} \left[\frac{1 - e^{(g-i)n+1}}{1 - e^{(g-i)}} \right]} \right\}$$

Equivalently:

$$Z \leq \frac{R_0}{P_o} \left[\frac{1 - e^{(r-i)n+1}}{1 - e^{(g-i)n+1}} \right] \left[\frac{1 - e^{(g-i)}}{1 - e^{(r-i)}} \right] \qquad (9)$$

Finally, as n approaches infinity ($n \rightarrow \infty$), Z becomes:

$$Z \leq \frac{R_0}{P_o}\left[\frac{1-e^{(g-i)}}{1-e^{(r-i)}}\right] \qquad (10)$$

Where:

$r < i$, and $g < i$.

Two assumptions are made regarding the relationships between g, r, and i in deriving equation 10. First, we assumed r is less than i. In equilibrium one could assume that the long-term growth rate of oil revenues, r, would be equal to the long-term reinvestment rate, i. However, we know that the output of oil, and thus oil revenues, will eventually decline to zero. Hence, in the long run we expect oil revenue growth to be somewhere between zero and the long-term reinvestment rate, i. Second, g is assumed to be 2 percent and less than i. This assumption is reasonable because the historical long-term average growth rate of humankind has been in the 2 percent range.[35]

Given the assumptions above, what does equation 10 mean for the Muslim oil-exporting countries? In other words, if countries were to establish such a Fund, what would each country's per capita constant real payout look like? To illustrate a range of possible per capita payout, Z, we present country-specific tables for different levels of r and g. In the calculations, as a proxy for the current period's oil revenues, R_0, we take the product of: (a) the simple average of the past five years of total oil output (this includes oil that was exported and that which was retained for domestic consumption) for each country[36]; and (b) the simple average of the past five years of oil prices. The average reinvestment rate i is assumed to be 8.0 percent per annum based on the weighted average of 30-year U.S. Treasury Yield and S&P 500 Index Yield over the past 25 years, assuming 75 percent and 25 percent allocation to bonds and stocks, respectively, and that rate is used for all six countries, with sensitivity analysis around this average figure. Also, as a proxy for the current population, P_0, we propose that a payout from the Fund is only made to citizens who are age 18 years and over.[37] In addition to these assumptions, we made further estimations for the purpose of calculation as follows: population is adjusted in order to account for "indigenous nationals" only; per capita GDP (PPP) for Iraq is based on authors' estimate; and in calculating two-year oil revenue, outputs of Iraq between 2003 and 2004 were adjusted to account for production disruption due

Table 11.3 Iran's annual per capita payout to citizens (in US$ and as a percent of per capita GDP)

	$r = 0.5\%$	$r = 1.5\%$	$r = 2.5\%$	$r = 3.5\%$	$r = 4.5\%$
$i = 6.0\%$	\$713 10%	\$868 12%	\$1,110 16%	\$1,546 22%	\$2,564 37%
$i = 7.0\%$	\$755 11%	\$887 13%	\$1,079 15%	\$1,381 20%	\$1,923 27%
$i = 8.0\%$	\$785 11%	\$901 13%	\$1,060 15%	\$1,289 18%	\$1,649 24%
$i = 9.0\%$	\$808 12%	\$911 13%	\$1,046 15%	\$1,230 18%	\$1,496 21%
$i = 10.0\%$	\$826 12%	\$919 13%	\$1,036 15%	\$1,190 17%	\$1,399 20%

Note: Used 2003 population of 68.2 million with 3% non-citizen, from 2005 United Nation's Human Development Report (UN HDR) and authors' estimate, respectively.

Table 11.4 Iraq's annual per capita payout to citizens (in US$ and as a percent of per capita GDP)

	$r = 0.5\%$	$r = 1.5\%$	$r = 2.5\%$	$r = 3.5\%$	$r = 4.5\%$
$i = 6.0\%$	\$1,559 46%	\$1,896 56%	\$2,425 71%	\$3,379 99%	\$5,603 165%
$i = 7.0\%$	\$1,649 48%	\$1,939 57%	\$2,358 69%	\$3,017 89%	\$4,203 124%
$i = 8.0\%$	\$1,715 50%	\$1,969 58%	\$2,315 68%	\$2,816 83%	\$3,602 106%
$i = 9.0\%$	\$1,765 52%	\$1,991 59%	\$2,286 67%	\$2,688 79%	\$3,269 96%
$i = 10.0\%$	\$1,805 53%	\$2,007 59%	\$2,264 67%	\$2,599 76%	\$3,057 90%

Note: Assumed population of 25 million, authors' estimate. Oil revenue of 2003 and 2004 was doubled to take account of production disruption due to wars.

to warfare. Tables 11.3 to 11.8 show a range of potential payouts to each citizen (Z calculated using equation 10 above) and citizen payout as a percentage of conventionally calculated GDP per capita (that is, GDP divided by total population and not citizens, or citizens over 18), depending on the combination of the oil revenue growth assumption (r) and the reinvestment rate assumption (i).

A number of assumptions and facts should be repeated before discussing these results. The calculation of Z is based on citizens

Table 11.5 Kuwait's annual per capita payout to citizens (in US$ and as a percent of per capita GDP)

	$r = 0.5\%$	$r = 1.5\%$	$r = 2.5\%$	$r = 3.5\%$	$r = 4.5\%$
$i = 6.0\%$	$32,788 182%	$39,876 221%	$51,016 283%	$71,067 394%	$117,857 653%
$i = 7.0\%$	$34,679 192%	$40,782 226%	$49,599 275%	$63,454 352%	$88,394 490%
$i = 8.0\%$	$36,066 200%	$41,410 229%	$48,697 270%	$59,224 328%	$75,768 420%
$i = 9.0\%$	$37,126 206%	$41,870 232%	$48,073 266%	$56,533 313%	$68,754 381%
$i = 10.0\%$	$37,963 210%	$42,221 234%	$47,615 264%	$54,670 303%	$64,291 356%

Note: Assumed population of 2.5 million with 70% non-citizen used, 2005 UN HDR and authors' estimate, respectively.

Table 11.6 Qatar's annual per capita payout to citizens (in US$ and as a percent of per capita GDP)

	$r = 0.5\%$	$r = 1.5\%$	$r = 2.5\%$	$r = 3.5\%$	$r = 4.5\%$
$i = 6.0\%$	$56,957 287%	$69,270 349%	$88,620 447%	$123,452 622%	$204,730 1,032%
$i = 7.0\%$	$60,242 304%	$70,844 357%	$86,158 434%	$110,226 555%	$153,551 774%
$i = 8.0\%$	$62,651 316%	$71,933 362%	$84,592 426%	$102,879 518%	$131,618 663%
$i = 9.0\%$	$64,493 325%	$72,732 367%	$83,508 421%	$98,204 495%	$119,434 602%
$i = 10.0\%$	$65,947 332%	$73,343 370%	$82,713 417%	$94,968 479%	$111,680 563%

Note: Assumed population of 700,000 with 75% non-citizen, 2005 UN HDR and authors' estimate, respectively.

over 18. In four of these countries, Saudi Arabia, and especially in Kuwait, Qatar, and the UAE, the percentage of non-citizens is extraordinarily high. Thus oil revenues and GDP per *citizen* are much higher than when the denominator is total population; this effect is magnified further when adult citizens are used. For the same reason, the payout as a percentage of conventional GDP per capita (the number reported in the tables) is significantly higher than the payout as a percentage of GDP per citizen. We should also repeat the obvious

Table 11.7 Saudi Arabia's annual per capita payout to citizens (in US$ and as a percent of per capita GDP)

	$r = 0.5\%$	$r = 1.5\%$	$r = 2.5\%$	$r = 3.5\%$	$r = 4.5\%$
$i = 6.0\%$	\$9,127 46%	\$11,100 56%	\$14,201 72%	\$19,782 100%	\$32,807 165%
$i = 7.0\%$	\$9,653 49%	\$11,352 57%	\$13,806 70%	\$17,663 89%	\$24,606 124%
$i = 8.0\%$	\$10,039 51%	\$11,527 58%	\$13,555 68%	\$16,486 83%	\$21,091 106%
$i = 9.0\%$	\$10,335 52%	\$11,655 59%	\$13,382 67%	\$15,737 79%	\$19,138 96%
$i = 10.0\%$	\$10,568 53%	\$11,753 59%	\$13,254 67%	\$15,218 77%	\$17,896 90%

Note: Assumed population of 23.2 million with 35% non-citizen, 2005 UN HDR and authors' estimate, respectively.

Table 11.8 The UAE's annual per capita payout to citizens (in US$ and as a percent of per capita GDP)

	$r = 0.5\%$	$r = 1.5\%$	$r = 2.5\%$	$r = 3.5\%$	$r = 4.5\%$
$i = 6.0\%$	\$35,410 158%	\$43,065 192%	\$55,094 246%	\$76,749 342%	\$127,280 568%
$i = 7.0\%$	\$37,452 167%	\$44,043 196%	\$53,564 239%	\$68,527 306%	\$95,462 426%
$i = 8.0\%$	\$38,950 174%	\$44,720 199%	\$52,591 235%	\$63,959 285%	\$81,826 365%
$i = 9.0\%$	\$40,095 179%	\$45,217 202%	\$51,916 232%	\$61,053 272%	\$74,251 331%
$i = 10.0\%$	\$40,999 183%	\$45,597 203%	\$51,422 229%	\$59,041 263%	\$69,431 310%

Note: Assumed population of 4 million with 78% non-citizen, 2005 UN HDR and authors' estimate, respectively.

fact that the calculated Z is the payout today. If a moving average is used to recalculate Z every year, next year if figures for oil revenues, rate of return on investments, or population projections change, then Z will change.[38]

Broadly speaking the absolute payout figures, and as a percentage of GDP per capita, are very impressive and could make a tremendous difference to the lives of the average citizens. But there are significant variations between the six countries. Based on our results, the six countries fall more or less into three categories: (1) Iran; (2) Iraq and Saudi Arabia; and (3) Kuwait, Qatar, and the UAE.

Iran has the lowest payout figures. In the case of Iran, the payout ranges from 10 to nearly 40 percent of GDP per capita. Iran's population is large (more than the other five countries combined, and Iran's expatriate population is relatively small) while its oil output is less than either Kuwait's or the UAE's. Iran's payout potential could improve dramatically (*more than double* over a decade) if it begins to exploit more aggressively its natural gas resources, as has Qatar.

Iraq is a unique case. It is a country that has gone back to the 1950s and is essentially starting all over again. It appears poorer than Iran because it has little in the way of modern infrastructure, but it is likely to be richer than Iran in terms of per capita endowment of oil. In our opinion, the payout figures in our table for Iraq are an underestimate if Iraq can move towards peace and improved governance. Iraq could approach the category of a Saudi Arabia in terms of oil revenues per capita; and Iraq can learn from the economic policy mistakes of Iran and Saudi Arabia.

For Saudi Arabia, the payout potential is significantly higher than that of Iran or even Iraq (given Iraq's current status and Iran's slow exploitation of its natural gas resources). The annual payout in Saudi Arabia would dramatically improve the lives of citizens, as the Saudi government has not delivered on economic growth and widespread prosperity. At the same time the Fund would provide a better guarantee of economic benefits to future generations.

Kuwait, Qatar, and the UAE are in another league. Simply said, they are rich beyond belief. Their annual payouts, even under the most conservative assumptions, are just staggering. Our calculations do not include their existing investments (in a fund for the future) abroad. In the case of the UAE the numbers are simply staggering. We estimate that UAE investments abroad are well over US$350 billion. Most of these funds do not belong to the entire UAE, but belong only to the Emirate of Abu Dhabi. We estimate that Abu Dhabi's investments abroad is over US$500 billion. The entire citizenry (of all ages, not just over 18) of Abu Dhabi is about 250,000. They are *all* effectively millionaires based on their existing foreign investments alone! Moreover, in our payout table for the UAE, if the emirate of Abu Dhabi were taken by itself, the payout figure would be three times that of the UAE as a whole. If the income from existing investments were added to current (and projected) oil revenues (the basis of our payout tables), then the annual payouts for the UAE would increase significantly from those shown in our tables; and for Abu Dhabi alone, the payout figures (including investment income) would be significantly higher than this figure. Qatar, with its rapidly growing gas revenues and citizenry of about 200,000, is likely be in the same fortunate position as Abu Dhabi. Kuwait still has significant foreign investments, even though it spent a large portion for its liberation and reconstruction; we estimate Kuwait's foreign holdings to be in the neighborhood of US$100 billion. In the case of Kuwait, Qatar, and the UAE the issue is not so much that citizens of these countries are likely to starve any time soon. Instead the issue is that the wealth of nationals should be preserved for them and for future generations in an *optimal*, *equitable*, and *transparent* manner. This depleting wealth should not be seen as the birthright of rulers (also in Saudi Arabia) to use in order to buy loyalty, to waste on grandiose projects and military hardware, and to support shortsighted economic policies.

We now turn to some of the operational, social, and economic issues.

11.2.2.1 Who is the Beneficiary?

It seems reasonable that only citizens should be the beneficiaries of any payout from the Fund as the oil belongs to citizens of all generations.[39] A pertinent question is whether payouts should be given to adults only? If payouts are given to all citizens regardless of age, is it reasonable to assume that a minor would be sufficiently responsible? Should the payment then be made to the parent or the guardian of a minor? If yes, then such a policy could encourage population growth (and the more children one has the larger the share of the Fund's payout). On the other hand, if the first payment (representing the accumulated annual payouts from the prior 16 or 18 years) to a citizen is set contemporaneous to the attainment of adulthood, would that expectation of such a financial "windfall" create moral hazards and result in unintended waste? For the purpose of our illustrative calculations, we assumed that annual payouts are made only to those over 18 years of age.

11.2.2.2 Moral Hazards and Conditionality

Given the moral hazard issue identified above, one could argue for instituting compensating factors that would serve to minimize unintended consequences. Specifically, the first payment from the Fund could be tied to some socially acceptable (or desirable) criteria. For instance, for those in the 18–30 age bracket, the first and subsequent payouts could be made conditional to the citizens' achieving a minimum level of educational proficiency, or indeed, for having a history of productive and legal employment if not attending school. Such a condition would encourage literacy amongst the populace and could support economic growth. Another condition that could be attached to a citizen's right to receive current and future payouts from the Fund is the maintenance of a clean civilian record. Depending on the nature of the offense, a felon may forfeit his or her right to further payouts from the Fund.[40]

A potentially interesting application of the Fund is to explore the design of the Fund to mimic the role that social security plays in the wealthier countries. Thus, payouts could be higher when a citizen reaches a certain given (retirement) age. These and other features could have a significant effect on a number of related factors, such as birth rates. For our limited illustrative purposes here we assumed none of the abovementioned options.

11.2.2.3 Societal Productivity

An obvious attack on any scheme is that individuals would become lazy, would not work and in the process society would become less productive. While this is a legitimate concern it need not become a fact of life. If governments develop effective institutions, adopt rational and consistent economic policies, and generally provide a supportive business climate, citizens will be more motivated (and will have the resources) to invest and invigorate private sector growth. At the same time the eligibility to receive payments from the Fund can be tied to definable, objective, and socially desirable achievements.

11.2.2.4 Investments, Payouts, and the Use of Funds

The payout objective must be set with the ultimate goal of making reasonably constant and fair payouts to current and future generations. To that end, the Fund should invest the unpaid balance into a portfolio of well-diversified real and financial investments across a broad range of countries, currencies, asset classes, and non-oil industries. The size of the payout would need to be recalculated periodically and the various input assumptions would need to be pegged to some predetermined moving average, as happens in the State of Alaska.

Another issue that could arise is government borrowing from the Fund (or collateralization of the Fund to borrow from third parties). We assumed no such borrowing or collateralization options in our calculation. We stress that the key tenet of our manifesto is the separation of all future oil and gas revenue from the hands of governments and ruling families in the Fund. To make the assets of the Fund available either directly or indirectly to these governments would open Pandora's box and undermine the effectiveness of the Fund.

11.2.2.5 Effective Tax Policy

The success of the Fund also depends on efficient income tax policy and an effective system of taxation in place. None of the Persian Gulf oil exporters have an effective income tax system to address social and economic needs (Iran has an ineffective tax system while the others do not have an income tax system in place). Given the waste of oil revenues over the last 30 or so years, it is clear that much more thought is required on how oil revenues should be used and what form of tax system would best meet the needs of current and future generations in order to address efficiency, simplicity, and fairness (social justice).

11.2.2.6 Fund Administration

The operations of the Fund must be totally transparent. A Fund needs to have clear independence and authority with respect to investment decisions and general management. The Fund's administrators must have direct reporting lines to the governing board, and their employment/succession, performance, and compensation must be determined solely by the board. The administration of the Fund and the formal processes it adopts should not be a part of the civil government structure, be reliant on any government entities, nor have any connection to ruling families and elites. Accordingly, the governments of oil-exporting countries will not have real or ostensible authority over the Fund's management.

11.2.2.7 Governance and Control

A fundamental concern with the establishing of a Fund is the governance structure of the Fund. There needs to be integrity among those who can influence strategy and financial performance. The governance body (possibly a Board of Directors not dissimilar to a modern corporation) should comprise individuals with a balance of skills, experience, and independence, appropriate for the management of the Fund.

Mandatory and periodic disclosures with respect to the Fund's balances, investment policies and results, flow of funds, material matters, and even personal financial disclosures of the board members would instill public confidence and minimize potential malfeasance. Further, the rights of citizens, the Fund's beneficiaries, need to be clearly articulated and upheld. Effective internal control mechanisms must be put in place to ensure the proper functioning and governance of the Fund.

11.2.2.8 The Transitional Phase

The cutback of oil revenues to the government may have to be made on a gradual basis over a transitional period of, say, ten years. Given the gross reliance of governments in oil-exporting countries on oil and gas revenues today, it would be unrealistic to expect a sudden withdrawal from it to be politically and structurally feasible. In our calculations in this chapter, we have assumed no transition phase.

11.2.2.9 Provision of Government Services

Some may find our proposal objectionable because crucial government services could be reduced or even eliminated. They argue that governments should have access to "some" oil revenues in order to provide services that are universally expected of a government: education, healthcare, retirement, and public safety. Our broad answer to this line of reasoning is that governments could provide at least some of these services *but* they should finance them through income taxes that are fair and efficient, as non-oil-exporters try to do. More specifically, in many of the countries, payouts from the Fund would be sufficient to cover private funding of education, healthcare, and retirement. In cases where they are insufficient, governments should provide them and they should be financed by taxation. The danger of allowing governments to take some oil revenues for "specific and noble causes" is that governments can then use funds from taxation in wasteful areas, as they have done in the past with oil revenues; money is, after all, the most fungible of commodities. It should also be remembered that we support a transition period of up to ten years for taking all oil revenues from governments.

* * * * *

Clearly, the range of potential issues in implementing an Oil Fund is far-reaching and different for each country, and a comprehensive assessment and analysis would in itself occupy a volume beyond this book.

11.3 PUBLIC EXPENDITURE

In a Muslim country, public expenditure should be focused on providing a level playing field where all citizens have the means and an equal chance to be productive and to improve themselves. Public expenditure must uphold the Islamic sense of social and economic justice. This would mean a concentration of expenditure on social and physical infrastructure, including world-class education, healthcare, and access to housing. In Table 11.1 we present public expenditure by major category. Is the distribution of expenditures Islamically appropriate in Muslim countries and especially in major oil and gas exporting countries?

As to be expected, the health and education expenditure as a percentage of GDP are low in OIC countries when compared to the advanced industrial countries. These countries have not provided the minimum for all individuals to thrive. All OIC countries need to do more to provide the basis for citizens to reach their full potential.

But this sub-par performance is also the case when the rich OIC oil-exporting countries are the basis of comparison to the advanced industrial countries. Clearly oil is not used to benefit the average citizen, directly or indirectly, as called for in Islamic teachings. These conditions may get even worse if oil and gas reserves are depleted without adequate safeguards and provisions to benefit future generations. We can only repeat our conclusion that a comprehensive oil fund that spans all generations is the only sure way that governments in oil-exporting countries can protect the financial and economic interests of all generations and practice the teachings of Islam. There can be little doubt that the oil exporting countries of the Persian Gulf have failed economically. While oil has supported government revenues, the pursuit of economic and social justice has failed. It is time for a change while oil and gas reserves last. A comprehensive oil fund will take easy money away from the hands of governments and of rulers, waste and corruption are likely to be reduced, there will be better chance of adopting and implementing rational economic policies, and equity across generations is more likely to become a reality. Careful considerations needs to be given in each country, on a country-by-country basis, to design a system that affords appropriate incentives to individuals to live productive lives and to contribute to national economic and social prosperity. Finally, rulers and elites in all of these countries will condemn the adoption of a fund as proposed here. It will become a reality if it is touted and supported by international agencies, NGOs and academics, and given international recognition by the media.

ENDNOTES

1 Part of this chapter is based on the excerpts from H. Askari, F. Abbas, G. Jabbour, and D. Kwon (2006), "An Economic Manifesto for the Oil Exporting Countries of the Persian Gulf," *BNL Quarterly Review*, LIX, no. 239. We are thankful to *BNL Quarterly Review* for their permission to use the excerpts.

2 Wilson, Rodney, "The Contribution of Muhammad Baqir Al-Sadr to Contemporary Islamic Thought," *Journal of Islamic Studies*, 9, no.1, (1998): 49.

3 See *Qur'an* 13:22 a similar phrasing is found in 35:29.

4 See *Qur'an* 70:24.

5 For example, this is the interpretation cited as primary by Joseph Schacht in the article on *Zakah* in the *Encyclopedia of Islam* (Leyden: E. J. Brill Ltd., 1934).

6 According to Schacht in the *Qur'an* 29:31, 55; 7:156; 21:73, etc.

7 As, for example, in the *Qur'an* 92:14.

8 Aghnides, Nicholas P., *Mohammedan Theories of Finance*, (New York: Columbia University Press, 1916): note 5: 203.

9 Ul Haq, Irfan, *Islamization of Economic Doctrines of Islam: A Study in the Doctrines of Islam and Their Implications for Poverty, Employment, and Economic Growth*, (Virginia: International Institute of Islamic Thought, 1996).

10 Askari, Hossein, John Thomas Cummings, and Michael Glover, *Taxation and Tax Policies in the Middle East*, (United Kingdom: Butterworth Publishers, 1982).

11 The terms "taxes" and "social spending" are used interchangeably throughout the *Qur'an*. See also *Qur'an* 59:7, which says that "*it [wealth] may not be [a benefit] going round and round among such as you may [already] be rich.*"
Source: Irfan Ul Haq, *Economic Doctrines of Islam: A Study in the Doctrines of Islam and Their Implications for Poverty, Employment, and Economic Growth.*

12 See *Qur'an* 9:60: "*The offerings given for the sake of God* (zakah) *are [meant] only for the poor and the needy, and those who are in charge thereof (who collect the tax), and those whose hearts are to be won over, and for the freeing of human beings from bondage, and [for] those who are overburdened with debts, and [for every struggle] in God's cause, and [for] the wayfarer: [this is] an ordinance from God—and God is All-Knowing, Wise.*"
See *Qur'an* 70:24–25: "*...in whose (the faithfuls') possessions there is a due share, acknowledged [by them], for such as ask [for help] and such as are deprived [of what is good in life]*." See *Qur'an* 51:19: "*[But,] behold, the God-conscious ... [would assign] in all that they possessed a due share unto such as might ask [for help] and such as might suffer privation.*"
The Prophet (pbuh) is also reported to have said that "charity is *halal* (permitted) neither for the rich nor the able-bodied." Source: Ibid.

13 Ul Haq, Irfan, *Economic Doctrines of Islam: A Study in the Doctrines of Islam and Their Implications for Poverty, Employment, and Economic Growth.*

14 Zaman, S. M. Hasanuz, *Economic Guidelines in the Quran*, (Islamabad: The International Institute of Islamic Thought, 1999).

15 Mirakhor, Abbas, "General Characteristics of an Islamic Economic System", in *Essays on Iqtisad: the Islamic Approach to Economic Problems*, eds. Baqir Al-Hasani and Abbas Mirakhor, (New York: Global Scholarly Publications, 2003).

16 Ul Haq, Irfan, *Economic Doctrines of Islam: A Study in the Doctrines of Islam and Their Implications for Poverty, Employment, and Economic Growth.*

17 The Prophet (pbuh) is reported to have said: "Nothing makes a poor man starve except that which a rich person avails in luxury." See: Abbas Mirakhor, *General Characteristics of an Islamic Economic System.*

See *Qur'an* 20:118–119, Adam is told: "*Behold, it is provided for thee that thou shalt not hunger here nor feel naked, and that thou shalt not thirst here or suffer from the heat of the sun.*"

The Prophet (pbuh) is reported to have said: "He is not a faithful who eats his fill while his neighbor [or fellowman] remains hungry by his side." Source: Ibid.

18 See *Qur'an* 30:39: "*And [remember]: whatever you may give out in usury so that it might increase through [other] people's possessions will bring [you] no increase in the sight of God—whereas all that you give out in charity, seeking God's countenance, [will be blessed by Him:] for it is they, they [who thus seek His countenance] that shall have their recompense multiplied!*"

See *Qur'an*: 3:92: "[*But as for you, O believers,] never shall you attain true piety unless you spend on others out of what you cherish yourselves; and whatever you spend—verily, God has full knowledge thereof.*"

See *Qur'an* 2:276: "*Allah ... will give increase for goods of charity.*" Source: Ed. Munawar Iqbal, *Distributive Justice and Need Fulfillment in an Islamic Economy* (Islamabad: International Institute of Islamic Economics, International Islamic University, 1986).

See *Qur'an* 2:177: "*True piety does not consist in turning your faces towards the east or the west—but truly pious is he who believes in God, and the Last Day, and the angels, and revelation, and the prophets, and* spends his substance—*however much he himself may cherish it—upon his near of kin, and the orphans, and the needy, and the wayfarer, and the beggars, and for the freeing of human beings from bondage; and is constant in prayer, and* renders their purifying dues (Zakah) ... *it is they that have proved themselves true, and it is they, they who are conscious of God.*"

19 Ed. Munawar Iqbal, *Distributive Justice and Need Fulfillment in an Islamic Economy.*

20 Mirakhor, Abbas, *General Characteristics of an Islamic Economic System.*

21 See *Qur'an* 9:60.

22 Aghnides, note 5: 296. For example, the Hanafi School held that gold, silver, and articles of trade were nonapparent property, while livestock and any otherwise nonapparent property taken outside the city were apparent property, with the obligation on agricultural produce held to be an obligation distinct from *Zakah*. On the other hand, the Shafi School included agricultural produce and the output of mines along with the livestock as apparent property.

23 See *Qur'an* 9:29. The word *jizyah* is derived from *jaza*, meaning compensation or requital for good or evil.

24 The Hanbali School held views similar to the Shafi, and the Maliki School straddled the issue.

25 This entire section is taken from H. Askari, F. Abbas, G. Jabbour, and D. Kwon, "An Economic Manifesto for the Oil Exporting Countries of the Persian Gulf," *Banca Nazionale Del Lavoro Quarterly Review*, LIX, no. 239.

26 The conceptual interpretation of NNP in an economy is that it represents the highest level of sustainable consumption. In the development of the conceptual framework of national income accounting, extractive industries were treated as any other source of national product. As a result, the value of the extracted resource was added to national product at the point of extraction. This method of valuing the contribution of extractive industries, as is now widely recognized, is ill-conceived and results in significant distortions. For the derivation of the required rate of savings see Appendix I in Hossein Askari, *Saudi Arabia: Oil and the Search for Economic Development*, (JAI Press, 1990), and for a calculation of the savings rate for individual oil exporting countries see Hossein Askari, Vahid Nowshirvani, and Mohamed Jaber, *Economic Development in the Countries of the GCC: The Curse and Blessing of Oil* (JAI Press, 1997).

27 Zagha, Roberto, Gobind Nankani, and Indermit Gill, "Rethinking Growth," *Finance and Development*, (Washington, DC: International Monetary Fund, March 2006): 8.

28 The exception are countries that are so rich that they can invest a large portion of current oil revenues in diversified assets (abroad) to give the government all the revenues it needs in the future without having to resort to taxation.

29 Solow, Robert M., "Intergenerational Equity and Exhaustible Resources," *The Review of Economic Studies*, 41, (Symposium on the Economics of Exhaustible Resources, 1974): 41.

30 For a review and discussion of the operation of many of these funds (stabilization and future generations) in Alberta, Algeria, Alaska, Chile, Iran, Kuwait, Kiribati, Norway, Oman, Papua New Guinea, and Venezuela, see Jeffrey Davis, Rolando Ossowski, James A. Daniel, and Steven Barnett, "Stabilization and Savings Funds for Nonrenewable Resources: Experience and Fiscal Policy Implications," in *Fiscal Policy Formulation and Implementation in Oil-Producing Countries*; see Martin Skancke, "Fiscal Policy and Petroleum Fund Management in Norway," see John Wakeman-Linn, Paul Mathieu, and Bert van Selm, "Oil Funds in Transition Economies: Azerbaijan and Kazakhstan".

31 For more detail on military expenditure and arms imports see Askari, H. and R. Taghavi, "Economic and Social Failure in the Middle East," *Banca Nazionale Del Lavoro Quarterly Review*, LIX, no. 236, March 2006.

32 Collier, Paul, V.L. Elliott, Håvard Hegre, Anke Hoeffler, Marta Reynal-Querol, and Nicholas Sambanis, *Breaking the Conflict Trap: Civil War and Development Policy*, (Washington, D.C.: World Bank and Oxford University Press, 2003).

33 Ibid., 182, for a five-point template.

34 Gini coefficient is used as a measure of inequality of income distribution; it is defined as a ratio with values between 0 and 1. A low Gini coefficient indicates more equal income distribution, with a value of 0 indicating perfect equality, and 1 indicating perfect inequality or with all income accruing to one individual.

35 There were exceptions to this observation. For a particular country, the population growth for a certain period of time may exceed (or indeed, be negative) this long-term growth rate. For example, it is not uncommon for population growth

to be abnormally high during post-war periods (for example, the U.S. "baby boom" after World War II).

36 Oil output and price used here are from the "BP Statistical Review of World Energy Full Report 2005."

37 For the purpose of calculation, however, age 15 years and over was used due to data availability.

38 We have assumed that the Fund can borrow (depending on projected oil revenue growth) at the same rate as the investment rate (i).

39 The definition of "citizen" is itself a complex topic. For instance, in most countries a non-citizen spouse of a citizen could elect for citizenship status. If that were the case, would the spouse who was recently granted citizenship be entitled to the same payout from the Fund in the same manner as the indigenous person? What about extended families of the spouse?

40 Here, the money that would have been paid out to felons may instead be redirected to law enforcement bodies and also to finance prisons, rehabilitation centers, and so on.

CHAPTER 12

The Scope of the Social Safety Net in Islam: A Case Study[1]

While, over the last few decades, the international community has adopted the position that broad-based economic growth is necessary for stemming the effects of systemic poverty, a growing consensus has emerged that social safety nets and social protection are also essential elements of any comprehensive framework for poverty alleviation. Not only are provisions that provide basic services, such as health and education, important in their own right, but also they are critical drivers for economic growth and development and essential to achieving an equitable distribution of income and wealth. An adequate social safety net is a central feature of Islamic economic doctrines, and is even more imperative in countries that generate a significant percentage of current revenues from society's depleting resources, oil and gas.

In the early 1980s, the general prescription for growth in developing countries was economic reforms, focusing on developing a prudent combination of policies to enhance stabilization and adjustment, while little attention was placed on the potential social costs of such reforms; reforms were largely for reforms sake and did not incorporate the particular conditions of individual countries. However, by the late 1990s (in the era of post Washington Consensus) the pendulum gradually shifted towards a model of economic growth that included more attention to relieving constraints that were binding to individual countries, including specific provisions for social welfare and protection. Over the years, it has also been recognized that safety nets alone cannot serve effectively as an instrument for alleviating poverty without sound macroeconomic policies that enhance sustainable growth. While restructuring efforts may create economic efficiency gains over the long term, they oftentimes also lead to social dislocation, particularly over the short term. As Persian Gulf oil-exporting countries[2] adopt much needed economic reforms to promote fiscal discipline (eliminate government waste, reduce harmful subsidies), build effective institutions (rule of law, reduce corruption), and promote economic justice in an effort to stimulate long-term growth, the development of a comprehensive structure to protect the vulnerable from declining deeper into poverty and improving the income distribution becomes even more pressing.

For social protection policies to be effective in the oil-exporting countries of the Persian Gulf, they should be complementary to the principles of economic justice as enunciated in Islam. We explore the more critical aspects of Islamic safety net arrangements, strategies for poverty alleviation, and equitable income distribution, and in this context we also explore how the oil-exporting countries can more efficiently allocate their oil wealth to minimize social dislocation and insure equity. We conclude by discussing the current role social safety net policies play in these countries.

Within the international discourse, there is little consensus as to the scope of policies and programs, both public and private, that constitute an optimal safety net. Such arrangements generally fall within the broad rubric of social protection, which describes all initiatives that provide income or consumption transfers, protect the vulnerable against the risks of losing their livelihood, and enhance the social status and rights of the marginalized. We define social safety nets as any formal or informal support mechanisms designed to mitigate the risk of vulnerable groups falling into or deeper into poverty and improving the economic status of the disadvantaged over time. Unlike social protection, safety net policies are almost exclusively confined to those provisions that are targeted towards the poor and vulnerable. These mechanisms can take many forms, including cash transfers (for oil exporters this could be directly financed from oil revenues) and consumer subsidies, fee waivers for healthcare and education, public works, and vocational training programs, as well as certain social insurance schemes including old-age pensions and unemployment insurance. Informal mechanisms, such as community-based insurance, *Zakah* (in the case of many Muslim countries), and social and familial networks, also play a crucial role in supporting the vulnerable.

Social safety nets play three primary roles: alleviating and reducing poverty, managing risk and protecting vulnerable groups against various shocks, and ensuring an acceptable level of wealth and income distribution. While separate policies and programs may strive to achieve only one of these objectives, they have a synergistic relationship with one another. For instance, some programs and policies are designed to facilitate equity in the distribution of wealth and resources between individuals exposed to different levels of vulnerability, thus reducing overall risk and acting as a conduit for poverty reduction. The purpose of public intervention may be to affect the mean income for the entire population, which consequently leads to improved income distribution and reduced levels of poverty.

Equity means different things to different people. The World Bank's 2006 World Development Report has defined equity as "having equal opportunities to pursue a life of their choosing and be spared from extreme deprivation in outcomes."[3] Institutions and policies, such as safety nets that foster equal opportunities, not only contribute to sustainable development and growth, but are also the custodians of justice and equality. The equal distribution of social goods—such as education, health, and shelter—is one of the many necessary elements at the core of meeting human needs and aspirations. Such equity is also central to a just society. With broad market distortions, which characterize the economies of most of the oil-exporting countries of the Persian Gulf, inequalities in income and influence lead to unequal opportunities, lost productive capacity, and an inefficient allocation of resources. While rectifying such market failures would be the ideal approach to ensuring an optimal level of income distribution, in some cases this is not feasible in the short run or simply far too costly. Some redistributive mechanisms—particularly those that fall under the rubric of social protection—afford all members of society equal access to services, assets, and political influence, and can enhance economic efficiency. In the longer term, an equitable and effective income tax system is an absolute necessity.

12.1 THE DESIGN AND EVALUATION OF SOCIAL SAFETY NETS

The design of an optimal safety net program should incorporate the composition of vulnerable groups, as well as financial, political, cultural, and institutional constraints.[4] Some key considerations in assessing the success of safety net arrangements include the extent to which benefits:

- Reduce poverty and the number of the poor from falling deeper into poverty
- Target the most vulnerable

- Protect the income and/or assets of the unemployed or working poor
- Impact equity and income distribution
- Are feasible and sustainable over the long term, given political and cultural realities

At the technical level, appropriate targeting is fundamental, and yet poses the greatest challenge to the success of reducing poverty and improving income distribution. In the World Bank's 2004 World Development Report it was noted that while governments allocate nearly one-third of their budgets to health and education, only a small proportion of those benefits actually accrue to the poor. Moreover, even when funds are appropriately targeted, poor incentives and delivery mechanisms largely explain the inconsistent relationship between social spending and poverty.

Targeting may be difficult for at least two reasons. First, identifying the poor and defining poverty is often incomplete, particularly in developing countries with little institutional and statistical capacity. There is a dearth of data on poverty and on human development for Persian Gulf countries. Second, the "middle-class capture" of existing benefits makes targeting a politically sensitive issue.[5] For instance, in all of the Persian Gulf oil-exporting countries, costly universal subsidies are provided to all, rich and poor alike, as an implicit incentive to buy public loyalty for autocratic regimes. Curtailing inefficient public expenditure is necessary for meaningful economic reform.

Successful targeting goes beyond simply preventing benefits from accruing to those that do not need assistance, it also requires that *all* the poor have access to safety net arrangements. Approaches to targeting include means-testing transfers, which is based on income and asset ceilings of households. In practice, such targeting instruments may not be feasible in economies because of criteria that tend to be contentious and because of the unavailability of detailed data on family incomes and expenditures. In many cases the administrative costs of means testing are also prohibitive. An approach to targeting, which tends to be more appropriate in the developing-country context, is to restrict benefits to those who are typically most vulnerable to shock, through regional targeting (for example, rural areas) or categorical targeting (for example, the elderly, nursing mothers, children), or a combination of the two approaches. Another strategy would be to provide subsidies only on inferior goods typically consumed by the poor.

In addition to choosing a well-targeted approach to deliver benefits, these provisions must also limit the distortionary effects of certain arrangements common to safety nets, such as subsidies. Not only are broad-based consumer subsidies (such as Iran's fuel subsidies) prohibitively expensive (depending on world oil prices, amounting to over 15 percent of Iran's GDP), they may also engender significant production disincentives, generate wasteful consumption patterns, and tend to be regressive (affording those financially better off a disproportionate share of the benefits).[6] While cash transfers can avail beneficiaries with a greater amount of choice and mitigate wasteful consumption (enhancing consumer welfare) and are thus more efficient, they may also leave them vulnerable to unexpected price increases for essential goods if cash transfers are not adequate.

The success of the public safety net system depends on the government's ability to administer the system efficiently while meeting the needs of the poor; needs which are invariably unique to that community or society. A number of Latin American countries have found that cash transfers are generally better targeted toward the most poor, whereas other safety net mechanisms, such as social insurance, are tied to formal sector employment and disproportionately accessible to those economically better off.

A number of studies indicate that conditional cash transfer (CCT) programs oftentimes result in increased school attendance, improved health and nutrition, and in increased female decision-making power within the household.[7] Yet these programs also tend to be limited by high administrative requirements and by a demand for a higher standard of health and education infrastructure than typically seen in many developing economies, including the oil-exporting countries of the Persian Gulf.

12.2 ISLAMIC ECONOMIC DOCTRINES AND SOCIAL SAFETY NET PROVISIONS[8]

Policymakers and politicians have questioned the prudence of placing Islam at the forefront of the Muslim world's development agenda given that many predominantly Islamic countries have had limited success in meeting their populations' basic needs. However, advocates of the establishment of an Islamic-inspired economy contend that since soon after the passing of the Prophet Mohammed (pbuh), governments throughout the Islamic world have made little attempt to systematically (without influence of politics and power) infuse their economic systems and institutions with the precepts laid out in the *sunnah* and the *Qur'an*. Ul Haq,[9] Chapra,[10] and others suggest that at the time of the Prophet (pbuh), when the community of believers (*Ummah*) were most closely abiding by these principles, their economies flourished to unprecedented levels. In fact, many Islamic historians agree that Islam played a critical role in the advancement of the Arab society and transformed it to such a remarkable extent that it not only overcame its own handicaps but also brought about a revolutionary change throughout the world.[11] The *Qur'an* not only offers guidance for addressing poverty, it has also influenced a great deal of thought and behavior regarding economic activity—poverty and economics went hand-in-hand in the early history of Islam.[12] Others have noted that although conventional economics addresses the issue of the allocation and distribution of resources, it lacks the spiritual or moral foundation to achieve these goals. The *Qur'an* assumes an economic system based on individual enterprise and reward and conventional economic principles, such as the laws of supply and demand, but set within a moral framework to ensure support for all.[13] The definition of Islamic economics afforded by the late Muhammad Baqir al-Sadr captures this essence:

> ... the way Islam prefers to follow in the pursuit of its economic life and in the solution of its practical problems in line with its concept of justice.[14]

Islam essentially superimposes its concept of social justice as the guiding principle. Today, the primary practical features that Muslim countries have adopted from Islamic economic teachings are limited and include a defunct, state-administered *Zakah* (purifying dues or alms giving) system and the prohibition of *riba* or usury.

We begin by providing a brief description of the foundation of an Islamic social safety net system.[15] To fully implement Islamic economics requires more than a simple paradigm shift away from classical economics. Rather, Islam conceptualizes human behavior with regard to the distribution of resources and the requisites for human welfare somewhat differently than does Western economic theory. For example, classical economics assumes that: individuals are rational actors in the economy; resources are scarce; and personal demands or wants are unlimited. However, the underlying factors determining the extent of poverty are unlimited wants, resource scarcity, and, to some degree, the distribution of output.

Similar to classical economic theory, Islam recognizes that individuals are rational actors, however in Islam the underlying cause of poverty is seen differently. Scarcity is not afforded an overriding importance in explaining poverty in Islam. Abbas Mirakhor summarizes this assertion:

> Islam asserts unambiguously that poverty is neither caused by scarcity and paucity of natural resources, nor is due to the lack of proper synchronization between the mode of production and the relation of distribution, but as a result of waste, opulence, extravagance, and nonpayment of what rightfully belongs to the less able segments of the society. This position is illustrated by the Prophetic saying that: "Nothing makes a poor man starve except that with which a rich person avails in luxury."[16]

That is to say that the right to advance ones own personal utility cannot impinge upon the rights of others. Corruption (the absconding of what belongs to society, such as oil), maldistribution of wealth and income, and the accompanied waste are seen as the root causes of poverty, deprivation, and need. Put somewhat differently, the principle is to protect against the eventual degeneration and disintegration of the community that result from placing narrow self-interests above ethical values. The *Qur'an* cautions the individual against allowing ephemeral worldly desires to subsume God's desires for humankind:

> (Q:28:58–59) *And how many a community that [once] exalted in its wanton wealth and ease of life have We destroyed, ... Yet, withal, thy Sustainer would never destroy a community ... unless its people are wont to do wrong [to one another].*

> (Q:9:24): ... *and the worldly goods which you have acquired and the commerce whereof you fear a decline, and the dwelling in which you take pleasure—[if all these] are dearer to you than God and His Apostles and the struggle in His cause, then wait until God makes manifest His will; and [know that] God does not grace iniquitous fold with His guidance.*

Thus in sharp contrast to classical economics, resource constraints are in fact not seen as the binding constraint to prosperity and economic welfare in Islam. Rather, God granted humankind enough to meet everyone's basic needs, however as a result of an unjust social and economic order there is an inequitable distribution of these resources between the artificial boundaries of the state and people within countries; with waste and poverty seen as the twin results. God's entrustment of these resources to humankind as a whole can only be duly discharged when everyone has enough to satisfy at least their basic needs.[17] This point is particularly relevant to the Persian Gulf oil exporters, as the states' survival and ability to provide their people with basic services has been up to now dependent on revenues from oil—a depleting natural resource entrusted to all (current and future generations). Accordingly, poverty in oil-exporting countries is a result of corruption, misallocation of resources, and the resulting waste:

> (Q:4:130–131): ... *God shall provide for each of them out of abundance... and unto God belongs all that is in the heavens and all that is on earth.*

> (Q:15:19–20): *And the earth—We spread it out wide, and placed on it mountains firm, and caused [life] of every kind to grow on it ... and provided thereon means of livelihood for you [O men] as well as of all [living beings] ...*

> (Q:27:16): *O you people! We have taught the speech of birds and have been given [in abundance] of all [good] things: ... !*

Islamic teachings limit humankind's material wants (unlike Western economic thought) if they adversely affect society's wellbeing: no one should be denied their basic needs or sustenance and live in poverty and deprivation. While vulnerability (disability, sickness, and so on) is a product of the human condition and prevalent in all societies, its attending impact, resulting in poverty, is fundamentally a consequence of humanity's deference to God's guidance.[18] In this regard, Islam calls on its believers to be content with their material lot in life, while also giving to charity, if the capacity exists, and not engaging in wasteful consumption. Although Islam envisages an established safety net system, it is not meant to replace the essential element of hard work. The Prophet(pbuh) repeatedly stressed God's disapproval towards those who depended on charity though they could earn enough to fulfill their livelihood through their own labor.[19]

(Q:16:71): ... *they who are more abundantly favored are [often] unwilling to share their sustenance with those whom their right hand possess, so that they [all] might be equal in this respect. Will they, then, God's blessings [thus] deny?*

(Q:34:39): *Behold, my Sustainer grants abundant sustenance, or gives it in scant measure, unto whomever He wills of His servants; and whatever it be that you spend on others ...*

The Islamic method to alleviate poverty and to realize an equitable distribution of income is fundamental to achieving the Islamic vision of a just social and economic order.[20] Injustice is believed to ultimately impede the realization of human welfare, exacerbate social unrest and malaise, and retard development.[21] Justice demands that all—regardless of race, color, sex, nationality,[22] and even religion—share the benefits of development equitably; and distributive justice is recognized as central to the Islamic vision of an economic system.

(Q:4:135) ... *Be ever steadfast in upholding equity, bearing witness to the truth for the sake of God, ... Whether the person concerned be rich or poor, God's claim takes precedence over [the claims of] either of them. Do not, then, follow your own desires, lest you swerve for justice ... !*

(Q:5:8) ... *Bearing witness to the truth in all equity; and never let hatred of anyone lead you into sin of deviating from justice. Be just: This is closest to being God-conscious ...*

(Q:16:90) *Behold, God enjoins justice, and the doing of good, and generosity towards [one's] fellow-men; and He forbids all that is shameful and all that runs counter to reason, as well as envy ...*

The principle of justice also demands an economic system that ensures equal access to basic needs that promote human well-being (including shelter, food, healthcare, and education) for all, thus creating a level playing field. For instance, equal access to education is essential to promoting equality of opportunity, as it minimizes social stratification and employment segmentation. Where provisions have been developed to ensure the individual's access to basic needs and equal opportunity, it is also under the state's authority to redistribute wealth. While Islam recognizes that some have been endowed with more worldly goods than others, it also creates mechanisms for redistribution, such as *Zakah*, calling on believers to engage in economic justice. *Zakah* is more than a simple tax:

> ... it is not only the end which is important, but also the means. This is why Islam provides for *Zakat*, a voluntary wealth tax which Muslims pay in recognition of their social responsibilities. This that fosters good behaviour by the more prosperous, by giving them a choice through its voluntary nature ... thus helps both rich and poor, and has a moral as well as material dimension ...[23]

According to the *Qur'an*, poverty and denial of assistance to the needy is forbidden. The *Qur'an* goes on to explain that material inequalities are not a manifestation of spiritual inequalities. Rather such inequalities should be overcome through human effort and are thus meant to foster brotherhood, again stressing the importance of *Zakah*.

> (Q: 43:32): ... *We who distribute their means of livelihood among them in the life of this world, and raise some of them by degrees above other, to the end that they might avail themselves of one another's help ...*

Islam also stresses the principle of economic prudence. With respect to the use of public funds and personal wealth, waste is forbidden. Islam views extravagant expenditure and conspicuous consumption with acute rapprochement.

> (Q:17:26–27) *And give his due to the near of kin, as well as the needy and the wayfarer, but do not squander [thy substance] senselessly. Behold squanderers are, indeed, of the ilk of the satans ...*

Islam enjoins the ethical principles discussed above with institutional measures to create a framework for poverty alleviation to ensure that basic needs can be met. The measures to alleviate poverty and achieve an equitable distribution of wealth and resources are threefold: the development of ethical and moral values such as justice, equality, honesty, and so on; economic tools and instruments such as *Zakah, sadaqah*, and inheritance and property laws; and lastly the development of the institutional capacity and political will to ensure that these principles and norms are adequately upheld.[24]

Similar to many publicly organized safety net systems, the purpose of *Zakah* is to guarantee a minimum standard of living by helping the poor meet the costs of basic needs, protecting the vulnerable against shock, and fostering an equitable income distribution. Its primary objective is to serve the cause of social justice and a moral purpose, not a mechanism for charity. According to Islam, the role of the state includes the administration of a social security system in which the religiously decreed *Zakah* assumes a central position. As one of the five pillars of Islam, the system levies a *Zakah*, or compulsory alms tax, on all Muslims who meet a minimum level of wealth to help finance eight categories of welfare that are mentioned in the *Qur'an*, including poverty alleviation, the emancipation of slaves, pilgrimage, and assistance to those serving Islam (Q:9:60). The tax rate ranges from 2.5 percent to 20 percent, depending on the assets and the method used to produce it.

In much of the literature on safety nets in the Muslim world, Islamic institutions such as *Zakah* are considered to be part of the informal safety net or on the fringes of a welfare system. While the *Zakah* system is a fundamental element and the cornerstone of social safety nets its effective implementation has been less than optimal. Recent evidence indicates that donors prefer to give (*sadaqah*) directly to private individuals or charities.[25] An Islamic safety net system constitutes a number of other institutional arrangements that facilitate voluntary spending for the needy. *Waqf* is another mechanism whereby an individual donates a certain asset, such as land and buildings, for a designated specific purpose under a legal deed, and has been useful in transferring wealth from private ownership to collective ownership to be used for social advancement. Loss of confidence between *Zakah* payers and *Zakah* institutions should lead Muslim countries to seek alternatives that are permissible in Islam, such as the taxation of income by the state.

What has been the success of Muslim countries in implementing Islamic principles and achieving an adequate social safety net? We now briefly assess the success of social safety nets in the six major oil-exporting countries of the Persian Gulf, incorporating the important role of exhaustible resources—oil and gas—in Islamic teachings.

12.3 CASE STUDY: OIL AND SOCIAL SAFETY NETS IN PERSIAN GULF OIL-EXPORTING COUNTRIES

The capacity for countries to address vulnerability and the social protection mechanisms vary significantly across Muslim countries. In the case of the major oil-exporting countries of the Persian Gulf, the ability to address social safety net issues would appear to be made easier by the availability of vast oil and gas revenues, which accrue in the first instance to the governments. However, because oil is a depletable resource, which must benefit all generations, governments must proceed with this fact in mind.

Economists have long ago addressed the issue of optimal and fair natural resource depletion on the theoretical level. One component of a just practice of resource depletion could be an adequate social safety net financed by oil and gas depletion (still this must be supplemented with reproducible capital to compensate for resource depletion), or alternatively the issue of a safety net and overall compensation for resource depletion may be addressed by taking oil revenues away from the government and creating a fund to address issues of equity (by giving the same real transfer payment to all current and future citizens).[26] Again, the management of exhaustible resources must be compatible with basic Islamic teachings on ownership rights of depletable resources and the role of the state. In the specific case of resources below the ground, Islam is unambiguous. Anything underground belongs to society at large, both *current* and *all future* generations. This view is supported by interpretations of the writings of Muhammad Baqir al-Sadr:[27]

> As indicated in the theory of distribution, the Islamic State possesses the sole right of ownership of natural resources. Consequently, it has absolute control over all aspects of economic activities ... The major objective of the Islamic State is to set up policies to develop the natural resources to the fullest extent to benefit the entire society.

While this may be al-Sadr's interpretation on the ownership and management of natural resources, he may have felt less inclined when it came to government intervention in general.[28] Others also support the same basic premise about natural resources and the role of the state:[29]

> Exhaustible resources, such as land, belong to present and future generations of Muslims. But unlike land, which if ruined can be reclaimed, exhaustible resources, if depleted today, will be unavailable to all future generations of Muslims. This is tantamount to saying that GNP of a country that is heavily based on natural resources is not comparable to other economies because economies that are not based on exhaustible resources can produce at the same rate as long as the capital base is not eroded. In this respect, the application of Islamic principles is even more important for an exhaustible resource as its extraction affects not only the present generation of Muslims but all future generations as well.

In our view, Solow's prescription is essentially the path that should be followed by these Muslim oil-exporting countries, a task which is clear but difficult. First, governments must take control of all minerals. Second, governments must make sure that they do not waste depleting mineral resources, because they are the birthright of all citizens and must be used productively. Third, as minerals are depleted, governments must make sure that they use their revenues in such a way that all citizens today and for all future time receive similar real benefits. Oil should benefit all members of the current generation equally (with optimal depletion and optimal compensation for depletion), with the implication of relatively even distribution of income given the overwhelming role of oil (as opposed to hard work and sound productive investments) in these economies, and that these benefits should be similar for *all* generations to come.

How can the oil exporters better address the needs of the disadvantaged in an Islamic context? Individual reforms that develop better targeting mechanisms, reduce wasteful government expenditure on subsidies and employment guarantees, and improve education and human resource capacity are an indispensable basis for creating an Islamic safety net system. However, such reforms will naturally have to be slow and progressive given the considerable political constraints. But unlike most other developing countries, the Persian Gulf oil exporters have an additional means to address the needs of all members of society, especially those of the disadvantaged. They can use current oil and gas revenues directly, but this solution may not benefit future generations. Alternatively, they can use oil revenues to establish an oil fund and use the earnings from the fund to meet social needs and possibly to supplement the income of even the nondisadvantaged, while treating all generations equitably.

Countries have set up separate funds to address the two main issues that arise from the depletion of exhaustible natural resources: uncertainty of revenues (and thus, difficulty of budgetary planning and exchange rate management), and intergeneration equity. To address these issues some funds were established with the objective of reducing the volatility of natural resource revenue income ("Stabilization Fund") while others have as an objective the saving of current natural resource revenue for the benefit of future generations ("Savings Fund"). Some oil-rich countries adopt a Stabilization Fund to absorb potential shocks from sudden increases or decreases in oil prices (and thus, revenue); excess oil revenues would be funneled to the Stabilization Fund when oil revenue is high and the fund will finance the budget shortfall when oil revenue runs low. The Savings Fund on the other hand receives a constant share of oil revenues over time. The fund will be saved for future generations so that when oil is exhausted future generations will receive the same benefit as the current generation.

In the Persian Gulf region, the first oil-financed funds were established by Kuwait and Abu Dhabi. The Kuwait Reserve Fund for Future Generations was established in 1976 with the objective of saving in order to provide for future generations with the depletion of resources (a savings fund). The fund receives 10 percent of total government revenue, accumulating along with the investment returns on its assets. There is no reason why the annual savings from government revenues should be 10 percent. The fund has no precise or established rules for withdrawals; the financing of the reconstruction of Kuwait after the First Gulf War, approved by the national assembly, was a major beneficiary. The Abu Dhabi Investment Authority (ADIA) established a fund in 1976 to manage the emirate's "excess" oil revenues. ADIA's rules for savings from government revenues and withdrawals are even more obscure than those of the Kuwait fund. It may be interesting to note that many diverse sources estimate the holdings of ADIA to exceed US$350 billion in 2006, with some putting the figure over US$500 billion. In sum, neither of the two Savings Funds (Kuwait and Abu Dhabi) have formal goals in establishing the size of savings from current oil revenues, nor are there formal provisions for withdrawals, let alone the distribution of cash payments to citizens or residents from these funds. Moreover, there is very little institutional transparency.

Iran established an oil stabilization fund (OSF) in 2000 to counter volatilities in oil revenues, impose fiscal discipline on the government, and to support exchange rate policies. Although the OSF has significant reserve holdings, the government of Iran has not adhered to the legislation establishing the operation of the fund; withdrawals from the fund have been made for the sake of political expediency.

If intergenerational equity in the depletion of oil and gas reserves is afforded importance, then a concurrent solution with a social safety net could be the establishment an "Oil Fund" that would provide cash transfers, financed through oil revenues, to all current and future citizens and residents. Currently, none of the six oil exporters have a formal mechanism to transfer oil wealth equitably across generations by means of annual checks to citizens and residents. Such annual financial transfers to citizens (or residents) for all future time, if large enough, could theoretically meet a country's safety net needs. While this may be a solution for the richer countries, it may have to be combined with a national safety net in the case of Iran, Iraq, and even Saudi Arabia. For these latter, more populous countries, an effective progressive income tax is an absolute necessity to address equity issues and to support government programs. What is clear is that oil and gas afford governments more options in designing a safety net to meet the needs of the general citizenry.

There are many ways that an oil fund could be designed, however a number of elements must be included to ensure the sustainable and equitable transfer of oil revenues. The amount of the cash transfer in real terms should be equitable across society and across all generations. The fund should be professionally managed by an independent entity accountable to the citizens of the country and with the appropriate mechanisms to ensure its transparency. Governments should have only limited access to the resources in the fund. An obvious shortcoming of this strategy is that individuals receiving large cash transfers may naturally become complacent, as they would have little incentive to engage in productive activities. However, this effect could be mitigated if transfers are given on the basis of meeting some conditionality, such as employment and education.[30]

In addition to the establishment of an oil fund and individual reforms, governments in the region should adopt policies that stabilize and diversify sources of revenues away from oil to protect intergenerational equity in the depletion of oil resources. A broader and more progressive tax base that raises government revenues efficiently and fairly would help to increase the overall sustainability of the current safety net, while improving intergenerational equity. Islam envisages and endorses a system of taxation where revenues are used to fulfill basic social needs. Yet none of the Persian Gulf oil exporters have an effective income tax system. (Iran has an ineffective tax system while the others do not have an income tax system in place.)

Some historical background will provide a context for the establishment of current social welfare policies in the Persian Gulf oil-exporting countries. The 1960s and 1970s marked a formative decade for many of these countries. Not only had they gained independence from colonial rule (with the exception of Iran), but this period also marked a dramatic increase in oil export proceeds. These two events gave rise to the development of an implicit social contract in which citizens exchanged political liberties for economic and social stability. Elements of the social contract essentially endorsed state paternalism and included a preference for equity and redistribution in social and economic policy and a preference for protectionism and state control of markets. The social contract was later consolidated through adoption of an elaborate welfare framework, financed entirely from oil revenues. However, the Islamic ethos of equity, equality, and justice had long deteriorated from the landscape of Arab and Iranian society—ruling class hierarchies, gender inequality, and other modalities of social stratification prevailed.

The entrenchment of these openhanded welfare policies has posed challenges to development and economic reform in the region. Despite the bloated and in some cases unsustainable safety net system, meaningful reforms would inevitably be met with fierce political opposition as citizens see transfers from oil wealth as part of their birthright. The wealthier oil-exporting countries are often criticized for offering generous cash transfers and subsidies, particularly in times of budgetary surpluses resulting from higher oil prices. For instance, in the last few years, while higher oil prices increased government revenues, in some countries in the region concurrent increases in spending on current expenditure and subsidies have more than offset revenue increases.[31] The International Monetary Fund (IMF) has recently cautioned countries such as Kuwait that despite the boom in oil revenues, depleted reserves is an imminent reality, which could force them to borrow at an unsustainable pace in an effort to maintain current living standards. For the Persian Gulf oil exporters in particular, the development of safety net mechanisms should be for the purposes of transferring oil wealth to their citizens in an equitable and sustainable manner and to alleviate poverty—not to maintain the current authoritarian system.

12.4 SOCIAL SAFETY NETS

In-depth analysis of poverty and income distribution for the six countries is at best difficult due to the dearth of data on key statistics. However, where data does exist we can get a sense of the progress made in poverty alleviation. Iran is the only country that has compiled and released data on income distribution and poverty. Statistics indicate that 2 percent of Iranians live on less the US$1 per day, and within the last decade about 7 percent of Iranians fell below the US$2 per day poverty line. However, national poverty rates often obscure pervasive distortions in relative depravation and inequalities in human development. For instance, *national poverty measures* (calculated on the basis of food intake of less than 2200 calories per day) reveals a more alarming picture of deprivation than the US$1 per day indicator: nearly 15 percent in urban areas and 17 percent of Iran's rural population. Moreover, while 10.4 percent of Iran's urban population lives below the *absolute poverty line*, 22.6 percent of rural inhabitants live in absolute poverty.[32] Although Iran has made remarkable improvements in poverty alleviation and in key human development indicators over time, these gains have primarily been achieved through charitable handouts and subsidies rather than through empowerment and employment.

The incidence of poverty in Iran (based on the US$1 or US$2 per day yardstick) is considerably lower than the Middle East and North Africa (MENA) regional average. About 2 percent of MENA's population live on the less than US$1 per day poverty line and nearly 20 percent live below the US$2 poverty line. Given the region's overall level of development, income poverty in MENA is actually low compared to the rest of the developing world (see Table 12.1 for regional comparisons). Poverty levels do vary significantly between the oil-rich countries and the resource-poor countries, signaling large regional disparities. Iraq is a special case, with extensive poverty that is likely to be higher than the MENA average. While data does not exist for the other four countries, it would be safe to conclude that they—especially Kuwait, Qatar, and the UAE—have an insignificant number of citizens living below the US$2 poverty line.

Table 12.1 Regional poverty comparisons

	Poverty headcount ratio at US$1 a day (PPP) (% of population)			Poverty headcount ratio at US$2 a day (PPP) (% of population)		
	1981	1990	2002	1981	1990	2002
East Asia and Pacific	57.7	29.6	11.6	84.8	69.9	40.7
Europe and Central Asia	0.7	0.5	2.1	4.7	4.9	16.1
Latin America and Caribbean	9.7	11.3	8.9	26.9	28.4	23.4
Middle East and North Africa	5.1	2.3	1.6	28.9	21.4	19.8
Sub-Saharan Africa	41.6	44.6	44.0	73.3	75.0	74.9

Source: World Bank, World Development Indicators 2006.

An important indicator of income distribution is the Gini index. Iran's Gini index provides a striking view of its skewed income distribution, with an index higher than even other countries in the MENA region which have less access to a steady revenue base from oil (see Figure 12.1). Moreover, figures on Iran's income distribution further indicate widespread disparities, with a 10.5 to 1 ratio between the income and consumption of the richest and the poorest 20 percent of the population, which places Iran among those countries with a

Figure 12.1 GINI coefficient: Select OECD and MENA countries

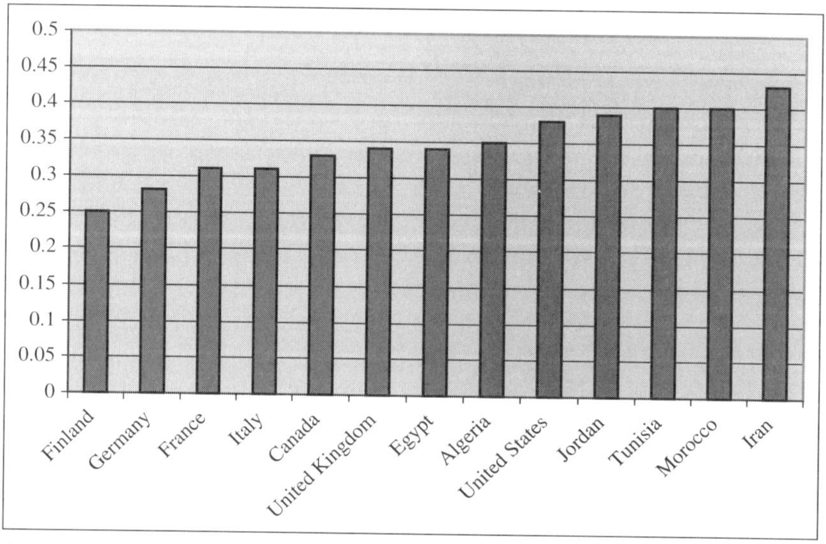

Source: World Bank, World Development Indicators 2006.

relatively high level of inequality. The fact that the wealthiest 20 percent of the population in the richest provinces consumes nearly 32 times that of the poorest 20 percent in the poorest provinces illuminates the regional challenges Iran faces in addressing income inequalities.[33] This disparity goes beyond income and consumption standards and as expected permeates into access to basic services. For instance, in the province of Sistan and Baluchistan (perhaps the poorest province in Iran), only 55 percent of the population has access to safe water, while the national average is 83 percent. The gaps between national and provincial literacy, nutrition, and birth registration indicators are similarly wide. While the labor-importing oil exporters (Kuwait, Qatar, Saudi Arabia, UAE) have not compiled indices on poverty and income distribution, such statistics may, in any case, be misleading. The wealthier oil exporters in the Persian Gulf are characterized as labor importers; that is, they rely on a large immigrant population for cheap labor. For instance, the composition of non-nationals ranges from a high of 80 percent in the UAE to a low of 27 percent of the total population in Saudi Arabia.[34] Immigrants, many of whom settled in the Gulf generations ago, are denied many of the basic rights of citizens; they are often excluded from official census data and surveys, and yet are clearly most affected by poverty and lack of access to basic services. While poverty in terms of income places these countries favorably compared to other developing regions, a bleaker picture is revealed in terms of what is defined as "poverty of opportunity."[35,36] Inequality of opportunities is one of the most pressing obstacles to achieving economic justice in the region. This point becomes particularly illuminated as we explore labor market and education outcomes.

Provisions that provide for basic needs such as quality healthcare, education, employment, and consumer goods play a vital role in reducing generational poverty and enhancing equal opportunities, particularly over the long term. Outcome indicators and government expenditure in the various areas of the social sector afford a sense of government priorities and the efficiency, sustainability, and equitability with which public funds are being spent. We examine these indicators for Persian Gulf oil-exporting countries relative to other comparator groups (comparators are based on the World Bank designated MENA region, and the low-income, middle-income, and high-income groupings) in the areas of health and education, and other components of the social safety net.

Formal social safety net programs—including employment guarantees, consumer subsidies, cash transfers, and universal health and education services—play a prominent role throughout the Persian Gulf oil-exporting countries. However, such programs are characterized as being regressive (that is, the rich receiving a larger share of the benefits than the poor), inefficient, and poorly targeted. Evidence from the region indicates that most programs providing direct assistance to the poor either cover only a small fraction of the poor or are too small to affect poverty rates. Given the relatively high levels of per capita income in the region, it is the misallocation and maldistribution of government social expenditure that have resulted in much of social malaise and lack of opportunity that afflict this group of countries.

12.4.1 Healthcare

A sound healthcare system not only maximizes health outcomes, but it also protects the population against the potentially devastating financial costs of healthcare, provides equitable and high-quality access to services, and is financially sustainable given anticipated economic growth and demographic factors. National health account estimates and indicators on health outcomes for the Persian Gulf oil exporters and the comparator groups reveal a telling trend with regard to the equitability, efficiency, and sustainability of resource allocation.

Table 12.2 provides a snapshot of national health accounts estimates for the six Persian Gulf countries. Internationally, total healthcare expenditure as a percentage of GDP has increased, while for the oil-exporting countries they have decreased. The relative reduction is most likely a result of GDP growth (particularly in the first part of this decade) outpacing growth in healthcare outlays, rather than a reduction in real terms. Healthcare expenditures as a percentage of GDP are also, on average, lower than the comparator groups and range from a low of 2.5 percent in Qatar to a high of 5.6 percent in Iran. Total per capita health expenditure for all of the Persian Gulf oil exporters (with the exception of Iraq) are higher than all the comparator groups, with the exception of the high-income group. Between the Persian Gulf oil exporters there is also a broad range in government outlays on healthcare as a percentage of total government expenditures: Iran and Saudi Arabia spend around 9.5 percent, while Iraq spends 4.6 percent. Overall, private sector healthcare expenditure as a percentage of total healthcare expenditure has increased

Table 12.2 National health accounts estimates

	Total expenditure on health (THE) % of GDP			General government expenditure on health (GGHE) % of THE			Private expenditure on health (PvtHE) % of THE			General government expenditure GGHE %			Net out-of-pocket spending on health (OOPs) % of PvtHE			THE per capita at exchange rate (US$)			GGHE per capita at exchange rate (US$)		
	1998	2001	2004	1998	2001	2004	1998	2001	2004	1998	2001	2004	1998	2001	2004	1998	2001	2004	1998	2001	2004
Iran[1]	5.9	6.3	5.6	44.6	44.5	46.7	55.4	55.5	53.3	10.9	11.5	9.6	94.6	94.7	94.5	53	81	142	24	36	66
Iraq[1]	2.3	1.6	3.1	51.0	27.1	79.6	49.0	72.9	20.4	1.9	1.2	4.6	100	100	100	11	12	28	6	3	22
Kuwait[1]	4.3	3.6	2.9	78.8	77.7	78.5	21.2	22.3	21.5	6.6	6.2	5.8	96.7	95.0	90.3	566	525	625	446	408	491
Qatar[1]	4.2	2.9	2.5	73.0	74.1	74.2	27.0	25.9	25.8	6.8	6.8	6.7	89.4	86.7	86.4	772	808	905	564	599	672
Saudi Arabia[1]	5.0	4.7	3.9	79.1	78.6	76.3	20.9	21.4	23.7	11.4	9.9	9.5	34.0	30.7	26.4	361	387	409	285	304	312
UAE[1]	4.1	3.7	3.1	78.4	78.3	71.1	21.6	21.7	28.9	7.9	7.7	8.0	71.1	69.4	71.4	688	737	684	539	577	486
MENA[2]	5.0	5.0	6.0	..	..	..	..	..	..	..	..	..	89.0	89.0	89.0	65	78	92	..	..	..
Low-income[2]	5.0	5.0	5.0	..	..	..	..	..	..	..	..	..	95.0	94.0	95.0	20	24	30	..	..	..
Middle-income[2]	6.0	6.0	6.0	..	..	..	..	..	..	..	..	..	76.0	79.0	78.0	99	103	116	..	..	..
High-income[2]	10.0	11.0	11.0	..	..	..	..	..	..	..	..	..	40.0	37.0	37.0	2,516	2,846	3,449	..	..	..

Source: 1 World Health Organization National Health Accounts Data, and World Development Indicators 2006.

over time for most of the oil-exporting countries; however private expenditure continues to be significantly lower than those provided by the government. Iran does not to follow this trend—despite high government expenditure on healthcare, private health expenditure is also the highest among the oil-exporting countries.

Even with varying expenditure on healthcare, basic health standards in areas such as infant mortality, immunization, and life expectancy rates have improved significantly in these oil-exporting countries (see Table 12.3). For all the Persian Gulf oil exporters (with the exception of Iraq), during the period 1990–2002 infant mortality has decreased, with rates lower overall than the MENA region and low-income group average, and with the exception of Iran and Iraq lower than the middle-income group average. During that same period, overall life expectancy has increased; rates are higher than the MENA, the low-income, and the middle-income group averages. Indicators also reveal significant improvement in child immunization, with the 2002 estimate higher than even the high-income comparator group of countries.

Table 12.3 Key health indicators

	Life expectancy at birth, total (years)		Mortality rate, infant (per 1,000 live births)		Immunization, DPT (% of children aged 12–23 months)		Immunization, measles (% of children aged 12–23 months)	
	1990	2002	1990	2002	1990	2002	1990	2002
Iran	64.65	69.28	54	34	91	99	85	99
Iraq	61.28	62.62	40	102	83	81	80	90
Kuwait	74.88	76.9	14	9	71	98	66	99
Qatar	72.22	74.94	19	11	82	96	79	99
Saudi Arabia	69	73.11	34	23	92	95	88	97
UAE	73.53	75.37	12	8	85	94	80	94
MENA	64.27	68.58	56.71	43.66	87.96	91.8	83.63	91.99
Low-income	56.78	58.86	92.68	78.56	63.5	64.63	57.27	64.73
Middle-income	68.25	69.82	40.01	30.23	88.05	85.15	89.21	80.07
High-income	75.94	78.19	8.08	5.4	86.42	95.17	75.9	89.91

Source: World Bank, World Development Indicators, 2004.

A balanced healthcare system is financed through an equitable contribution from the various partners, including insurance providers, households, and governments. Provisions for universal healthcare coverage ensure more than 90 percent of the population is given access to at least basic health services.[37] However, full healthcare coverage is also incomplete. For instance, in Saudi Arabia free healthcare is considered a right for all expatriates employed by the public sector and all Saudi citizens. Health coverage for non-nationals employed in the private sector is the responsibility of their employers and/or sponsors. Similarly, Iran faces difficulties in meeting its commitment to universal healthcare; nearly all Iranians have access to public healthcare services and limited curative care, and yet a significant portion of the population lacks access to the full range of care through Iran's various health networks. Like most safety net arrangements in these countries, public expenditure for healthcare and health coverage are regressive. In some cases, government-financed outlays often accrue to high-tech hospitals that provide expertise and services for diseases that typically afflict the affluent. Government facilities are usually the social safety nets for the poor and other vulnerable groups. However, such facilities often provide incomplete and insufficient care, particularly in the rural areas where facilities face severe budgetary limitations. For most of these oil-exporting countries contribution from private insurance provides only modest financing and is out of reach for the impoverished seeking quality care. While Iran does provide universal healthcare coverage, those who can afford it seek services from private sources because of the quality difference between private- and public-sector healthcare services. Iran's overall high expenditure on private healthcare (as a percentage of total healthcare expenditure) is almost definitely a result of the rich seeking higher quality healthcare services.

The issue of sustainability of the healthcare sector is a critical dimension. Improved healthcare standards are associated with significant population growth, which in turn has placed greater pressure on public healthcare systems in the region. Without adequate healthcare system controls that improve efficiency and coverage, population growth can threaten the sustainability of the entire healthcare system. For instance, at the current average annual rate of growth in population, Saudi Arabia's population is expected to grow by 75 percent by the year 2020. Population aging alone will require total per capita spending to increase by 12 percent.[38] Given the public sector's dominance in the healthcare sector, it is unlikely governments in the oil-exporting countries will be able to continue to provide free cradle-to-the-grave healthcare indefinitely. Despite current overall levels of healthcare spending comparable to international standards and improved health indicators, demographic trends and the resulting shifts in the disease burden threaten to increase cost pressures, exacerbating inefficiencies in the healthcare systems and jeopardizing the healthcare safety net.

12.4.2 Education

In today's information age, it is clear that the knowledge gap, rather than the income gap, determines a country's competitiveness in the global economy. Education is essential to expanding human capacities and opportunities, as well as a tool for reducing poverty.[39] Moreover, there can be no mistake made about the prominence and importance Islam places on the acquisition of knowledge. The *Qur'an* calls on humankind to use intellect, to reflect and to think, because the objective of life is to seek and discover truths.[40] Throughout the Middle East, most countries have adopted a policy of universal education, however for a number of the oil-exporting countries this has not necessarily resulted in increased school performance and access.

Overall, education expenditure in the Persian Gulf oil-exporting countries (Table 12.4) is higher than the comparator groups, averaging between 5 and 8 percent of GDP. In some countries (Iran, Saudi Arabia, and Kuwait), expenditure on education (as a percentage of GDP) is higher than the average for the MENA region as a whole and even the middle-income group of countries. Indicators that measure the quality of education, such as outlays for education at each level (primary, secondary, tertiary), reveal a similar trend; both Saudi Arabia and Kuwait spend far more per student at the primary level (31.4 and 28.3 percent of per capita GDP respectively) than the MENA regional average of 14.5 percent and the middle-income group of countries average of 13.1 percent. In Kuwait, expenditure per student on tertiary education are particularly high: 178 percent of GDP per capita. While in Iran outlays for tertiary education are on average 39 percent, expenditure in the UAE are far lower, averaging just 2.2 percent of per capita GDP (in part because of the large expatriate community who are counted for the purpose of GDP per capita calculations, GDP per capita is high, and many go abroad for tertiary education). In contrast, expenditure for tertiary education are 32.5 percent for the middle-income group and are even lower for the high-income group of countries.

Table 12.4 Education financing and outcome indicators

	Education financing							Education outcomes					
	Public spending on education (% of total gov't expend.)		Public spending on education, (% of GDP)		Expenditure per student, primary (% of GDP per capita)	Expenditure per student, secondary (% of GDP per capita)	Expenditure per student, tertiary (% of GDP per capita)	Primary enrollment rate (net)		Secondary enrollment rate (net)		Tertiary enrollment rate (gross)	
	1991	2002[1]	1991	2002	2002	2002	2002	1991	2002	1991	2002	1991	2002
Iran	22.4	22	4.1	4.8	11.3	12	38.6	92.4	86.7	..	78.1[a]	10.2	19.3
Iraq	..	..	..	..	..	..	..	94.0	87.7[a]	..	37.9[a]	..	12.5
Kuwait	3.4	17.4	4.8	8.2[a]	25.9[a]	28.3[a]	178.1[a]	49.0	84.9	..	77.6	..	22.3[a]
Qatar	..	..	3.5	3.6[a]	..	..	..	89.4	93.5	69.6	76.2	23.2	19.7
Saudi Arabia	17.8	..	5.8	8.3[a]	31.9[c]	31.4[c]	..	59.3	59.2	30.9	55.3	10.3	22.5
UAE	15.0	22.5	1.9	1.5	7.7	13.3	2.2	99.0	74.7	59.6	67.3	7.6	23.3
MENA	4.5	..	19.1	4.5[d]	14.5	20.5	..	83.5	91.2	..	..	12.6	23.3[b]
Low-Income	..	..	3.20	3.1[c]	..	..	..	..	78.9	..	..	5.2	8.7
Middle-Income	16.2	..	3.9	4.4	13.1	16.3	32.5	92.4	..	..	..	11.3	24.3
High-Income	14.3	12.7[e]	5	5.6	19.1	24.7	28.9	95.4	94.8	84.8	89.6	46.3	66.6

Notes: [a]2004, [b]2003, [c]2000, [d]1999, [e]2001

Source: World Bank, World Development Indicators, 2004 and UNESCO Country Factsheet.

While there is limited availability of data on equity within the education systems in the region, we can make some broad conclusions based on the data that is available. Overall, high expenditure on education has done little to enhance and ensure potential spillover and safety net effects. Admittedly, adult and youth literacy rates have improved markedly for all countries in the region. However, greater expenditure on education have not been met by demand-side policies that raise the overall enrollment rates and supply-side policies that raise the quality of education. In Iran the net primary school enrollment rate has actually decreased significantly from about 92 percent in 1991 to 87 percent in 2002, and in the UAE this figure has also decreased from 99 to about 75 percent during those same years. Saudi Arabia's net primary school enrollment rates have remained steady, however enrollment is significantly lower than the comparator groups (see Table 12.4).

Inefficiencies constrain the education system's ability to provide quality and well-targeted education in nearly all spheres of education management, including financing and delivery mechanisms. The public school system's inability to provide students with critical high-order cognitive and analytical skills jeopardizes the oil-exporting countries' international competitiveness as they attempt to move away from oil-export-led economic growth. Government spending on public education is often highly concentrated on tertiary education and vocational training. Yet despite high expenditure, the quality of education in its current form is incapable of generating the caliber of employees required by the private sector. As we will see, high investment in tertiary education has not been met with positive labor market outcomes, signaling a low or even negative return on education expenditure. For instance, while enrollment rates in tertiary education have outpaced enrollment into primary and secondary schools, Iran continues to have the highest level of unemployment among the six oil-exporting countries (excluding Iraq) in the Persian Gulf. Moreover, the rate and the number of women enrolling in higher education institutions is higher than that of men (in 2000–01 88,000 men versus 90,000 women), and yet women face an inordinately difficult time finding employment.[41]

While initially proportionally higher investment on tertiary education may be associated with lower unemployment rates and employment in skill-intensive jobs, such untargeted policies are in reality regressive, diverting public resources away from broad-based educational opportunities. Subsidies on higher education tend to produce inequitable outcomes because students who pursue university tend to be from higher income levels.

12.4.3 Employment and Labor

Initiatives that help to generate employment tend to have an equalizing effect across society, one of the core goals of the safety net. Equality in wage-earning opportunity is one of the most important strategies for poverty reduction.[42] For the oil-exporting countries of the Persian Gulf, labor market distortions are quite possibly one of the most formidable challenges to achieving sustainable levels of equity and poverty alleviation. Labor force growth in the Persian Gulf oil-exporting countries is one the highest in the world. While population growth has been high in the last 25 years, averaging roughly 2.9 percent for the oil exporters, labor force growth has been on average even higher at about 3.2 percent. This has resulted in an increasing percentage of young people in the population seeking employment. According to some estimates, Iran will have to create at least half a million new jobs per year over the next decade to keep up with the pace of new entrants into the labor force. The challenges presented by this growth include developing a labor market with the needed absorptive capacity and fostering human resource development that will be competitive in international and domestic markets. Successfully facing such challenges requires reforms in education and labor market policies, as well as policies that generate private sector growth.

Among these oil exporters, the employment generation and the social safety nets program of choice has historically been the guarantee of employment in the public sector. Public sector employment has created "deficit financed" jobs to absorb the excess supply of labor, thereby acting as a welfare program for those who could not successfully integrate into the private sector. Even as oil prices began to rise and structural reforms were implemented, employment among nationals and job creation in the private sector remain low, in part because the public sector continues to be the employer of last resort resulting in significant labor market distortions.

As indicated in Figure 12.2, the wage bill consumes a high of 55 percent of total current expenditure in Saudi Arabia and a low of 20 percent in the UAE. Even for the low this is a considerably high figure. The wage bill finances generous salary and benefits packages, which for new college graduates working in the public sector are on

Figure 12.2 2004 government wage bill

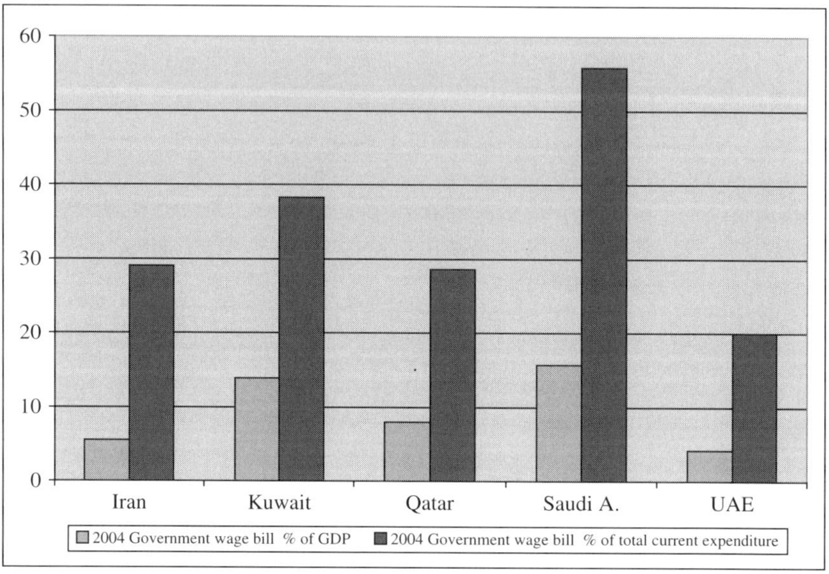

Source: Relevant IMF Country Reports.

average 46 percent greater than for those expatriates working in the UAE's private sector. In 1995, nearly 90 percent of UAE nationals and 22.6 percent of expatriates were employed in the public sector, while only 7.7 percent of nationals and 57 percent of expatriates were employed in the private sector.[43] In Kuwait, the public administration sector alone employed 52 percent of the total workforce, 79 percent of the national workforce, and 46 percent of expatriates, and in Saudi Arabia foreign workers accounted for 75 percent of the private sector workforce.[44]

While overall unemployment is low among the labor-importing countries (Kuwait, Qatar, Saudi Arabia, and UAE), unemployment rates among nationals are much higher. This may be a sign of the public sectors' limited absorptive capacity and the skill irrelevance among nationals. For instance, according to 2004 estimates, the total unemployment rate in Kuwait was 1.7 percent, however unemployment among the citizen population was 4.9 percent; and in the UAE total unemployment was 3 percent, but unemployment among Emirati citizens accounted for 11.4 percent of the total national labor force. In Iran, the official unemployment rate (an underestimate of the true rate) has grown from 9 percent in 1996 to 12.2 percent in 2005, and continues to grow as a result of a population bulge between the ages of 10 and 20 and the emergence of women entering into the workforce.

Not only do employment guarantees strive to promote the redistribution of wealth, they also attempt to protect a sizable portion of the workforce from the consequences of economic volatility. However, these policies fall short in a number of crucial areas. First, they are offered at the expense of the development of a vibrant private sector that can absorb the expanding labor capacity through legitimate market mechanisms. Second, as is the problem with other safety net policies in the region, government sector employment tends to be extended to those in more educated and wealthier portions of the population;[45] these policies are regressive and suffer from poor targeting. Promotions on the job are often based on tribal affiliation. Finally, while some of the smaller and wealthier countries—such as the UAE, Qatar, and Kuwait—may have sufficient resources to pay a reasonable salary to new entrants in the government sector, this strategy results in gross inefficiencies and acts as a disincentive for citizens to seek gainful employment in more productive sectors of the economy and to gain skills that are actually relevant to the private sector's needs. Statistics indicate for instance that only 33 percent of Emiratis and 66 percent of non-nationals who graduated from university pursued degrees in fields that were most relevant to the private sector, such as engineering, medicine, and the sciences.[46] Similarly, Saudi Arabia and Qatar had the lowest percentages of science graduates in higher education (17 and 18 percent respectively) in the MENA region, while Iran had the highest (61 percent).[47] Similar employment guarantee policies are simply unsustainable in the more populous oil-exporting countries, namely Iran, Iraq, and Saudi Arabia; as a result these countries are faced with rising unemployment rates coupled with falling living standards.

In more recent years government authorities have begun to institute a number of strategies to increase the employment of nationals in the private sector, such as sector-specific quotas and active labor market policies. Some examples of reform initiatives include Saudi Arabia's Human Resource Development Fund (HRDF) and the UAE's National Human Resource and Employment Authority (TANMIA). The objective of HRDF is to increase private-sector employment among nationals by providing temporary wage subsidies and financial assistance for training. Perhaps one of the major obstacles to this approach is that many young Saudi Arabians resist taking blue-collar jobs as a matter of social status—such attitudes first need to change.[48] Reforms continue to need to be made in public-sector employment in the areas of recruitment, linking wages and productivity, and rationalizing public-sector wages and benefits.

12.4.4 Subsidies

Nearly all of the oil-exporting economies of the Persian Gulf provide generous subsidies on basic goods such as water, electricity, fuel, and food. The most common policy provision is to create a price ceiling, making goods and services more affordable to all households. Consumer subsidies and transfers are one of the most formidable mechanisms through which these oil-exporting countries attempt to transfer oil wealth that accrues initially to the government then to its citizens. But, like most safety net policies in the region, subsidies are untargeted, highly regressive, and drain public resources from those most in need. Moreover, as a result of shifts in demographic trends (population growth) and depleting oil reserves, estimates indicate that it will become increasingly difficult for Persian Gulf oil-exporting countries to continue to support the demands for high living standards for future generations. The lack of fiscal sustainability, inefficiency, and regressiveness highlight the need for the oil exporters to reevaluate and reform their current subsidy policies.

The composition of these subsidies is critical for evaluating their impact on poverty alleviation and income distribution. Qatar recently announced a waiver on electricity and water, which will cost the government nearly US$400 million annually,[49] and nearly 25 percent of Kuwait's budget is allocated towards public subsidies and transfers, the lion's share of which also went towards water and electricity.[50] Iran's implicit fuel subsidy accounts for nearly 15.5 percent of GDP[51]—that is more than government expenditure on health and education combined, and the highest in the region. In contrast, very little is spent on subsidies that are typically targeted towards the most vulnerable and poor or that have higher social returns. Iran spent only 2 percent of GDP on subsidies for welfare and social security, and in 2004 both Qatar and Saudi Arabia spent less than 1 percent of total expenditure on social services (subsidy).

In the case of energy subsidies, the price of domestically produced commercial energy is set considerably below market levels. Since consumption is generally higher among the wealthier segment of the population, a higher portion of the subsidy accrues to them. The leakage rate for Iran's fuel subsidy—that is, the proportion of the subsidy transferred to the economically more advantaged—is 94 percent in Iran's urban areas and 89 percent in its rural areas.[52] Moreover, of the poorest 10 percent of households less than half receive general welfare benefits in cash or in kind, and only one-quarter of assistance accrues to the second poorest segment of the population. In addition to being regressive, subsidized gasoline has resulted in the illegal smuggling of gasoline to neighboring countries. Recently, authorities in Iran have proposed reforms to its fuel subsidies in an attempt to reduce its fiscal burden and the environmental degradation caused by overconsumption.[53] The proposed program offers a "smart card" to all car owners, fixing the subsidized fuel allowance and forcing consumers to pay market prices when consumption exceeds the amount rationed.[54] The scheme has shortcomings. The very poor have no cars, while others will exchange their smart card for cash or other goods at a disadvantageous exchange ratio. Moreover, economic inefficiencies associated with high administrative costs and leakages to the economically more advantaged could be mitigated if the public was simply provided with a cash transfer and gasoline prices raised to prevailing world market prices.

12.5 CONCLUSION

Policies in the Persian Gulf oil-exporting countries have not broadly reflected the social welfare principles enunciated in Islam. The *Qur'an* and the *sunnah* provide both normative and ethical guidance on how to develop a just economic order—with justice at the center of the paradigm. Islam clearly demands that basic needs are met, that equality of opportunity is achieved, and that depletable resources are used to benefit all members of current and future generations equitably.

While governments in the oil-exporting countries of the Persian Gulf region may arguably have designed safety net mechanisms that meet the basic needs of some of their population, such policies cannot be said to be fully Islamic for a number of reasons. Perhaps most crucially, state paternalism comes at an enormous cost to the population at large—the costs ultimately being a loss of political and economic freedoms and the opportunity to achieve upward mobility through education and hard work, fundamental Islamic principles. The combination of universalized, untargeted, and regressive subsidies, and high expenditure and poor-quality services results in a safety net system that is inefficient and wasteful. Finally, those institutional features of an Islamic economic system, such as *Zakah*, that do exist are poorly administered by the state, and many throughout the Muslim world have lost confidence in the ability of these institutions to alleviate poverty and distribute income equitably. It is critical that the major oil exporters devise a more efficient social safety net system that incorporates a better means of transfering oil wealth to their citizens and a progressive income tax system that addresses gross income inequalities. This would be a major departure from state paternalism designed to keep rulers in power.

ENDNOTES

1 An earlier version of this chapter appeared as H. Askari and Noora Arfaa, "Social Safety Net in Islam: the Case of Persian Gulf Oil Exporters," *British Journal of Middle Eastern Studies*, 34, no. 2 (2007): 177–202. We are thankful to BJMES for their permission to use this article. For further information, see http://www.informaworld.com.

2 The major Persian Gulf oil-exporting countries that are the focus of this chapter are Iran, Iraq, Kuwait, Qatar, Saudi Arabia, and the United Arab Emirates (UAE).

3 World Bank, World Development Report 2006: Equity and Development, (New York: Oxford University Press, 2005).

4 Gupta, Sanjeev and Henry Ma Schiller, "Privatization, Social Impact and Social Safety Nets," International Monetary Fund Working Paper No. 99/58 (1999).

5 Chu, Ke-young and Sanjeev Gupta, "Social Safety Nets: Issues and Recent Experiences," (Washington, DC: International Monetary Fund, 1998).

6 Ibid.

7 Skoufias, Emmanuel and Susan W. Walker, "Conditional Cash Transfers and Their Impact on Child Work and Schooling: Evidence from the Progresa Program in Mexico', FCND Discussion Paper No. 123, (Washington, DC: International Food Policy Research Institute, 2001).

8 Qur'anic quotes taken directly from: Muhammad Asad, *Message of the Quran* (Fons Vitae of Kentucky, Incorporated, 2005).

9 Ul Haq, Irfan, *Islamization of Economic Doctrines of Islam: A Study in the Doctrines of Islam and Their Implications for Poverty, Employment, and Economic Growth*, (Virginia: International Institute of Islamic Thought, 1996).

10 Chapra, M. Umer, "Islam and Economic Development: A Discussion Within the Framework of Ibn Khaldun's Philosophy of History," from proceedings of the Second Harvard University Forum on Islamic Finance into the 21st Century, (Cambridge, MA: Harvard University, October 9–10, 1998): 23–30.

11 Ibid.

12 Bonner, Michael, "Poverty and Economics in the Qur'an," *Journal of Interdisciplinary History*, xxxv:3, (winter 2005): 391–406.

13 Iqbal, Munawar, "Distributive Justice and Need Fulfillment in an Islamic Economy," (Islamabad: International Institute of Islamic Economics, 1986): 79.

14 Wilson, Rodney, "The Contribution of Muhammad Baqir Al-Sadr To Contemporary Islamic Thought," *Journal of Islamic Thought*, 9, no. 1 (1998) 46,

quoting from Muhammad Baqir al-Sadr, Iqtisaduna: *Our Economics*, 2, part 2: 6, (Tehran: World Organization for Islamic Services, 1982).

15 For a general discussion of the fundamentals of Islamic economics, see Hossein Askari and Roshanak Taghavi, "The Principal Foundations of an Islamic Economy," *Banca Nazionale Del Lavoro Quarterly Review*, LVIII, no. 235 (December 2005).

16 Mirakhor, Abbas, "General Characteristics of an Islamic Economic System," in *Essays on Iqtisad: the Islamic Approach to Economic Problems*, eds. Baqir Al-Hasani and Abbas Mirakhor, (Nur Corporation, 1989): 25.

17 Ahmad, Ziauddin, *Islam, Poverty, and Income Distribution*, (Leicester: The Islamic Foundation, 1991).

18 Ul Haq, Irfan, *Islamization of Economic Doctrines of Islam: A Study in the Doctrines of Islam and Their Implications for Poverty, Employment, and Economic Growth*.

19 Ahmad, Ziauddin, *Islam, Poverty, and Income Distribution*, (Leicester: The Islamic Foundation, 1991).

20 Ibid.

21 Chapra, M. Umer, "Development Economics: Lessons That Remain to be Learned," *Islamic Studies*, 42, no. 4 (2000).

22 Ibid.

23 Wilson, Rodney, "The Contribution of Muhammad Baqir Al-Sadr to Contemporary Islamic Thought," *Journal of Islamic Thought*, 9, no. 1 (1998): 49.

24 Iqbal, *Distributive Justice and Need Fulfillment in an Islamic Economy*: 79.

25 Salih, Siddig Abdelmageed, "Challenges to Poverty Alleviation in IDB Member Countries," (Islamic Development Bank, 1999).

26 This suggestion has been made elsewhere. See Hossein Askari, Faranghees Abbas, George Jabbour, and Dohee Kwon, "An Economic Manifesto for the Oil-exporting countries of the Persian Gulf: Oil Depletion, Economic Efficiency and Intergenerational Equity," *Banca Nazionale Del Lavoro Quarterly Review*, LIX, no. 239 (December 2006).

27 Aziz, T. M. *An Islamic Perspective of Political Economy of Muhammad Baqir al-Sadr*, Chapter 8, http://www.al-islam.org/al-tawhid/politicaleconomy/title.htm.

28 Wilson, Rodney, "The Contribution of Muhammad Baqir Al-Sadr to Contemporary Islamic Thought," *Journal of Islamic Thought*, 9. no. 1 (1998): 48–59.

29 Mustafa, Ahmad and Hossein Askari, "The Economic Implications of Land Ownership and Land Cultivation in Islam," paper given at the Second International Conference on Islamic Economics held in Islamabad, Pakistan, 1983, and printed in *Distributive Justice and Need Fulfilment in an Islamic Economy*, ed. Munawar Iqbal, (Leicester: International Institute of Islamic Economics, 1998): 128.

30 See Askari et al., "An Economic Manifesto for the Oil-exporting Countries of the Persian Gulf: Oil Depletion, Economic Efficiency and Intergenerational Equity" for the mathematical derivation of the required annual transfers from oil and gas revenues and the estimated size of payments in these six countries.

31 Various IMF reports and country data.

32 United Nations, "United Nations Common Country Assessment for the Islamic Republic of Iran," 2003.

33 Ibid.
34 Andrzej, Kapiszewski, "Arab Versus Asian Immigrant Workers in the GCC Countries," United Nations Expert Group Meeting on International Migration and Development in the Arab Region, United Nations, Beirut, May 15–17, 2006.
35 UNESCO defines poverty of opportunity "as a multidimensional concept. It embraces not only critical elements of lack of education, proper health and economic assets, but also social exclusion and political marginalization."
36 United Nations Development, "Human Development Report 2002: Deepening Democracy in a Fragmented World," (New York: Oxford University Press, 2002).
37 World Bank, "Reducing Vulnerability and Increasing Opportunity: Social Protection in the Middle East and North Africa," (Washington, DC: World Bank, 2002).
38 Various World Health Organization reports.
39 United Nations Development Program, "Arab Human Development Report 2003: Building a Knowledge Society," (New York: Oxford University Press, 2003).
40 Knowledge (*ilm*) and its derivatives are mentioned 811 times in the *Qur'an*, the same number as faith (*iman*) and its derivatives.
41 United Nations, "United Nations Common Country Assessment for the Islamic Republic of Iran" (2003).
42 Roemer, John, *Equality of Opportunity*, (Cambridge: Harvard University Press, 1999).
43 Various IMF reports and country data.
44 Ibid.
45 Yousef, Tarik M., "Employment, Development and the Social Contract in the Middle East and North Africa," (World Bank, October 2004). http://siteresources.worldbank.org/INTLM/Resources/390041-1103750362599/MENA_paper.pdf.
46 Various IMF reports and country data.
47 Fergany, Nader, "Arab Higher Education and Development, An Overview," (Almishkat Center for Research, Cairo, 2000).
48 Mellehi, Kamel, "Human Resource Development Through Vocational Education in Gulf Cooperation Countries: the Case of Saudi Arabia," *Journal of Vocational Education and Training*, 52 (2000) no. 2.
49 El-Rashidi, Yasmine, "In Kuwait, Oil Wealth Dulls Economic Change," *The Wall Street Journal*, (November 4, 2005). http://www.post-gazette.com/pg/05308/600837.stm.
50 Various IMF reports and country data.
51 Ibid.
52 Iqbal, Farrukh, "Sustaining Gains in Poverty Reduction and Human Development in the Middle East and North Africa," (Washington, DC: World Bank, 2006).
53 Universal fuel and energy subsidies have resulted in some of the worst environmental degradation and pollution in the world. According to the World Resources Institute, Tehran is one of the most polluted cities in the world as a result of excessive fuel consumption.
54 World Bank (Middle East and North Africa Region, Office of the Chief Economist), "Middle East and North Africa Economic Developments and Prospects 2006: Financial Markets in a New Age of Oil," (Washington, DC: World Bank, 2006).

References

Abed, G. T., and H. R. Davoodi, *Challenges of Growth and Globalization in the Middle East and North Africa*, (Washington, DC: International Monetary Fund, 2003).

Abed, G. T., and S. Gupta, *Governance, Corruption and Economic Performance,* (Washington, DC: International Monetary Fund, 2002).

Abu-Lughod, J., *Before European Hegemony, The World System AD: 1250–1350,* (New York, NY: Oxford University Press, 1989).

Abu-Lughod, J., "Discontinuities and Persistence." *The World System, Five Hundred Years or Five Thousand?,* (London and New York: Routledge, 1994).

Acemoglu, D. and V. Guerrieri, "Capital Deepening and Non-Balanced Economic Growth," *NBER Working Paper* No. 12475, (Cambridge, Massachusetts: National Bureau of Economic Research, 2006).

Acemoglu, D. and S. Johnson. *Institutions, Corporate Governance, and Crises,* (Oxford University Press: 2002).

Acemoglu, D. and S. Johnson, "Unbundling Institutions," *NBER Working Paper* No. 9934, (Cambridge, Massachusetts: National Bureau of Economic Research, 2003).

Acemoglu, D., S. Johnson, and J. Robinson, "Institutions as the Fundamental Cause of Long-Run Growth," *NBER Working Paper* No.10481, (Cambridge, Massachusetts: National Bureau of Economic Research, 2004).

Ackerman, Bruce A., *Economic Foundation of Property Law*, (Boston: Little, Brown and Company, 1975).

Adelson, Howard L., "Early Medieval Trade Routes," *The American Historical Review,* 65 (2), (1996): 271–287.

Aghnides, Nicholas P., *Mohammedan Theories of Finance*, (New York: Columbia University Press, 1916): note 5, 203.

Ahmad, Ziauddin, *Islam, Poverty, and Income Distribution*, (Leicester: The Islamic Foundation, 1991).

Aizenman, J., "Financial Opening: Evidence and Policy Options," *NBER Working Paper* No. 8900, (Cambridge, Massachusetts: National Bureau of Economic Research, 2002).

Aizenman, J. and Y. Jinjarak, "Globalization and Developing Countries—A Shrinking Tax Base?" *NBER Working Paper*

No.11933, (Cambridge, Massachusetts: National Bureau of Economic Research, 2006).

Aizenman, J., J. B. Pinto, and A. Radziwill, "Sources for Financing Domestic Capital—Is Foreign Saving a Viable Option for Developing Countries?," *NBER Working Paper* No.10624, (Cambridge, Massachusetts: National Bureau of Economic Research, 2004).

al-Abidin, Imam Zayn, and Ali ibn al-Husayn, *Risalat Al-Huquq*, trans., William C. Chittick, *The Treatise of Rights*, (QUM: Foundation of Islamic Cultural Propagation in the world, 1990).

Albuquerque, R., "The Composition of International Capital Flows: Risk Sharing Through Foreign Direct Investment," *Journal of International Economics*, 1 (2), (2003): 353–383.

Alesina, A. and E. La Ferrara, "Who Trusts Others?" *Journal of Public Economics*, 85 (2002): 207–234.

Alfaro, L., "Why Doesn't Capital Flow from Rich to Poor Countries? An Empirical Investigation." *NBER Working Paper* 11901, (Cambridge, Massachusetts: National Bureau of Economic Research, 2005).

Alfaro, L., A. Chanda, S. Kalemli-Ozcan, and S. Sayek, "How Does Foreign Direct Investment Promote Economic Growth? Exploring the Effects of Financial Markets on Linkages," *NBER Working Paper* No. 12522, (Cambridge, Massachusetts: National Bureau of Economic Research, 2005).

Al-Hassani, B. and A. Mirakhor, *Essays on Iqtisad*, (New York, NY: Global Scholarly Publications, 2003).

Ali, Salman S., "Islamic Modes of Finance and Associated Liquidity Risks," paper presented at Conference on Monetary Sector in Iran: Structure, Performance and Challenging Issues Tehran, February 2004.

Ali, Salman S., *Financial Distress and Bank Failure: Lessons from Ihlas Finans Turkey*, Islamic Economic Studies, 14 (2), (2007): 1–52.

Ali, Salman S. and Ahmad, Ausaf, "An Overview," in ed. Salman S. Ali and Ausaf Ahmad, *Islamic Banking and Finance: Fundamentals and Contemporary Issues*, (Jeddah: IRTI, 2006).

Ali Al-Jarhi, Mabid, "A Short Discourse on Markets in an Islamic Economic System," draft paper presented to the Round Table on Islamic Economics, May 26–27, 2004.

Ali Khan, M., "Review: Journal of King Abdul Aziz University," *Islamic Economics*, 3, (1991): 97–177.

Ali Khan, M., "On Trust as a Commodity and on the Grammar of Trust," *Journal of Banking and Finance* 26, (2002): 1719–66.

Al-Misri, Rafik Younis, "Definition of Islamic Economics," *Review of Islamic Economics*, 4 (1), (1995): 36.

Al-Sadr, Shaheed, *Our Economics*, (Beirut: The House of Knowledge for Publication).

Al-Suwailem, Sami, "Hedging in Islamic Finance," Occasional Paper No. 10, (Jeddah: IRTI, 2006).

Amin, S., "The Ancient World-Systems Versus the Modern Capitalist World-System." *The World System, Five Hundred Years or Five Thousand?* (London and New York: Routledge, 1994): 247–276.

Ammer, J., S. B. Holland, D. C. Smith, and F. E. Warnock, "Look at Me Now: What Attracts U.S. Shareholders?," *NBER Working Paper* No. 12500, (Cambridge, Massachusetts: National Bureau of Economic Research, 2006).

Anderson, J. N. D., and N. J. Coulson, "The Moslem Ruler and Contractual Obligations," *N.Y.V. Law Review*, 33 (7), (1958).

Antunes, A. R., and V. C. Tiago, "Corruption, Credit Market Imperfections, and Economic Development," *Working Paper 17-0, 3* (Banco de Portugal, Economic Research Department, 2003).

Archer, Simon, and Riffat Abdul Karim, "Agency Theory, Corporate Governance and the Accounting Regulation of Islamic Banks," *Research in Accounting Regulation, Supplement 1*, Special International Edition, (1997): 97–114.

Arfoe, L., "Cedar Forest to Silver Mountain: Social Change and the Development of Long-Distance Trade in Early Near Eastern Societies," eds. M. Rowlands, M. Larsen and K. Kristiansen, *Centre and Periphery in the Ancient World*, (Cambridge Massachusetts: Cambridge University Press, 1987): pp. 25–35.

Arrow, J. A., *The Limits of Organization*, (New York: W.W. Norton & Company, 1974).

Arrow, Kenneth, et al., "Are We Consuming Too Much?," *The Journal of Economic Perspective*, 18 (3), (Summer 2004): 147–172.

Arthur, John, and William H. Shaw, *Justice and Economic Distribution*, Second edition, (Prentice Hall, 1990).

Asad, Mohammad, *The Message of Quran*, (USA: The Book Foundation, 2004). http://www.thebook.org.

Asad, Muhammad, *Message of the Quran*, (Fons Vitae of Kentucky, Incorporated, 2005).

Ashraf, N., B. Iris, and P. Nikita, "Decomposing Trust and Trustworthiness," *Working Paper*, (Harvard University: Department of Economics, 2005).

Ashtor, E., "Levant Trade in the Later Middle Ages," (Princeton, NJ): 3–64.

Ashtor, E., "The Volume of Levantine Trade in the Later Middle Ages." *Journal of European Economic History* 4, (1975): 573–612.

Ashtor, E., *A Social and Economic History of the Near East in the Middle Ages*, (London: Collins, 1976).

Askari, Hossein, *Saudi Arabia: Oil and the Search for Economic Development*, (JAI Press, 1990).

Askari, Jaafar, "The performance of Gharzul-hasaneh funds in Iran," the 2nd Seminar on Monetary and Foreign Exchange Policies, Monetary & Banking Research Institute, (Tehran, 1992).

Askari, Hossein, Faranghees Abbas, George Jabbour, and Dohee Kwon, "An Economic Manifesto for the Oil-exporting countries of the Persian Gulf: Oil Depletion, Economic Efficiency and Intergenerational Equity," *Banca Nazionale Del Lavoro Quarterly Review*, LIX, (239), (December 2006).

Askari, Hossein, John Thomas Cummings, and Michael Glover, *Taxation and Tax Policies in the Middle East*, (UK: Butterworth Publishers, 1982).

Askari, Hossein, Vahid Nowshirvani, and Mohamed Jaber, *Economic Development in the Countries of the GCC: The Curse and Blessing of Oil*, (JAI Press, 1997).

Askari, Hossein, and Roshanak Taghavi, "The Principal Foundations of an Islamic Economy," *Banca Nazionale Del Lavoro Quarterly Review*, LVIII, (235), (December 2005).

As-Sadr, M. Baqir, *Our Philosophy*, translated by Sham S. C. Inati, (London: Muhammadi Trust, 1987).

Atje, R. and B. Jovanovic, "Stock Markets and Development," *European Economic Review*, 37, (1993): 632–640.

Atkins, Derek, Ian Bates, and Lynn Drennan, *Reputational Risk: A Question of Trust*, (UK: Financial World Publications, 2006).

Aurelio, M. M., "Going Global: The Changing Pattern of U.S. Investment Abroad," *Federal Reserve Bank of Kansas Economic Review*, (third quarter, 2006).

Ayub, Muhammad, *Understanding Islamic Finance*, (Singapore: John Wiley & Sons (Asia), 2007).

Ayyagari, M. and R. Kosova, "Does FDI Facilitate Domestic Entrepreneurship? Evidence from the Czech Republic," (George Washington University: Department of International Business and School of Business and Public Management (SBPM) Working Paper Series, September 14, 2006).

Ayyagari, M., et al., "What Determines Protection of Property Rights? An Analysis of Direct and Indirect Effects," *Robert H. Smith School Research Paper No. RHS 06–032*, (2006).

Aziz, Azrulnizam Abdul, "The Evolution of Islamic Hedging Solutions," *Islamic Finance News*, (Kuala Lumpur, Singapore: Red-Money, 2007).

Aziz, T. M., *An Islamic Perspective of Political Economy of Muhammad Baqir al-Sadr*, Chapter 8. http://www.al-islam.org/al-tawhid/politicaleconomy/title.htm.

Bailey, W., C. X. Mao, and K. Sirodom, "Investment Restrictions and the Cross-Border Flow of Information: Some Empirical Evidence," *Journal of International Money and Finance*, 26, (2007).

Balassa, B., "Exports and Economic Growth: Further Evidence," *Journal of Development Economics*, (1978).

Baldwin, W. W., *Social Justice*, (Oxford: Pergamon Press, 1966).

Baldwin, K., "Risks Management in Islamic Banks," eds. S. Archer and Rifaat Ahmed Abdel Karim, *Islamic Finance*, (London UK: *Euromoney*, 2002).

Balgati, B., P. Demitriades, and S. H. Law, "Financial Openness and Institution: Evidence from Panel Data," paper presented at the Conference on New Perspective on Financial Globalization, sponsored by the Research Department, (Washington, DC: International Monetary Fund, 2007).

Batra, G., D. Kaufmann, and A. H. W. Stone, *Investment Climate Around the World*, (Washington, DC: World Bank, 2003).

Bank, Deutsche, "Pioneering Innovative Shari'a Compliant Solution," Deutsche Bank Academic Paper, Deutsche Bank.

Bashir, Abdel-Hameed M., "Property Rights in Islam," Conference Proceedings of the Third Harvard University Forum on Islamic Finance, (Cambridge, MA: Harvard University, 1999): 71–82.

Beck, T., A. Demirgüç-Kunt, and R. Levine, "Finance, Inequality and the Poor," *Journal of Economic Growth*, (2007).

Beck, T. and R. Levine, "Legal Institutions and Financial Development," eds. Claude Menard and Mary Shirley *Handbook of New Institutional Economics*, (Dordrecht: Kluwer, 2004).

Bekaert, G., "Emerging Equity Market and Economic Development," *NBER Working Paper* 7763, (Cambridge, Massachusetts: National Bureau of Economic Research, 2000).

Bekaert, G., "Emerging Equity Markets and Economic Development," *Journal of Development Economics* 66, (2001): 465–504.

Bekaert, G., "Does Financial Liberalization Spur Growth?," *Journal of Financial Economics* 77 (1), (2005): 3–56.

Bekaert, G., and R. L. Lumsdaine, "The Dynamics of Emerging Market Equity Flows," *Journal of International Money and Finance* 21(3), (2002): 295–350.

Bekaert, G. and C. Lundblad, "Growth Volatility and Financial Liberalization," *Journal of International Money and Finance* 25, (2006): 370–403.

Bekaert, G., and M. S. Urias, "Diversification, Integration and Emerging Market Closed-End Funds," *The Journal of Finance* 51 (3), (1996): 835–869.

Berg, J., D. John, and K. McCabe, "Trust, Reciprocity, and Social History," *Games and Economic Behavior*, 10, (1995): 122–142.

Bernardelli, H., "The Origins of Modern Economic Theory," *Economic Record*, 37, (1961): 320–38.

Beugelsdijk, Sjoerd, Henri L. F. de Groot, and Anton B.T. M. van Schaik, "Trust and Economic Growth: a Robustness Analysis," *Oxford Economic Papers* 56, (2004): pp. 118–134.

Bhattacharya, S., "Aspects of Monetary and Banking Theory and Moral Hazard," *Journal of Finance* 37 (2), (1982): 371–384.

Bonner, Michael, "Poverty and Economics in the Qur'an," *Journal of Interdisciplinary History*, xxxv (3), (Winter 2005): 391–406.

Borensztein, E., J. de Gregorio, and J. W. Lee, "How Does Foreign Direct Investment Affect Economic Growth?" *Journal of International Economics* 45 (1), (1998): 115–135.

Broner, F. A., and J. Ventura, "Globalization and Risk Sharing," *NBER Working Paper* No. 12482. (Cambridge, Massachusetts: National Bureau of Economic Research, 2006).

Bushman, R. M., and J. D. Piotroski, "Financial Reporting Incentives for Conservative Accounting: The Influence of Legal and Political Institutions," *Journal of Accounting and Economics*, (2005).

Byrne, E. H., "Genoese Trade with Syria in the Twelfth Century," *American Historical Review* 25, (1920): 191–219.

Byrne, E. H., *Genoese Shipping in the Twelfth and Thirteenth Centuries* (doc. dated 1250), (Cambridge, Massachusetts: 1930): 85–88.

Calderon, C., A. Chong, and A. Galindo, "Development and Efficiency of the Financial Sector and Links with Trust: Cross-Country Evidence," *Economic Development and Cultural Change,* (University of Chicago, 2002): 189–204.

Cardoso, F., and V. G. da Cunha, "Household Wealth in Portugal," *Working Paper 4–05*, (Banco de Portugal, Economic Research Department, 2005).

Carens, Joseph M., *Equality, Moral Incentives, and the Market,* (Chicago and London: The University of Chicago Press, 1981).

Carlson, Mark A. and Leonardo Hernández, "Determinants and Repercussions of the Composition of Capital Inflows," IMF Working Paper No. 02/86, (May 2002). Available at SSRN: http://ssrn.com/abstract=879621.

Caselli, Francesco, and Nicola Gennaioli, "Economics and Politics of Alternative Institutional Reforms," *NBER Working Papers* 12833, National Bureau of Economic Research, Inc., (2007).

Chang, Ha-Joon, *Bad Samaritans: The Myth of Free Trade and the Secret History of Capitalism*, (UK: Random House, 2007).

Chari, A. and B. Henry, "Firm-Specific Information and the Efficiency of Investment," *NBER Working Paper* No. 12186, (Cambridge, Massachusetts: National Bureau of Economic Research, 2006).

Chinn, M. D., and H. Ito, "Capital Account Liberalization, Institutions and Financial Development: Cross Country Evidence," *NBER Working Paper* No. 8967, (Cambridge, Massachusetts: National Bureau of Economic Research, 2002).

Chittick, William C., *The Treatise on Rights*, (Qum: Foundation of Islamic Cultural Propagation in the World).

Cho, Y. J., "Inefficiencies from Financial Liberalization in the Absence of Well Functioning Equity Markets," *Journal of Money, Credit, and Banking*, 17 (2), (1986): 191–200.

Choudhry, N. N., and A. Mirakhor, "Indirect Instruments of Monetary Control in an Islamic Financial System," *Islamic Economic Studies*, 4 (2), (1997).

Chu, Ke-young, and Sanjeev Gupta, "Social Safety Nets: Issues and Recent Experiences," (Washington, DC: International Monetary Fund, 1998).

Čihák, Martin, and Heiko Hesse, "Islamic Banks and Financial Stability: An Empirical Analysis," IMF Working Paper WP/08/16, (Washington, DC: International Monetary Fund, 2008).

Claessens, S., "The Emergence of Equity Investment in Developing Countries Overview," *The World Bank Economic Review* 9, (Washington, DC: World Bank, 1995): 1–17.

Claessens, S. and E. Feijen, "Financial Sector Development and the Millennium Development," *World Bank Working Paper* No. 89, (Washington, DC: World Bank, 2006a).

Claessens, S. and E. Perotti, "The Links between Finance and Inequality: Channels and Evidence," Background paper for the *World Development Report* 2006, (Washington, DC: World Bank, 2006b).

Clarke, G. R. G., "How the Quality of Institutions Affects Technological Deepening in Developing Countries," *World Bank Policy Research Working Paper* 2603, (Washington, DC: World Bank, 2004).

Clementi, G. L., and G. MacDonald, "Investor Protection, Optimal Incentives, and Economic Growth," *Journal of Economics*, (August 2004): 1131–1175.

Clifford, W. and Smith, Jr., "Risk Management in Banking", ed. Robert J. Schwartz and Clifford W. Smith, Jr., *Advanced Strategies in Financial Risk Management*, (New York: New York Institute of Finance, 1993): pp. 147–162.

Coleman, J. S., "Social Capital in the Creation of Human Capital," *The American Journal of Sociology*, Vol. 94 Supplement, (University of Chicago, 1988): 95–120

Coleman, J. S., *Foundations of Social Theory*, (The Belknap Press of Harvard University Press, 1990).

Coldwell, Bruce, "Does Methodology Matter? How Should it be Practiced?" *Finnish Economic Papers*, 3 (1), (1990).

Collier, Paul, V. L. Elliott, Havard Hegre, Anke Hoeffler, Marta Reynal-Querol, and Nicholas Sambanis, *Breaking the Conflict*

Trap: Civil War and Development Policy, (World Bank and Oxford University Press, 2003).

Coval, J. D., "Home Bias at Home: Local Equity Preference in Domestic Portfolios," *The Journal of Finance*, 54 (6), (1999).

Crafts, N., *Globalization and Economic Growth: A Historical Perspective*, (London: London School of Economics, 2003).

Creane, S., Rishi Goyal, A. Mushfiq Mobarak, and Randa Sab (2003), *Financial Development in the Middle East and North Africa*, (Washington, DC: International Monetary Agency, 2003).

Cummings, John Thomas, Hossein Askari, and Ahmad Mustafa, "Islam and Modern Economic Change," ed. John L. Esposito *Islam and Development: Religion and Sociopolitical Change*, (New York: Syracuse University Press, 1980).

Primitive, Archaic, and Modern Economics: Essays of Karl Polanyi, edited by George Dalton, 1971.

Dasgupta, P., "Trust as a Commodity," *Economic Theory Discussion Paper* No. 101, (University of Cambridge, April 1986).

Dasgupta, P. and I. Serageldin, *Social Capital: A Multifaceted Perspective,* (Washington, DC: World Bank, 1999).

Davis, Jeffrey, Rolando Ossowski, James A. Daniel, and Steven Barnett, "Stabilization and Savings Funds for Nonrenewable Resources: Experience and Fiscal Policy Implications," *Fiscal Policy Formulation and Implementation in Oil-Producing Countries.*

Day, J., *The Levant Trade in the Middle Ages, the Economic History of Byzantium: From the Seventh Through the Fifteenth Century*, (Dumbarton Oaks Research Library and Collection, 2002).

De Alessi, Louis, "Property Rights, Transaction Costs, and X-Efficiency: An Essay in Economic Theory," *American Economic Review*, 73, (March 1983): 64–81.

Dehesa, M., et al., "Relative Price Stability, Creditor Rights, and Financial Deepening," *IMF Working Paper*, (Washington, DC: International Monetary Fund, 2007).

Del Mar, Alexander, *History of Monetary Systems in Various States*, (New York: Angustus M. Kelly): 163–99.

DeLorenzo, Yasuf Talal, "Certifying *Sharj'ah* Compliance in Financial Products: The Role of Islamic Values in Financial Decision Making," Paper presented at Islamic Finance in Southeast Asia: Local Practice, Global Impact, Organized by National Bureau of

Asian Studies (NBR) on October 18, 2007 at the Georgetown University, Washington, DC, USA.

Demirgüc-Kunt, A., T. Beck, and R. Levine, "Small and Medium Enterprises, Growth, and Poverty: Cross-Country Evidence," *World Bank Policy Research Working Paper* 3178, (Washington, DC: World Bank, 2006).

De Somogyi, J., "Trade in Classical Arabic Literature in the Muslim World," (1965): 131–134.

Doidge, C., A. G. Karolyi, and R. M. Stulz, "Why are Foreign Firms Listed in the U.S. Worth More?" *Journal of Financial Economics* (2004): 205–238.

Dziobek, C. and C. Pazarbasioglu (1997), "Lessons from Systemic Bank Restructuring: a Survey of 24 Countries," IMF Working Paper 97/161, (Washington, DC: 1997).

Ebrahim, Muhammed-Shahid and Safadi, Akram, "Behavioral Norms in the Islamic Doctrine of Economics: A Comment," *Journal of Economic Behavior and Organization*, 27, (1995).

Eccles, Robert G., Scott C. Newquist, and Roland Schatz, "Reputation and Its Risks Identify, quantify, and manage the risks to your company's reputation long before a problem or crisis strikes," *Harvard Business Review*, February (2007).

Edison, H. J., and F. E. Warnock, "Cross-Border Listings, Capital Controls, and Equity Flows to Emerging Markets," *NBER Working Paper* No. 12589, (Cambridge, Massachusetts: National Bureau of Economic Research, 2006).

Ehrenkreuz, A., "Studies in the Monetary History of the Near East in the Middle Ages." *JESHO*, 2 (1959): 128–161; 6 (1963): 243–277.

Eggertsson, Thranin, *Economic Behavior and Institutions*, (Cambridge: Cambridge University Press, 1990).

El-Erian, M. A., "Dealing with Global Fluidity," *Finance and Development*. A compilation of articles from Finance and Development, (Washington, DC: International Monetary Fund, 2007).

El-Erian, Mohamed, and Monmohan Kumar, "Emerging Equity Markets in the Middle Eastern Countries," Working Paper No. 94/103, (Washington, DC: International Monetary Fund, 1994).

Elfakhani, Said, M. Kabir Hassan, and Yusuf Sidani, "Comparative Performance of Islamic Versus Secular Mutual Funds," *Working Paper* WP 10–2006, (New Orleans, LA: University of New Orleans, 2007).

El Gamal, Mahmoud, *Islamic Finance: Law, Economics and Practice*, (New York: Cambridge University Press, 2006).

El-Hawary, Dahlia, Wafik Grais, and Zamir Iqbal, *Regulating Islamic Financial Institutions: The Nature Of The Regulated*, Policy Research Working Paper No. 3227, (Washington, DC: World Bank, 2004).

El-Rashidi, Yasmine, "In Kuwait, Oil Wealth Dulls Economic Change," *The Wall Street Journal*, November 4, 2005. http://www.post-gazette.com/pg/05308/600837.stm.

Erbas, N. and A. Mirakhor, "The Equity Premium Puzzle, Anbiguity Aversion, and Institutional Quality," IMF Working Paper: work in progress, (Washington, DC: International Monetary Fund, 2007).

Ernst & Young, "Ernest and Young's The Islamic Funds and Investments Report (IFIR) 2007," The World Islamic Funds and Capital Markets Conference, Dubai, (2007).

Errico, Luca and Mitra Farahbaksh, *Islamic Banking: Issues in Prudential Regulations and Supervision*, IMF Working Paper WP/98/30, (Washington, DC: International Monetary Fund, 1998).

Euromoney "The 2007 guide to Opportunities and Trends in Islamic Finance" (London: *Euromoney* Institutional Investor PLC, 2007).

Euromoney Magazine (Islamic Finance), January 1, 2008.

Evans, M. and V. Hnatkovska, "International Capital Flows Returns and World Financial Integration," *NBER Working Paper 11701*, (Cambridge, Massachusetts: National Bureau of Economic Research, 2005).

Exenberger, A., "The Cradle of Globalization: Venice's and Portugal's Contribution to a World Becoming Global," *Working Papers in Economics 2004/02,* (Austria: University of Innsbruck, 2004).

Faria, A. and P. Mauro, "Institutions and the External Capital Structure of Countries," *IMF Working Paper* WP/04/236, (Washington, DC: International Monetary Fund, 2004).

de Faria, Andre Lince, and Paolo Mauro, "Institutions and the External Capital Structure of Countries," *IMF Working Papers* 04/236, (Washington, DC: International Monetary Fund, 2005).

Faria, A., P. Mauro, M. Minnoni, and A. Zaklan, "External Financing of Emerging Market Countries: Evidence from Two Waves of Financial Globalization," *IMF Working Paper* WP/06/205, (Washington, DC: International Monetary Fund, 2006).

Fearson, W. E., S. R. Foerster, and D. B. Keim, "General Tests of Latent Variable Models and Mean-Variance Spanning," *The Journal of Finance*, 48 (1), (1993): 131–155.

Fehr, Ernst, and Simon Gächter, "Fairness and Retaliation: The Economics of Reciprocity," *The Journal of Economic Perspective*, 14 (3), (summer 2000): 159–81.

Finance and Development, "Globalization: The Story Behind the Numbers," a compilation of articles from Finance and Development, (Washington, DC: International Monetary Fund, 2007).

Financial Times reports: Islamic Finance, May 24, 2007.

Fischel, W., "The Origin of Banking in Medieval Islam," *Journal of the Royal Asiatic Society*, (1933): 339–352, 568–603, also published in *Islamic Culture*, Vol. XIV, by the Bureau of Compilation, Translation and Publication, Cairo.

Fischel, W., *Jews in the Economic and Political Life of Mediaeval Islam*, (London: 1937).

Frank, A. G., "The Thirteenth Century World System: A Review Essay," *Journal of World History* 1 (2), (1990): 249–256.

Frankel, J. A., and A. K. Rose, "Currency Crashes in Emerging Markets: Empirical Indicators," *CEPR Discussion Papers* 1349, (1996).

Fremond, Olivier, and Mierta Capaul, "The State of Corporate Governance: Experience from Country Assessments," World Bank Policy Research Working Paper No. 2858, June (2002). Available at SSRN: http://ssrn.com/abstract=636222.

French, K. R., and J. M. Poterba, "Investor Diversification and International Equity Markets," *American Economic Review*, 81 (2), (1991): 222–226.

Fukuyama, F., *Trust, The Social Virtues and the Creation of Prosperity*, (Free Press Paperbacks: 1996).

Garretsen, H., R. Lensink, and E. Sterken, "Growth, Financial Development, Societal Norms and Legal Institutions," *International Financial Markets, Institutions and Money*. (June 2003).

Gelos, R. G., and S. J. Wei, "Transparency and International Investor Behavior," *NBER Working Paper No. 9260*, (Cambridge, Massachusetts: National Bureau of Economic Research, 2002).

Gills, B. K., "World System Cycles, Crises, and Hegemonic Shifts, 1700 BC to 1700 AD," *The World System, Five Hundred Years or Five Thousand?*, (London and New York: Routledge, 1994): 143–199.

Gills, B. K., and G. A. Frank, "The Cumulation of Accumulation," *The World System, Five Hundred Years or Five Thousand?*, (London and New York: Routledge, 1994): 81–114.

Glaeser, E. L., "Measuring Trust," *The Quarterly Journal of Economics,* (August 2000): 811–846.

Glaeser, E. L., D. Laibson, J. A. Scheinkman, and C. L. Soutter, "What is Social Capital? The Determinants of Trust and Trustworthiness," *Working Paper 7216*, NBER, (Cambridge, Massachusetts: National Bureau of Economic Research, 1999).

Godwin, Michael, and Irma Freese, *Banks zero in on reputational risk*, (2005). http://www.camagazine.com/2/7/6/1/0/index1.shtml.

Goitein, S. D., "From the Mediterranean to India," *Speculum*, 29, (1954): 181–197.

Goitein, S. D., "The Cairo Geniza as a Source for the History of Muslim Civilization," *Studia Islamica,* (1955): 168–197.

Goitein, S. D., "The Main Industries of the Mediterranean Area as Reflected in the Records of the Cairo Geniza." *JESHO*, 4, (1961): 168–197.

Goitein, S. D., *Jewish Education in Muslim Countries, Based on Records of the Cairo Geniza* (Hebrew), (Jerusalem: 1962).

Goitein, S. D., "Commercial and Family Partnerships in the Countries of Medieval Islam," *Islamic Studies*, 3, (1964): 318–319.

Goitein, S. D., *A Mediterranean Society, The Jewish Communities of the Arab World as Portrayed in the Documents of the Cairo Geniza*, Vol. I. (Berkeley and Los Angeles: Economic Foundations, 1967).

Goitein, S. D., and B. Shemesh, *A Muslim Law in Israel* (Hebrew), (Jerusalem: 1957).

Goldberg, P. K., and N. Pavcnik, "Distributional Effects of Globalization in Developing Countries," *NBER Working Paper* No. 12885, (Cambridge, Massachusetts: National Bureau of Economic Research, 2007).

Goodhart, C., *Financial Development and Economic Growth, Explaining the Links*, British Association for the Advancement of Science Books, (NY: Palgrave Macmillan, 2004).

Grais, Wafik, and Zamir Iqbal, "Corporate Governance Challenges of Islamic Financial Institutions," 7th Harvard Forum on Islamic Finance, Boston, USA, April 22–23, 2006.

Grais, Wafik, and M. Pellegrini "Corporate Governance and Shariah Compliance in Institutions Offering Islamic Financial Services,"

World Bank Policy Research Working Paper 4054, (November 2006).

van Greuning, Hennie, "Legal and *Sharia* Issues on Misconduct and Negligence in Islamic Finance," paper presented at a conference Challenges Facing the Islamic Financial Services Industry, April 6–7, 2005, Tehran, Islamic Republic of Iran.

van Greuning, Hennie, and Zamir Iqbal, *Risk Analysis for Islamic Banks*, (Washington, DC: World Bank, 2007).

Guiso, Luigi, Paola Sapienza, and Luigi Zingales, "People's Opium: Religion and economic attitudes," *Journal of Monetary Economics,* 50, (2003): 225–282.

Guiso, L., P. Sapienza, and L. Zingales, "The Role of Social Capital in Financial Development," *The American Economic Review* 94 (3), (2004).

Guiso, L., et al.., "Trusting the Stock Market," *NBER Working Paper* No. 11648, (Cambridge, Massachusetts: National Bureau of Economic Research, 2005).

Gupta, Sanjeev, and Henry Ma Schiller, "Privatization, Social Impact and Social Safety Nets," International Monetary Fund Working Paper No. 99/58, (1999).

Güth, Werner and Axel Ockenfels, "Evolutionary Norm Enforcement," *Journal of institutional and Theoretical Economics,* 156, (2000): 335–47.

Habachy, S., "Property, Right, and Contract in Muslim Law," *Columbia Law Review I,* 62 (3), (1962).

Halaissos, M. and C. Bertaut, "Why do so Few Hold Stocks?" *The Economic Journal,* 105 (432), (1995): 1110–1129.

Hall and Jones, "Why do Some Countries Produce so Much More Output per Worker than Others?" *Quarterly Journal of Economics,* 114 (1), (February 1999): 83–116

Hands, D. Wade, "Thirteen Theses on Progress in Economic Methodology," *Finnish Economic Papers,* 3 (1), (1990).

Harasanyi, J. C., "Morality and the Theory of Rational Behavior," *Social Research* 44: 623–56.

Harrison, A., "Globalization and Poverty," *NBER Working Paper* No. 12347, (Cambridge, Massachusetts: National Bureau of Economic Research, 2006)

Hasanuz Zaman, S. M., "Definition of Islamic Economics," *Journal of Research in Islamic Economics*, 1 (2), (Winter 1984): 55–60.

Hasanuz Zaman, S. M., *Economic Guidelines in the Quran*, (Islamabad: The International Institute of Islamic Thought, 1999).

Hassan, Kabir, "Cost, Profit And X-Efficiency Of Islamic Banks In Pakistan, Iran And Sudan," ed. Tariqullah Khan and Dadan Muljawan, *Islamic Financial Architecture: Risk Management and Financial Stability,* (Jeddah: IRTI, 2006).

Hassan, Abul, and Antonios Antoniou, "Equity Fund's Islamic Screening: Effects on its Financial Performance," in ed. Salman S. Ali and Ausaf Ahmad, *Islamic Banking and Finance: Fundamentals and Contemporary Issues,* (Jeddah: IRTI, 2006).

Häusler, G., "The Globalization of Finance," *Finance and Development*, a compilation of articles from Finance and Development, (Washington, DC: International Monetary Fund, 2007).

Helliwell, J. F., and R. Putnam, "Economic Growth and Social Capital in Italy," *Eastern Economic Journal*, Summer, 21 (3), (1995): 295–307.

Henderson, J. V., Z. Shalizi, and A. J. Venables, "Geography and Development," *Journal of Economic Geography,* 1, (2001): 81–106.

Henisz, W. J., "The Institutional Environment for Economic Growth," *Economics and Politics* 12, (2000): 1–31.

Henry, P. B., "Do Stock Market Liberalizations Cause Investment Booms?," *Journal of Financial Economics* 58 (1–2), (2000a): 301–334.

Henry, P. B., "Stock Market Liberalization, Economic Reform, and Emerging Market Equity Prices," *Journal of Finance* 55 (2), (2000b): 529–564.

Hicks, John, "Rational Behavior—Observation or Assumption?" edited by Israel M. Kirzner, *Subjectivism, Intelligibility and Economic Understanding*, (New York: New York University Press, 1986).

"Holders: No Need for Panic," *Turkish Daily News*, Feb. 14., as reported in Starr and Yilmaz (2006).

Hong, H., J. D. Kubik, and J. C. Stein, "Social Interaction and Stock-Market Participation," *The Journal of Finance,* 54 (1), February (2004): 137–163

Honohan, P., "Financial Sector Policy and the Poor: Selected Findings and Issues," *World Bank Working Paper* No. 43, (Washington, DC: World Bank, 2006).

Hourani, G. F., "Two Theories of Value in Medieval Islam," *The Muslim World*, XLIX, (1959): 269–78.

Huberman, Gur, "Familiarity Breeds Investment," *The Review of Financial Studies*, 14 (3), (2001): 659–680.

Huberman, Gur, and S. Kandel, "Mean-Variance Spanning," *The Journal of Finance*, 42 (4), (1987a): 873–888

Huberman, Gur, S. Kandel, and R. F. Stambaugh, "Mimicking Portfolios and Exact Arbitrage Pricing," *The Journal of Finance*, 42 (1), (1987b): 1–9

Hussein, K. A., "Operational Efficiency in Islamic Banking: The Sudanese Experience," Islamic Development Bank Working paper Series No.1, (Jeddah: IRTI, 2003).

Hussein, Khaled A., "Islamic Investment: Evidence From Dow Jones and FTSE Indices," 6th International Conference on Islamic Economics and Banking, Jakarta, Indonesia, November 2005.

Imad Ali, M., "In the Mirror of History Were the Earlier Generations Smarter or Are We?" *Finance in Islam,* (2005).

Imamuddin, S. M., "Bayt Al-Mal and Banks in the Medieval Muslim World," *Islamic Culture,* January 1960.

IMF, Global Financial Stability Report (GFSR). International Monetary Fund (IMF), Washington, DC, USA, (2007).

IMF, World Economic Outlook 2007, p. 59.

Iqbal, Munawar, "Distributive Justice and Need Fulfillment in an Islamic Economy," (Islamabad: International Institute of Islamic Economics, 1986): 79.

Iqbal, Zamir, "Financial Engineering in Islamic Finance," *Thunderbird International Business Review*, 41 (4/5), (July-October 1999): 541–560.

Iqbal, Zamir, "Portfolio Choices and Asset Pricing in Islamic Framework," ed. Habib Ahmed *Theoretical Foundations of Islamic Economics*, (Jeddah: IRTI, 2002).

Iqbal, Zamir, "Financial Intermediation and Design of Financial System in Islam," International Seminar on Economics, Malaysia, Sep. 22–24, (2004).

Iqbal, Farrukh, "Sustaining Gains in Poverty Reduction and Human Development in the Middle East and North Africa," (Washington, DC: World Bank, 2006).

Iqbal, Zubair, and Abbas Mirakhor, Islamic Banking: Occasional Paper No. 49, (Washington, DC: International Monetary Fund, 1987).

Iqbal, Zamir, and Abbas Mirakhor, "Progress and Challenges of Islamic Banking," *Thunderbird International Business Review*, 41(4/5) (1999): 381–405.

Iqbal, Zamir, and Abbas Mirakhor, "Development of Islamic Financial Institutions and Challenges Ahead," eds. Simon Archer and Rifaat Abdel Karim *Islamic Finance: Growth and Innovation*, (London: *Euromoney* Books, 2002).

Iqbal, Zamir, and Abbas Mirakhor, "A Stakeholders Model of Corporate Governance of Firm in Islamic Economic System," *Islamic Economic Studies*, 11 (2), March (2004).

Iqbal, Zamir, and Abbas Mirakhor, *An Introduction to Islamic Finance: Theory and Practice,* (Singapore: John Wiley & Sons (Asia), 2007).

IRTI and IFSB, *Islamic Financial Services Industry Development: Ten-Year Framework and Strategies*, Islamic Development Bank, (Jeddah: IRTI, 2006).

ISI Analytics, Islamic Financial Services Industry, (London: ISI Emerging Markets, 2007).

Ismail, Arshad, "Emergence and Growth of the Sukuk Market," in ed. Kamar Jaffer and Sohail Jaffer, *Investing in the GCC Markets: Regional Opportunities and Challenges*, (Dubai: CPI Financial Books, 2007).

Islamic Financial Information Services (ISI Emerging Markets, 2007).

John, R., Presley and John G. Sessions, "Islamic Economics: The Emergence of a New Paradigm," *Economic Journal*, 104 (424), (May 1994): 584–596.

Johnson, S., J. McMillan, and C. Woodruff, "Property Rights and Finance," *The American Economic Review,* 92 (5), (2002): 1335–1356.

Jones, B. F., and B. A. Olken, "Do Leaders Matter?" *NBER*, July 2004.

Ju, J., and S. J. Wei, "A Solution to Two Paradoxes of International Capital Flows," *IMF Occasional Paper* No.178, (Washington, DC: International Monetary Fund, 2006).

Kamali, Mohammad Hashim, "Islamic Commercial Law: An Analysis of Futures," *American Journal of Islamic Social Sciences*, 13 (2), (Summer 1996): 197–224.

Kamali, Mohammad Hashim, "Prospects for an Islamic Derivatives Market in Malaysia," *Thunderbird International Business Review*, 41, (July–October 1999): 523–540.

Kaminsky, G. and S. Schmuckler, "Short-Run Pain, Long-Run Gain: The Effects of Financial Liberalization," unpublished working paper, (Washington, DC: International Monetary Fund, 2002).

Kapiszewski, Andrzej, "Arab Versus Asian Immigrant Workers in the GCC countries," United Nations Expert Group Meeting on International Migration and Development in the Arab Region, United Nations, Beirut, May 15–17, 2006.

Karolyi, A. G., "The Role of American Depositary Receipts in the Development of Emerging Equity Markets," *The Review of Economics and Statistics,* August, 86 (3) (2004): 670–690.

Kassem, Mahmoud, and Anita Greil, Dow Jones Newswires, "Islamic Banking Reputation Suffers In Wake of September 11," *WSJ*, Nov. 6, 2001.

Kaufman, D., A. Kraay, and M. Mastruzzi, "Governance Matters: Governance Indicators for 1996–2004," (Washington, DC: World Bank, 2005).

Kenneth, J. and Arrow, "Economic Theory and the Hypothesis of Rationality," *The World of Economics* (p. 198).

Khalil, Elias L., "Is Justice the Primary Feature of the State? Adam Smith Critique of Social Contract Theory," *European Journal of Law and Economics*, 6 (3), (November 1988): 215–30.

Khalil, Elias L., "Beyond Self-Interest and Altruism" *Economic and Philosophy*, 6 (1), (April 1990): 255–73.

Khalil, Elias L., "On the Scope of Economics: What is the Question?" *Finnish Economic Papers*, 8 (1), (Spring 1995): 40–55.

Khan, Mohsin, "Islamic Interest-Free Banking: A Theoretical Analysis," eds. Khan and Mirakhor, *Theoretical Studies in Islamic Banking and Finance*, (Houston: IRIS Books, 1987).

Khan, Ali, "Globalization of Financial Markets and Islamic Financial Institutions," *Islamic Economic Studies*, 8 (1) (2000): 52.

Khan, Fahim, "Macro Consumption Function in an Islamic Framework," *Journal of Research in Islamic Economics*, 1 (1).

Khan, Tariqullah, and Habib Ahmed, *Risk Management an Analysis of Issues in Islamic Financial Industry*, Occasional Paper No. 9, (Jeddah: Islamic Development Bank, 2001).

Khan, M. and A. Mirakhor, "Islamic Interest-Free Banking: A Theoretical Analysis," eds. Khan and Mirakhor *Theoretical Studies in Islamic Banking and Finance*, (Houston, TX: IRIS Books, 1987).

Khan, Mohsin, and Abbas Mirakhor, "The Financial System and Monetary Policy in an Islamic Economy," *Journal of Research in Islamic Economics,* (1988).

Khan, Mohsin, and Abbas Mirakhor: "Islam and the Economic System," *Review of Islamic Economics*, 2 (1), (1992): 1–30.

Khurshid, Ahmad, "Islamic Finance and Banking: The Challenges and Prospects," *Review of Islamic Economics* No. 9, (Leicester: The Islamic Foundation, July 2000): 59.

Kho, B. C., R. M. Stulz, and F. E. Warnock, "Financial Globalization, Governance, and the Evolution of the Home Bias," *NBER Working Paper* No. 12389, (Cambridge, Massachusetts: National Bureau of Economic Research, 2006).

Klein, M. W., "Capital Account Liberalization, Institutional Quality and Economic Growth: Theory and Evidence," *NEBR* unpublished working paper, (Cambridge, Massachusetts: National Bureau of Economic Research, 2005).

Knack, S. and P. Keefer, "Does Social Capital Have an Economic Payoff? A Cross-Country Investigation," *The Quarterly Journal of Economics*, (November 1997): 1251–1288.

Kolm, Serge Christopher, "The Buddhist Theory of 'No Self'," *The Multiple Self*, ed. Jon Elster, (Cambridge University Press): 233–63.

Komijani, Akbar, and Ali Askari, "Structure and performance of interest free loan funds and their place in the financial and banking system of Iran," Tahghighate Eghtesadi, No. 44, (1991).

Kose, A., "Financial Integration and Macroeconomic Volatility," *IMF Working Paper* WP/03/50, (Washington, DC: International Monetary Fund, 2003).

Kose, A., "The Macroeconomic Implications of Financial Globalization: A Reappraisal and Synthesis," *IMF Working Paper* WP/01/180, (Washington, DC: International Monetary Fund, 2005).

Kose, A. and M. Terrones, "How Does Financial Globalization Affect Risk Sharing? Patterns and Channels," IMF, Research Department

(Washington, DC: International Monetary Fund, 2007).

Kose, A., et al. "Financial Globalization: A Reappraisal," *IMF Working Paper* WP/06/189, (Washington, DC: International Monetary Fund, 2006).

Kourides, P. N., "The Influence of Islamic Law on Contemporary Middle Eastern Legal System: the Foundation and Binding Force of Contracts," *Columbia Journal of Transnational Law*, 9 (2), (1970): 384–435.

Kovářík, Tomáš and Pavel Nevický, *Reputational Risk Management and Reputational Capital*, (DTTI, 2007). http://www.deloitte.com/dtt/article/0,1002,sid=11629&cid=141087,00.html?list=gfsi-risk.

Krueger, A. O., "Trade Policy as an Input into Development," National Bureau of Economic Research, Working Paper Series (U.S.); No. 466 (1980): 288–92.

Kuran, Timur, "Islamic economics and the Islamic Subeconomy," *Journal of Economic Perspectives*, 9, (Fall 1995): 155–173.

Kuran, Timur, "The Discontents of Islamic Morality," *American Economic Review*, 86 (2), (May 1996): 438–442.

Kuran, Timur, "Islam and Under-Development: An Old Puzzle Revisited," *Journal of Institutional and Theoretical Economics*, 153, (1997): 41–71.

Kurre, Frank, *Assessing Reputational Risk*, (2007). http://www.nacubo.org/x8958.xml?ss=pf.

Labib, S. Y., 1969. "Capitalism in Medieval Islam," *The Journal of Economic History*, 29 (1), (The Tasks of Economic History, 1969): 79–96.

Laiou, A. E., "The Byzantine Economy in the Mediterranean Trade System: Thirteenth–Fifteenth Centuries," *Gender, Society and Economic Life in Byzantium*, (Hampshire, 1992): 177–223.

Laiou, A. E., "The Levant Trade in the Middle Ages, The Economic History of Byzantium: From the Seventh through the Fifteenth Century," *Dumbarton Oaks Research Library and Collection*, No. 39, (2002).

Lane, F. C., "Venetian Bankers, 1496–1533: A Study in the Early Stages of Deposit Banking," *The Journal of Political Economy*, 45, (1937): 187–206.

Lane, F. C., "Family Partnerships and Joint Ventures in the Venetian Republic," *The Journal of Economic History*, 4 (2), (1944): 178–196.

Langholm, Odd, *Price and Value in the Aristotelian Tradition*, the Norwegian Research Council for Science and The Humanities, 1979, distributed by Columbia University Press.

Langlois, Richard, *Economics as a Process: Essays in the New Institutional Economics*, (Chicago: The University of Chicago Press, 1986).

La Porta, Rafael, Florencio Lopez-de-Silanes, Andrei Shleifer, and Robert W. Vishny, "Agency Problems and Dividend Policies Around the World," *NBER Working Paper 6594*, (1998).

Lavoie, Don, ed. *Economics and Hermeneutics*, (London: Routledge, 1991).

Lawal, Muhammad, Ahmad Bashar, "Price Control in an Islamic Economy," *Journal of King Abdul Aziz University: Islamic Economics*, 9, (1997): 29–52.

Leibenstein, Harvey, "Property Rights and X-Efficiency: Comment," *American Economic Review,* 73, (September 1983): 831–45.

Levchenko, A. and P. Mauro, "Do Some Forms of Financial Flows Help Protect from Sudden Stops?" *IMF Occasional Paper* No. 202, (Washington, DC: International Monetary Fund, 2006).

Levine, R., "Financial Development and Economic Growth," *Journal of Economic Literature* 35, (1997): 688–726.

Levine, R. and S. Zervos, "Stock Market, Banks and Economic Growth," *American Economic Review* 88, (1998): 537–558.

Lewis, K. K., "Consumption, Stock Returns, and the Gains from International Risk-Sharing," *NBER Working Paper* No. 5410, (Cambridge, Massachusetts: National Bureau of Economic Research, 1996).

Lieber, A. E., "Eastern Business Practice and Medieval European Commerce," *Economic History Review,* 2 (21), (1968): 230–243.

Lieberman, David, "Adam Smith on Justice, Rights, and Law," *Boalt Working Papers in Public Law*, paper No. 67, (Berkeley: University of California, 1999).

Lightstone, John, "Quantitative Methods of Stock Selection in the Construction of Sharia-Compliant Portfolios," Fifth Harvard University Forum On Islamic Finance, Harvard University, (Cambridge, Massachusetts: April 2002).

Lindert, P. H., and J. G. Williamson, "Does Globalization Make the World More Unequal?" *NEBR Working Paper* 8228, (Cambridge, Massachusetts: National Bureau of Economic Research, 2001).

Little, David, John Kelsey, and Abdulaziz Sachedina, *Human Rights and the Conflicts of Culture: Western and Islamic Perspectives on Religious Liberty,* (South Carolina: University of South Carolina Press, 1988): 26.

Lopez, R. S., "The Dollar of the Middle Ages," *Journal of Economic History*, (1951): 209–234.

Lopez, R. S., "The Trade of Medieval Europe: The South," *The Cambridge Economic History of Europe*, 2, (Cambridge: 1952): 257–354.

Lopez, R. S., "East and West in the Early Middle Ages: Economic Relations," *Relazioni del X Congresso Internazionale di Scienze Storiche* (6 Vol., Florence) III, (1955a): 129–137.

Lopez, R. S., and I. W. Raymond, *Medieval Trade in the Mediterranean World*, Records of Western Civilization Series, (Columbia University Press, 1955b).

Lopez, R. S., *The Commercial Revolution of the Middle Ages, 950–1350*, (Cambridge University Press, 1976).

Lopez-de-Silanes, F., R. F. La Porta, A. Shleifer, and R. W. Vishny, "Trust in Large Organizations," *The American Economic Review*, 87 (2), papers and proceedings of the Hundred and Fourth Annual Meeting of the American Economic Association (1997): 333–338.

Lorenz, E., "Trust, Contract and Economic Cooperation," *Cambridge Journal of Economics*, 23, (1999): 301–315.

Louisot, Jean-Paul, "Managing reputation risks," *Risk Management: An International Journal*, 6 (3), (2004): 35–50

Lucas, R., Jr., "Why Doesn't Capital Flow From Rich to Poor Countries?" *American Economic Review Papers and Proceedings*, 8-0, (1990): 92–96.

Lucas, R., Jr., "Some Macroeconomics for the 21st Centurym," *Journal of Economic Perspectives*, 14 (1), (2000): 159–178.

Majid, M. A., N. G. M. Nor, and F. F. Said, "Efficiency of Islamic Banks in Malaysia," Conference Proceedings: The Fifth International Conference on Islamic Economics and Finance, Vol. II, Bahrain, Oct. 7–9, (2003).

Mäki, Uskali, "Methodology of Economics: Complaints and Guidelines," *Finnish Economic Papers*, 3 (1), (1990).

Marcus Noland, "Religion, Culture, and Economic Performance," *Institute for International Economics,* (2004).

Martin, Mathew, "The Globalization of Islamic Banking," *Middle East Economic Digest*; 51 (36), (September 7, 2007): 33–36.

Martson, David, and V. Sundararajan "Unique Risks Of Islamic Banks: Implications For Systemic Stability," ed. Tariqullah Khan and Dadan Muljawan, *Islamic Financial Architecture: Risk Management and Financial Stability,* (Jeddah: IRTI, 2006).

McClosky, Donald, *The Rhetoric of Economics*, (University of Wisconsin Press, 1985).

Mehra, R., "The Equity Premium: Why is it a Puzzle?," *Financial Analysts Journal*, (2003): 54–69.

Mehra, R., "The Equity Premium in India," *NBER Working Paper* No. 12434, (Cambridge, Massachusetts: National Bureau of Economic Research, 2006).

Mehra, R. and E. C. Prescott, "The Equity Premium: A Puzzle." *Journal of Monetary Economics* 15, (1985): 145–161.

Mellehi, Kamel, "Human Resource Development Through Vocational Education in Gulf Cooperation Countries: the Case of Saudi Arabia," *Journal of Vocational Education and Training*, 52 (2), (2000).

Merton, Robert, *Financial Innovation and the Management and Regulation of Financial Institutions*, National Bureau of Economic Research, Working Paper No. 5096, (Cambridge, MA: NBER, 1995).

Michie, R. C., *The Global Securities Market: A History*, (Oxford University Press, 2007).

Minsky, H., *Inflation, Recession and Economic Policy,* (London: Wheatsheaf Books, 1982).

Mirakhor, Abbas, "Islamic Economic System," in *Essays on Iqtisad* by Al-Hassani and Mirakhor, (MD, USA: Nur Publications, 1989a).

Mirakhor, Abbas, "Muslim Contribution to Economics," presented at the Annual Meeting of the South-Western Economic Association, March 1983 and reproduced from *Essays on Iqtisad* by Al-Hassani and Mirakhor, (MD, USA: Nur Publications 1989b).

Mirakhor, A., "Outline of an Islamic economic system," Zahid Husain Memorial, Lecture Series, No. 11, 22 March 1995, State Bank of Pakistan.

Mirakhor, Abbas, "Cost of Capital and Investment in a Non-interest Economy", *Islamic Economic Studies,* 4 (1) (December 1996).

Mirakhor, Abbas, "Outline of an Islamic Economic System," Zahid Husain Memorial, Lecture Series, No. 11, State Bank of Pakistan, March 22, 1997.

Mirakhor, Abbas, "Muslim Contribution to Economics," first presented at the Midwest Economic Association Meeting, April 7–9, 1983, and reprinted in *Essays on Iqtisad* by Al-Hassani and Mirakhor, (New York, NY: Global Scholarly Publications, 2003a).

Mirakhor Abbas, "The General Characteristics of an Islamic Economic System," in Al-Hassani, B., and Mirakhor A., (ed.), *Essays on Iqtisad,* (New York, NY: Global Scholarly Publications, 2003b).

Mirakhor, Abbas, "Islamic Finance and Instrumentalization of Islamic Redistributive Institutions," paper presented at Ibn Rushd Memorial Lecture, London, (April 2004).

Mirakhor, Abbas, "A Note on Islamic Economics," Lecture delivered at the Islamic Development Bank for Research in Islamic Economics, Saudi Arabia, April (2005a).

Mishkin, F. S., "Is Financial Globalization Beneficial?," *NBER Working Paper* No. 11891, (Cambridge, Massachusetts: National Bureau of Economic Research, 2005).

Mirakhor, Abbas, "Globalization and Islamic Finance," paper presented in the Sixth International Conference on Islamic Economics and Finance, Jakarta, Indonesia, (November 21–24, 2005b).

Mirakhor, A. and I. Zaidi, "Profit-and-loss Sharing Contracts in Islamic Finance" *Handbook of Islamic Banking*, eds. M. K. Hassan and M. K. Lewis, (Cheltenham, UK and Northampton, US: Edward Elgar, 2007): 49–63.

Modigliani, F., and M. H. Miller, "The Cost of Capital, Corporate Finance, and the Theory of Investment," *American Economic Review,* 48 (3), (1958): pp. 261–297.

Mody, A., and Antu Panini Murshid, "Growing up with Capital Flows," *Journal of International Economics*, 65 (2005): 249–266

Mohajerani, Mostafa, and Jaafar Askari, "Gharzul-hasaneh funds" ed. by Bagher Namazi *Traditional and Voluntary Associations in Iran*, (Tehran: Hamyarane Ghaza Institute, 2002).

Mohamad, N., Alchaar, "Developments In International Financial Reporting: Implications For Islamic Banks," eds. Tariqullah Khan and Dadang Muljawan *Islamic Financial Architecture: Risk Management and Financial Stability*, (Jeddah: IRTI, 2006).

Muhammad, W. and Islam, "Al-Mal: The Concept of Property in Islamic Legal Thought," *Arab Law Quarterly*, (1999): 361–368.

Munro, J., "The Late-Medieval Origins of the Modern Financial Revolution: Overcoming Impediments from Church and State." *Working Paper No. 2*, (2003). Online version: http://www.chass.utoronto.ca/ecipa/wpa.html. University of Toronto: Department of Economics and Institute for Policy Analysis.

Mustafa, Ahmad, and Hossein Askari, "The Economic Implications of Land Ownership and Land Cultivation in Islam," paper given at the Second International Conference on Islamic Economics held in Islamabad, Pakistan, 1983, and printed in *Distributive Justice and Need Fulfilment in an Islamic Economy*, ed. Munawar Iqbal, (Leicester: International Institute of Islamic Economics, 1998): 128.

North, Douglass C., "Economic Performance Through Time," *The American Economic Review* 84, (June 1994): 359–68.

Oakley, David, "Capital Takes a Leading Role," FT Report—Islamic Finance, May 23, 2007, *Financial Times* (London, UK).

Obstfeld, M., "International Risk Sharing and Capital Mobility—Another Look," *Journal of International Money and Finance* 11, (1992): 115–121.

Obstfeld, M., "Risk-Taking, Global Diversification, and Growth," *The American Economic Review*, 84 (5), December (1994): 1310–1329.

Obstfeld, M. and A. Taylor, *Global Capital Markets: Integration, Crisis and Growth*, (Cambridge: Cambridge University Press, 2003a).

Obstfeld, M., et al., "Globalization and Capital Markets," eds. M. D. Bordo, A. M. Taylor, and J. G. Williamson *Globalization in Historical Perspective*, (Chicago, IL: NEBR, University of Chicago Press. 2003b).

O'Hara, K., *Trust from Socrates to Spin*, (Duxford, UK: Icon Books, 2004).

Okeahalam, Charles C., *The Political Economy of Bank Failure and Supervision in the Republic of South Africa*, African Journal of Political Science, 3 (2), (1998): 29–48.

O'Rourke, Kevin H., "Globalization and Inequality: Historical Trends," University of Dublin, Trinity College; Centre for Economic Policy Research (CEPR), CEPR Discussion Paper No. 2865, July (2001).

Parker, Mushtak, "Dow Jones Citigroup Sukuk Index Launched," *Arab News*, (2006).

Payandeh, A., *Nahjulfasahah: Collected Short Sayings of the Messenger*, (Tehran: Golestanian, 1984).

Perotti, E. C., "Credible Privatization," *American Economic Review* 85, (1995): 847–859.

Perotti, E. C., and P. van Oijen, "Privatization, Political Risk and Stock Market Development in Emerging Economies," *Journal of International Money and Finance* 20, (2001): 43–69.

Phelps, Edmond, "Distributive Justice," *World of Economics*, (The McMillan Press, 1991): 164–67.

Phillips, Samuel T., "Some Economic Implications of John Rawl's Theory of Justice" in *Public Finance Quarterly*, 3 (1), January (1975).

Pinkowitz, L., R. M. Stulz, and R. Williamson, "Do Firms in Countries with Poor Protection of Investor Rights Hold More Cash?" NEBR unpublished working paper, (Cambridge, Massachusetts: National Bureau of Economic Research, 2004).

Posen, A. S., "A Strategy to Prevent Future Crises: Safety Shrink the Banking Sector," *Peter G. Peterson Institute for International Economics*, (2001).

Postan, M., "Credit in Medieval Trade," *The Economic History Review*, 1 (2), (1928): 234–261.

Postan, M., "Partnership in English Medieval Commerce," *Studi in Onore Di A. Sapori*, 1, (Milan: 1957): 521–549.

Prasad, E., K. Rogoff, S. Wei, and M. A. Kose, "Effects of Financial Globalization on Developing Countries: Some Empirical Evidence," *IMF Occasional Paper* 220, (Washington, DC: International Monetary Fund, 2004).

Presley, J. R., and J. G. Sessions, "Islamic Economics: The Emergence of a New Paradigm," *The Economic Journal: the Quarterly Journal of the Royal Economic Society*, 104 (424): (May 1994): 584–596.

Prychitko, David L., "Individuals, Institutions, Interpretations: Hermeneutics Applied to Economics," (Aldershot: Avebury Publishing, 1995).

Rajan, R. G., "Has Financial Development Made the World Riskier," *NBER Working Paper 11728*, (Cambridge, Massachusetts: National Bureau of Economic Research, 2005).

Rajan, R. G., and L. Zingales, "The Great Reversals: The Politics of Financial Development in the Twentieth Century," *Journal of Financial Economics* 69, (2003): 5–50.

Ramadan, Tariq, *Western Muslims and the Future of Islam*, (Oxford University Press, 2004).

Ranciere, R., A. Tornell, and F. Westermann, "Decomposing the Effects of Financial Liberalization: Crises vs. Growth," *NBER Working Paper* No. 12806, (Cambridge, Massachusetts: National Bureau of Economic Research, 2006).

Ranyer, Jenny, *Managing Reputational Risk: Curbing Threats, Leveraging Opportunities*, Institute of Internal Auditors Risk Management Series, (UK: John Wiley & Sons, 2003).

Rashid, Salim, "An Agenda for Muslim Economists: A Historico-Inductive Approach," *Journal of King Abdul Aziz University*, 3, (1991): 45–55

Ravallion, M., "Competing Concepts of Inequality in the Globalization Debate," *World Bank Policy Research Paper* 3243, (Washington, DC: World Bank, 2004).

Ravallion, M., "Inequality is Bad for the Poor," *World Bank Policy Research Working Paper* 3677, (Washington, DC: World Bank, 2005).

Ravallion, M. and S. Chen, "How did the World's Poorest Fare in the 1990s?," *Review of Income and Wealth* Series, 47 (3), (2001): 283–300.

Reder, Melvin W., *Economics: The Culture of a Controversial Science*, (The University of Chicago Press, 1999).

Robert, J., Barro and Rachel McCleary, "Religion and Political Economy in an International Panel," *Working Paper No. 8931,* National Bureau of Economic Research, (May 2002).

Robert, M. and Solow, "Intergenerational Equity and Exhaustible Resources," *The Review of Economic Studies*, Volume 41, Symposium on the Economics of Exhaustible Resources, (1974): 41.

Robins, Michael H., *Promising, Intending, and Moral Autonomy,* (Cambridge University Press, 1984).

Robinson, Joan, "What are the Questions?" *Journal of Economic Literature*, 15 (4), (December 1977): 1318–39.

Roemer, John, *Equality of Opportunity,* (Cambridge: Harvard University Press, 1999).

Rodrik, D., "Getting Institutions Right," unpublished working paper, (Cambridge, MA: Harvard University 2004).

Röpke, Wilhelm, *A Humane Economy: The Logical Framework of the Free Market*, (Chicago, IL: Henry Regnery Company, 1960, reprinted in 1971), first published in German in 1958.

Ross, S. A., "The Arbitrage Theory of Capital Asset Pricing," *Journal of Economic Theory*, 13, (1976): 341–360.

Ross, S. A., "Mutual Fund Separation in Financial Theory—The Separating Distributions," *Journal of Economic Theory*, 47, (1978): 254–286.

Sachedina, Abdulaziz, *The Islamic Roots of Democratic Pluralism*, (New York: Oxford University Press, 2001): 23–24.

Sachs, J. and A. Warner. "Economic Reform and the Process of Global Integration," *Brookings Papers on Economic Activity*, 1, (1995): 1325–1343.

Sadr, Kazem, "Financing And Institutions," paper presented at the First International Conference on Inclusive Islamic Financial Sector Development: Enhancing Islamic Financial Services for Micro and Medium Sized Enterprises (MMEs) held during April, 17–19, 2007 in Negara Brunei Darussalam.

Sakr, A. A., "Individual and Social Responsibility in Islamic Thought," Ph. D. dissertation, (New York University, 1966): 167–175.

Saleh, Nabil A., *Unlawful Gain and Legitimate Profit in Islamic Law: Riba, Gharar, and Islamic Banking*, 2nd Ed., (London: Graham & Trotman, 1992).

Samad, H., and M. K. Hassan, "The Performance of Malaysian Islamic Banks during 1984–1997: An Exploratory Study," *International Journal of Islamic Financial Services*, 1 (3), (1999).

Sauer, J. B., "Metaphysics and Economy—The Problem of Interest. A Comparison of the Practice and Ethics of Interest in Islamic and Christian Cultures," *International Journal of Social Economics*, 29 (1 and 2), (2002): 97–118.

Schacht, Joseph, *Zakah, Encyclopedia of Islam*, (Leyden: E. J. Brill Ltd., 1934).

Schmidt, D., "Globalization at Work," *Finance and Development*, A compilation of Articles from Finance and Development, (Washington, DC: International Monetary Fund, 2007).

Schmukler, S., "Financial Globalization: Gains and Pain for Developing Countries," *Economic Review* Second Quarter, (Federal Reserve Bank of Atlanta, 2004): 39–66.

Scholes, M., Key Note Address, Risk 2000 Conference, Boston, MA, USA, June 13–14, 2000.

Sen, Amartaya, "Well-Being, Agency and Freedom," *The Journal of Philosophy*, LXXXII, (4) (April 1985): 169–221

Serjeant, R. B., "The Constitution of Medina" *Islamic Quarterly*, 8–9, (1964–65): 3–16.

Shiller, R. J., *The New Financial Order: Risk in the 21st Century*, (Princeton: Princeton University Press, 2003).

Shirazi, Imam Muhammad, *War, Peace, and Non-Violence: An Islamic Perspective* (2004).

Shleifer, Andrei, "Establishing property rights," *Proceedings of the World Bank Annual Conference on Development Economics*, 1994, published by the World Bank in 1995.

Shleifer, A. and D. Wolfenson, "Investor Protection and Equity Markets," *Journal of Financial Economics* 66, (2002): 3–27.

Siddiqi, Mohammad Nejatullah, *Muslim Economic Thinking*, (Leicester: The Islamic Foundation, 1981).

Siddiqi, Mohammad Nejatullah, *Recent Works on History of Economic Thought in Islam: A Survey*, (Jeddah: International Center for Research in Islamic Economics, King Abdul Azziz University, 1982).

Siddig, Abdelmageed Salih, "Challenges to Poverty Alleviation in IDB Member Countries," (Islamic Development Bank, 1999).

Siddiqi, Mohammad Nejatullah, "Shariah, Economics and the Progress of Islamic Finance: The Role of Shariah Experts," Seventh Harvard Forum On Islamic Finance, Cambridge, Massachusetts, USA, April 21, 2006.

Siegel, J., "Can Foreign Firms Bond Themselves Effectively by Renting U.S. Securities Laws?," *Journal of Financial Economics* 75, (2005): 319–359.

Simsek, Yalcin, "Special Finance Institutions," Urge Ihlas Holding Savings, (2001).

Singer, C., "East and West in Retrospect," edited by Singer et al. *A History of Technology*, (Oxford, 1956).

Skoufias, Emmanuel, and Susan W. Walker, "Conditional Cash

Transfers and Their Impact on Child Work and Schooling: Evidence from the Progresa Program in Mexico," FCND Discussion Paper No. 123, (Washington, DC: International Food Policy Research Institute, 2001).

Smarzynska, B. K., and S. J. Wei, "Corruption and the Composition of Foreign Direct Investment: Firm-Level Evidence," *NBER Working Paper* 7969, (Cambridge, Massachusetts: National Bureau of Economic Research, 2000).

Sole, Juan, "Introducing Islamic Banks into Conventional Banking Systems," *IMF Working Paper* No. 07/175, (Washington, DC: International Monetary Fund, 2007).

Spikes, Sarah, "Qatar Islamic Unit Wins UK banking license," *Financial Times*, February 3, 2008.

Spuler, B., "Trade in the Eastern Islamic Countries in the Early Centuries," *Islam and the Trade in Asia*, (1970): 11–20.

Standard & Poor's, *Standard & Poor's Islamic Finance Outlook 2008*, (New York: Standard & Poor's, 2008).

de Ste Croix, G. E. M. "Greek and Roman Accounting," edited by A. C. Littleton and B. S. Yamey *Studies in the History of Accounting*, (1956).

Stulz, R., "International Portfolio Flows and Security Markets," ed. Martin Feldstein *International Capital Flows*, (Chicago, IL: University Chicago Press, 1999a).

Stulz, R., "Globalization, Corporate Finance, and the Cost of Capital," *Journal of Applied Corporate Finance* 12 (3), (1999b): 8–25.

Stulz, R., "The Limits of Financial Globalization," *The Journal of Finance*, 60 (4), August (2005).

Stulz, R., "Financial Globalization, Corporate Governance, and Eastern Europe," *NBER Working Paper* No. 11912, (Cambridge, Massachusetts: National Bureau of Economic Research, 2006).

Starr, Martha A., and Rasim Yilmaz, "Bank Runs in Emerging-Market Countries: The Experience of Turkey's Islamic Banks in the 2001 Crisis," Working Papers 2006–08, (Washington, DC: American University, Department of Economics 2006).

Stiglitz, J., "Money, Credit and Business Fluctuations," *Economic Record*, 64 (187), (1988): 307–322.

Stiglitz, Joseph E., *Whither Socialism?*, (The MIT Press, 1996).

Stiglitz, J., *Globalization and its Discontents*, (New York: W.W. Norton, 2003).

Stiglitz, J., *Making Globalization Work,* (New York: W.W. Norton, 2006).

Stiglitz, J. and A. Weiss, "Credit Rationing in Markets with Imperfect Information," *American Economic Review*, 71 (3), (1981): 333–421.

Sundararajan, V., "Risk Measurement, Risk Management, and Disclosure in Islamic Finance," Seminar on Comparative Supervision of Islamic and Conventional Finance, December 7–8, 2004, Beirut, Lebanon.

Sundararajan, V., and Luca Errico, "Islamic Financial Institutions and Products in the Global Financial System; Key Issues in Risk Management and Challenges Ahead," *IMF working paper WP/02/192*, IMF, November (2002).

Tamari, Meir, "With All Your Possessions: Jewish Ethics and Economic Life," *The Free Press,* (New York, 1987).

Tayyebi, Komail, and Amir Hertmani, "Examining new developments in Gharzul-hasaneh fund in Isfahan Province," 15th Islamic Banking Seminar, Banking Institute of Iran, Tehran, (2004).

Tesar, L. L., "Evaluating the Gains from International Risk-Sharing," *Carnegie-Rochester Conference Series on Public Policy*, 42, (June 1995a): 95–143.

Tesar, L. L., "Home Bias and High Turnover," *Journal of International Money and Finance,* 14, August (1995b): 467–492.

Thaler, Richard H., and H. M. Sherfin, "An Economic Theory of Self-Control," *Journal of Political Economy*, 89 (2), (1981): 392–406.

The Banker (2007), Special Supplement: Top 500 Financial Islamic Institutions, November 01, 2007.

Tornell, A., F. Westermann, and L. Martinez, "The Positive Link Between Financial Liberalization, Growth, and Crises," *NBER Working Paper* 10293, (Cambridge, Massachusetts: National Bureau of Economic Research, 2004).

Tschoegl, Adrian E., "The Key to Risk Management: Management," Working Paper, (Philadelphia, PA: The Wharton Financial Institutions Center, 2000).

Tuma, E. H., "Early Arab Economic Policies," *Journal of the Central Institute of Islamic Research*, 4 (1), (Karachi: 1965): 1–24.

Turnbull, Nigel, "Internal Control: Guidance for Directors on the

Combined Code (the 'Turnbull Report')," (London: The Institute of Chartered Accountants in England & Wales, 1999).

Udovitch, A. L., "At the Origins of the Western Commenda: Islam, Israel, Byzantium?," (1962): 198–207.

Udovitch, A. L., "Credit as a Means of Investment in Medieval Islamic Trade," *Journal of the American Oriental Society*, 87 (3), July–September (1967a): 260–264.

Udovitch, A. L., "Labor Partnership in Medieval Islamic Law," *Journal of Economic and Social History of the Orient*, 10, (1967b): 64–80.

Udovitch, A. L., "Commercial Techniques in Early Medieval Islamic Trade," *Islam and the Trade of Asia*, ed. D. Richards, (1970a): 37–62.

Udovitch, A. L., *Partnership and Profit in Medieval Islam*, (Princeton: Princeton University Press, 1970b).

Ul Haq, Irfan, *Economic Doctrines of Islam: A Study in the Doctrines of Islam and Their Implications for Poverty, Employment, and Economic Growth*. Virginia, The International Institute of Islamic Thought, 1996: 65

Ul Haq, Irfan, *Islamization of Economic Doctrines of Islam: A Study in the Doctrines of Islam and Their Implications for Poverty, Employment, and Economic*, (Virginia: International Institute of Islamic Thought, 1996).

Ul Haque, Nadeem, and Abbas Mirakhor, "Optimal Profit-Sharing Contracts and Investment in an Interest-Free Economy" ed. Mohsin Khan and Abbas Mirakhor, *Theoretical Studies in Islamic Banking*, (Houston, Texas: Institute for Research and Islamic Studies, 1987).

Ul Haque, Nadeem, and Abbas Mirakhor, "The Design of Instruments for Government Finance in an Islamic Economy," International Monetary Fund (IMF) Working Paper no. WP/98/54 (Washington, DC: International Monetary Fund, 1998).

Ul Haque, Nadeem, and Abbas Mirakhor, "The Design of Instruments for Government Finance in an Islamic Economy," *Islamic Economic Studies*, 6 (2), (1999).

Umer Chapra, M., *Economic System of Islam*, (London: Islamic Council of Europe, 1975).

Umer Chapra, M., *Objectives of the Islamic Economic Order*, (Leicester: The Islamic Foundation, 1979).

Umer Chapra, M., "What Is Islamic Economics," Islamic Development Bank Winner's Lecture Series No. 9, (Jeddah: 1996): 25–26.

Umer Chapra, M., "Islam and Economic Development: A Discussion Within the Framework of Ibn Khaldun's Philosophy of History," from proceedings of the Second Harvard University Forum on Islamic Finance Islamic Finance into the 21st Century, (Cambridge, MA, Harvard University, October 9–10, 1998): 23–30.

Umer Chapra, M., "Development Economics: Lessons That Remain to be Learned," *Islamic Studies,* 42 (4), (2000a).

Umer Chapra, M., *The Future of Economics*, (UK: The Islamic Foundation, 2000b).

Umer Chapra, M., and Habib Ahmed, *Corporate Governance in Islamic Financial Institutions*, Occasional Paper no. 6. (Jeddah: IRTI 2002).

Umer Chapra, M., "Financial Stability: The Role of Paradigm and Support Institutions" ed. Tariqullah Khan and Dadan Muljawan, *Islamic Financial Architecture: Risk Management and Financial Stability*, (Jeddah: IRTI, 2006).

Umer Chapra, M., and Tariqullah Khan, *Regulation and Supervision of Islamic Banks*, Occasional Paper no. 3, (Jeddah: IRTI, 2000).

United Nations Development, "Human Development Report 2002: Deepening Democracy in a Fragmented World," (New York: Oxford University Press, 2002).

United Nations Development Program, "Arab Human Development Report 2003: Building a Knowledge Society," (New York: Oxford University Press, 2003).

United Nations, "United Nations Common Country Assessment for the Islamic Republic of Iran," 2003.

Usmani, Muhammad Taqi, *Sukuk* and their Contemporary Applications, (Bahrain: AAOIFI, 2007).

Vaitheswaran, R., "The Evolution of Economic Theory of Justice from Sidgwick to Rawls and Hayak," paper presented at the Midwest Economic Association Meetings, April 7–9, 1983.

Van Wincoop, E., "Welfare Gains from International Risk Sharing," *Journal of Monetary Economics* 34, (October 1994): 175–200.

Van Wincoop, E., "How Big are Potential Welfare Gains from International Risk Sharing?" *Journal of International Economics* 47,

(February 1999): 109–235

Walter, Ingo, "Reputational Risk and Conflicts of Interest in Banking and Finance: The Evidence So Far," (December 20, 2006). Available at SSRN: http://ssrn.com/abstract=952682.

Watkins, K., "Making Globalization Work for the Poor: Point, Counterpoint," *Finance and Development*. A compilation of articles from Finance and Development, (Washington, DC: International Monetary Fund, 2007).

Wei, S. J., "Why is Corruption Much More Taxing than Tax? Arbitrariness Kills," *NBER Working Paper No. 6255*, (Cambridge, Massachusetts: National Bureau of Economic Research, 1997).

Wei, S. J., "How Taxing is Corruption on International Investors?" *Review of Economics and Statistics*, 82, (February 2000a): 1–11.

Wei, S. J., "Local Corruption and Global Capital Flows," *Brookings Papers on Economic Activity: 2*, (Washington, DC: Brookings Institution, 2000b): 303–354.

Wei, S. J., "Natural Openness and Good Government," *NBER Working Paper No. 7765*, (Cambridge, Massachusetts: National Bureau of Economic Research, 2000c).

Wei, S. J., "Domestic Crony Capitalism and International Fickle Capital: Is there a Connection?" *International Finance*, 4, (Spring 2001): 15–46.

Wei, S. J., "Connecting Two Views on Financial Globalization: Can We Make Further Progress?" prepared for the 18th Annual TRIO Conference, organized by Shin-ichi Fukuda, Takeo Hoshi, Takatoshi Ito, and Andrew Rose, University of Tokyo, Japan, (2005).

Wei, S. J., and Y. Wu, "Negative Alchemy? Corruption, Composition of Capital Flows, and Currency Crises," eds. Sebastian Edwards and Jeffrey Frankel, *Preventing Currency Crises in Emerging Markets*, (University of Chicago Press, 2002a): 461–501.

Wei, S. J., and Y. Wu, "The Life-and-Death Implications of Globalization," paper presented at the National Bureau of Economic Research Inter-American Seminar in Economics, Monterrey, Mexico, November, *IMF Working Paper*, (Washington, DC: International Monetary Fund, 2002b).

Williams, Geoffrey Alan, and John Zinkin, "Doing Business with Islam: Can Corporate Social Responsibility be a Bridge between Civilisations?," (October 2005), http://ssrn.com/abstract=905184.

Williamson, Oliver E., "Institutions and Governance of Economic Reform" *Proceedings of the World Bank Annual Conference on Development Economics*, (1994): 171–97.

Wilson, Rodney, "The Contribution of Muhammad Baqir Al-Sadr To Contemporary Islamic Thought," *Journal of Islamic Thought*, Vol. 9, No. 1, (1998): 46–, quoting from Muhammad Baqir al-Sadr, Iqtisaduna: *Our Economics*, Vol. 2, Part 2: 6, (Tehran: World Organization for Islamic Services, 1982).

Wilson, Rodney, "Islamic Finance in Europe," RSCAS Policy Papers No. 2007/02, (Florence: Robert Schijman Centre for Advanced Studies, European University Institute, 2007).

World Bank, "Reducing Vulnerability and Increasing Opportunity: Social Protection in the Middle East and North Africa," (Washington, DC: World Bank, 2002).

World Bank, World Development Report 2006: Equity and Development, (New York: Oxford University Press, 2005).

World Bank (Middle East and North Africa Region, Office of the Chief Economist), "Middle East and North Africa Economic Developments and Prospects 2006: Financial Markets in a New Age of Oil," (Washington, DC: World Bank, 2006).

Yartey, C. A., "The Stock Market and the Financing of Corporate Growth in Africa: The Case of Ghana," *IMF Occasional Paper* No. 201, (Washington, DC: International Monetary Fund, 2006).

Yousef, Tarik M., "Employment, Development and the Social Contract in the Middle East and North Africa," (World Bank, October 2004).

Yudistira, D., "Efficiency in Islamic Banking: An Empirical Analysis of Eighteen Banks," *Islamic Economic Studies*, 12 (1), (Jeddah: IRTI, IDB, 2004).

Zagha, Roberto, Gobind Nankani and Indermit Gill, "Rethinking Growth," *Finance and Development*, (Washington, DC: International Monetary Fund, March 2006): 8.

Zak, Paul, "The Neurobiology of Trust," article in *Corante Tech News*, (2003).

Zak, Paul, and S. Knack, "Trust and Growth," *The Economic Journal*, 111, (April 2001): 295–321.

Zaman, Hasanuz, *The Economic Functions of the Early Islamic State*, (Karachi: International Islamic Publishers, 1981).

Zaman, Arif, *Reputational Risk: How to Manage for Value Creation*, (UK: *Financial Times*/Prentice Hall, 2003).

Zubaida, Sami, "The Politics Of The Islamic Investment Companies In Egypt," *Bulletin (British Society for Middle Eastern Studies)*, 17 (2). (1990), 152–161.

Index